# LIST OF EDITORS

Rajib Shaw
*Graduate School of Global Environmental Studies,*
*Kyoto University, Kyoto, Japan*

Hari Srinivas
*United Nations Environmental Programme, Osaka, Japan*

Anshu Sharma
*Sustainable Environment and Ecological Development Society, Delhi, India*

## EDITOR'S PROFILE

**Rajib Shaw** is an Associate Professor in the Graduate School of Global Environmental Studies of Kyoto University, Japan. He worked closely with the local communities, NGOs, governments and international organization, including United Nations, especially in the Asian countries. He is currently the Chair of the United Nations Asia Regional Task Force for Urban Risk Reduction. His research interests are: community-based disaster risk management, climate change adaptation, urban risk management, and disaster and environmental education.

**Hari Srinivas** is the Chief of Urban Management section of the United Nations Environment Programme (UNEP). A trained urban planner, he has worked for United Nations University and academic positions before joining UNEP. He has written extensively on urban environmental management, and runs the website Global Development Resource Center (GDRC), as a nonprofit think tank that carries out initiatives in the spheres of environment, urban, community, economy, and information.

**Anshu Sharma** is the board member of SEEDS, a nonprofit organizations having wider community-based operation in developing countries in Asia. An urban planner by training, his main work is in India in post-disaster reconstruction programs and pre-disaster educational activities. He is also a trainer for professionals, and also the global tutor of Oxford Brooks University of UK. He has written widely in different journals and has edited several publications.

# BRIEF INTRODUCTION OF THE SERIES

Community, Environment, and Disaster Risk Management

This series connects academic research to field practice, strengthening the links between the environment, disaster, and community. The series will be developed on field evidences and community practices, and thus will provide specific guides to professionals, which are grounded in rigorous academic analysis. The series will have specific focus on community-based disaster risk management, urban environmental management, human security, water community, risk communication, climate change adaptation, climate disaster resilience, and community-based practices.

# BRIEF INTRODUCTION OF THE VOLUME

Urban Risk Reduction: An Asian Perspective

As cities all over the world have or are being urbanized rapidly, most cities have confronted environmental problems and resulted disaster risk issues. In the context of urban cities in the developing world, it can be narrowed to the quality of life of living population, where disaster risk reduction and environmental management are closely interrelated. Needless to say that Asia has the largest population, as well as urban population at risk. This book brings the lessons from innovative urban risk management approaches in Asian cities, focusing on both disaster risk reduction and environmental risk management, drawing the lessons from eight Asian countries. The authors of the chapters consist of wider spectrum of stakeholders: from academicians to policy makers, international agencies, including United Nations and NGO practitioners.

# PREFACE

Urban risk is increasing and will increase for next several years. For the first time in the history, the urban population is more than the rural population in the world. The speed of urbanization is highest in Asia, and consequently unplanned development, migration from rural areas and increasing vulnerabilities are the characteristic features of urbanization in Asia. Urbanization is increasingly located in the developing countries: in 1970s, 50% of urban residents lived in developing countries, whereas it is increased to 66% in 1990s, and is projected to be 80% by 2020. The key issue of Asian urbanization is its variation. Each country has its characteristic context and the nature and issues of urbanization is different from the others.

Although urban areas face both environment and disaster risks, it is often treated separately. There are several publications available on urban risk reduction. However, the need of a comprehensive publication with specific examples of field practices was always felt. This book is an attempt to focus on an integrated approach to environment and disaster risks in Asia. The book not only emphasizes emerging issues of urban environment (both small, medium, and megacities), it also provides lessons on innovative urban risk management approaches, drawing lessons from nine Asian countries. The uniqueness of the work lies in two aspects: overall analysis of urban risk issues, and specific attempt to capture lessons learned from case studies of Asian cities.

The book is divided into two parts: Part I has six chapters. Chapter 1 provides an overview of issues and challenges of urban risk, while Chapters 2, 3, and 4 provides three specific tools of risk reduction (risk assessment, environmental risk reduction, and education and communication). Chapter 5 provides a mapping of urban risk reduction initiatives in Asia, and Chapter 6 once again revisit different disaster and environmental issues of urban risk reduction. Significant and unique part of the book is the issues described in Part II, which has three sections. Six disaster risk reduction case studies are presented from different parts of Asia, which consists of different disasters like earthquake, flood, typhoon, and tsunami. The next section provides three case studies on environmental risk management, and the last section provides three case studies on disaster–environment linkages. All these case

:sults of specific field based project implementation. As exemplified in the list of contributors, the authors come from different background: academic, government, international agencies such as United Nations and NGO practitioners.

In conclusion, urban risk reduction in Asia needs a balanced mix of policy implementation, regulatory measures and education-awareness programs through community-based approaches. There are already several frameworks on which urban risk reduction initiatives can build on. The Millennium Development Goal (2000–2015) emphasizes several basic issues of development, which are linked to urban risk reduction. The Hyogo Framework for Action (HFA: 2005–2015) also emphasizes the integrated approach of disaster risk reduction. The United Nations International Strategy for Disaster Reduction (UN ISDR) is starting a campaign of urban safety for the year 2010–2011. We hope that the concept, approaches, and methods described in this book will gain momentum through all these international initiatives.

Finally, the idea of this book was generated in 2006 through the Action Workshop titled "Participatory Urban Risk Management," organized by Kyoto University, UNEP, and SEEDS, and funded by the Asia/Pacific Cultural Center for UNESCO (ACCU). Discussion of the workshop highly benefits the concept and framework of the book, and this is highly acknowledged. The book is dedicated to the practitioners, professionals, and researchers in the environment and disaster field, especially those who are dealing with urban risk. We will be very happy if it serves their purpose.

Rajib Shaw
Hari Srinivas
Anshu Sharma
*Editors*

# PART I

# CHAPTER 1

# INTRODUCTION TO URBAN RISK REDUCTION

Hari Srinivas, Rajib Shaw and Anshu Sharma

## ABSTRACT

*Cities and urban areas are increasingly becoming the settlement of choice for a majority of humans.*

*Many of the global environmental problems that we are now facing have their precedence and causes in the cities and urban areas we live in.*

*Lessons in understanding urban risk are now emerging – urban hazards and risk are predominantly human-induced, and exacerbate natural events. Various economic, social, and economic aspects compound the risks that urban residents face.*

*Urban lifestyles and resource consumptions can be directly or indirectly attributed to the many environmental consequences that we are seeing – both within the city, as well as the entire hinterland or urban watershed that it is located in.*

## 1. CRITICALITY OF URBAN ENVIRONMENTS

The criticality of urban environments is highlighted by the fact that most of today's global environmental problems can find their precedence and causes, directly or indirectly, in urban areas and urban lifestyles – which have

Urban Risk Reduction: An Asian Perspective
Community, Environment and Disaster Risk Management, Volume 1, 3–12
Copyright © 2012 by Emerald Group Publishing Limited
All rights of reproduction in any form reserved
ISSN: 2040-7262/doi: 10.1108/S2040-7262(2009)0000001005

referred choice of settlement for a majority of humanity. urban centers have far-reaching and long-term effects not only on its immediate boundaries, but also on the entire region in which it is positioned.

The world's cities take up just 2% of the Earth's surface, yet account for roughly 78% of the carbon emissions from human activities, 76% of industrial wood use, and 60% of the water tapped for use by people.

The world is steadily becoming urban. The UN report on World Urbanization Prospects projects that more than 50% of the world's population will be dwelling in cities and almost all the growth of the world's population between 2000 and 2030 is expected to be absorbed by the urban areas of less developed regions. According to UN projections, the urban population in Asia is expected to become nearly double and the percentage of people living in urban areas in India will be 41.4 against the current figure of 28%.

Along with the benefits of urbanization and agglomeration come environment and social ills, including lack of access to drinking water and sanitation, pollution and carbon emissions, etc. It is, in fact, a two-way street – -while cities and urban areas are directly or indirectly causing global environmental problems, climate change has impacts that are being felt at the micro and urban levels.

Clearly, there are cyclical links between urban areas, lifestyles and consumption patterns on one hand, and global environmental problems on the other. The outlook is even grimmer if we consider the accumulated effects and synergy between environmental deterioration and poverty.

## 2. INTERPOLATING GLOBAL PROBLEMS TO THE LOCAL LEVEL

Considering the complex range of global environmental problems we are facing today, one key factor will be to rethink the way we look at urban areas. Global environmental problems can be traced back, directly or indirectly, to urban areas and the urban lifestyles we lead today. The forces and processes that constitute "urban activities" have far-reaching and long-term effects not only on its immediate boundaries, but also on the entire region in which it is positioned.

But in order to begin to understand what needs to be done, it is clear that the global problems have to be scaled down to the level of an individual and the household. This is because everyday decisions taken by everyone of us, overlap and cumulate, creating eventually the global environmental problems we are seeing today.

This is the reason why cities and the built environment is receiving increasing attention from the environmental front. Living in cities provides not only opportunities (such as higher earning potential, medical care, transportation facilities, better education for children, entertainment and culture, etc.), but also present risks and hazards (such as deteriorating air quality, congestion and traffic, garbage and waste, security risks, reduced social interaction, etc.).

Cities are also creating an "ecological overshoot." To be sustainable, the average per capita area required for everyday comfortable living (known as a "footprint") should be 1.9 hectares. However, the average person now actually requires or uses 2.2–2.3 hectares to support his or her needs. For example, the average footprint in developed nations is typically between 4 and 6 hectares, or more.

## 3. CASCADING RIPPLES OF URBAN PROBLEMS

These lifestyle patters at the individual level creates patterns of problems at the urban level too. For the first time in human history, a majority of the world's six billion people will live in cities. The world is facing explosive growth of urban population, particularly in the developing world.

Many cities, confronted with hyper growth, are failing to cope with the challenges of generating employment, providing adequate housing, and meeting the basic needs of their citizens. Many cities also face problems such as an ageing population, urban decay, unsustainable use of resources, and the inability to adapt and change. But there are also "problems-behind-problems" that cause such a situation, including lack of political will, decision-making support systems, inadequate financial resources, etc.

A key to effective policy formulation and allocation of resources to project components is to understand the scale of urban environmental problems. This helps us in a variety of ways: to identify the causes and effects of environmental problems; to collect appropriate data and information at the appropriate level, to allocate resources and stakeholders

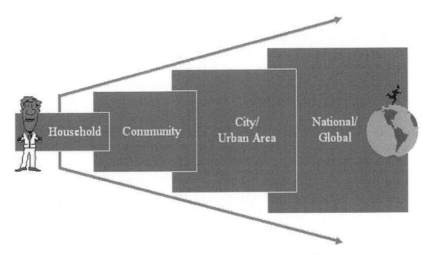

*Fig. 1.* Perspective of Environmental Problems.

that function and are involved at the particular scale, and to formulate policy and take appropriate action at the appropriate level.

Environmental problems can be scaled by using a spatial scale, which includes household, community, city, and region/nation (Fig. 1). At each level of the spatial scale, the characteristic problems and the related infrastructure and services needed to address such problems need to be specified. The consideration of the spatial scale of impacts reveals several important issues:

- health impacts are greater and more immediate at the household or community level and tend to diminish in intensity as the spatial scale increases;
- equity issues arise in relation to (a) the provision of basic services at the household or community scale and (b) inter temporal externalities at the regional and global scale – particularly the intergenerational impacts implicit in non-sustainable resource use and global environmental issues; and
- levels of responsibility and decision-making should correspond to the scale of impact, but existing jurisdictional arrangements often violate this principle.

A deeper understanding of urban problems and its causes and effects, helps us in developing appropriate management options for the problem. For example, pollution of groundwater resources, and its depletion, is an urban

| | | | | |
|---|---|---|---|---|
| Water pollution | Loss of habitat, biodiversity and species endangered | **Region/Nation** | Soil erosion and increased salinity | Toxic run-off and acid rain |
| Amenity loss | Traffic congestion | **City** | Loss of heritage and historical buildings | Reduced property and building values |
| Accidents and disasters | Polluted land | **Community** | inappropriate and inadequate technology use | Inadequate tax/financial revenues |
| `Flooding and surface drainage | Trash dumping | **Household** household health, garbage generation, air/water/noise pollution, spread of diseases | Lack of understanding of environmental problems | Lack of, and inappropriate, laws and legislation |
| Toxic and hazardous wastes/dumps | Flooding | Noise pollution | Natural disasters | High living densities |
| Loss of agricultural land and desertification | Air pollution | Water pollution | Inadequate supply and transmission loss of electricity | Misguided urban governments and management practices |
| Natural and man-made hazards and disasters | Land clearance and loss of forest cover | Effects of climate change and global warming. | | |

*Fig. 2.* Complexity of Urban Issues and Problems.

problem facing many cities of developing countries (Fig. 2). The *effects* of groundwater pollution include human health problems; reduced water quality from saline intrusion, biochemical seepage; and economic costs of additional treatment, new sources of supply and health costs. Some of the *causes* of these problems include – pricing policies; unclear property rights; poor regulations and/or enforcement; unsustainable extraction; sanitation, municipal, and industrial waste disposal practices; and poor demand management. Management options available to solve these problems include – regulations, standards, licensing, charges; waste management; appropriate technology; demand management; controls on land use; and education and awareness generation.

## 4. CITIES AND CLIMATE CHANGE: THE BEGINNINGS OF URBAN VULNERABILITY

These scenarios and patterns translate directly into environmental problems for cities – for example, carbon dioxide ($CO_2$) and green house gas (GHG) emissions. Scientists have predicted that the level of $CO_2$ will increase by at least 25% of current levels in the next decade or so. The level of energy consumption and waste production will also increase by at least 30%, based on current development patterns. This will only worsen, since there will be a significant rise in energy demand for private and public consumption, and for economic activities.

$CO_2$ and GHG emissions include direct, indirect, and embodied emissions. Direct emissions come from emissions of GHGs within the city proper from various urban activities. Indirect emissions emerge from activities taking place outside the city boundary, but resulting from urban activities (e.g., coal/oil burned to produce electricity used in cities).

Embodied emissions, on the other hand, result from external goods and services consumed within an urban area.

What drives these urban emissions of $CO_2$ and GHGs? We are now back to the usual culprits that are often quoted – urban demography, economic development, urban physical infrastructure and technology, urban forms and function, behavioral and societal factors, globalization, etc.

Urban areas not only provide a number of socio-economic opportunities for jobs and income generation, but are also simultaneously becoming increasingly risky places to live, especially for low-income residents of cities in developing countries. Exposure to environmental risk and hazard is a result of physical processes creating these hazards (e.g., building construction, urban planning, infrastructure provision, or transportation), and human processes that lead to vulnerabilities (e.g., lifestyle choices and consumption patterns). These issues have cumulatively creating different impacts in different areas of a city or cities, depending on its socio-spatial structure.

Urban areas are not disaster prone by nature; rather the socio-economic structural processes that accelerate rapid urbanization, population

movement, and population concentrations substantially i
vulnerability, particularly of low-income urban dwellers. Migrants, ioi
example, settle in areas either originally unsafe (susceptible to floods, land
slides, etc.), or create the potential of man-made disaster (environmental
degradation, slum fires, health hazards). Urban vulnerabilities are not
limited to just low-income residents – a flood or a typhoon does not
distinguish between residents, affecting everyone in its path. Even "natural"
disasters always have social, cultural, institutional, and technical aspects
involved, which ultimately determine if a natural hazard becomes a disaster.

Therefore, while urban vulnerabilities are created *directly* by global
change such as sea level raise and flooding (more than 80% of cities are on
river basins or close to a coast, or both), a number of *indirect* causes, such as
household and hazardous/toxic wastes, pollution, etc. are responsible as
well, resulting in potentially higher impacts owing to concentrations of
infrastructure, government, population, and economic activity.

In the context of climate change, for example, risks from natural events
result from a combination of the nature of the hazard itself, and the intrinsic
vulnerability of the affected society and territory. The Intergovernmental
Panel on Climate Change (IPPC) Working Group II has defined
vulnerability as the extent to which a natural or social system is susceptible
to sustaining damage from climate change. Vulnerability therefore implies
not only exposure to hazard factors but also the capacity to recover from
their effect (Fig. 3). Vulnerability in an urban context should not be
conceived as a fixed feature of a specific society or territory, but as a process,
whose intensity can be reduced through adequate policies.

Thus a changing urban environment, brought about by both man-made
factors and natural factors creates vulnerabilities in cities that need to be

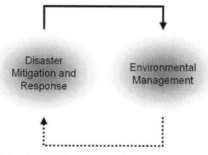

*Fig. 3.* Environment Disaster Linkages.

prevented (control the source), protected (build to withstand) and controlled (land use planning and zoning).

The criticality of integrating environment and disaster risk reduction is now being highlighted by a number of international initiatives, including the Hyogo Framework of Action (2005–2015), the Millennium Declaration (2002), UN Millennium Ecosystem Assessment, and others.

This common understanding has drawn our attention to the fact that environmental management is a crucial element to reduce disaster risks and to adapt to climate change. Healthy local environments increase a community's resilience to hazards, and therefore, disaster risk considerations should be integrated into sustainable development planning. Thus, environment policies, strategies, and tools need to incorporate risk reduction, and vice-versa, disaster planning needs to take into account the risks and hazards that the local environment faces.

## 5. CONTEXTUALIZING URBAN VULNERABILITIES

Urban hazards and risks do not happen in isolation. The key to understanding urban risk reduction and vulnerabilities is to contextualize it within the broader perspectives of disaster management and urban development in general.

As the case studies in the following chapters show, we need to consider a number of precedence and preconditions in cities and urban areas. These can contribute to and influence, both positively and negatively, to urban risks. Examples include:

- Urban hazards and risks, and urban disasters have to be understood from the perspective of both the larger disaster event and the secondary impacts that they create (e.g., a typhoon or cyclone that created flooding in the city as a result of poor run-off drainage systems).
- Various economic, social, and other aspects compound the risks from actual disaster events (e.g., the propensity of lower-income households to stay on low-lying flood-prone areas or river banks due to availability of low- or no-cost land).
- Urban hazards and vulnerabilities may be a cause of lopsided policies or planning and development processes and programs that do account the resulting risks that could be generated (e.g., the ding sites and streets, water works engineering, pavement at prevent or impede effective drainage of flood waters;

degraded environments in slums and squatter settlements that present a fire or health hazard).

- Urban lifestyles and resource consumptions, as explained earlier, can be directly or indirectly attributed to the many environmental consequences that we are seeing – both within the city, as well as the entire hinterland or urban watershed that it is located in. But such resource consumption patterns also create hazards and risks of their own (e.g., deforestation for timber use in cities indirectly causing erosion, landslides, and flooding in remote mountains and forests; or un-disposed household wastes blocking city drains that lead to flooding).
- Involvement of a number of stakeholders and organizations is critical for the reduction of disaster risk, not only to effectively respond to disaster events, but especially in mitigating and preventing/preparing for such events. Many of these stakeholders and targets of disaster risk reduction initiatives are based in cities and urban areas (e.g., implementing building codes and planning guidelines by architects and engineers for the retrofitting of buildings; or identification of a system of sharing waste disposal trucks to clear disaster debris among neighboring cities).
- Many of the key steps in urban disaster risk reduction involve good governance – particularly in implementing laws and legislation, strong role and responsibilities for local governments. These issues, supported by the information and knowledge resident in educational and research institutions have to be dovetailed into larger processes of disaster information and knowledge management at the national and regional levels, involving national governments and organizations (e.g., the ASEAN Secretariat assisting its member-countries to implement urban risk reduction projects).

It is with this thinking that Part one of this book, containing the first six chapters, is presented with the various components that together form an approach to reducing and mitigating urban vulnerabilities and risks.

Chapter 2, written by Phong Tran and coauthors looks at the issue of risk analysis as a starting point for a better understanding of urban risk. The chapter also outlines the next stage of action planning for risk management – a systematic process that enables urban stakeholders to plan the development of risk reduction action, followed by the issue of implementation management – from both the perspectives of the local target communities as well as external interventions. This is followed by Hari Srinivas in Chapter 3, presenting the various facets of decision-making that will have to be undertaken once the action plan is ready. Chapter 4 by Rajib Shaw and Manu Gupta covers critical and complementary elements of educational and communication aspects, respectively. Chapter 5 provides an outline of the Hyogo Framework for Action (HFA), which deals with action programs for undertaking risk reduction measures from a local government or city perspective. Finally, the Chapter 6 by Hari Srinivas et al. provides future perspective of risk reduction activities. Taken together, the five chapters (Chapters 2–6) present a continuum of risk management components that will have to be taken up for effective urban risk reduction and mitigation as case studies.

# CHAPTER 2

# URBAN DISASTER RISK ANALYSIS, ACTION PLANNING AND IMPLEMENTATION MANAGEMENT

Phong Tran, Fumio Kaneko, Rajib Shaw, Lorna P. Victoria and Hidetomi Oi

## ABSTRACT

*Risk assessments are the very basis on which planning and implementation are carried out. In the context of urban risk management, the assessment processes are complex to understand as they involve multi-sectoral parameters. Many of the issues involved are of technical nature, but this also requires focus on the principles behind the assessment process including participatory assessment tools.*

*Action planning is a participatory, short-term, visible, output-oriented process that enables urban community groups to plan the development of risk reduction actions in their locality and to lead the implementation of the action plans.*

*There are three kinds of actions that emerge from an action planning process: (i) those that can be implemented by the community groups themselves, (ii) those that need some external help for implementation, and (iii) those that can only be implemented by specialized agencies from*

Urban Risk Reduction: An Asian Perspective
Community, Environment and Disaster Risk Management, Volume 1, 13–36
Copyright © 2012 by Emerald Group Publishing Limited
ISSN: 2040-7262/doi: 10.1108/S2040-7262(2009)0000001006

*outside the community. Implementation management processes thus need*
*to look at how internal systems can be established to operationalize self-*
*action, and to coordinate external interventions.*

## 1. INTRODUCTION

Current unplanned urbanization in developing countries is growing at an
alarming rate that poses challenges for development planning and disaster
risk management (DRM). The ever-growing vulnerability of large urban
populations contributes to increasing urban risks in the face of which
natural hazards are compounded into frequent disasters. Many recent major
disasters have occurred in densely populated human settlements leading to
high levels of human, economic, social, and environmental loss with a
consequent severely negative impact on national and regional development
(Wisner, Blaikie, Cannon, & Davis, 2004).

When disasters strike in cities, the effects can be worse than in other
environments, and it is the communities of the poor and the marginalized in
the developing world, that face the greatest risks (International Decade for
Natural Disaster Reduction [IDNDR], 1990). The disaster impacts may be
direct, indirect, or systemic. Direct impacts are openly visible and reported.
However, in cities and urban areas, the majority of losses are often from
secondary or indirect impacts. Cities and large urban complexes,
particularly those in developing countries, often demonstrate a high degree
of vulnerability to disaster precisely because they have a high concentration
of activities, dependence on infrastructure, reliance on a money economy,
concentrations of poverty, political competition, etc. (United Nations
Human Settlemtns Program [UNHSP], 2004).

With growing urbanization and more and more small- and large-scale
disasters occurring in urban areas, years of development effort and labor are
continually being destroyed and eroded (Sanderson, 2000). Thus, public
policies and disaster response measures are increasingly being tested beyond
their capacities, with tragic consequences (Mitchell, 1999). In response to this
development, it is essential to determine what kind of pre-disaster initiatives
can help to mitigate disaster risk, especially in urban, low-income, and informal
settlements. "Urbanization affects disasters just as profoundly as disasters can
affect urbanization" (Pelling, 2003). However, urban growth, whether planned
or unplanned, is seldom carried out with a view to reduce disaster risk.

In urban context, therefore, risk assessment information is very important
for authorities and communities to determine what risks they face and to

what degree and will determine what actions need to be taken and what resources are required. Implementing actions and accessing resources before such an assessment is undertaken may lead to waste and duplication. A comprehensive disaster risk assessment will help to identify what actions need to be taken to reduce the likelihood of a threatening event as well as actions that need to be taken to reduce the impact when an event has taken place (UNHSP, 2004).

Risk assessment consisting of hazard analysis and vulnerability analysis is a basic instrument of DRM that is used to study the factors of disaster risk and provides the basis for planning and implementing measures to reduce risks and impacts of disasters. Action Planning is the follow-up process that engages with the local stakeholders and leads to actionable plans that are based on the assessed risk and focus to reduce it, and that are more dependent on local aspirations and capacities than external support. Finally, implementation management is the key process that translates the plans into ground reality, and needs to be founded on principles that are in tandem with those of action planning so as to ensure implementation that is true to the essence of local plans and is sustainable beyond project durations. This chapter will focus on the concepts of risk analysis (RA), action planning, and implementation management from the point of view of urban disaster risk. RA is used here to refer to a method of determining the quantitative or qualitative degree of risk. The terms "risk analysis," "action planning," and "implementation management" have the underlying concept of "participative approaches." This means that the affected target population is involved in the various stages of all of these processes.

## 2. DISASTER RISK MANAGEMENT AND ITS COMPONENTS

DRM is part of disaster management, focusing on the before (RA, prevention, preparedness) of the extreme natural event, and relating to the during and after of the disaster only through RA (Fig. 1). DRM is an instrument for reducing the risk of disaster primarily by reducing vulnerability, based on social agreements resulting from RA. These social agreements are the result of a complex social process in which all social strata and interest groups participate. They are a necessary basis for resisting the future effects of extreme natural events (prevention, preparedness). The primary area of action of a DRM is reducing vulnerability and strengthening self-protection capabilities (Fig. 2).

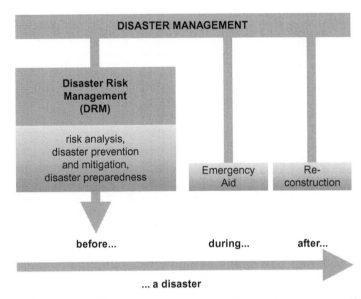

*Fig. 1.* Disaster Risk Management as Part of Disaster Management. (Adapted from Kohler, Jülich, & Bloemertz, 2005.)

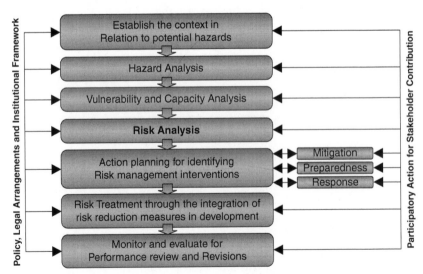

*Fig. 2.* Process of Disaster Risk Management. (Adapted from a Primer: Disaster Risk Management in Asia, ADPC & USAID.)

The DRM takes into account and links technical, social, political, socioeconomic, ecological and cultural aspects. This involves networking the various DRM components and the various aspects listed above to form an integrated system. This integration is what enables the DRM to reduce the risk to a level that a society can cope with. Some of the components to consider in DRM in urban areas include the following.

## *2.1. Urban Governance*

According to UNHSP (2004), urbanization – the growth of the proportion of the population living in urban areas – does not, by itself, increase vulnerability. However, vulnerability does increase in the face of poor governance, witnessed through bad planning and weak institutions. An emphasis on good governance, including the issues of participatory decision-making, transparency and accountability, and its integration in development could have a substantially positive effect in managing urban risks and vulnerability. In the absence of good governance, many poorer urban dwellers find themselves living in areas of high disaster risk that are frequently highly polluted and without adequate services, including health facilities, sanitation, clean water, and waste management.

## *2.2. Housing and Shelter*

Many of the casualties from disasters resulting from natural hazards are associated with collapsing buildings. The quality of housing construction and infrastructure is an essential element of disaster risk reduction. Very few countries have developed construction regulations that relate to their hazard profile and often, if the regulations exist, they are not enforced. The construction materials used often do not take account of the hazard profile (UNHSP, 2004).

## *2.3. Infrastructure*

Urban infrastructure assists in providing society's basic needs such as water, electricity, health care, and sanitation. Rapid urbanization outstrips the ability to provide adequate infrastructure. Infrastructure is often designed without taking into account disaster risks and other urban risk factors. This may lead, for example, to a lack of space for evacuations or for a rescue effectively. There are examples from Asia of infrastructure sited in disaster-prone areas while parks and recreational facilities are located in safer areas. Securing infrastructure requires effective maintenance, a knowledge and understanding of the hazardousness of the environment and an aware local government and community with the resources to access.

### 2.4. Urban Poverty

The poorest often live in the lowest quality housing located in the lowest quality environments and these locations are frequently highly disaster-prone. There is a close link between poverty and urban vulnerability and disaster risk reduction in such a context is as much about poverty reduction as any other measures. Poverty often migrates from rural to urban areas and if opportunities exist in the urban environment, those who move to urban areas often cannot take advantage because they lack the investment capacity. They also tend to live in areas that lack basic facilities and infrastructure. However, through the informal sector, the urban poor are often providers of many essential low-cost services.

City governments are concerned to avoid investment in poor and highly vulnerable areas where the potential for disaster is high. On the other hand, in many of these areas risk becomes institutionalized with local governments giving services to poorer, hazard prone communities as part of a process of political legitimization or convenience. However, if poverty reduction is an important development objective, then these highly vulnerable areas need significant attention, which may also, in turn, lead to a healthier and more, secure population and greater economic and political stability.

## 3. ANALYZING URBAN DISASTER RISK

Urban disaster risks are complex. These risks may already be established or may be newly constructed as a result of economic, political, and development decision-making. In addition, the economic, social, and environmental deprivation of nonurban areas, compounded by disasters, may lead to migrations to urban centers, thus increasing the number of lives at risk and overwhelming an already stressed urban infrastructure. There is no universally valid definition of risk, precisely because perceptions differ between individuals and cultures. In the context of DRM, the following definition has been "agreed":

> Risk is the probability of harmful consequences, or expected losses (deaths, injuries, property, livelihoods, economic activity disrupted or environment damaged) resulting from interactions between natural or human-induced hazards and vulnerable conditions. Conventionally risk is expressed by the notation: Risk = Hazards × Vulnerability. Some disciplines also include the concept of exposure to refer particularly to the physical aspects of vulnerability. (United Nations Inter-Agency Secretariat of the International Strategy for Disaster Reduction [UN/ISDR], 2004)

To perceive, understand and assess risk requires experience with or knowledge about risks, i.e., experience of something in the past. Risk is something that has not happened yet, something that is projected into the future. If a risk is perceived as too great, there are two possibilities: eliminate the risk or reduce it as far as possible. However, with growing poverty there are more and more situations in which the affected population accepts a high level of risks and locate in urban population centers, steep slopes, or flood areas. There are also those who, e.g., live near industrial zones or atomic power plants, and do not want to move away because they would lose their job or other benefits. How high the risk is judged to be also depends on the available information about possible hazards. Adequate provision of information relating to hazards helps increase awareness and perception of risks.

Beyond expressing a possibility of physical harm, it is crucial to recognize that risks are inherent or can be created or exist within social systems. It is important to consider the social contexts in which risks occur and that people therefore do not necessarily share the same perceptions of risk and their underlying causes. The wide range of actual and potential urban disaster risks is important to recognize as measures to reduce risks. Some risks will be easier to address than others. Risks arising from disasters resulting from natural hazards may present good potential for risk reduction.

### 3.1. Concept of Risk Analysis

RA consists of hazard analysis and vulnerability analysis, together with analysis of protective capabilities. Some authors treat the analysis of the protective capabilities of the local population (coping strategies) as part of vulnerability analysis, others as a third component of RA, others see it as an additional chapter, and as such a component of risk assessment and not RA. Here, the analysis of self-protection capabilities is treated as part of vulnerability analysis (Fig. 3).

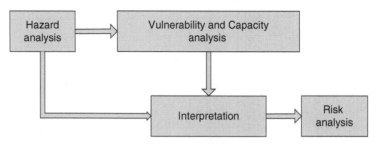

*Fig. 3.* Concept of Risk Analysis. (Adapted from Kohler et al., 2005.)

RA is based on the recognition that risk is the result of the link between hazard and vulnerability of elements affected by the hazard. The goal of RA is to use this link to estimate and evaluate the possible consequences and impacts of extreme natural events on a population group and their basis for life. This involves impacts at the social, economic, and environmental levels. Hazard and vulnerability analyses are parts of RA, and are inseparable activities – vulnerability analysis is not possible without hazard analysis, and vice versa. Thus, risk is understood here as the expected value of the loss of human life or damage to objects, infrastructure and the environment. Determining the disaster risk as a result of the RA is analytically based on documenting and assessing the hazard, followed by valuation of the vulnerability of a population or region to this hazard. In determining the overall risk, all the elements at risk (e.g., population, property, infrastructure, economic activities, etc.) are taken into account with their specific vulnerability. In urban context, disaster RA needs to include environmental risk that considers environmental hazard as an additional element rather than natural hazard.

## 3.2. Hazard Analysis

A hazard analysis investigates, identifies, and documents natural hazards (drought, floods, landslides, earthquakes, etc.), their causes and impact chains. In hazard analysis, natural disasters (droughts, floods, landslides, earthquakes, etc.) and their causes and the resulting impact chains are identified, analyzed, and documented. Knowledge of the types of hazard is essential for analyzing and assessing risks. The resources required for an analysis depend on the situation. A simple analysis with modest data input may be sufficient, or comprehensive investigations and elaborate studies may be required to document hazard potentials.

To be able to estimate and evaluate the degree of risk and the characteristics and scale of possible loss from extreme natural events, it is necessary not only to estimate the probability of occurrence but also to investigate the force and duration of the event. However, before this detailed study it is necessary to establish how far population groups and their bases for life are potentially affected by the event, i.e., how susceptible they are to the event and how vulnerable they are to this hazard. If there are no vulnerable populations or elements at the site of the hazard, no hazard analysis is required, as in this case the extreme natural event does not constitute a hazard. These are the first steps in vulnerability analysis, and they are needed before any detailed hazard analysis. Hazard analysis is not a linear sequence of analytical steps relating to the hazard; it is constantly being interrupted by steps in the vulnerability analysis, and supplemented by the learning loops and results generated by this.

The most important tasks and steps in hazard analysis are:

- The first stage in hazard analysis is to identify the types of hazards. There are many ways to classify hazard types, e.g., natural events occurring suddenly or gradually, of an atmospheric, seismic, geological, volcanic, biological and hydrological nature while others summarize mass movements under the heading of "geo-morphological hazards."
- Depending on the types of hazard identified, the process may need to be continued on a separate basis for each type of hazard or group of hazard types. Earthquakes, for example, require different instruments and specializations for analysis than, e.g., landslides or floods. The analytical methodology must be adapted for the hazard types and data available.
- Identification and characterization of hazard prone locations.
- Identification and determination of the probabilities of occurrence on an ordinal scale (high – medium – low).
- Estimate or calculate the scale (strength, magnitude) of the hazardous event, also on an ordinal scale.
- Identify the factors influencing the hazards, e.g., climatic change, environmental destruction and resource degradation, major infrastructural facilities such as dams, etc. In the case of hydro-meteorological hazards, there is a close connection between weather and floods. The weather determines the precipitation, which in turn determines the runoff of the waters. Floods are determined by the specific characteristics of the catchment area, by regional climatic factors, and the physical conditions of the city which are often different from rural flooding (see Box 1).

_..._ .. _.ypes_ of Flooding in Urban Areas (*Source:* ActionAid, 2006).

- *Localized flooding* occurs many times a year in slum areas because there are few drains, most of the ground is highly compacted and pathways between dwellings become streams after heavy rain. Such drains and culverts are often blocked by waste and debris.
- *Small streams in urban areas* rise quickly after heavy rain, but often pass through small culverts under roads. Although adequate when designed, changes in the urban area and in storm intensity now produce higher flows that exceed capacity. Channels may also have so much debris in them that they are effectively smaller than they were two decades ago.
- *Major rivers* flowing through urban areas are affected by land use changes and engineering works upstream. Dams can trap sediment, causing rivers to erode their banks downstream. Dam operation may lead to high flows when stored water is released suddenly. Often, urban growth has expanded over some of the floodplain, making parts of the city below flood level and reducing the area into which floods can naturally overflow. Levees have been raised artificially, but with the risk that they may be breached and cause devastating urban flooding.
- In lowland and coastal cities, *wet season flooding* may affect some areas for two or more months, because rain and river water combine to raise the levels of water in swamps that would have naturally been inundated at certain times of the year. Dumping of waste beneath dwellings in these areas tends to help raise levels further. Storm waves can also bring flooding to such areas.

Hazard analysis describes and assesses the probability of occurrence of an extreme natural event at a specific place, at a specific time, and with a specific intensity and duration, for a vulnerable population and their vulnerable basis for life. It describes and evaluates the degree to which the population, animals, structures, and goods would be at risk.

### 3.3. Vulnerability and Capacity Analysis

Vulnerability analysis studies the ability of a system (or element) to withstand, avoid, neutralize, or absorb the impacts of hazardous natural events. Before starting an analysis of the vulnerability of a p and its bases for living, the extreme natural events and th threaten must be identified and studied. Without extreme natural events as a hazard, there are no vulnerable elements, and hence no risk. Conversely, without threatened locations with vulnerable elements, there is no risk, and hence no need for either hazard or vulnerability analysis.

The vulnerability of a group of people or region is inseparably linked to the social, cultural, and economic processes developing there and the agricultural and ecological transformation of the region. Vulnerabilities are created, they are the product of social development or faulty development; they reflect deficits, shortages, or disruptions within social development.

Vulnerability is assessed by the potential loss resulting from a natural event. It expresses the degree of possible loss or damage to an element threatened by a natural event of specific force. Damage can be to the population (life, health, wellbeing), material assets (buildings, infrastructure), or natural assets (woods, forest, agricultural land).

The most important tasks and steps in vulnerability analysis are:

- Identification of potentially vulnerable individuals or elements (e.g., agricultural production, buildings, health, agricultural land, and waters). In this, basic data is collected on population (age, density, gender, ethnic structure, socioeconomic status), location (buildings, important facilities such as schools, hospitals, emergency centers, environment, economy, structures, history), self-protection capability in terms of capacities for disaster preparedness – emergency response capability, training, prevention program, and early warning systems.
- Identification and analysis of factors influencing or resulting in vulnerability or vulnerability factors for each hazard type. Analysis of risk perception and the factors determining this (e.g., education, access to information, poverty) and investigation of the vulnerability factors and their linkage and interdependencies.
  - *Physical vulnerability factors*: location, technical construction type and quality of the settlements and buildings, population growth and density.
  - *Social factors*: education, legal reliability, human rights, participation of civil society, social organizations and institutions, legal framework, statutes, politics, corruption, gender aspects, minorities, dependent population (old, young, sick), traditional knowledge systems, power structures, access to information and social networks.
  - *Economic factors*: socioeconomic status, poverty, food insecurity, lack of diversity of seed and economic activities (e.g., monoculture in

agriculture), lack of access to basic infrastructure (water, energy, health, transport), lack of reserves and financing.

  – *Environmental factors*: arable soil, usable water, vegetation, biodiversity, land under forest (logging, land degradation), and stability of the ecosystems.

- Development and identification of indicators for identifying vulnerabilities and estimating the degree of vulnerability (quality and location of buildings and basic infrastructure, education, access to information, diversity of agriculture and seed, preventive infrastructure, etc.).
- While considering RA, we need to focus on resilience of community through the analysis of self-protection capabilities: identification of indicators to show or measure capacity for preparedness (protective and preventive infrastructure, early warning and forecasting systems, etc.). Here, strategies and measures are identified and investigated at the various levels (family, village, community, district, province, country).
- Estimate of accepted risk (risk level) and hence residual risk. Preventive measures are taken to reduce the risk to a socially and culturally accepted risk.

### 3.4. Products of Risk Analysis

RA involves estimating damage, loss, and consequences arising out of one or more disaster scenarios. It attempts to estimate the probability and magnitude of damage and loss caused by extreme natural events. Its results are conventionally presented in risk maps created manually or using geographical information systems (GIS). As already mentioned, the two analytical stages of hazard and vulnerability analysis are not separate procedures, but rather interactive steps. At the end we get the risk assessment products – risk maps, scenarios, forecasts, risk assessment tables, etc. RA is not a static one-time process, but rather a dynamic process which is constantly adjusting to changing vulnerabilities, hazards, and risks.

### 3.5. The Goal of Risk Analysis

- To identify participative possible hazards and vulnerabilities of population groups to natural events, to analyze these and to estimate and assess both the probability of occurrence and the possible potential damage of such natural events; to identify and study possible weaknesses and gaps in existing protective and adaptive strategies.

- To formulate realistic recommendations for measures to overcome weaknesses and reduce the identified and assessed disaster risks, and to agree these with those affected. It is particularly important here to identify and improve existing capacities as well as protective strategies.
- To ensure and enhance the feasibility, effect, and efficiency of protective measures by working from the RA to (a) balance the various interests, (b) consider the reasonability of measures, and (c) make possible social agreements on strategies and measures to reduce disaster risks.

RA is also expected to contribute to the following:

- Other planning, and specifically spatial and land use planning. This makes it possible to take into account the risks of natural hazards in land use and other activities with spatial impact, including development and zoning plans of communities, agencies, and specialist institutions which are formulated using the information from RA and whose implementation contributes to reducing disaster risks.
- Planning for emergency aid measures, by making it possible to create the conditions for sustainable reconstruction work and development measures.
- Efforts to integrate DRM into the various areas of development.

## 3.6. Expected Products of Risk Analysis

In the context of RA, highly advanced technologies for remote sensing and GIS have in recent years led to the development and improvement of numerous instruments and methods for hazard mapping and analyzing the physical aspects of vulnerability. By contrast, the integration of social, economic, and environmental variables into GIS models, risk maps, and RA generally still remains a challenge.

The products most frequently created in risk analyses include hazard maps and so-called risk maps. Different authors and regions use different names for risk or hazard maps. They also have different levels of data accuracy, and can be subdivided into three categories:

- Hazard maps: these are maps which give qualitative and quantitative information on natural hazards, e.g., by presenting the expected danger or maximum level of danger or the event, e.g., slopes at risk from landslides.

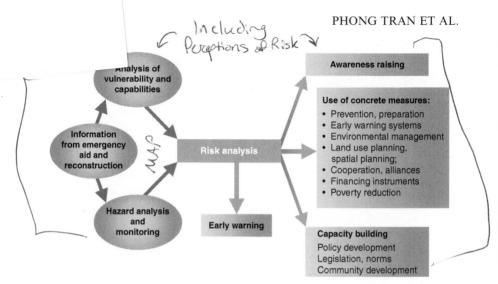

*Fig. 4.* Inputs and Outputs of Risk Analysis. (Adapted from Kohler et al., 2005.)

- Risk zone maps: these provide information on the probability of occurrence (in the case of earthquakes, the contain the building standards needed for disaster reduction). They are generally the result or product of a hazard analysis.
- Risk maps are risk zone maps which also contain quantitative information on the risk and the impacts on people, property, environment, etc. Typically, they take into account the physical aspects of vulnerability, but not the social, economic, and political aspects (Fig. 4).

# 4. DISASTER RISK MANAGEMENT

Participatory DRM planning follows participatory disaster risk assessment – hazard assessment, vulnerability assessment, capacity assessment, and understanding people's perception of the risks. Through the risk assessment process and results, the community and various stakeholders come to a common understanding of the disaster risks in the locality or sector. Participatory DRM planning then unites the various stakeholders in commitment and *actions* to reduce disaster risk and vulnerabilities and enhance capacities to prevent, mitigate, or prepare for hazards and its damaging impacts. Using the results of the participatory disaster risk assessment, a wide range of courses of risk reduction solutions and options, interventions, measures, actions and

activities, strategies, projects and programs are identified and \
protect people, their assets and the built and natural envir _____ ___
planning process focuses on the proactive disaster management activities of
Prevention, Mitigation, and Preparedness.

Prevention covers activities to provide outright avoidance of the adverse
impact of hazards and means to minimize related environmental,
technological, and biological disasters (UNISDR, 2004, p. 17). While
natural hazards may not be prevented, human-induced hazards such as
those associated with industries, technological failures, pollution, and civil
strife can be prevented. Prevention covers measures to provide permanent
protection from disasters or reduce the intensity and frequency of a
hazardous event so that it does not become a disaster (NDCC-UNDCR
Core Group, 2003). These include safety standards in industries, provision
of basic wellbeing services such as preventive health care, education, and
poverty reduction schemes.

Mitigation covers structural and nonstructural measures undertaken to
limit the adverse impact of natural hazards, environmental degradation, and
technological hazards (UNISDR, 2004, p. 17). Mitigation reduces and limits
the destructive and disruptive effects of hazards on the elements at risk.
Measures range from the physical such as engineering works (bridges,
protective dikes, embankments) and safe building design to the nonstructural
interventions such as risk assessment, risk reduction planning, land use
planning and zoning, building codes, risk communication and public
awareness, strengthening institutional arrangements and coordination,
environmental management, food and livelihood security, and micro-finance
programs.

Preparedness involves activities and measures taken in advance to ensure
effective response to the impact of hazards, including the issuance of timely
and effective warnings and the temporary evacuation of people and
property from threatened locations (UNISDR, 2004, p. 17). Preparedness
measures are taken in anticipation of the disaster event to ensure that
appropriate and effective actions are taken during the emergency. Aside
from systems for early warning and evacuation, preparedness measures
include coordination and institutional arrangements, emergency operations
center management, public awareness, disaster drills and simulation, and
logistics and stockpiling.

Disaster risk reduction planning is referred to with various names – DRM
planning, disaster preparedness and mitigation planning, disaster mitigation
planning, counter disaster planning, DRM action planning, risk reduction

action planning. All reflect the focus on the disaster risk reduction on prevention, mitigation, and preparedness:

- How to stop the potentially damaging event? How to stop the harmful event from being a disaster? How to stop all the harmful effects of an event?
- How to make the hazard event smaller? How to reduce the harmful effects of the event?
- What can be done before, during, or after the event?

DRM as used in this chapter is similar to concept of Risk Counter-measures or Risk Treatment (ADRC, 1995, pp. 16–20), which is concerned with what can and will be done in combining risk control and risk finance:

- To avoid the risk (e.g., land use planning and zoning; relocation).
- To reduce the risk (e.g., retrofitting of buildings, drills and simulation exercises; public awareness, early warning system; safe building design).
- To transfer the risk (e.g., reinsurance; catastrophic bond).
- To retain the risk (e.g., disaster or calamity fund; self-insurance).

The safety of urban population, infrastructure, and assets is inextricably linked with the general wellbeing of the people, state of the built and natural environment, and level of economic, social, and physical development. The general goal of disaster risk reduction is to transform at-risk communities and groups to safe and disaster resilient communities, which can withstand and recover from stresses and shocks from the natural/physical and socioeconomic political environment. Resilience is the capacity of the system, community, or society potentially exposed to hazards to adapt, by resisting or changing, in order to reach and maintain an acceptable level of functioning and structure (UNISDR, 2004, p. 16). The image that easily explains the concept of resilience is that of the bamboo that sways and bends with battering of heavy wind and rain but then remains firmly rooted after the storm. Simply put too, the goal of DRM is to have safe and disaster resilient urban communities can be translated into having safe, livable, vibrant, and developed city or urban area.

## 5. ACTION PLANNING FOR DISASTER RISK MANAGEMENT

The DRM plan is the road map or guide in transforming the at-risk locality to be disaster resilient. The DRM plan charts the course of the locality, sector, or community's progression toward safety, disaster resilience, and sustainable development. It unites the various stakeholders, most especially the community actors in commitment and actions in proactive (instead of reactive) disaster management activities of prevention, mitigation, and preparedness with the following results:

- Avoid loss, rather than replace loss
- Avoid social dislocation
- Protect assets of households, community, government
- Protect community safety nets (family, health, food supply, business, education, culture)

Similar to the participatory risk assessment, the process to craft the Disaster Management Plan follows a participatory process. Similar to the results of participatory risk assessment which mainly provide a snapshot of the community at a certain time, comprehensive planning for the disaster risk reduction of the locality may take too long or be too tedious a process for communities. Even with this in mind, the community is usually not able to put the results of the disaster risk reduction planning into an elaborate Disaster Management Plan. However, the community is easily able to document the results of the disaster risk reduction action planning.

DRM action planning is a participatory, short-term, visible, output-oriented process that enables urban community groups to plan risk reduction actions or development in their locality and to lead the implementation of such action plans.

The action planning process recognizes that planning itself is a process of progressive improvements with risk reduction as a long-term goal to be approached incrementally but surely, ensuring that local capacities are mobilized and strengthened and not undermined.

Action Planning is like preparing for a long road trip. The plan serves as the road map. "Where are we going?" and "How do we know we have arrived?" describe the goals and objectives of DRM at the community level, and the expected outcomes of this process. "How do we get there?" refers to the measures, strategies, and risk reduction activities. "Who is coming along?"

ieed to get there?" details resources and task responsibilities to
get actions going.

### 5.1. Identifying Relevant and Adequate Risk Reduction Measures

Using the results of the Participatory Disaster Risk Assessment ensures that
the relevance and adequacy of the Action Plan.

1. Identify the hazard. Assess vulnerabilities (weaknesses) and capacities
   (resources).
2. Determine the elements at risk (people and health; property; livelihood
   and economic activities; communities structures; critical facilities;
   environment) and possible damages from the hazard.
3. Determine conditions and factors of vulnerability. Why will the elements at
   risk be damaged (physical, economic, social, institutional, attitudinal
   reasons).
4. Identify existing coping strategies and capacities/resources (material,
   human, institutional/organizational, social, motivational).
5. Identify measures or solutions to reduce the vulnerability of the elements
   at risk. How to protect and strengthen the elements at risk and how to
   reduce the impact of the hazard?
6. Rank and prioritize risk reduction measures to undertake into immediate,
   short-term, based on resources available, skills, organizational mandate,
   and other criteria agreed upon.
7. Reach consensus on the measures to undertake immediately, in the short,
   medium, and long term.

## 6. IMPLEMENTATION MANAGEMENT

Implementation management is an important part of the participatory risk
management process that is often overlooked. Most implementing agencies
involve beneficiaries to some degree through the assessment process, and
some also through the planning process, but then they implement the
projects on their own without beneficiary participation. It is important to
clarify and emphasize the need for participatory implementation management, and to illustrate ways of achieving it.

There are three kinds of actions that emerge from an action planning
process: (i) those that can be implemented by the community groups
themselves, (ii) those that need some external help for implementation, and

(iii) those that can only be implemented by specialized agencies from outside the community. Participatory approaches focus most on the first set, and least on the third set of options. Implementation management processes thus need to look at how internal systems can be established to operationalize self-action, and to coordinate external interventions. It is for these reasons that formation of community based organizations or strengthening of existing organizations to take up the task of implementation of the Action Plans is a must for ensuring proper translation of the plans into action, and for sustaining the momentum.

### 6.1. Forming a Community Disaster Management Organization

A Community Disaster Management Organization (CDMO) has to be formed in communities where such an organization does not already exist. Where such an organization exists but is dormant, the existing one can be revived. There are quite a few countries where CDMOs were formed in the past in accordance with the law, but have been dormant for years for various reasons.

A CDMO is usually formed in the course of workshops held in the initial stages of a risk reduction project. Workshops are held further to develop capacity of CDMOs for fulfilling the functions as mentioned below.

The functions of a CDMO include:

- Decision making
- Planning of activities before, during, and after disaster
- Activities are tabulated in Table 1.

These functions are to be fulfilled in cooperation with local/central government and other concerned organizations. The CDMO holds meetings periodically, usually once a month, or as and when the necessity arises.

***Table 1.*** Detailed Activites of CDMO Before, During, and After Disaster.

| Before | During | After |
|---|---|---|
| • Awareness raising<br>• Conducting drills<br>• Activities for prevention/mitigation | • Early warning<br>• Damage/need assessment<br>• Search/rescue/first aid<br>• Evacuation/shelter management<br>• Reception/distribution of food and other relief items<br>• Epidemic surveillance | • Assistance to affected people<br>• Reconstruction<br>• Evaluation of activities for "during" phase |

## 6.2. Structure of CDMO

The structure of the CDMO varies from community to community. Usually, a Community Disaster Management Committee (CDMC) is set up, which consists of a secretariat and commissions for different functions. The Committee is registered in the municipal administration. The president of the committee and the coordinators of the commissions are elected by community people. They work voluntarily without remuneration. "Start simple" is the principle in building community organizations.

In areas where the society is complex and has different social classes, religions and races, it is important to involve all the different groups in the process. This is particularly so in conflict areas.

## 6.3. Plans and Implementation

The CDMO should have a plan that covers the four phases of a disaster management cycle (response, rehabilitation, prevention, preparedness). In practice though, a Plan for Emergency and a Plan for Disaster Risk Reduction are the two documents prepared in most cases.

In order to implement these plans, an Annual Work Plan is prepared, specifying activities considering the priorities and resources available internally and from outside. The work plan is implemented in cooperation with various supporting actors, especially the central and local governments.

## 6.4. Sustainability

The key aspect of community participation is sustainability. It is often observed that community activities are successful during the project period with external support, but gradually diminish as the years pass. Sustainability is an issue of long-term concern, and to achieve it is really a big challenge. There are many reasons for this, of which the following are the most fundamental and should be so recognized for meeting the challenge of achieving sustainability:

- *Lack of resources.* Even though awareness is enhanced through implementation of such projects, it is difficult for the communities to continue the activities if necessary resources are not available. In most countries, municipalities are responsible for continuing support to the

CDMOs, however, there are few municipalities that are able to fulfill such a responsibility because they themselves are often suffering from lack of resources. Appropriate arrangements to ensure sustainability, especially in terms of finance, should be made before the project terminates.

- *Disaster reduction is not always the top priority agenda* in communities due to a number of pressing issues they face. In communities where the majority of people are very poor, activities should not be limited to disaster reduction but should cover daily survival issues. As far as they remain very poor, CDMOs may not find it possible to implement activities successfully in a sustainable manner.
- *Disaster is not a frequent event.* Some communities suffer from disasters frequently, while for others it is not a frequent event, occurring at an interval of years or even decades. In such cases, it is difficult for local people to maintain readiness for such an event throughout the nonoccurrence period.
- It is often observed that *"Political influence"* hinders sustainability. Each time the government changes through elections, the responsible officials of central and local governments may also be replaced, resulting in no consistency in policy, no continuation in activities and no accumulation of experience and knowledge. It sometimes happens that the CDMO starts with members belonging to the political party in power and diminishes when the other party takes power. Institutional strengthening to make political influence less might be one way toward solving this problem.

### 6.5. Monitoring and Evaluation

Monitoring is a part of project management, focusing on two aspects: process and effect. "Process monitoring" focuses on the use of inputs and the progress of activities and takes records in order to ensure that inputs deliveries, work schedules, and target outputs are proceeding according to the plan. This should be a regular activity involving stakeholders on a weekly, monthly, or quarterly basis according to the duration and nature of the project. "Effect monitoring" focuses on progress toward achieving the objectives and on the impacts made in relation to these objectives. This can also be used as an internal self-evaluation mechanism besides the formal evaluation that is conducted usually in the middle and at the end of the project.

Evaluation is conducted to see to what extent the project objectives have been achieved. It is normally by experts not directly involved in the project. It is usually carried out two times: in the middle of the project term to improve activities still in progress, and at the end of the project to find out whether the project has been successful or not. Evaluation is usually made in accordance with Project Design Matrix (PDM).

Evaluation of a CDMO project is not easy. Disasters take place at different places, with different magnitudes, at intervals of long time periods, usually longer than the project term. In view of such capricious nature of disaster events, it is not easy to identify an appropriate index to evaluate the achievements in the context of "risk reduction," "vulnerability reduction," "capacity development" as usually set out under goals and objectives. While in other sectors like education and water supply the goal can be expressed in numerical figures and achievements evaluated quantitatively, a CDMO project is difficult to evaluate purely in numerical figures and its evaluation is thus not as clearly understood.

Evaluation of CDMO projects have been carried out in various ways, but qualitatively using participatory processes in most cases. In addition to this, quantitative evaluation is also recommended for the following reasons:

(1) It is possible to identify priority communities for the project from among various communities proposed, by comparing their numerical results of the evaluation.

(2) It is possible to evaluate achievements and effectiveness of the project by conducting the evaluation twice, at the beginning of and after the termination of the project, and comparing the results of the two evaluations. "Is a CDMO project really effective in risk reduction?" is a question sometimes raised by financial authorities and others. Clear answers are necessary for gaining wider support for CDMO projects.


## 7. CONCLUSION

RA is not a static one-time process, but rather a dynamic process, which is constantly adjusting to changing vulnerabilities, hazards, and risks. RA is particularly important to:

• Identify possible hazards and vulnerabilities of population groups to natural events, to analyze these and to estimate and assess both the probability of occurrence and the possible potential damage of such natural events; identify and study possible weaknesses and gaps in existing protective and adaptive strategies.

- Formulate realistic recommendations for measures to overcome weaknesses and reduce the identified and assessed disaster risks, and to agree these with those affected. It is particularly important here to identify and improve existing capacities as well as protective strategies.
- Ensure and enhance the feasibility, effect and efficiency of protective measures by working from the RA to balance the various interests; consider the reasonability of measures; and make possible social agreements on strategies and measures to reduce disaster risks.
- To contribute to meeting priority two of the HFA.

RA is the first and important steps in DRM process. It means the results of risk assessment should be used at latter phase of DRM.

The stage that follows RA is one of planning, that uses the analysis outcome to develop disaster risk reduction plans. Action Planning is a participatory way of making such risk reduction plans that engages the local stakeholders and ensures that the plan is appropriate for local needs, capacities, and context. There are various participatory tools that can be used, keeping the principle of participatory and local actions in focus.

Implementation of Action Plans is a complex and often ignored process. The most appropriate way of implementation is through Community Disaster Management Organizations that are truly local in nature and have a sense of ownership as well as a long-term presence. This ensures greater accountability, dedication, and sustainability of the interventions.

# ACKNOWLEDGMENTS

Phong Tran highly acknowledges the scholarship of Government of Japan, Ministry of Education Sport Culture Science and Technology (MEXT), and the support of the Gradate School of Global Environmental Studies, Kyoto University for this study. Part of this study was drawn from Kyoto University inputs to ISDR technical note number 2 and 3. Rajib Shaw acknowledges the support from MEXT projects (CASIFICA, Vietnam Kaken, and Water Communities) and ACCU/UNESCO grant to conduct the training workshop on Urban Risk.

# REFERENCES

ActionAid. (2006). Climate change, urban flooding and the rights of the urban poor in Africa Key findings from six African cities.

Asian Disaster Reduction Center. (1995). *Total disaster risk management: Good practices.* Kobe: Asian Disaster Reduction Center.

International Decade for Natural Disaster Reduction (IDNDR). (1990). *Cities at risk: Making cities safer ... before disaster strikes.* Geneva: IDNDR.

Kohler, A., Jülich, S., & Bloemertz, L. (2005). Guidelines risk analysis – A basis for disaster risk management, GTZ.

Mitchell, J. (Ed.) (1999). *Crucibles of hazards: Mega-cities and disasters in transition.* Tokyo: United Nations University Press.

NDCC-UNDCR Core Group. (2003). Contingency planning for emergencies: A manual for local government units (2nd ed.). Manila: United Nations High Commissioner for Refugee Liaison Office Manila with the National Disaster Coordinating Council-Office of Civil Defense.

Pelling, M. (2003). *The vulnerability of cities.* London: Earthscan.

Sanderson, D. (2000). Cities, disasters and livelihoods. *Environment and Urbanization, 12*(2), 93–102.

United Nations Human Settlements Program (UNHSP). (2004). Reducing urban risk and vulnerability: A thematic paper submitted for discussion at the UN-HABITAT/UN-ISDR. Working meeting on vulnerability assessment and reducing urban risk, Madrid, 7–9 September 2004.

United Nations Inter-Agency Secretariat of the International Strategy for Disaster Reduction (UN/ISDR). (2004). *Living with risk: A global review of disaster reduction initiatives.* New York: United Nations Publications.

UNISDR (United Nations International Strategy for Disaster Reduction). (2004). Living with risk: A global review of disaster reduction initiatives. Geneva: United Nations.

Wisner, B., Blaikie, P., Cannon, T., & Davis, I. (2004). *At risk second edition: Natural hazards, people's vulnerability, and disasters.* London: Routledge.

# CHAPTER 3

# ENVIRONMENTAL RISK REDUCTION IN URBAN AREAS

Hari Srinivas

## ABSTRACT

*Decision-making is an important step in the risk management process. Decisions often need to be based on incomplete information, and have to carry an element of sound judgment with them. Decision-making is usually a prerogative of government agencies in change of development and disaster management. But it also needs to be included in participatory processes involving citizens – which is far more than mere consent of the public to decisions taken by others.*

*The most critical components of decision-making are participation and consensus building. In fact these two elements are often in conflict with each other. In the spirit of participation, a wider consultation is needed, and when participation widens, it becomes difficult to arrive at consensus. Simple tools can be very useful in evolving consensus within the planning groups, civil society actors and the government.*

*The content of this chapter focuses specifically on environmental risk and its potential to exacerbate the negative impacts of a disaster event. It also looks more closely on the built environment and the role that effective decision-making can play in not only mitigating urban risk, but also to preserve/conserve the local environment. They key message of the cyclical interrelationships between good environmental management and reducing disaster risk, lies at the core of this paper.*

Urban Risk Reduction: An Asian Perspective
Community, Environment and Disaster Risk Management, Volume 1, 37–54
Copyright © 2012 by Emerald Group Publishing Limited
All rights of reproduction in any form reserved
ISSN: 2040-7262/doi: 10.1108/S2040-7262(2009)0000001007

# 1. INTRODUCTION

Across the world, environmental decisions are constantly being taken. Their settings vary, as do the people and groups involved. Environmental decisions occur within neighbourhoods, small businesses, corporate boardrooms, and in the offices of local, state and national governments. They involve different people with different backgrounds. There is a constant need for understanding the various processes, actors and preconditions of decision-making processes for environmental management and risk reduction.

Environmental decisions particularly at the local level anchor themselves on three entities – businesses, government and the civil society at large. Facilitating interaction between them, and focusing on sustainable use of earth's resources, have been key challenges for developed and developing countries alike. What directions should research and development take? What specific roles should be played by the different actors so that innovation and creativity in environmental decisions can be fostered? How can environmental decision-making at various levels be supported and promoted?

It is clear that a culture of understanding and awareness needs to be developed, that is primarily focused on ecological processes, and on man's environmental footprint (which, in most cases, is increasing the risk posed by disasters). Environmental research needs to be geared towards mitigating current problems, and securing the earth for future generations. What changes, modifications and adjustments are necessary for a turnaround to refocus our efforts on sustainable lifestyles? What decision-making patterns need to be adopted for this to happen?

Research insights, monitoring and evaluation results, and information dialogues need to be incorporated into environment and development projects, so that demonstrable successes can be an inspiration for further action and replication.

What is the nature of decisions that are taken with respect to urban and environmental risk? How can information for decisions be better managed for effective decision-making? What skills will be needed for such processes?

# 2. THE DECISION-MAKING PYRAMID

Decision-making related to environmental risk, in reality, is a complex, multi-faceted process, needing multi-sectoral and multi-stakeholder involvement at various levels of governance from local to global (Fig. 1).

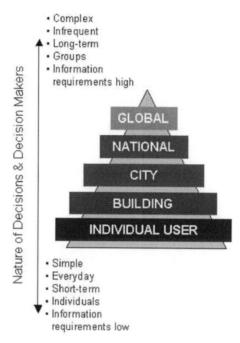

*Fig. 1.* The Decision-Making Pyramid.

This is particularly true for decisions that need to be taken for managing the environment. As mentioned earlier, the focus of the pyramid is on environmental decision-making and the built environment, and the user is encouraged to be more aware of this process and extrapolate its implication to risk management as well.

In our daily lives, 'simple' decisions and choices taken by individuals on a daily basis cumulatively have a global impact – whether direct or indirect, immediate or long-term. Vice versa, global decisions have to be broken down into smaller frequent decisions and choices at the individual level.

An example of this process is to break down a 'global' environmental problem such as desertification (that is a major cause of droughts and other disasters) into individual causes, for example, deforestation, water extraction, agricultural practices, and then further to choices and decisions that influences these causes (including, e.g. lifestyle choices, consumption patterns, technology development etc.), ending up with options that can be taken up at the local level by individuals, for example, choice of the foods we eat.

The pyramid has the individual level at the bottom level, and the global level at the top. In between are aligned other levels of decision-making: a community, city and national.

While the bottom reflects simple decisions taken everyday, the top represents complex decisions taken more infrequently. Cyclically, activities at the local/micro level influences the global levels, and activities at the global level influences the local/micro level.

The pyramid is actually a continuum: as we go from the bottom (micro level) to the top (macro level), we see that

• individual decisions are replaced by decisions taken by groups, the largest (i.e. 'everyone') at the topmost
• decisions become more complex covering a broader range of different aspects
• quality and quantity information required for decision-making increases
• short-term decisions are replaced by longer-term decisions.

The link between the top and the bottom of the sections of the pyramid is in fact cyclical: the everyday choices and preferences at the bottom of the pyramid influences policies developed at the global level.

On the other hand, decisions and agreements made at the global level clearly influences action at the bottom of the pyramid. For example, the Montreal Protocol on ozone depletion at the global level has an influence on an individual's product choices at the local level.

Thus, outputs generated at the top of the pyramid – the global level – are policy oriented and have indirect impacts on everyday life, while outputs generated at the bottom of the pyramid – the individual level – are action-oriented and have direct impacts on everyday life.

Buildings, and urban systems that link these buildings, are a key factor in increasing risk and vulnerability in cities and urban areas. What happens when we apply the decision-making pyramid to a specific sector, say the building and construction sector? How can we break down a decision that needs complex long-term multi-stakeholder involvement, into smaller frequent individual decisions to be taken at the micro level on a daily basis?

In the example here, we start with a global goal: 'Vulnerability levels need to be reduced'. We then see how this global goal impacts other levels and generates action, initiated and carried out by multi-stakeholder partnerships (Table 1).

The key message of the analysis enabled by the decision pyramid is clear. (1) We need to ensure that global goals and objectives are translated to viable

***Table 1.*** Characteristics of Decisions Taken at Different Levels, But on the Same Topic.

*Level: Global*

| | |
|---|---|
| Actions and implications at this level | At the global level, much attention is paid to trends in understanding vulnerability, and disaster risk; how transnational trade and other globalization processes are increasing urban activities and growth patterns, and consequently increasing vulnerabilities. Causes and effects are also outlined, with targets and plans of action for national governments. |
| Stakeholders involved | UN and international organizations, universities and research institutions, international NGOs. |

*Level: National*

| | |
|---|---|
| Actions and implications at this level | The commitment that national governments make at global/ UN forums to 'reduce vulnerability' is converted into national policies and programmes where support and guidance, in the form of rules, regulations legislation, research and development, financial support etc. is outlined and implemented. |
| Stakeholders involved | National government ministries, agencies and departments; research and training institutions; universities; business and industry associations; chambers of commerce. |

*Level: City*

| | |
|---|---|
| Actions and implications at this level | Cities and local governments take advantage of the special arrangements made at the national level to implement it locally, by integrating the goals and objectives within their own environmental management plans. Local ordinances, regulations, etc. are combined with information campaigns and other means of informing the local communities of the need to reduce vulnerability in the city. Campaigns can include special subsidies for developers, transportation planning, guidelines and checklists etc. |
| Stakeholders involved | Local government agencies and departments, business and industry associations, local chambers of commerce, financial institutions, NGOs and community groups, local universities and research institutions etc. |

*Level: Building*

| | |
|---|---|
| Actions and implications at this level | This is the critical step where the guidelines, checklists and regulations are converted to planning and design specifications that help in reduced $CO_2$ emissions from buildings, and the activities that are undertaken within them. Material specifications, design features, technology choices and building usage procedures have a key role to play in achieving reducing $CO_2$ levels. |
| Stakeholders involved | Individual users, clubs and NGOs, management teams. |

**Table 1.** (*Continued*)

| | |
|---|---|
| *Level: Individual* | |
| Actions and implications at this level | Much of the action at this level concerns the day-to-day use of the building. It is these activities that cumulatively have a substantial impact on the environment, and provide the most critical opportunity for action. Reducing electricity usage, minimizing the amount of water used and wastes generated, espousing the 3Rs – reduce/reuse/recycle are some of the actions taken at this level. These can follow strict procedures laid out by the management or can be self-persuasion through education and awareness building. |
| Stakeholders involved | Individual users, clubs and NGOs, management teams. |

local actions that cumulatively help achieve the objectives. (2) Appropriate stakeholders should be involved at the right level, and partner with each other for the purpose of taking the right action at that level. (3) Proper communication among stakeholders – between levels and within a particular level is very important.

# 3. INFORMATION FOR DECISION-MAKING

Providing the right information at the right time to the right person at the right level of subsidiary is needed in order to ensue that the right decision is taken (Box 1). As a first step, let us take a quick look through the critical stages of decision-making and the management of information needed for the purpose.

## 3.1. Defining the Problem

Take time to properly define the problem. What is the issue to be covered? What is the problem? What decisions need to be taken? A fishbone diagram will sometimes help in understanding the complex interlinkages that create a particular 'problem'. For each of the causes or its effects, make a list of information or data that will be required, and clarify how that information will lead to a better decision.

What causes a particular effect or problem is usually a combination of factors – causes and sub causes-that need to be analysed and studied to get the whole picture (Fig. 2).

**Box 1.** Principles of Decision-Making

There are 11 principles of collaborative problem-solving. Such collaboration is an inclusionary process that promotes lateral communication and shared decision-making. It helps stakeholder groups to develop policy recommendations on a variety of public issues. The 11 principles are listed below.

1. Purpose-driven: People need a reason to participate in the process.
2. Inclusive, not exclusive: All parties with a significant interest in the issues should be involved in the collaborative process.
3. Educational: The process relies on mutual education of all participants.
4. Voluntary: The parties who are affected or interested participate voluntarily.
5. Self-designed: All parties have an equal opportunity to participate in designing the collaborative process. The process must be explainable and designed to meet the circumstances and needs of the situation.
6. Flexible: Flexibility should be designed into the process to accommodate changing issues, data needs, political environment and programmatic constraints such as time and meeting arrangements.
7. Egalitarian: All parties have equal access to relevant information and the opportunity to participate effectively throughout the process.
8. Respectful: Acceptance of the diverse values, interests and knowledge of the parties involved in the collaborative process is essential.
9. Accountable: The participants are accountable both to their constituencies and to the process that they have agreed to establish.
10. Time limited: Realistic deadlines are necessary throughout the process.
11. Achievable: Commitments made to achieve the agreement(s) and effective monitoring are essential.

*Source:* Natural Resources Research Institute.

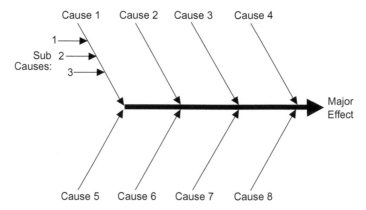

*Fig. 2.* The Decision-Making Pyramid. *Note:* Remember that sometimes, the real cause can lie hidden behind the 'visible' causes ...

## 3.2. Finding the Information

Determine the sources from where information needed for decision-making can be obtained. What information needs to be taken? Who has that information? Why is that information being collected by the source? Which component of the problem at hand will it help? Evaluate the sources to see which of them can provide the best information, and identify the mode and format in which the information is presented. Keep in mind that different sources provide information in different formats (for different reasons!).

Besides looking at books, articles etc. we also need to look at the full information pyramid – including intermediate information products and raw data (Fig. 3).

## 3.3. Processing the Knowledge

This where the information gathered is matched with the problem in hand. The relevant information from each source is extracted and information from multiple sources is organized. Which parts of the information collected needs to be used? What additional data or information is needed? How can information be best presented to be able to understand the situation and take decisions? The collected information is evaluated and integrated for its relevance, validity and interconnectedness.

The actual info needed for a decision comes from the collected info, but also from other additional info and from experiences and knowledge. The

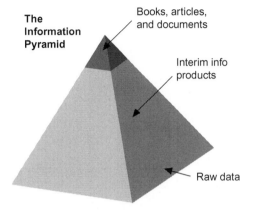

The Information Pyramid

Books, articles, and documents

Interim info products

Raw data

| Information you know you have | Information you know you don't have |
|---|---|
| Information you don't know you have | Information you don't know you don't have |

*Four states of info possession*

*Fig. 3.* The Information Pyramid. *Note:* Remember that information can also lie in experiences and insights that are not 'recorded'. Also look at the information pyramid to see if all levels are covered ...

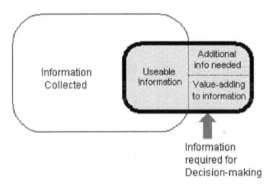

Information Collected

Useable Information

Additional info needed

Value-adding to information

Information required for Decision-making

*Fig. 4.* Information Procession for Decision-Making. *Note:* Remember that it is critical to package the information to fit the audience using the right medium: presenting the right information at the right time to the right audience ...

useable info is extracted from the info collected – additional information needed is identified and ways to add value to the information collected is also determined. This will be the information required to take the decision (Fig. 4).

### 3.4. Making the Decision

In an interactive and inclusive process involving all the concerned parties, form an opinion from the information collected for its effectiveness and

*Fig. 5.* The Problems-Decisions Cycle. *Note:* Remember that implementing the decision (actors and actions), as well as monitoring and evaluating the actions taken, are integral parts of the decision.

efficiency. Use it to take the decision. Has the decision taken help in solving the problem at hand? Was the decision satisfactory and took into account all the views of concerned parties? A decision taken may need to be examined closely and refined, and modified to meet differing needs over time. Many times, a decision may have to be broken down into smaller decisions, to be taken by different entities. Decision-making for problem-solving is always a cyclical process – each feeding the other (Fig. 5).

# 4. SKILLS FOR ENVIRONMENTAL DECISION-MAKING

There are a number of skills we need in order to take the appropriate decision to solve a particular problem.

## 4.1. Knowledge and Understanding

We take decisions everyday, as a part of our lives, our work, our future, and every one of these decisions have an impact on environment and risk mitigation, one way or another. Understanding the impact of our decisions on the environment, and taking decisions on proper management of the environment is a critical skill that we all have to possess, irrespective of our formal qualifications or jobs that we hold.

We will need competent knowledge and understanding of environmental decision-making and relevant key concepts and how different perspectives and motivations of different people and groups affect environmental decision-making. A knowledge of the principles of sustainable development will have to be combined with formal environmental decision-making techniques, including the role of models, monitoring and auditing; and abilities to define, plan and carrying out information gathering for decision-making.

## 4.2. Cognitive Skills

Cognitive skills remain an important component of the sliver of skills of a competent environmental decision-maker. The ability to analyse problems, sifting the irrelevant from the relevant and expressing the results using standard formalisms and notations, needs to be tempered with the ability to integrate knowledge and skills from various sources into a coherent whole. This includes developing appropriate scenarios to produce conclusions, and to critically assess/evaluate proposed solutions. A good decision-maker should also be able to deal with complex issues both systematically and creatively, making informed judgements in the absence of complete data and demonstrate self-direction and originality in tackling and solving problems.

## 4.3. Practical and/or Professional Skills and Attributes

Skills for effective decision-making are developed on a daily basis, from practical experience and from our understanding of the impacts of our everyday actions, on the environment around us (and also the 'invisible' environment far away, which has produced the goods/services we consume). A professional who has to take decisions affecting the environment will have to be able to prepare cases advocating the appropriate use of environmental systems approaches. He/she will also have to be able to appraise technical or environmental systems developments and assess their applicability and implications to a particular area that requires action.

Legal issues are an integral part of this – and we have to demonstrate an awareness of the legal and ethical implications associated with environmental and risk issues, show a detailed knowledge of the importance and application of environmental issues to businesses and society; and also formulate an audit of an organization for proper environmental management that includes risk aspects.

*4.4. Other Key Skills*

Many other key skills go together to aid effective environmental decision-making. Communication is one of the foremost of them – to be able to communicate knowledge, ideas and conclusions effectively using written presentations, producing detailed critiques, coherent project reports and other appropriate media, for specialist and non-specialist audiences. This includes the ability to seek relevant information from appropriate sources.

Numeracy skills and ability to interpret statistical data will also be important. The use of IT tools and skills, specifically retrieving information from the internet, transferring information by e-mail and using commercial software packages, is now becoming an important part of the portfolio of key skills.

Ultimately, it will be a combination of formal knowledge along with everyday experiences and common sense that will facilitate good decision-making. A good decision-maker will have to be able to advance his/her own knowledge and understanding through independent learning, develop problem-solving skills and apply them independently to tasks, projects or functions; work independently, reflecting on own actions and thoughts; making effective use of constructive feedback; and also work with others to refine ideas leading to an improved understanding of key concepts within an environmental context.

## ANNEX 1. TO DO OR NOT
## TO DO: DECISION-MAKING AND
## RISK FROM BUILDINGS

The reduction of greenhouse gases (GHGs) is central to a number of multilateral environmental agreements, including the climate change convention. A number of human activities are responsible for the release of GHGs, and for its consequent man-made hazards and risks, but a recent key area of focus has been the building and construction sector that forms a core part of the development of any city.

The processes involved in a building's lifespan – conceptualization, design, construction, use, maintenance and demolition – have immense implications for the GHGs produced in terms of resources and energy consumption. Building and construction processes can be subject to the principles of sustainability and risk reduction. What would this mean to users, professionals or local governments? What are the key elements of a

***Table A1.*** Common Reasons for Lack of Action and Strategies for Change.

| Common Reasons for Lack of Action | Strategies for Change in Decision-Making Processes |
|---|---|
| 'I don't benefit from making this building disaster resistant' | Some construction companies now provide services directed at the full life cycle of a building, thus benefiting, for example, from making provisions for disaster resistance in design. Professional ethics may force us to think of all stages of a building, not only on the stage we are concerned with. |
| 'Each stakeholder pursues his/her own goals, ignoring others' | We may want to work in collaborative teams to ensure better understanding of other stakeholders. We have a responsibility sometimes to 'educate' the client, whether it is the developer, financier or user, to think of disaster risk issues as well. Providing services of all stages of the building's life cycle may, in itself, be a business opportunity. |
| 'Social or economic returns is more important than environmental risk issues' | Many times, action needed for solving environmental problems can generate income or create jobs! Environmental management has many externalities in reducing risks, ensuring good health, better air quality or efficient water usage. |
| 'One person (or one building) cannot make a difference!' | But by embracing sustainability or risk principles, we can be leaders and role models in the field! All action starts small – one step at a time – which eventually leads to its broad adoption within the entire industry sector. Proper publicity and media coverage may educate clients to 'copy' a good design for disaster resistance, or a sustainable building – the best pressure that can put pressure on building and construction professionals to take action. |
| 'It's too expensive' | Some initial costs may be high, or may be perceived as unnecessary 'extras'. But money will be saved in the long term from overall risk reduction, energy efficiency, costly remedial action, maintenance etc. Costly litigation may be saved by ensuring all aspects of a building's environmental impacts are considered (including the activities that take place within a building – e.g., through an ISO 14001 certification process). |
| 'Building codes (functional efficiency, comfort…) are not favourable towards disaster risk reduction' | This is changing, and international action towards this issue is increasing. Sometimes current building codes and standards have to be interpreted to extract its sustainability roots. |

**Table A1.** (*Continued*)

| Common Reasons for Lack of Action | Strategies for Change in Decision-Making Processes |
| --- | --- |
| 'Banks and clients always focus on bottom lines and high profits' | Banks and clients need to be made aware of disaster resistance and sustainability's positive externalities and long-term costs of not taking action. |
| | Environmental and sustainability aspects need to be included in budgeting and investment processes, and can in itself be used as a 'selling' point. |
| 'Professional ethics is very weak, so using sustainability or risk reduction principles is difficult' | Disaster risk reduction and sustainability has to made an integral part of the education of professionals involved in building and construction sector. |
| | Continuing education programmes, on-the-job training, awareness building workshops etc. should be used to place emphasis on sustainability principles. |

sustainable building and construction policy? What policies and programmes are needed to ensure the success of such a policy? Who needs to be
involved – up and down the supply chain, besides the local government
itself?

Incorporating risk reduction and sustainability principles in the building
and construction sector is critical, but the decision-making process is
fraught with mind-sets that resist the change towards greater sustainability.
Table A1 illustrates the common reasons for resisting action towards risk
reduction and sustainability, and some of the strategies and justifications we
can adopt in facilitating appropriate decision-making.

# ANNEX 2. ENVIRONMENTAL MANAGEMENT TOOLBOX

The Environmental Management (EM) Tool Box includes a range of
decision support tools that can assist decision makers to improve the
environmental outcomes of their management decisions (Table A2).

Understanding the differences between the different decision support tools
can help you decide which tool you should use in a particular situation. For
example, while an EIA is typically undertaken to gain regulatory approval
for a project, an ERA is voluntary and can be carried out at any time.

**Table A2.** Environmental Management Tools.

*Scoping Stage*

The initial phase of policy making, planning and project design, when the broad dimensions of the initiative, critical success factors and sources of significant risk are identified and elaborated through a consultative process with stakeholders, and used subsequently to make recommendations and decisions as to the conceptual design and overall economic viability, social acceptability and environmental sustainability of the proposed activity.

Strategic Environmental Assessment (SEA)

A systematic process for evaluating the environmental consequences of policies, plans, programmes or proposals, to ensure that they are addressed early in the decision-making process and on par with economic and social considerations and. Undertaking SEAs can also contribute to sustainable development goals, promote accountability and credibility among the general public and specific stakeholders and lead to broader policy coherence.

Life Cycle Assessment (LCA)

Facilitates evaluation of how and to what extent a process or product system impacts on the environment, for all stages of its life cycle. The typical life cycle consists of a series of stages running from extraction of raw materials, through design and formulation, processing, manufacturing, packaging, distribution, use, reuse, recycling and, ultimately, waste disposal. With the entire product life cycle as the focus for the assessment, a complicated picture can often emerge, with environmentally significant inputs and outputs to air, water and soil identified at every life cycle stage. Unexpected impacts, or benefits, will often be associated with some of the co-products or by-products which are produced by a given process.

Environmental Technology Assessment (ETA)

A systematic procedure whereby a proposed technology intervention is described and appraised in terms of its potential influence on the environment, the implications for sustainable development and the likely cultural and socio-economic consequences. The assessment process requires consideration of alternative technologies, and other options, thereby providing a mechanism for comparing the impact of a variety of possible interventions. Thus EnTA helps planners, decision-makers in government, the private sector, communities and other stakeholders, to reach a consensus on the technology intervention that is expected to be the most environmentally sound, socially acceptable and economically viable, for a specified location and application.

## Table A2. (Continued)

*Design and Approval Stage*

The phase of policy making, planning and project design and approval when the specific details of the proposed activity, including the desired end results, are developed and described, taking into account the objectives, stakeholder views, regulatory and other requirements and best practices in design and implementation.

Environmental Impact Assessment (EIA)

A structured procedure designed to help ensure that development and investment proposals, activities, projects and programmes are environmentally sound and sustainable. EIA facilitates identification, analysis and evaluation of the significance of the potential environmental impacts and the identification and elaboration of measures that will avoid, remedy or mitigate any adverse impacts. It allows informed decision-making as to whether a proposal should proceed and, if so, under what conditions. It also establishes a monitoring and environmental management regime for implementing mitigation measures, monitoring impacts for compliance and ascertaining if impacts are as predicted.

Social Impact Assessment (SIA)

If there is a need for a more comprehensive, in-depth and rigorous determination of the impacts a given policy, plan, programme, project, activity or action may have on the social aspects of the environment, SIA is an appropriate tool. A basic part of SIA is to analyse who wins and who loses with each alternative considered, and to determine whether an alternative may have high and disproportionate adverse environmental or health effects on a low-income population or a minority population. Impact equity must be considered in close and sympathetic consultation with affected communities, neighbourhoods, and groups, especially low-income and minority groups.

Environmental Risk Assessment (ERA)

All decisions and actions have environmental consequences, many of which are unintended. Thus no part of existence is risk free. Risk is the likelihood that a harmful consequence will occur as a result of an action. EnRA determines the potential impact of a chemical or physical agent on ecosystems, habitats and other ecological resources, and on human health and well-being. The assessment can be either qualitative or semi-quantitative. Two further steps are integral to risk assessment, namely risk management and risk communication. The use of EnRA in environmental planning and management is fast becoming a

## *Table A2.* (*Continued*)

standard practice, either as a stand-alone procedure or as a support or complement to an EIA. Appropriate use of EnRA will identify situations of potential environmental concern and allow decision-makers to select management options with the least, and still acceptable level of risk.

Cost Benefit Analysis (CBA)

This is one way to organize, evaluate and present information that will improve the quality of decision-making, by using as a metric a monetary measure of the aggregate change in environmental (including human) well-being resulting from a decision. Individual welfare is assumed to depend on the satisfaction of individual preferences, and monetary measures of welfare change are derived by observing how much individuals are willing to pay, that is willing to give up in terms of other consumption opportunities. This approach can be applied to non-market 'public goods' like environmental quality or environmental risk reduction as well as to market goods and services, although the measurement of non-market values is more challenging. Because of this need to place monetary values on attributes of human well-being for which no market prices exist, CBA is often complicated, expensive and somewhat controversial.

*Operational Stage*

The implementation stage, when policy is made, plans are developed and projects are undertaken. Throughout this stage monitoring and review procedures are used to foster a process of continual improvement, by identifying and reinforcing successful activities and actions, and by identifying and revising or halting unsuccessful activities and actions.

Environmental Management Systems (EMS)

A systematic way to ensure environmental issues are managed consistently and systematically throughout an organization. An EMS can also assist an organization to address environmental issues in a comprehensive manner, sending positive signals to clients, consumers, regulators and other stakeholders indicating that environmental issues are being seriously considered. Effectively applied, an EMS can help integrate environmental considerations with an organization's overall management system. It sets out environmental policies, objectives and targets for an organization, with pre-determined indicators that provide measurable goals, and a means of determining if the performance level has been reached. Often these are the same performance indicators that are chosen for strategic reasons.

*Table A2.* (*Continued*)

Environmental Reporting (ER)

Reporting on environmental policies, targets, performance and plans to improve, whether it be by a company an institution, a country or some other entity, can help improve environmental and wider reputations, aid communication with a wide variety of stakeholders, play a major role in improving management of risk and help identify opportunities for savings in resources used, wastes produced and operating costs. Several codes and some major organizations are moving towards wider sustainable development reporting. This also covers social and economic impacts. Many companies are finding that others in their supply chains want to do business with like-minded suppliers and are beginning to ask for evidence of environmental engagement. Investors too are increasingly aware of environmental performance. Organizations that do not report on environmental performance will likely have more difficulty gaining access to capital, while those that can demonstrate attention to environmental management may well benefit from easier credit and lower insurance premiums.

Environmental Audit (EA)

A systematic, periodic and documented verification process that obtains and evaluates objectively the available evidence, to determine whether specified activities, events, conditions, equipment, management systems and organizations, or information about these matters, conform with EA criteria. The results of this process are communicated to the client and other appropriate stakeholders. An EA will often facilitate management control of environmental practices and assess compliance with policies that would include meeting or exceeding regulatory requirements.

# CHAPTER 4

# INFORMATION, EDUCATION, AND COMMUNICATION FOR URBAN RISK REDUCTION

Rajib Shaw and Manu Gupta

## ABSTRACT

*Risk management is one of the most important means of achieving sustainable development, while education is the most basic intervention required for addressing attitudes and changing community practice. Education for sustainable development is in this light a relatively passive yet extremely important intervention for ensuring long-term urban risk management, particularly if we want such risk management to be participatory and deeply engrained in community level practices. Information and communication management is the backbone of all the participatory processes involved in urban risk management. It is a cross cutting theme that touches each stage of the urban risk management process and is critical for ensuring that all the various stakeholders engaged in the activities operate in a coordinated, efficient, and effective manner. Education for sustainable development needs to identify and target such stakeholders who will, in the long run, make a sizeable difference by bringing about sustainability factors within urban field practice. Information and communication management is a means of smoothening the problems in the participatory processes, and for ensuring collectivity.*

Urban Risk Reduction: An Asian Perspective
Community, Environment and Disaster Risk Management, Volume 1, 55–75
Copyright © 2012 by Emerald Group Publishing Limited
ISSN: 2040-7262/doi: 10.1108/S2040-7262(2009)0000001008

# 1. INTRODUCTION

Education, including formal education, public awareness and training, should be recognized as a process by which human beings and societies can reach their fullest potential. Education is critical for promoting sustainable development and improving the capacity of the people to address environment and development issues.

While basic education provides the underpinning for any environment and development education, the latter needs to be incorporated as an essential part of learning. Both formal and non-formal education is indispensable to changing people's attitudes so that they have the capacity to assess and address their sustainable development concerns.

Education is crucial for achieving environmental and ethical awareness, values and attitudes, skills and behavior consistent with sustainable development and for effective public participation in decision-making. To be effective, environment and development education: should deal with the dynamics of both the physical/biological and socio-economic environment and human (which may include spiritual) development; should be integrated in all disciplines; and should employ formal and non-formal methods and effective means of communication.

– Chapter 36 of Agenda 21, on "Education, Awareness and Training" (1992)

The vision of education emphasizes a holistic, interdisciplinary approach to developing the knowledge and skills needed for a sustainable future, as well as the necessary changes in values, behaviors, and lifestyles. However, education for sustainable development in not restricted to the transmission of knowledge and skills. It should be about learning how to obtain and synthesize the knowledge that equips us, individually and collectively, to forge a sustainable coexistence with our social and ecological environments.

Providing basic education to all is definitely a challenge to us, and this is reflected in the Millennium Development Goals (MDGs), which calls for "achieving universal primary education" by 2015 (MDG, 2000). However, there is another challenge to bridge the gap between knowledge and practice. In all the countries, higher education focuses on research and development on different issues, but little part of that research outputs are transmitted to the need of the society. Thus, the gap between the need (the question) and the solution (the answer) exists, and expands. This gap can only be reduced through proactive and participatory education, where the implementation issues should be incorporated from the planning stage. Karl Marx called for the unity of "*Head and Hand*," and this is very much linked to the proactive education, and unity of knowledge (*head*) and implementation or practice (*hand*).

In this chapter, the issue of proactive education is discussed based on the risk management perspective, with specific focus on disaster and environment. The chapter is divided into four parts. The first section will focus on political declaration and its context for the UN Decade of Education for Sustainable Development. In the second and third section, there will be two case study experiences on disaster and environmental education respectively from different parts of Japan. The fourth and the last part will describe the future direction of proactive risk education, based on the case study experiences.

## 2. INFORMATION AND COMMUNICATIONS IN THE DISASTER MANAGEMENT CYCLE

Typically, the disaster management (DM) cycle has four aspects; Information and communication management and its associated activities may be bundled along with the fours stages of the DM cycle (Fig. 1).

During the time before a disaster, when a warning may have been received or a disaster is impending (such as rising water levels in rivers), Gathering correct information on likely disaster and communicating the same to the last, most vulnerable person becomes critical. Associated activities relate to building a platform, in which information is interpreted by scientists, conveyed to decision-makers and/or administrators who in turn reach out to

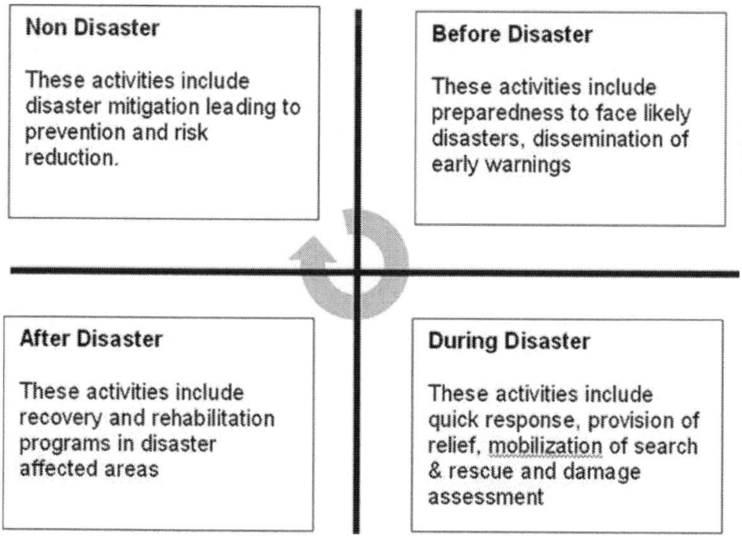

**Non Disaster**

These activities include disaster mitigation leading to prevention and risk reduction.

**Before Disaster**

These activities include preparedness to face likely disasters, dissemination of early warnings

**After Disaster**

These activities include recovery and rehabilitation programs in disaster affected areas

**During Disaster**

These activities include quick response, provision of relief, mobilization of search & rescue and damage assessment

*Fig. 1.* The Disaster Management Cycle.

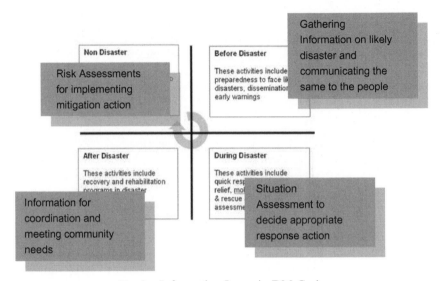

*Fig. 2.*    Information Issues in DM Cycle.

the community with differential levels of outreach based on the different available capacities of the community (Fig. 2).

When disaster strikes, chaos prevails and at this stage getting correct information on the extent of damage, the spread of damage, and assessment of needs for relief, search, and rescue is important. In different disasters, often communication systems along with other critical infrastructure do collapse. However, realizing how important it is to react quickly and appropriately, a dynamic system of communication that can quickly switch and adapt to alternatives and that remains reliable is needed (Fig. 3).

Following a disaster, Information is needed for coordination and meeting community needs. There are interest groups and stakeholders which have a common interest in assisting the community that has faced the disaster. Its important to obtain information on humanitarian assistance as well as changing needs of the community undergoing recovery, and all this needs to be mapped and coordinated so that needs are met right and overlapping is avoided thus preventing redundancy of resources.

An important aspect both before, during, and immediately after a disaster is to prevent spread of "misinformation." Almost parallel to the attempts to share correct information among stakeholders, there is always inevitable spread of rumors and false information leading to panic and confusion. In an information age, this has accelerated further going beyond spread

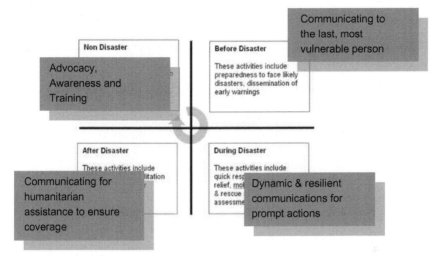

*Fig. 3.* Communication Issues in DM Cycle.

through word of mouth. Such "misinformation" often undermines and even runs counter to the good efforts being made for safety of the community.

During "Non-Disaster times," scientific information together layered with participatory risk assessments hold the key to preventing possible impact of hazards in future. This information has several uses. It can potentially guide developmental action specially in areas vulnerable to natural hazards. It can also form the content for advocacy, awareness, and training programs to create an environment for a culture of prevention.

# 3. UN DECADE OF EDUCATION FOR SUSTAINABLE DEVELOPMENT

The United Nations General Assembly proclaimed the 10-year period from 2005 to 2014 as the United Nations Decade of Education for Sustainable Development (DESD, 2005). Governments around the world are invited to use the Decade to integrate education for sustainable development into their national educational strategies and action plans at all appropriate levels.

UNESCO is designated as the Lead Agency in the promotion of the Decade, and is required to consult with the United Nations and other relevant international organizations, governments, nongovernmental organizations, and other stakeholders to develop a draft international implementation scheme for the Decade, bearing in mind the relationships between education for sustainable development and current international educational priorities.

The Rio Declaration from the World Conference on Environmental and Development 1992 began by stating:

> Human beings are at the centre of concerns for sustainable development. They are entitled to a healthy and productive life in harmony with nature.

The Johannesburg Declaration at the World Summit on Sustainable Development in 2002 built on this aspiration and expressed the commitment of world leaders "*to build a humane, equitable and caring global society cognizant of the need for human dignity for all.*" Sustainable development is a dynamic and evolving concept with many dimensions and interpretations and reflects locally relevant and culturally appropriate visions for a world in which development "*meets the needs of the present without comprising the ability of future generations to meet their own needs.*" The MDGs provide targets for international actions to bring such visions into reality by: overcoming poverty; improving child, maternal and sexual health; expanding educational provision and redressing gender inequalities in education; and developing national strategies for sustainable development.

The Secretary General of the United Nations, Mr Kofi Annan, has argued that:

> Our biggest challenge in this new century is to take an idea that sounds abstract – sustainable development – and turn it into reality for all the world's people.

Making the abstract real, and developing the capacities of individuals and societies to work for a sustainable future is, essentially, an educational enterprise. Indeed, the four principles for achieving sustainable human development enunciated at the World Summit for Sustainable Development in 2002 reflect the four pillars of education described in the Delors Report as in Table 1 (Delors, 2002).

*Table 1.*   Four Pillars of Education Described in Delros Report.

| Achieving Sustainable Development Requires | Education Provides the Skills for |
|---|---|
| Recognition of the challenge | Learning to know |
| Collective responsibility and constructive partnership | Learning to live together |
| Acting with determination | Learning to do |
| The indivisibility of human dignity | Learning to be |

Thus, education is the primary agent of transformation toward sustainable development, increasing people's capacities to transform their visions for society into reality. Education not only provides scientific and technical skills, it also provides the motivation, justification, and social support for pursuing and applying them. The international community now strongly believes that we need to foster – through education – the values, behavior, and lifestyles required for a sustainable future. Education for sustainable development has come to be seen as a process of learning how to make decisions that consider the long-term future of the economy, ecology, and equity of all communities. Building the capacity for such future-oriented thinking is a key task of education.

Education for Sustainable Development has four major domains, reflecting diverse goals and audiences: promotion and improvement of: (1) *basic education*, (2) *reorienting existing education* at all levels to address sustainable development, (3) *developing public understanding and awareness of sustainability*, and (4) *training*. Thus, the focus of DESD activities will be advocacy, communication, and networking directed at facilitating all educators to include sustainable development concerns and goals in their own programs. These issues constitute the priorities for planning programs and activities that will support the objectives of DESD, and include: (1) overcoming poverty, (2) gender equality, (3) health promotion, (4) environmental conservation and protection, (5) rural transformation, (6) human rights, (7) intercultural understanding and peace, (8) sustainable production and consumption, (9) cultural diversity, and (10) information and communication technologies (ICTs). These many areas of overlap and common interest, both in approaches to education and in areas of substantive objectives, suggest that joint initiatives across DESD can add value to the common effort of each individually (Table 2).

To achieve these goals and target these diverse issues, it is essential to promote the DESD through partnership. Partners in the DESD include all those organizations, networks, bodies, and alliances that share the conviction that sustainable development depends to a large extent on broad-based awareness through educational and learning processes. The following table shows, there are partners at all levels – subnational (local, community) level, national, regional, and international levels, and from all spheres – governmental, civil society and NGOs, and private.

With such an enormous and diverse group of potential partners, there is a need to focus on networks and alliances. Three key principles are:

- *Vision*: If each partner is to play its role within the DESD, it is essential that they are able to articulate clearly what the vision of ESD is in two

*Table 2.* ESD at Different Levels with Different Stakeholders.

| | Governmental | Civil Society and NGOs | Private |
|---|---|---|---|
| Subnational | Provincial/state/district departments of education and development sectors<br>Municipal authorities<br>Schools, adult learning programs | Community-based organizations<br>Local sections of NGOs<br>Faith-based groups<br>Village development committees<br>Adult learning groups | Local business<br>Clans and families<br>Individuals |
| National | National government departments of education and development sectors<br>Universities and research institutes<br>EFA networks | National NGOs and NGO coalitions<br>Branches of international NGOs<br>Faith-based organizations<br>Teachers' associations and trade unions | Private sector businesses<br><br>Business associations |
| Regional | Regional intergovernmental groupings<br>Regional EFA networks | Regional CS and NGO groupings and networks | Regional business associations |
| International | CSD<br>EFA High-Level and Working Groups<br>UNDG member agencies<br>Millennium Project Task Forces<br>Official/semiofficial watchdog bodies | Sustainable development education networks<br>NGO UNESCO Liaison Committee<br>CCNGO/EFA<br>Global Campaign for Education<br>International env. NGO | International associations of businesses (e.g., in the extractive sector)<br>TNCs (e.g., media corporations) |

ways: first, the overall vision of ESD to which all partners subscribe, and second, the particular vision for ESD within the parameters of their own aims, concerns, and programs.

- *Demonstration programs:* Ultimately the DESD aims to see ESD implemented in thousands of local situations on the ground. This will not involve ESD as a stand-alone program, but the integration of ESD into a multitude of different learning situations.
- *Networking:* As has been mentioned, sustainable development links with most aspects of life and development. From the outset, therefore, the orientation of DESD partners must be outward looking, seeking to make connections with initiatives, programs, groupings, and networks through whom ESD will be further promoted and implemented.

One indicator of the success of the DESD will be the extent to which ESD becomes part of the development dialogue at community level. Spaces for dialogue generally exist at community level – associations, school support groups, cooperatives, faith-based groupings, self-help groups, development committees, and many more. Giving maximum voice to local community level raises two significant challenges:

- *What kind of support is needed to stimulate and sustain the process?*
- *How can community voices be heard beyond the local level?*

In other words, a fundamental approach of the DESD should be to foster cooperation at all levels with the aim of strengthening local-level effectiveness. Sustainable development requires active and knowledgeable citizens and caring and informed decision-makers capable of making the right choices about the complex and interrelated economic, social, and environmental issues facing human society. To achieve this requires the broader process of social change known as "social learning," which is described as "enhancing societal capacity for the environment." This involves not only specific education and training programs but also the use of policy and legislation as opportunities for teaching and encouraging new forms of personal, community, and corporate behavior (Fien, 2004). Social learning also involves reflection – often stimulated by leaders and the media. The social learning states:

- Sustainable development is perhaps more a moral percept than a scientific concept, linked as much with human and ecology.
- While sustainable development involves the natural science, policy, and economics, it is primarily a matter of culture.

- Sustainable development requires us to acknowledge the interdependent relationship between people and the natural environment.

Hagiwara (2004) described the initiatives of building a city of sustainable development in Okayama, Japan. With a population of 630,000, the Okayama has a series of unique community-based environmental projects, which include a broad range of environmental preservation activities in which citizens participate voluntarily. Environmental partnership project includes voluntary environmental development activities of citizens in their communities (eco-volunteer activities) and activities that reduce the environmental burden steaming from corporate actions (Green Company Activities). A similar concept is also observed in the city of Nishinomiya (Yoshizumi & Miyaguchi, 2005), where a local NGO called LEAF initiated the community education process together with the city government, citizens, private sectors, and elementary schools (Yoshizumi, 2006).

Cappon (2004) described the community-based education as the key to the sustainable human development. The key issues of "action, commitments, and partnerships" are those that are crucial not only for the promotion of education for sustainable development, but also for the sustainability of the learning systems. As we move gradually toward a knowledge society, the ways we learn and the ways we educate will necessarily change, and will result in the need for new partnerships and new commitments. This will enhance to the role of citizen, people, and community in solving their own problems in a collective way through more community-oriented education.

# 4. DISASTER RISK EDUCATION: PROBLEMS AND PROSPECT

Disaster risk education has different components and challenges. There are two specific types of risk education: one is to show the occurrence of hazards, which is more as the physical phenomena. Most parts of these are taught in schools as a part of geography curriculum. The other is to know the social environment, and to understand the impacts of disasters, which is more like a process-based education.

Two major issues related to earthquake disaster pose the real challenge to the earthquake professionals. The first one is the nature of the event, which, unlike flood or typhoon, cannot be predicted in advance. The other issue is its occurrence, which, again unlike other events, occurs once in 10 or 50 or even 100 years. Thus, the priorities of preparing for the earthquake disaster in advance is relatively low in many countries. For the developing countries, while the post-disaster reconstruction exercise provides an opportunity for development, pre-disaster preparedness and mitigation measures are the only solution for earthquake risk reduction. However, the painful question is: "how to motivate an individual and/or community to take pre-disaster risk reduction actions?"

This question is not only critical for the developing countries, but also found to be relevant for the developed country like Japan, which has a high risk of earthquake, experiences of major earthquake disasters, and significant technical expertise and resources. Still the question arises: "Is Japan prepared for the next big one?" The same question will possibly be valid for other developed countries, and obviously for the developing countries as well.

Japan faced one of its most tragic natural disasters in recent years, when the earthquake hit the city of Kobe on January 17, 1995. Total number of casualty crossed 6,400, with numerous injuries and victims of other collateral damages. Buildings and infrastructures were severely damaged, and more than 200,000 people had to find temporary shelter in different parts of the city. Only within Kobe city administrative area, 70,000 buildings were completely collapsed, and 55,000 were seriously damaged. Public facilities like city offices, schools, and hospitals were also damaged extensively, which made the city services paralyzed for several days.

From the experiences of the Kobe earthquake, it was observed that many people were rescued by their friends, families, and neighbors, particularly in the places, where the community ties were strong. Also, the neighborhoods, which had higher social capital, the reconstruction and rehabilitation were smooth and faster, with better collective decision-making among the communities and better cooperation of the community and local government (Nakagawa & Shaw, 2004). Thus, the lesson is that community and individual awareness are important, and to sustain the community initiatives is crucial to achieve a safer and sustainable society. Culture of disaster preparedness plays an important role in this regard. To build this culture, education is one of the key tools, and thus focusing the school children is considered as an essential element to understand the development of the culture. To understand the direction of education for effective earthquake risk reduction actions, a survey was undertaken with the first grade high school students (15–16 years) in five prefectures of Japan: Aichi, Hyogo, Osaka, Shizuoka, and Wakayama (Shaw, Shiwaku, Kobayashi, & Kobayashi, 2004). Among these prefectures, Hyogo and Osaka have experienced the damages due to the Kobe earthquake, while Aichi, Shizuoka, and Wakayama are expecting a big earthquake called

Tokai earthquake. In total, there were 28 classes from 12 schools, and total number of students was 1,065.

A set of questionnaires was prepared based on a model as shown in the adjoining figure. In the model, knowledge, awareness, and code of conduct are perceived in the sequence of: Knowing, Realizing, Deepening, Decision, and Action, as the gradual change in behavior from knowing to code of conduct. Knowledge comes from two sources: experience and education. Experience here denotes not only experiences of damaging earthquakes, but also general experience of earthquake. Education has four parts: school, family, community, and self-education. School education is divided into two parts: education from teachers (S), and proactive education with participation of teachers and students (ST). Family education (F) originates from parents, and other family members. Community education (C) is related to education in the neighborhood, community organizations, NGO activities, research workers, and voluntary activities etc. Self-education (Se) is acquired from books, internet, newspaper, TV, and other sources through student's own initiative. All these lead to "Knowing" about earthquakes and its impacts (Fig. 4).

The next step after "Knowing" is "Realizing," which is denoted as Perception. After "Realizing," comes "Deepening," which is divided into two parts: Deepening A (which is considered as wish to deepen the knowledge), and Deepening B (which is considered as actual deepening). The next step is "Decision," which is the wish to take action and disseminate

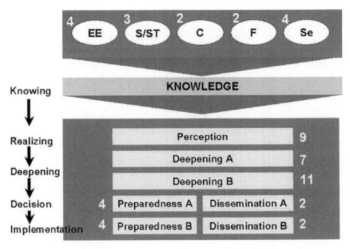

*Fig. 4.*   Conceptual Model of Disaster Risk Education.

knowledge, denoted as Preparedness A and Dissemination A respectively. "Acton" comes after it, which are Preparedness B and Dissemination B. In summary, the steps described above have following meaning:

Knowledge: Sources of information and knowledge about earthquake and its impacts

- Perception: Realizing about the earthquakes and its possible counter-measures
- Deepening A: Intending to deepening understanding of earthquake risk
- Deepening B: Deepening understanding of earthquake risk
- Preparedness A: Intending to take action on preparedness for earthquake
- Preparedness B: Actions to prepare for earthquake/mitigation measures
- Dissemination A: Intending to disseminate earthquake information and experiences
- Dissemination B: Disseminate earthquake information and experiences.

Thus, through this model gradual change in student's behavior is visualized, from knowing through realizing and deepening and ultimately brining it to code of conduct (action). The gap between the knowledge and code of conduct is actual challenge for earthquake disaster, and it is related to the risk perception and other socio-economic-cultural issues, which are described in the earlier section.

Analysis was done by cross tabulation with earthquake experiences and education. Details of each analysis are described in Shaw et al. (2004). The degree of effect of one factor on other is calculated, and the process is repeated for each set of questions for experience and education. Picking up the maximum values from each set of questions (experience, and different sources of education (S, ST, C, F, and Se)), a graph is produced showing the effects of experience and education on perception of earthquake risk. This shows that school education (S) and self-education (Se) have the most prominent effect on perception, followed by active education in school (ST) and earthquake experiences (EE). Similar exercises were conducted for other sets of parameters: Deepening A, B, Preparedness A, B, and Dissemination A and B. Integrated results are shown in the figure in the previous page.

Some interesting observations can be made from this figure. While, earthquake experience and school education (S) are important to develop perception of earthquake risk, active school education (ST) and community and family education play more crucial role in developing the wish and interest to deepening knowledge. Self-education is also an equally important factor in this aspect. However, actual deepening of knowledge is observed through intensive community education. Experience and school education play relatively smaller role in this regard. This is possibly attributed to enhancing perception and deepening through active participation of different types of community activities in the neighborhood. In contrast, when the wish for preparedness is concerned, family education is the most influential factor, followed by self-education. For actual preparedness, it is the community and family education, which are most important. This is attributed to importance of family and neighborhood level preparedness, which is possibly mainly through family and community education. Wish to disseminate experience is enhanced by active school education (ST) and family education, while actual dissemination is promoted by community and family education. In both cases, school education's (S) role is not so prominent (Fig. 5).

## 5. ENVIRONMENTAL EDUCATION

### 5.1. Basics of Environmental Education

Environmental education is the process of recognizing values and clarify concepts in order to develop skills and attitudes necessary to understand and appreciate the interrelatedness among man, his culture and his bio-physical surroundings. It also entails practice in decision-making and self formulation of code of behavior about problems and issues concerning environmental quality. IUCN(1970)

Environmental Education incorporates a human component in exploring environmental problems and their solutions. Environmental solutions are not only scientific – they include historical, political, economic, and cultural perspectives. This also implies that the environment includes both built and natural environment.

Following are the main characteristics of environmental education (Shrivastava, 2004):

• It refers to the knowledge and understanding of physical, biological, cultural, and psychological environment and to perceive its relevance for real life situation.
• It identifies the imbalances of environment and tries to improve it in view of sustainable development.
• It entails practice in decision-making and self-formulation of a code of behavior about problems and issues concerning environmental quality.
• It involves people's investigation and systematic exploration of his own natural and social environment and prepare themselves to solve problems to improve quality of life.

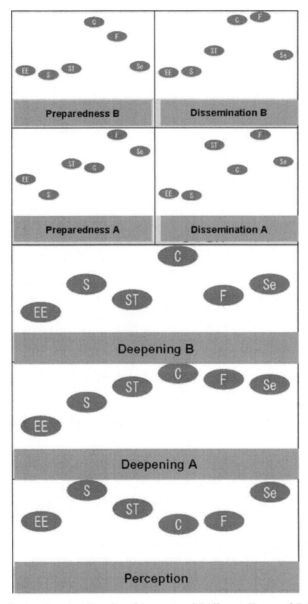

*Fig. 5.* Comprehensive Results of Impacts of Different Types of Education.

- It develops skills, attitudes, feeling, and values needed to play productive roles in improving lives and values.
- It provides the basis for construction and creative skills for the practice of healthy living and improvement.
- It is problem centered, interdisciplinary, value and community oriented, and concerns with people's survival and development. It concerns present and future.
- It utilizes educational approaches, methods, and techniques of teaching to identify the real causes of environmental problems and practice problem-solving skills in formal and nonformal situations.
- It is a process of recognizing the interrelatedness among people, its cultural and biological surroundings.
- It involves both theoretical and practical aspects of environment to improve the imbalances and prevent the deterioration or pollution.
- It appears to be a process that equips human beings with awareness, skills, attitudes, values, and commitments to improvement in environment.

The role for educators in addressing the affective domain is not always easy. Educators should make it clear that differing personal values exist, that these values can color the facts, and that controversy is often motivated by differing value systems. Environmental Education includes opportunities to build skills that enhance learners' problem-solving abilities, such as (Sato, 2005):

- Communication: listening, public speaking, persuasive writing, graphic design;
- Investigation: survey design, library research, interviewing, data analysis; and
- Group process: leadership, decision-making, cooperation.

### 5.2. Toward Standardization: Contents versus Process

The standardization of environmental education is best known as "Kids ISO 14000," which is a set of standard educational materials for different levels of education for primary, middle high school, and high school children. The most characteristic part of the Kids ISO is that it promotes environmental actions, and links the education and actions. Certification from ISO, UNEP, and UNU are also value addition and incentives to the students (ArTech, 2005).

While discussing the standardization process, it is required to keep in mind the wider cultural, social, and geo-political issues around Asia and the

Pacific region. There is a strong need to standardize the process, rather than the contents of the environmental education. A standard process of environmental education will be helpful to different countries to develop its own contents, and to unitize the process to monitor and review the educational impacts to the children.

# 6. PROBLEMS RELATED TO INFORMATION AND COMMUNICATION

Recent fiasco in response management have clearly revealed that a lot more needs to be done for better information and communication in order to save precious lives. The problems as evident from some of the cases studied in this paper indicate the following:

*Knowledge exists but not communicated!* There is enough intelligence information to guide suitable pre-emptive action. However, multiple problems ranging from attitudinal to efficiency prevent effective generation and flow of information. The last most vulnerable person is still unaware of the risks he is threatened with. There are too many missing links in the chain of communication flow. The knowledge that is generated in some of the most sophisticated real time and modeling systems thus remains in the hands of a chosen few which have little to do with the actual situation on the ground.

*Emergency systems, legal systems, rules etc. are set, yet citizens remain disempowered:* The current system of information and communication is overtly guarded by the public authorities. This prevents systems to work at the right time. Worse still the citizens remain disempowered. In absence of any clear directions, rumors and false news take precedence. Decisions are made on the basis of incorrect or incomplete information available from unreliable sources. This leads to chaos and further difficulty in efficient disaster reduction or response.

*We wait for crisis to happen:* One problem often faced by disaster managers, is that DM is still considered lower in priority compared to other problems. The day-to-day crisis of solid waste management, traffic, and other issues seem to take precedence until the disaster actually strikes. The net result is that protocols are not set nor rehearsed in time.

*Too many cooks...* The problem of multiplicity of agencies acting in several parallel layers is a sure recipe of disaster. Each agency has its own reporting mechanisms and mandate. This creates overlaps at one end and voids at the other. The issue of urban risk reduction often falls within the void, while disaster response is heavily overlapped.

## 7. FUTURE PERSPECTIVE

The crucial issue of environmental and disaster education is the gap between knowledge and practice. Over the past 30–40 years, there has been significant development in the knowledge base on environmental issues. However, when it comes to the practice, there still remains a significant gap. "School Education," in its strict sense cannot fill this gap. It needs to be "learning," which should involve family, community, and self-learning. The key emphasis is "learning by doing," where proactive actions should be taken in real life scenario. Then only, the environmental education can achieve its goal and objective.

There are all different types of models of education, summarized in Table 3.

Summarizing the above discussion, it can be concluded that following are a few major issues to be considered in the future perspective of community-based education:

- *Holistic approach:* While we discuss the environment education, it can not be separated from disaster education or development education.

*Table 3.*   Types of Environment and Disaster Education.

| Model Types | School | Communities |
| --- | --- | --- |
| School promoted education: Promoted by school, linked to community, professionals | Part of school curriculum, example: Maiko High School of Kobe, Japan | Linked to communities |
| NGO promoted education (with local government): Promoted by NGO, and sustainability ensured by linking this to local government education department | Part of school curriculum, example: Nishinomiya School education by LEAF | Linked to communities |
| NGO promoted education (with schools): Promoted by NGO, linked to school and local community | Part of extra curriculum activities, example: KIDS ISO environmental education program by ARTECH | Linked to communities |
| Local government promoted: Started by local government education department | Part of extra curriculum activities, example: Saijo disaster education | Linked to communities |
| Spontaneous community education: Existed in the community over time in terms of culture and tradition | Not part of school program, example: Shirakawa-go community | Linked to community activities |

A holistic approach should be taken to integrate disaster environment and development learning.

- *Process oriented:* The key issue of the education or learning is the process, and the involvement of different groups of the society. Events at the local communities, schools, and neighborhoods are the key vehicle for this.
- *Partnership-based:* The crucial issue of the education and development can not be solved by the community or NGO or local government alone. We need a healthy partnership among different sectors.
- *Expanded urban management:* The urban issues can not be solved only within the city boundary, and should be linked to the rural issues. For effective urban management, urban–rural linkage is extremely important.

The problems and experience provide us directions for developing sound information and communication systems:

*Establishing a participatory information system for intelligence as well as dissemination:* Considering the challenge of information needs in disaster situations, a participatory system can work well within the acceptable parameters of reliability and speed. As information sources in such a scenario would be multiple, standardization is required. However, the system allows scope for incorporating local knowledge and understanding that goes a long way in better targeting of disaster reduction and response interventions.

*Layering citizens' information with scientific information:* Citizen source information is often not substantiated with enough facts. This is because of the limitations of access at the level of ordinary citizens. However, the citizens' information layered with secondary scientific sources can provide an ideal combination for developing appropriate interventions. Participatory information gathering can also be enhanced by providing easy-to-use scientific instruments, to obtain desired levels of scientific database.

*Applying a communications structure:* In current scenarios, the information needs of multiple stakeholders has to be understood and a communication system designed to addressed such a need. In disaster situations, communication flows have to be natural, however, facilitated to ensure reliability and targeting. Doing so requires establishment of an agreed upon coordination mechanism with a predefined terms of reference.

*Recognizing role of government, CSOs, and citizens:* Effective coordination can only be possible if each stakeholder recognizes and respects the role of the other. No hierarchies can be followed in communications flow. The information communicated should be free and easy to access. This will create greater transparency and conducive environment for unified action.

*Simulation exercises*: Disasters happen at the most unexpected times. Only regular drills and simulation exercises can help in maintaining adequate levels of preparedness among stakeholders. In many regions around the world, citizens are regularly engaged in citywide drills testing preparedness against disasters such as earthquakes.

Developing a reliable and sound communication and information system is the key to disaster reduction and response exercise. In the current context, with a plethora of technologies available, communications still do fail at vital times. The choices have actually made the task of designing a sound system far more complicated than was the case with limited technologies. The conclusion thus remains the same – the key to success lies in recognizing that the individual citizen and his neighbor are the best disaster managers and that a sound information and communication management system should be able to reinforce this strength.

## ACKNOWLEDGMENT

The authors acknowledge the support of UNESCO ACCU to conduct the workshop, where this chapter was presented as a training module.

## REFERENCES

Agenda 21. (1992). Agenda 21/Chapter 36: Promoting education, public awareness and training. Accessed from http://www.un.org/esa/sustdev/documents/agenda21/english/agenda21chapter36.htm, accessed on 31st of January 2008.

ArTech. (2005). KIDS ISO Program for environmental education. Accessed from http://www.artech.or.jp/english/kids/envedu/index.html on 31st of January 2008.

Cappon, P. (2004). The sustainability of education: A prerequisite for sustainable human development. In: *Educating for a sustainable future: Commitments and partnership*, UNESCO Publication, pp. 35–42.

Delors. (2002). UNESCO Task Force on Education for the 21st Century. Accessed from http://www.unesco.org/delors/, accessed on 31st of January 2008.

DESD. (2005). Decade of education for sustainable development. Accessed from http://www.desd.org/, accessed on 31st of January 2008.

Fien, J. (2004). A decade of commitments: Lessons learnt from Rio to Johannesburg. In: *Educating for a sustainable future: Commitments and partnership*, UNESCO Publication, pp. 75–138.

Hagiwara, M. (2004). Building a city of sustainable development. In: *Educating for a sustainable future: Commitments and partnership*, UNESCO Publication, pp. 183–194.

IUCN. (1970). Environmental education workshop, Nevada, USA.

MDG. (2000). Millennium Development Goals 2 "Achieve universal primary education". Accessed from http://www.un.org/millenniumgoals/, accessed on 31st of January 2008.

Nakagawa, Y., & Shaw, R. (2004). Social capital: A missing link to disaster recovery. *International Journal of Mass Emergency and Disaster, 22*(1), 5–34.

Sato. (2005). Similarity of the conceptual development process between EE through a series of international discussion and ESD in DESD-IIS. Accessed from www.yc.musashi-tech. ac.jp/~kiyou/no8/3-09.pdf, accessed on 31st of January 2008.

Shaw, R., Shiwaku, K., Kobayashi, H., & Kobayashi, M. (2004). Linking experience, knowledge, perception and earthquake preparedness. *Disaster Prevention and Management, 13*(1), 39–49.

Shrivastava, K. K. (2004). *Environmental education: Principles, concept and management* (p. 465). New Delhi, India: Kanishka Press.

Yoshizumi, M. (2006). *Town-watching: Tool of community based disaster and environmental management*. Environmental Education Workshop, Danang, Vietnam.

Yoshizumi, M., & Miyaguchi, T. (2005). Realizing education for sustainable development in Japan: The case of Nishinomiya city in changes and challenges. *Current Issues in Comparative Education, 7*(2), 22–31.

# CHAPTER 5

# HYOGO FRAMEWORK FOR ACTION AND URBAN RISK REDUCTION IN ASIA

Yuki Matsuoka, Anshu Sharma and Rajib Shaw

## ABSTRACT

*The pace of urbanization in the developing world is led by Asia. Over the next 25 years, Asia's urban population will grow by around 70% to more than 2.6 billion people. An additional billion people will have urban habitats (ADB, 2006).*

*The "Hyogo Framework for Action 2005–2015: Building the Resilience of Nations and communities to disasters" (HFA) was adopted at the UN World Conference on Disaster Reduction (January 2005, Kobe, Japan). The HFA specifies that disaster risk is compounded by increasing vulnerabilities related to various elements including unplanned urbanization. Across the HFA, important elements on urban risk reduction are mentioned as one of crucial areas of work to implement the HFA. In particular incorporating disaster risk reduction into urban planning is specified to reduce the underlying risk factors (Priority 4).*

Urban Risk Reduction: An Asian Perspective
Community, Environment and Disaster Risk Management, Volume 1, 77–104
Copyright © 2012 by Emerald Group Publishing Limited
All rights of reproduction in any form reserved
ISSN: 2040-7262/doi: 10.1108/S2040-7262(2009)0000001009

# 1. INTRODUCTION

In 1950, some 733 million people, or 29% of the world's population, lived in urban areas. By 2005, the urban population had grown to an estimated 3,172 million or 49% of the population. By 2030, it is estimated that 4,945 million people – almost 61% of the world's population – will be urban. The urban population is set to increase by more than 55%, or 1,770 million, in the next 25 years, while the rural population is estimated to decline by 3% or 96 million. Between 1950 and 2030, the population of the world will change from about 70% rural to 60% urban (ADB, 2006).

In the year 1950, New York City was the only city with a population of over 10 million persons. By 2015, it is expected that there will be 22 cities with populations over 10 million. Of these, 17 will be in developing countries, 13 of them in the Asia-Pacific region (UNESCAP, 2005). Asia's urbanization trend, its disaster events, and numbers of people exposed to risk are all growing rapidly.

Most of the urban dwellers in Asia's bustling cities live in substandard conditions. The economic imperative drives them to live in areas earlier left uninhabited as they were too unsafe to live in. Slums and squatters can be seen sprawling the drain-banks, riverbeds, low-lying marshy lands, steep slopes, and other hazardous locations in Mumbai, Jakarta, Dhaka, Kathmandu, Manila, Bangkok, and most other Asian cities. Their numbers are only growing, and much faster than the supply of livable spaces. This trend manifests in the increasing numbers and impacts of disasters, both in the form of shocks, i.e., rapid onset, high impact events, and stresses, i.e., day-to-day small scale but widespread difficulties.

Urban disasters vary considerably compared to their rural counterparts. They are not only represented by one-off events like earthquake or cyclones but also get exaggerated due to high population concentrations and hindrances in accessing basic services.

# 2. HYOGO FRAMEWORK FOR ACTION AND ISDR SYSTEM

"Hyogo Framework for Action 2005–2015: Building the Resilience of Nations and Communities to Disasters" (HFA) was formulated as a comprehensive, action-oriented response to international concern about the growing impacts of disasters on individuals, communities and national development. Based on careful study of trends in disaster risks and practical experience in disaster risk reduction, and subjected to intensive negotiations during 2004 and early 2005, the HFA was finally brought to fruition and adopted by 168 Governments at the World Conference on Disaster Reduction (January 2005 in Kobe, Hyogo, Japan), and was endorsed anonymously by all the United Nations Member States at the United Nations General Assembly in the same year. The expected outcome of the HFA is substantive reduction of disasters losses in lives and in the social, economic, and environment assess of communities and countries. This is further elaborated into three Strategic Goals and five Priorities for Action.

Following the adoption of the HFA, global efforts have been accelerated to reduce disaster risks and to tackle with vulnerabilities to natural hazards. In the context of the International Strategy for Disaster Reduction (ISDR) system, a number of steps have been taken to promote and support the implementation of the HFA at international, regional, national, and community levels. HFA has the five priorities for action:

(1) Making disaster risk reduction a priority,
(2) Improving risk information and early warning,
(3) Building a culture of safety and resilience,
(4) Reducing the risks in key sectors, and
(5) Strengthening preparedness for response.

### 2.1. ISDR System

ISDR is a system of partnerships. These partnerships are composed of a broad range of actors, all of which have essential roles to play in supporting nations and communities to reduce disaster risk. These partners include governments, intergovernmental and nongovernmental organizations, international financial institutions, scientific and technical bodies and specialized networks as well as civil society and the private sector.

A secretariat – the UNISDR Secretariat – supports and assists the ISDR system in implementing the HFA (Fig. 1).

The overall objective of the ISDR system is to generate and support a global disaster risk reduction movement to reduce risk to disasters and to build "a culture of prevention" in society as part of sustainable development.

In pursuit of this objective, the ISDR system supports nations and communities to implement the HFA through widened participation of governments and organizations in the ISDR; raising the profile of disaster reduction in the priorities and programs of organizations; and building a

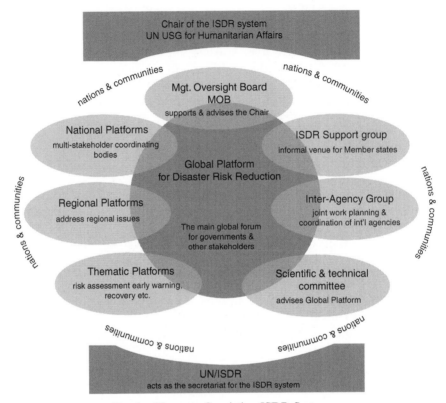

*Fig. 1.*   Elements Consisting ISDR System.

stronger, more systematic and coherent international effort to support
national disaster reduction efforts.


## 2.2. ISDR Asia Regional Task Force on Urban Risk Reduction

Recognizing that there is a growing need to address the subject of urban risk
reduction (URR) with concerted and coordinated efforts among stakeholders, in particular in the Asia region that is urbanizing at a dramatic
pace, the UNISDR Hyogo Office together with close partners took an
initiative to establish the Asia Regional Task Force (RTF) on URR as a
thematic platforms of the ISDR system in Asia to facilitate and accelerate
efforts and actions for URR.

The Asia RTF on URR was established in January 2008. The RTF is represented by 16 (ADPC, ADRC, CITYNET, EMI, IRP Secretariat, JICA, Kobe University, Kyoto University, NSET, SEEDS, UNCRD, UNEP, UN-HABITAT, UNISDR, UNU, and WHO) member organizations and is expected to expand further. The RTF aims at strengthening the linkages of the community of urban planners, architects, and engineers who are engaged in shaping the future of urban growth to ensure that disaster risk reduction is incorporated in urban development planning as well as future urban development trends are incorporated in disaster risk reduction strategies. The goal of the RTF is to enhance decisive actions to reduce risk and increase community resilience in the urban areas of the Asian region, with specific objectives such as acting as an advocacy vehicle to major urban policy bodies, providing a platform for collective information, and knowledge development and sharing, and facilitating interactions and cooperation among related organizations and stakeholders.

To facilitate concerted efforts among stakeholders to enhance prompt actions toward risk reduction and to increase community resilience in the urban areas in the Asian region, the RTF-URR has been carrying out several activities since its establishment, including the below concrete joint activities:

(i)   Developing the guideline for local governments for implementing HFA.
(ii)  "RADIUS plus 10" as the follow up project of the original RADIUS[1] project.
(iii) Production of Mapping of Urban Risk and Resilience in the Asia Region (as agreed by the Ministerial Meeting on Disaster Risk Reduction in Delhi in November 2007), starting with production of a status report on URR and inventory of initiatives and activities on URR in Asia. (The publication "Reducing Urban Risk in Asia: Status Report and Inventory of Initiatives" was launched at the second session of the Global Platform on Disaster Risk Reduction in Geneva, 16–19 June 2009).

UNISDR is going to launch its next global DRR campaign 2010–2011 focusing on URR. The global campaign should aim at creating an enabling environment of risk reduction in urban areas and enhancing the resilience of people and communities. The RTF-URR is committed to serve as the advocacy vehicle to advance the concerted efforts to address the challenges in URR in Asia.

# 3. OVERALL TRENDS AND ANALYSIS
# ON URBAN RISK REDUCTION IN ASIA REGION

The world is steadily becoming more urban (Boulle, Vrolijks, & Palm, 1997), although, urbanization rates vary across the world. The level of urbanization is far higher in countries like the United States and the United Kingdom compared to China, India, or Vietnam, but annual "urbanization rate" is much slower. Many consider urbanization as an irreversible process and thus urban vulnerability becomes a reality (Quarantelli, 2003). In Asian context, the combinations of economic and environmental pressures increasingly keep forcing the rural poor to search alternative living in nearby towns or cities. Supply of developed and safe land is always short of demand in urban areas and often result is mushrooming of informal settlements, slums, and squatters through encroachment on public and private land. Cities' commercial, industrial, and residential locations prove to be livelihood center for urban poor, who left with no choice but to settle on dangerous locations subject to natural or man-made hazards.

To understand the urban risk and its impacts on local environment, it may be appropriate to deconstruct the underlying factors making urban risk more critical than in any other built environment. These factors may be summarized as follows (Surjan & Shaw, 2009):

*Urban population*: By 2050, the world population is expected to grow by 3 billion people. By 2030, 1 in 4 persons will live in a city of 500,000 people; and 1 in 10 persons will live in a city of 10 million population. Data shows that some 1.5 billion extra people will live in urban areas of various sizes during the period of 1994 to 2025 (UNESCAP, 2005). Urban areas are characterized by high-density population, which results to higher exposures. Combination of high vulnerability and exposure causes higher degree of urban risk.

*Urban setting and urban planning*: The tendency of cities to be located and expanded on river banks or coastal areas for economic reasons makes them more vulnerable to disasters. Number of densely populated areas in the world is in river deltas, coastal areas, seismically active zones, etc. In fact, population started growing in productive floodplains and coastal zones, fertile volcanic slopes, etc. as these offered most lucrative piece on the earth to settle in. The major cities in Asia are either located in the flood plain or in the coastal areas. Recent study shows that nations with largest urban population in the Low Elevation Coastal Zone (LECZ) are China, India, and Japan (id21 insights 71, 2008).

*Urban structures*: In most of the countries in Asia, the cities have poor infrastructures, with specific problems in water and electricity supply, sanitation and drainage system. Moreover, the vital infrastructures in many Asian cities have poor quality, which is shown in several recent disasters in the earthquake of 2005 in northern Pakistan, 2008 in Wenchuan earthquake in China.

*Compact urban forms*: Even in large urban areas, population density varies and determines the severity concentration in specific pockets of the city. Moreover, daytime and nighttime density varies significantly. In downtown or in commercial and office areas, daytime population concentration is very high on working days. In case of Mumbai, although average city density is 27,000 people per sq km for the city, some areas have density astronomically high as 114,001 people per square kilometers.

*Urban dependence on rural areas*: Urbanization has its origin since industrialization gradually emerged in different parts of the world. The environmental impact of city on its adjoining areas kept growing resulting in larger "environmental footprint" than ever. The ecological footprint of Tokyo is five times of Japan's land area.

*Urban primacy*: Many cites including Asian megacities are increasingly becoming the concentration of a particular country's major functions including physical, economic, social, political, and cultural assets, which are being exposed to different types of disaster risks. For example, a hazardous event in a mega city like Manila, which is the hub of political, administrative, and economic activities of Philippines, may lead to complete disruption in the country as a whole. This makes Manila more vulnerable compared to other cities. A major earthquake striking in a city like Tokyo could have global impact specially damaging economy.

*Urban informal settlements*: The form and structure of informal settlements can vary from one urban context to another, however they remain "illegal constructions." In the urban megacities in Asia, like Manila, Mumbai, and Jakarta, almost 25–30% of the population lives in these informal settlements, and are exposed to different types of disasters like flood and typhoons.

*Urban economic imbalances*: As discussed earlier, poor tend to live in an unsafe environment. They live in most vulnerable housing, in absence of or degraded environmental conditions and hazard prone locations with very poor personal assets to help themselves in even minor emergencies. The socio-economic opportunities provided by Asian cities enable people from a wide range of income brackets not only to interact and live, but also to create vulnerabilities resulting from lack of access to urban goods and services.

*Urban services*: Bigger the city, more complex is the infrastructure service systems it will have. In developed countries, urban services generally consists of complicated network spread across city and are dependent on high energy inputs and require sophisticated technology to fix problems. Dependency on infrastructure in developed world is much higher compared to developing nations. The intricate web of services makes it difficult and expensive to repair but needs attention during disasters. Provision of water supply, sanitation, become more crucial in disaster struck regions.

*Urban environment*: Urbanization itself, in most cases, is proved detrimental to local and regional environment. Once ecologically fragile areas now have been swallowed by expanding cities resulting in loss of biodiversity, disrupted balance of ecosystems, and threat of extinction to many living organisms. In addition to this, ground subsidence, underground excavations, surface and ground water contamination, water table reduction, are some of the counter products of urbanization. In the city of Bangkok, the land subsidence is a crucial issue. In some places, the subsidence rate is almost 25–30 cm per year, which is caused due to over exploitation of underground water. The urban eco-system is characterized by interplay of the built, natural, and socio-economic environment, which separately and collectively generate much of the risk that cities face today.

*Urban management*: Urbanization as a result of complex socio-economic process, poses a daunting task of managing cities. Heterogeneous societal structure, opportunist political system, lack of administrative capacities, very poor resource generation capabilities, archaic urban planning, and development legislation, etc. contribute collectively in making city more vulnerable to poor management and disaster risks. Appropriate governance and decision-making system is the core of risk reduction in urban areas. Special focus should be given to vital infrastructures like schools, hospitals, and key public buildings.

In the above context, urban risks will be there in Asia, and we need to cope with these risks. Cities in developing countries of Asia also face cascading vulnerabilities that go beyond the original risk or hazard. The relevance of low probability and high consequence events should be increasingly recognized.

Climate change is becoming a threat to the urban environment. The uncertainty arises due to the changing climate, needs to be considered in the overall urban risk management framework. Climate change impacts are increasing accelerating these risks, and it is required to focus on the adaptation measures with specific emphasis on community-based approaches.

In several countries, new approaches to community-based risk reduction have been practiced and its importance is realized. In spite of different threats, communities have their inherent capacities to cope with different types of disasters. Community resilience should be considered as an asset of risk reduction in the urban areas. An eco-community approach for informal settlement in Mumbai has proved to be effective during catastrophic flood in 2005. Similarly, the community-based preparedness and neighborhood watching in Manila, Kuala Lumpur, Danang has proved to be useful to raise resident's interest in collective problem solving.

The forces and processes that constitute "urban activity" have far-reaching and long-term effects not only on its immediate boundaries, but also on the entire region in which it is positioned. The causes of urban growth are varied and complex, but among the main ones are economic and environmental pressures driving people to seek a living in the towns.

# 4. STATUS ON URBAN RISK IN ASIA

The publication "Reducing Urban Risk in Asia: Status Report and Inventory of Initiatives" produced under the RTF-URR looks at the dimensions of urban risk, with their causative factors and determinants, and at ways and means that have emerged through pilot interventions on addressing risk through innovative means such as community led disaster risk reduction (DRR) initiatives.

## 4.1. Explosion of Urban Population in Asia

At the world level, the 20th century saw an increase from 220 million urbanites in 1900 to 2.84 billion in 2000. The present century will match this absolute increase in about four decades. Developing regions as a whole will account for 93% of this growth, Asia and Africa for over 80%. Between 2000 and 2030, Asia's urban population will increase from 1.36 billion to 2.64 billion, Africa's from 294 million to 742 million, and that of Latin America and the Caribbean from 394 million to 609 million. As a result of these shifts, developing countries will have 80% of the world's urban population in 2030. By then, Africa and Asia will include almost seven out of every ten urban inhabitants in the world (UNFPA, 2007).

By 2050, Asia will host 63% of the global urban population, or 3.3 billion people. In Asia, the urban transition will occur even earlier than Africa, owing to rapid urban growth rates in China, a country that is expected to be 70% urban by 2050. Urban growth rates in India will be slower; by 2050, 55% of its population, or 900 million people, will live in cities (UNHABITAT, 2008).

### 4.2. Experience of Urban Disasters and the Emerging Risk in Asia

An earthquake striking a metro city, large scale inundation of dense urban population, or the wiping out of a coastal city due to storm surge or cyclone are parts of serious simulation exercises. The indications from the region's history of disasters are a grim reminder of what could be in store. The catastrophic flooding of Mumbai in 2005 took the city by surprise, both on account of the unprecedented amount of rainfall in record time, and the lack of preparedness of the civic infrastructure and emergency systems to manage the disaster.

Cities are highly vulnerable to disasters induced by natural hazards. Sudden supply shortages, heavy environmental burdens, or major catastrophes can quickly lead to serious emergencies. The consequences of such crises are multiplied by poorly coordinated administration and planning.

Disasters induced by natural hazards have become more frequent and more severe during the last two decades, affecting a number of large cities. The United Nations Environment Programme (UNEP) reports that, between 1980 and 2000, 75% of the world's total population lived in areas affected by a disaster. In 1999, there were over 700 major disasters, causing more than US$ 100 billion in economic losses and thousands of victims. Over 90% of losses in human life from disasters around the world occurred in poor countries.

The impacts of Global Environmental Change (GEC), particularly climate-related hazards, disproportionately affect poor and vulnerable people – those who live in slum and squatter settlements on steep hillsides, in poorly drained areas, or in low-lying coastal zones. Until recently, intensity and frequency patterns of natural hazards followed natural variations in global temperatures and tectonic activity. Today, while the scale of seismic and volcanic activity reflects these long time-scale variations, it appears that frequency and intensity of hydro-meteorological hazards is being affected by a changing climate.

Although it is very difficult to show scientific evidence of these changes, projections for the future invite concern, as shown by the findings of the Intergovernmental Panel on Climate Change (IPCC). In some ways, societies are not only responsible for their own socio-economic vulnerability, but also are increasingly responsible for shaping new trends in hazard occurrence.

### 4.3. Shocks and Stresses

Risks, particularly when viewed from a developmental perspective, can be viewed as the probability of shocks and stresses affecting people, or in a more focused way, households. The Household Livelihoods Security model has taken the approach of linking households, livelihoods, access to resources, basic needs and building of assets to the capacity of a household for dealing with shocks and stresses (Sanderson, 2000). The same model, when viewed in the light of climate change, can be interpreted in terms of shrinking resource base, stronger barriers in accessing resources, greater struggles for meeting basic needs, diminished assets, and increased exposure to the risk of shocks and stresses.

Shocks, in this approach, are the low probability but rapid onset and high impact events that cause immediate and visible damage to lives, property, and environment. These include earthquakes, cyclones, tsunamis, flash floods, fires, and accidents. Stresses, on the other hand, are slow onset and low impact processes that are of high probability, particularly in the context of the urban poor, and case a day-to-day continuum of hardships. Stresses include loss of livelihood due to water-logging and disease, small scale building damage due to rains, chronic illnesses related to poor public health, social conflicts and tensions within small communities, environmental degradation, pollution, and other such local small scale adverse conditions.

### 4.4. HFA Urban Risk Reduction

The "Hyogo Framework for Action 2005–2015: Building the Resilience of Nations and communities to disasters" (HFA) was adopted at the World Conference on Disaster Reduction (January, 2005, Kobe, Japan). The HFA specifies that disaster risk is compounded by increasing vulnerabilities related to various elements including unplanned urbanization.

Five priorities of the HFA are: (1) making disaster risk reduction a priority, (2) improving risk information and early warning, (3) using knowledge and education to building a culture of safety and resilience,

(4) reducing the underlying risk factors, and (5) strengthening preparedness for effective response.

Across the HFA, various important elements on URR are mentioned as part of crucial area of work to implement disaster risk reduction policies and actions. In particular, incorporating disaster risk reduction into urban planning is specified to reduce the underlying risk factors (Priority 4).

This section aims at analyzing crucial areas of work and identifying means to address them in the area of URR in the context of five priority areas in the HFA.

### 4.4.1. HFA Priority 1: Making Disaster Risk Reduction a Priority
HFA Priority Action 1 focuses on ensuring that disaster risk reduction is a national and a local priority with a strong institutional basis for implementation.

*Urban Risk Reduction within National and Local Policies and Techno-Legal Framework.* There are many practical ways to reduce the risk of disasters. Ways to reduce climate-related disaster risk include (ISDR, 2007):

1. Careful assessment of areas where hazards and socio-economic vulnerability combine to produce the greatest risks;
2. Public education to help people avoid areas of risk, protect their communities, and know what to do when disaster threatens;
3. Building codes tailored to local conditions to ensure resistance to storms;
4. Good land use management and flood controls to reduce the levels of flooding in settlements;
5. Early warning systems that provide all people with meaningful information, and well-organized public services with the mandate to reduce disaster risks.

Disaster risk reduction is critically important for adapting to changing climate as climate change will increase frequency and intensity of climate-related hazards.

Urban management occupies an important place in the disaster management policy framework as the dense populations and the migrant poor and the under-privileged are highly affected on account of calamities/disasters. The techno-legal regime of a nation has direct implications on the disaster management framework. In India, the approach has been translated into a national disaster framework covering institutional mechanism, disaster prevention strategy, early warning systems, disaster mitigation preparedness and response including human resource development. Disaster prevention is defined to encompass activities designed to provide permanent protection from disasters, which will include engineering and other physical protective measures, and also legislative measures controlling land use and urban planning (Ministry of Home Affairs, National Disaster Management Division and Ministry of Housing & Urban Poverty Alleviation, Building Materials & Technology Promotion Council, Government of India).

The goals of prevention are:

(a) to ensure that all new buildings are designed and constructed with proper engineering intervention taking due care for safety against natural hazards in urban as well as in rural areas so that no unsafe buildings are added to the huge existing stock of unsafe buildings;

(b) to ensure upgrading the safety of buildings in the public sector by retrofitting techniques and encourage similar action regarding buildings in the private sector and individually owned houses.

National standards/codes on disaster resistant structures including the National Building Code of the country are of highest standards in technical contents. However, to make their use mandatory, proper enabling provisions are required in the legal framework.

Laws pertaining to planning, development, and building construction are very important to achieve planned and safe development in urban and rural areas. Building standards/regulations are derived from various laws pertaining to planning and development of different states. They provide the mandatory techno-legal framework for regulating building activity from planning, design to completion of construction. While many Asian countries already have, or are in the process of developing acts, policies, institutional frameworks, and plans in the area of disaster management, many of these are still to get translated to real action and change on the ground. Implementation needs to follow institutionalization, and will finally determine the success of otherwise sound frameworks.

*Institutional Basis for Implementation.*   Institutionalizing community-based disaster risk management (CBDRM) is a multi-sector, multilevel, and participatory process based on agreed values leading to permanence, regularization, and sustainability through integration into the socio-economic development processes (ADPC, 2004).

From the perspective of community groups and organizations, "institutionalization" is a state in which their roles are recognized by the government, their efforts are supported, and the roles and functions of various stakeholders are defined.

In different organizational and cultural contexts the process is referred to by different names. These include: institutionalize, mainstream, scale-up, normalize, legitimize, integrate, adopt, replicate, or sustain.

Institutionalization of CBDRM is required to:

- Achieve the vision of disaster-resilient communities.
- Scale-up the impact (more people, more communities, more risks addressed).
- Enhance learning (more stakeholders, more cases, more lessons).
- Sustain the gains (more structural, more permanent improvements).
- Recognize that strategic success lies in the hands of people in communities.
- Position CBDRM as a viable approach to sustainable development.
- Mobilize partner resources for disaster risk management.

While Asian countries show evidence of the initiation of DRR mainstreaming, it is so far restricted to few sectors, and limited extent. Much of this has been on the international agenda in the form of DRR mainstreaming and URR mainstreaming efforts. The levels of mainstreaming achieved so far, however, are short of desirable levels, particularly due to the inter-sectoral complexities involved therein. Mainstreaming of URR in a country involves ministries and departments such as urban affairs, housing, water resources, environment, transport, home/internal affairs, power, communications, municipal governance, etc., making it a comprehensive and elaborate task to ensure interagency coordination. While DRR mainstreaming in many of these related sectors is sluggish, mainstreaming in the core urban planning and management sectors is lagging in particular.

*4.4.2. HFA Priority 2: Improving Risk Information and Early Warning Assessment and Monitoring of Risks.* Risk assessments include detailed quantitative and qualitative understanding of risk, its physical, social, economic, and environmental factors and consequences. It is a necessary first step for any serious consideration of disaster reduction strategies.

Its relevance for planning and development of disaster risk reduction strategies was explicitly addressed during the United Nations International Decade for Natural Disaster Reduction (IDNDR, 1990–1999). "In the year 2000, all countries, as part of their plans to achieve sustainable development should have in place comprehensive national assessments of risks from natural hazards, with these assessments taken into account in development plans."

This was also outlined in Principle 1 of the 1994 Yokohama Strategy and Plan of Action for a Safer World. "Risk assessment is a required step for the adoption of adequate and successful disaster reduction policies and measures". This approach was carried forward by HFA. HFA Priority Action 2 focuses on assessment of risks and talks of identifying, assessing, and monitoring risks.

Assessment and understanding of urban risk in Asia is still in early stages. It is not a priority issue for urban authorities yet, and does not figure on the agendas of urban planning, management or emergency response agencies. There have been cases of academic research on this subject, but that too is limited to in extent of coverage and depth of content.

Risk assessment encompasses the systematic use of available information to determine the likelihood of certain events occurring and the magnitude of their possible consequences. As a process, it is generally agreed that it includes (ISDR, 2004):

• identifying the nature, location, intensity, and probability of a threat;
• determining the existence and degree of vulnerabilities and exposure to those threats;
• identifying the capacities and resources available to address or manage threats; and
• determining acceptable levels of risk.

Key dimensions of hazard assessments are the presentation of the results and assuring the understanding of the added value of hazard mapping and awareness by policy makers. Maps can be prepared manually using standard cartographic techniques or electronically with GIS (ISDR, 2004). This, and other means, constitutes Risk Communication, which is an integral part of effective risk assessment. This is particularly true for Asian countries wherein the impact of disasters is felt most by the poor, who are often impacted because of the fact that they remain left out of many communication and warning dissemination nets. As a result, there are numerous cases of disasters hitting communities hard because the risk was not assessed or communicated at the community level.

*Early Warning.* Effective early warning requires the below important components.

• Risk Knowledge: Risks arise from both the hazards and the vulnerabilities that are present. What are the patterns and trends in these factors? Risk assessment and mapping will help to set priorities among early warning system needs and to guide preparations for response and disaster prevention activities. Risk assessment could be based on historic

experience and human, social, economic, and environmental vulnerabilities (UNU & ISDR, 2006).
- Warning Service: A sound scientific basis for predicting potentially
  catastrophic events is required. Constant monitoring of possible disaster
  precursors is necessary to generate accurate warnings on time.
  Approaches that address many hazards and involve various monitoring
  agencies are most effective.
- Communication and Dissemination: Clear understandable warnings must
  reach those at risk. For people to understand the warnings they must
  contain clear, useful information that enables proper responses. Regional,
  national, and community level communication channels must be
  identified in advance and one authoritative voice established.
- Response Capability: It is essential that communities understand their
  risks; they must respect the warning service and should know how to
  react. Building up a prepared community requires the participation of
  formal and informal education sectors, addressing the broader concept of
  risk and vulnerability (UNU & ISDR, 2006).

A global survey of early warning systems was undertaken by the United
Nations Secretary-General, pursuant to the request of the General Assembly
in its resolution 61/198, with a view to advancing the development of global
early warning system capacities for all natural hazards. The report on the
survey was finalized in September 2006 (ISDR, 2006). It concluded that while
some warning systems were well advanced, there were numerous gaps and
shortcomings, especially in developing countries and in terms of effectively
reaching and serving the needs of those at risk. The survey report
recommended the development of a globally comprehensive early warning
system, rooted in existing early warning systems and capacities. It
also proposed a set of specific actions toward building national people-
centered early warning systems, filling in the main gaps in global early
warning capacities, strengthening the scientific and data foundations for
early warning and developing the institutional foundations for a global early
warning system. The present report, submitted in response to resolution 61/
198, outlines the survey process and its conclusions and makes recommendations for follow-up actions by Member States and the United Nations system.
   Despite the focus and understanding on the need for effective early
warning formulation and dissemination, this has remained one of the
biggest challenges in Asia, leading to repeats of disasters that could have
been avoided through warning systems. Cyclone Nargis, that hit Myanmar
in 2008, is one of the most recent examples of a well-formulated forecast

that failed to reach the target community in time, and led to huge loss of lives and property.

The Early Warning Conferences (EWC) at Potsdam in 1998 and Bonn in 2003 highlighted the gap between urban vulnerabilities and warning dissemination systems in Asia. As cities are growing, additional populations are settling in areas that were earlier left unoccupied due to their high hazard exposure. As a result, there is a proliferation of slums and squatters along riverbeds, drains, low-lying lands, steep slopes, and busy traffic routes. As much as four fifths of the urban population in some cities is living in substandard housing and poorly organized and developed colonies. Not only are they more prone to disasters, but also their coverage in the early warning net is particularly poor as they are outside the formal outreach of warning systems due to their illegal or quasi-legal status.

One of the cases covered by the Early Warning Conference was of Delhi, where slums inside the Yamuna riverbed, on the wrong side of the embankments, are exposed to frequent floods but get very inadequate and sketchy warnings despite an elaborate forecast formulation system at the city, national, and regional level. While satellite-based forecasting, a national network of rain-gauge and river level monitoring system, and an established flood control system are administered by the government, the slums in the riverbed are not connected due to the missing "last mile" of communication. The same phenomenon is observed in other cities in the region, including Dhaka, Bangkok, Manila, and Kuala Lumpur.

### 4.4.3. HFA Priority 3: Using Knowledge and Education to Building a Culture of Safety and Resilience

In line with HFA Priority 3, the application of knowledge and innovation for risk reduction in urban context is a very important field. It is, however, still emerging as a comprehensive and viable subject, and has to catch up with the ever-increasing demands imposed by rapid increase in urban risk dimensions and magnitude that accompany growth trends and climate change. A number of initiatives have been taken up in the Asian region over the past decade on the creation and dissemination of risk knowledge. These pilots show the way forward for a knowledge-based approach to urban development, and the mainstreaming of risk reduction in the development processes. The relevance of participatory approaches in the planning, development, management, and monitoring of development and risk reduction processes in the urban sector is a critical factor that emerges across the regional initiatives. The use of indigenous knowledge in conjunction with appropriate technologies offers viable options for risk reduction along with climate change adaptation.

Priority emphasis must be given to education as an essential part of disaster reduction strategies. Education is a crucial means within local communities around the world to communicate, to motivate, and to engage, as much as it is to teach. Awareness about risks and dangers needs to start in early education before abilities to address them can become part of growing civic and professional responsibilities as people mature. The various dimensions of disaster risk within a community can be addressed and continuously reinforced, passed between generations, through formal educational programs and professional training.

People's understanding and the exercise of their professional skills are essential components of any risk reduction strategy. An investment in human resources and increasing individual capabilities across generations are likely to have more lasting value than any specific investments made in technical measures to reduce risks.

The following aspects of risk reduction education are critical for such purposes (ISDR, 2004):

- basic role of education and training;
- primary and secondary schooling;
- disaster and risk management training centers;
- academic and educational programs;
- professional trades and skills training; and
- capacity-building.

DRR education is one area that has emerged as a leading area of recent action in Asia. There have been cases of school safety work, inclusion of disaster management in school curriculum, inclusion of specific relevant aspects of DRR in the curriculum of various streams of higher education, informal education, and IEC materials for public education have emerged from various countries, and many of these target urban audiences. The Asian Urban Disaster Mitigation Programme of Asia Disaster Preparedness Center (ADPC), the Urban Earthquake Vulnerability Reduction Programme of UNDP and Government of India, the School Earthquake Safety Programme of NSET Nepal, the School to Community Safety Programme of SEEDS, public education works of Bangladesh Disaster Preparedness Centre, community DRR programs of Practical Action and many other such programs have proved the viability of the approach and set benchmarks for countries to follow.

### 4.4.4. HFA Priority 4: Reducing the Underlying Risk Factors

It is crucial to integrate disaster risk reduction in key sectors in urban development and planning, as vulnerability to natural hazards is increased in many ways in the process of development. Sustainability and climate change adaptation is one of the key areas to which urban planners need to pay their attention.

*Sustainability Issues and Climate Change.* Climate change and its ramifications on urban processes cover a wide spectrum. Climate-related disasters are increasing in frequency and magnitude. Their consequences will depend on a number of factors, including the resilience and vulnerability of people and places.

Climate conditions have always shaped the built environment. Since the 1950s, however, traditional patterns adapted to local climatic conditions have been increasingly abandoned (UNFPA, 2007). Globalization and rapid technological developments tend to promote homogenized architectural and urban design, regardless of natural conditions. With this cookie-cutter architecture comes increased energy consumption from the transportation of exogenous materials and from the utilization of a single building design in a variety of environments and climatic conditions without regard to its energy efficiency. In some places, energy is too cheap to motivate energy-efficient design; in other cases, developers ignore the costs, since sale prices do not reflect the future savings from higher energy efficiency.

Human health in urban areas may suffer as a result of climate change, especially in poor urban areas whose inhabitants are least able to adapt. They already suffer from a variety of problems associated with poverty and inequity. Climate change will aggravate these. For example, poor areas that lack health and other services, combined with crowded living conditions, poor water supply and inadequate sanitation, are ideal for spreading respiratory and intestinal conditions, and for breeding mosquitoes and other vectors of tropical diseases such as malaria, dengue, and yellow fever. Changes in temperature and precipitation can spread disease in previously unaffected areas and encourage it in areas already affected. Changes in climate and the water cycle could affect water supply, water distribution, and water quality in urban areas, with important consequences for water-borne diseases.

The work on climate and sustainability-related risks in Asian cities is catching attention fast, but is still in its nascent stages in terms of development of methodologies, application across the region, and ownership of processes by governments. The Climate Disaster Resilience Initiative of

Kyoto University and partners is a leading effort in this regard. The follow up of actions in response to initial knowledge generation, however, is an area that will need tremendous political commitment, resource allocation, and action in coming times.

### 4.4.5. HFA Priority 5: Strengthening Preparedness for Effective Response

Preparedness for response is a focus area under Priority 5 of the HFA. Urban emergency response preparedness in Asia is an area that far lags minimum standards. The emergency response capacities of cities, both in the policing functions as well as fire fighting and specialized emergency response are very low despite the high levels of risk in these cities.

In addition to the low overall emergency response capacity, the capacity of Asian cities to respond to dynamic risks such as those of climate change impact, migration storms, and social stresses related to rapid growth, are also very low. This is largely due to the fact that the knowledge base, general awareness, and informed political will on these issues are very low.

A viable capacity in addition to high-end and technology-based emergency management that has emerged through pilot initiatives in the region is of community-based emergency response preparedness. In a project on URR in India, implemented by SEEDS in partnership with the Indian Institute of Public Administration an Oxford Brookes University under the DFID Knowledge and Risk program, Risk Assessment was carried out in a squatter settlement in the Yamuna riverbed in Delhi, taking into account citizens' perceptions and expert views (SEEDS, 2007). It comprised identification of inventories of vulnerabilities and capacities of institutions, communities, and infrastructure; key hazards, risks, and perceptions of risks by key actors, etc. Action Planning Exercises were subsequently conducted within the community. The technique was to combine the rapid development of action-oriented initiatives (in the form of a community action plan) with sustainable risk-reduction measures. The measures that were listed at the end of the workshop included physical improvement, strengthening of community structures and the identification of community led environmental improvement initiatives. Utilizing action planning ensured the involvement of all key actors in decision making: community members, government authorities, and NGOs.

One of the major concerns that came out was of fire risk in the settlement. Through the workshop an action plan was prepared by the community and a task force was set up for fire safety. The Action Plan involved building local fire-fighting capacity. A number of alternatives were explored, in collaboration with local authorities and the fire-fighting department. The task force, with support from SEEDS, finally opted for a Community Fire Post, with independent water and power supply. The fire post was commissioned in October 2000.

The Community Fire Post was a first of its kind in the area. Not only was it a community led initiative in terms of planning and establishment of the facility, but it was also manned and maintained by a trained community task force. The local residents had pitched in for the construction work on the post, and held responsibility for its proper maintenance and use. There was a distinct sense of ownership and pride, and they were keen to establish a network of such fire posts to cover the entire settlement. The settlement was later relocated out of the riverbed as part of the city's redevelopment scheme, and gained access to formal fire-fighting services. The planning to action skill sets and the spirit, however, will remain with the community for long.

# 5. INVENTORY OF URBAN RISK REDUCTION INITIATIVES IN ASIA

## 5.1. Urban Risk Reduction Initiative Compilation

As one of the initiatives under the RTF-URR, inventory of initiatives on URR in Asia was produced to review and understand trends and demands, and identify gaps in the area of URR activities by various stakeholders. The collection of the information from various stakeholders and its compilation aims at providing analysis and input to this thematic reporting exercise.

A questionnaire template was developed for the purpose of collecting concise information, in consultation with the RTF. The template was designed, and aimed to get basic information consistently across the various actors working on URR. Information compiled through the template includes context, nature of risk addressed, mechanism, organizational systems, indicators of success, challenges, lessons learnt, and human-interest stories. The template was disseminated mainly through the RTF and ISDR partner networks. Then, submitted initiatives were compiled and analyzed.

## 5.2. Analysis on the Initiatives on Urban Risk Reduction

Over 40 responses were received from across the region. The inventory covers cases from many of the vulnerable Asian countries, including

Bangladesh, China, Japan, India, Indonesia, Malaysia, Nepal, Pakistan, Philippines, Republic of Korea, Singapore, Sri Lanka, Tajikistan, and Vietnam. It also includes over a dozen cases that are multicountry in coverage. It covers activities such as capacity development, school and hospital safety, and appropriate city development planning as initiated by a multitude of stakeholders. The inventoried cases have been categorized and analyzed on the lines of the five priorities of the HFA.

### 5.2.1. HFA Priority 1. Making Disaster Risk Reduction a Priority
In order for making disaster risk reduction a priority, this category includes the following types of methodologies:

(1) Engaging in multi-stakeholder dialogue to establish the foundations for disaster risk reduction,
(2) Creating or strengthening mechanisms for systematic coordination for disaster risk reduction,
(3) Assessing and developing the institutional basis for disaster risk reduction, and
(4) Prioritizing disaster risk reduction and allocating appropriate resources.

This category can be described as the following key terms: participation and mutual learning, cluster composition, institutionalizing disaster reduction, and strengthening capacity on disaster management and disaster risk reduction.

As an example of a project for this category, a project on participatory environment and disaster management through and mutual learning can be cited. Setting its core concept as "Water Environment," the project discusses the urban management from community perspective, and specifically focuses on water-related environment and disaster issues in Kuala Lumpur (Malaysia), Saijo (Japan), and Danang (Vietnam). Through participatory learning process of the local communities (by town watching, community workshops, questionnaire survey, focus group discussion) and local governments, the project targets field-based actions as local level.

### 5.2.2. HFA Priority 2. Improving Risk Information and Early Warning
This category includes the following activity components:

(1) Establishing an initiative for countrywide risk assessments,
(2) Reviewing the availability of risk-related information and the capacities for data collection and use,

(3) Assessing capacities and strengthening early warning systems, and
(4) Developing communication and dissemination mechanisms for disaster risk information and early warning.

Referring to the inventoried case studies, all of the cases related to improving risk information and early warning system follow the above steps (1)–(4) listed in this category. For the case of an early warning system project in Shanghai, China, it starts from establishing a multiagency response platform on severe weather disaster; then it carries out hazard trend warning on weather- and climate-related disaster through monitoring; it proceeds to establishment of a multiagency sharing database on a unified standard, but distributed accesses; and in the end it establishes a multiagency response mechanism and conducts experiment on community safety.

### 5.2.3. HFA Priority 3. Building a Culture of Safety and Resilience
The components for building a culture of safety and resilience include the following activities:

(1) Developing programs to raise awareness of disaster risk reduction,
(2) Including disaster risk reduction in the education system and the research community's work,
(3) Developing disaster risk reduction training for key sectors, and
(4) Enhancing the compilation, dissemination, and use of disaster risk reduction information.

This category can be represented by broad range of activities, including human resource development, school safety, disaster learning program development, community-based disaster management, elaboration of disaster scenarios, disaster risk studies, and hazard mapping.

For example, there is a school safety project in India, which aims at developing a culture of disaster safety in schools with broad objectives of sensitization of students and teachers toward safety issues and making schools premises safe against impending disasters. Its methodology includes sensitization of teachers, students, and parents; identification of hazards and vulnerabilities at school level; preparation of school disaster management plans; constitution of teams within the schools to carry out tasks on disaster management; and organization of regular mock drills.

Another interesting case on building a culture of safety and resilience can be done by the distance learning program on disaster risk management which is a series of online courses designed to develop a broader understanding of disaster risk management among local government decision makers, policy makers, city managers, administrators, and other key stakeholders.

### 5.2.4. HFA Priority 4. Reducing the Risks in Key Sectors
This category includes activities such as:

(1) Environment: Incorporating disaster risk reduction in environmental and natural resources management,
(2) Social needs: Establishing mechanisms for increasing resilience of the poor and most vulnerable,
(3) Physical planning: Establishing measures to incorporate disaster risk reduction in urban and land-use planning,
(4) Structures: Strengthening mechanisms for improved building safety and protection of critical facilities,
(5) Stimulating disaster risk reduction activities in production and service sectors,
(6) Financial/economic instruments: Creating opportunities for private-sector involvement in disaster risk reduction, and
(7) Disaster recovery: Developing a recovery planning process that incorporates disaster risk reduction.

From the inventory cases, the ones which were introduced as key sectors are the environment and climate change issues, health, construction, housing conditions, and infrastructure.

There is an project by WHO Kobe Centre which puts health at the heart of the climate change, expecting to promote research with Member States and appropriate UN organizations, other agencies, and funding bodies for assessing the risks to human health from climate change and implementing effective response measures.

A project in Tajikistan aims at reducing vulnerability of the capital city residents to strong and catastrophic earthquakes through the implementation of building inventory and development of earthquake damage scenarios and action plans, targeting to benefit the total population of the city of Dushanbe. Special attention will be given to primary facilities, such as schools and hospitals.

### 5.2.5. HFA Priority 5. Strengthening Preparedness for Response
This category includes activities such as:

(1) Developing a common understanding and activities in support of disaster preparedness,

(2) Assessing disaster preparedness capacities and mechanisms, and
(3) Strengthening planning and programming for disaster preparedness.

The activities for strengthening preparedness for response include public education, disaster risk management master planning, urban development planning, capacity enhancement, e-learning, disaster risk reduction training programs, and disaster mitigation with multi-stakeholder involvement.

There is a case from Singapore which focuses on public education and community outreach programs in order to engage and involve the population in preparing for emergencies through a multipronged approach targeted at different groups, such as the residential sector, the commercial and industrial workplace sector, and the school population.

In order to strengthen the preparedness for response, Kathmandu Risk-Sensitive Land Use Planning aims to ensure that the detailed land use plan of the Kathmandu Metropolitan City (KMC) of Nepal effectively integrates disaster risk reduction within its spatial and physical development strategies including regulatory and non-regulatory planning tools, bylaws, regulations, and procedures. Specifically, the Project aims to provide technical assistance to the Urban Development Department of KMC in terms of incorporating risk information and parameters in KMC's planning process and procedures.

# 6. RECOMMENDATIONS AND CONCLUSIONS

In conclusion, URR in Asia need a balanced mix of policy formulation, implementation, regulatory measures, and education-awareness programs through community-based approaches. A few conclusive statements can be as follow (Shaw, Srinivas, & Sharma, 2009):

- URR poses a challenge for effective distribution and management of global resources.
- For effective URR, there is a need to strike a balance between natural and built environments and a balance between ecological and economic objectives.
- There is a need to develop a structure of goals/visions and a methodology to achieve URR in order to identify the action that has to be taken.
- Steps need to be taken that are relevant in the short term in order to gain wider acceptability, but keeping long-term goals in mind.
- Access, sharing, and dissemination of information has to be a priority to achieve greater understanding of the issues involved.

- Collaborative efforts in "knowledge transfer" at the community-to-community level and city-to-city level has to be encouraged, particularly between developed and developing cities.
- There is a need to understand and enact the concept of sustainable development and sustainable living, in all its varied definitions, to achieve URR objectives.
- Development of new technologies that are clean, green, and practical has to be encouraged and exchanged between national and city/local governments to combat environmental problems.

The urban risk issue in Asia is being addressed by various institutions at various levels through regional programs by regional entities, through national programs by country governments, and through city-level and local-level activities by community-level entities. The Asia Region is uniquely positioned to have a synergy of activities of UN, bilateral donors, governments, and specific activities by civil society organizations and academic institutions. It is crucial to create an enabling environment of risk reduction in urban areas and enhancing the resilience of people and communities.

UNISDR is going to launch its next global DRR campaign 2010–2011 focusing on URR. The key issue of urban campaign is suggested to promote the action agenda, and to enhance sustainable resilient practices within different types of urban areas, including small, medium sized, and mega cities.

Specific activities of urban campaign could include:

- Advocacy: Awareness raising of people, communities, and decision makers
- Forum and Events: Workshops, Conferences, Public Forum on specific issues of URR
- Flagship Projects: Demonstrative projects on specific geographic and thematic locations
- Tools and Guidelines: Development and implementation of
- Higher Education: Specific courses and diploma programs related to higher education in the related field.

The campaign should compose a process and product on URR. Process should include participation of different stakeholders in advocacy, projects, and education. Products should include tools, guidelines, trained personnel and professionals, and creating an enabling environment of URR. It is needless to say that the Campaign will not solve all the problems in the urban areas. However, the expected outcome is to enhance the enabling environment of risk reduction in urban areas.

# NOTE

1. The Secretariat of the International Decade for Natural Disaster Reduction (1990–1999, predecessor of the UNISDR Secretariat) had conducted the RADIUS (*R*isk *A*ssessment Tools for *Di*agnosis of *U*rban areas against *S*eismic Disasters) project in 1997–1999.

# ACKNOWLEDGMENT

Yuki Matsuoka, Anshu Sharma, and Rajib Shaw highly acknowledge the support and contribution from the members of the Asia Regional Task Force on Urban Risk Reduction. The production of the status report and inventory of initiatives as the concerted efforts under the Asia Regional Task Force on Urban Risk Reduction was useful exercise to understand the status of the urban risk reduction in Asia.

# REFERENCE

ADB. (2006). *Urbanization and sustainability in Asia: Case studies of good practice.* In: B. Roberts & T. Kanaley (Eds). Available at: http://www.adb.org/Documents/Books/ Urbanization-Sustainability/urbanization-sustainability.pdf

ADPC (2004). Building disaster risk reduction in Asia (available at: http://www.adpc.net/ infores/kobe.pdf), p. 9.

Boulle, P., Vrolijks, L., & Palm, E. (1997). Vulnerability reduction for sustainable urban development. *Journal of Contingencies and Crisis Management*, 5(3), 179–188.

IDS, University of Sussex. (January 2008). Id21 insights #71: Climate change and cities. Available at: http://www.id21.org/insights/insights71/insights71.pdf

ISDR. (2004). Living with risk: A global review of disaster reduction initiatives, 2004 version (Chap. 2.2 Emerging trends in hazards, vulnerability patterns and the impact of disasters, p. 47; Cha. 2.3 Risk assessment, p. 63, 66; and Chap. 4.3 Education and training, p. 236) (available at: http://www.unisdr.org/eng/about_isdr/bd-lwr-2004-eng.htm).

ISDR. (2006). Global survey of early warning systems: An assessment of capacities, gaps and opportunities towards building a comprehensive global early warning system for all natural hazards. UN Publication.

ISDR. (2007). Reducing risks of disaster posed by climate change at United Nations Joint Press Kit for Bali Climate Change Conference 3–14 December 2007 (available at: http:// www.un.org/climatechange/pdfs/bali/isdr-bali07-20.pdf).

Ministry of Home Affairs, National Disaster Management Division and Ministry of Housing & Urban Poverty Alleviation, Building Materials & Techonology Promotion Council, Government of India, Building a New Techno-Legal Regime for Safer India (available at: http://www.bmtpc.org/pubs/unpriced_pub_contents/Building%20Techno-Legal%20 Regime.pdf).

Quarantelli, E. L. (2003). Urban vulnerability to disasters in developing countries: Managing risks. In: A. Kreimer, M. Arnold & A. Carlin (Eds), *Building safer cities: The future of disaster risk*. Washington, DC: The World Bank.

Reducing Urban Risk in Asia: Status Report and Inventory of Initiatives. (2009).

Sanderson, D. (2000). Cities, disasters and livelihoods. *Environment and Urbanization, 12*(2), 93–102.

SEEDS. (2007). Our experiments with community planning.

Shaw, R., Srinivas, H., & Sharma, A. (2009). Urban risk reduction: Way ahead. In: R. Shaw, H. Srinivas & A. Sharma (Eds), *Urban risk reduction: An Asian perspective*. Bingley, UK: Emerald Publication.

Surjan, A., & Shaw, R. (2009). Urban risk and disaster risk reduction. In: R. Shaw & R. Krishnamurthy (Eds), *Disaster management: Global challenges and local solutions*. University Press.

UNESCAP. (2005). *Urban environmental governance for sustainable development in Asia and the Pacific: A regional overview*. Bangkok: UN Publication.

UNFPA. (2007). *State of world population 2007: Unleashing the potential of urban growth* (pp. 7–8, 58, 60–61). Available at: http://www.unfpa.org/swp/2007/presskit/pdf/sowp2007_eng.pdf

UNHABITAT. (2008). (available at: http://www.unhabitat.org/downloads/docs/presskit-sowc2008/regional%20updates%20Asia.pdf), p. 1.

UNU & ISDR. (2006). Early warning systems in the context of disaster risk management (available at: http://www.unisdr.org/ppew/info-resources/basic-documents.htm).

# CHAPTER 6

# FUTURE PERSPECTIVE OF URBAN RISK REDUCTION

Hari Srinivas, Rajib Shaw and Anshu Sharma

## ABSTRACT

*Urbanization is a complex dynamic process playing out over multiple scales of space and time. It is both a social phenomenon and a physical transformation of landscape that is now clearly at the forefront of defining current and future trends of development. The key challenge for effective urban risk reduction and mitigation will be to identify the points of intersection for urban vulnerability and risk reduction in order to localize and contextualize the components, so that it can be customized to the unique needs of each urban area. This requires a critical revisit to the way we look at cities and urban areas, and is a useful starting point to contextualize the urban risk management components presented earlier. Taken together these points of intersection put cities in a unique position to generate both the problem and the solution. The concentration of politico-economic decision-making processes in cities of Asia, particularly capital mega cities, provide greater opportunities to meet the urban vulnerability challenge. For effective urban risk reduction, there is a need to strike a balance between natural and built environments and between ecological and economic objectives.*

Urban Risk Reduction: An Asian Perspective
Community, Environment and Disaster Risk Management, Volume 1, 105–115
Copyright © 2012 by Emerald Group Publishing Limited
All rights of reproduction in any form reserved
ISSN: 2040-7262/doi: 10.1108/S2040-7262(2009)0000001010

# 1. FOCUS ON URBANIZATION

Urbanization is a complex dynamic process playing out over multiple scales of space and time. It is both a social phenomenon and a physical transformation of landscape that is now clearly at the forefront of defining current and future trends of development. This phenomenon is now being accelerated by the rapid globalization and expansion of local economies, especially in Asia. Thus, vulnerability caused due to urbanization is also increasing, which is reflected in different major disaster in recent times in urban areas.

Virtually all of the world's future population growth is predicted to take place in cities and their urban landscapes – the UN estimates a global increase from the 2.9 billion urban residents from 1990s to a staggering 5.0 billion by 2030. By 2030, 1 in 4 persons will live in a city of 500,000 people and 1 in 10 persons will live in a city of 10 million population. Most of this growth will occur in the developing countries of Asia, mainly in small- and medium-sized cities and also in the megacities.

As engines of economic growth, cities offer opportunities for sustainability, but at the same time they also present many challenges, such as poverty, pollution, and disease. Therefore, without focusing on the urban areas, it is difficult to reduce the impacts of poverty and disasters. Urbanization effects should be considered in relation to the insufficient adaptation of the infrastructure to the phenomenon of rapid economic activities.

Urban landscapes represent probably the most complex mosaic of land cover and multiple land uses of any landscape and as such provide important large-scale probing experiments of the effects of global change on ecosystems (e.g., global warming and increased nitrogen deposition). Urbanization and urban landscapes have recently been identified by the Millennium Ecosystem Assessment as focus areas where significant knowledge gaps exist. Due to its high stake on built environment, the urban areas are prone to both geological hazards like earthquake and landslides, as well as hydro-meteorological disasters like typhoons (cyclone) and flooding.

# 2. POINTERS FOR POLICY DIRECTIONS

The earlier chapters provided a set of approaches in order to understand the different stages and components of managing urban risk. The issues presented in the chapters address a stark reality that urban residents of today face – of the vulnerable situation that they are in, and the action that needs to be taken to reduce such vulnerabilities and risks. The components form part of a continuum for managing urban risk. These range from risk assessment and action planning, to decision-making and implementation management, placing them within the cross-cutting issues of education, and information and communication management. The significance of the various components presented in the chapters are discussion below.

In the context of urban risk management, risk assessment processes are complex as they involve multi-sectoral parameters. They are the basis on which planning and implementation is carried out. Many of the issues involved are of technical nature, but this also requires focus on the principles behind the assessment process including participatory assessment tools.

Action Planning is a participatory, short-term, visible output-oriented process that enables urban community groups to plan the development or risk reduction actions in their locality and to lead the implementation of the action plans. It carries a strong element of participatory governance, including problem identification, solution search, prioritization, consensus building, reality checks, budgeting, scheduling, and task force formation for action planning.

The most critical components of decision-making are participation and consensus building. In fact these two elements are often in conflict with each other. In the spirit of participation, a wider consultation is needed, and when participation widens, it becomes difficult to arrive at consensus. Decision-making strategies can be very useful in evolving consensus within the planning groups, and then between the civil society actors and the government.

Implementation management is an important part of the urban risk management process that is often overlooked. Most implementing agencies involve beneficiaries to some degree through the assessment process, and some also through the planning process, but then projects are implemented on their own without participation of the beneficiary community. It is therefore important to clarify and emphasize the need for participatory implementation management, and to illustrate ways of achieving it.

Urban risk management has numerous constituent themes. Physical risk reduction, urban social systems, urban economies and livelihood issues, and governance are some of the key thematic areas of consequence. Education for sustainable development needs to address these subjects in an integrated and cross-cutting way. Targeting the key stakeholder is also of critical importance to ensure effective results. There is a clear need to identify and target such stakeholders who will, in the long run, make a sizeable difference by bringing about sustainability factors within urban field practice.

Information and communication management is the backbone of all the participatory processes involved in urban risk management. It is a cross-cutting theme that touches each stage of the urban risk management process and is critical for ensuring that all the various stakeholders engaged in the activities operate in a coordinated, efficient, and effective manner. There is a need to achieve balance between information technologies and "people's" technologies, depending on the operational context.

The key challenge for effective urban risk reduction and mitigation will be to identify the points of intersection for urban vulnerability and risk reduction in order to localize and contextualize the components, so that it can be customized to the unique needs of each urban area. This requires a critical revisit to the way we look at cities and urban areas, and is a useful starting point to contextualize the urban risk management components presented earlier.

## 3. POINTS OF INTERSECTION

To better understand the intrinsic linkages between the environments we are living in and the risk we face in cities, it is useful to look at cities as "ecosystems" that uses resources and emits wastes in a production and consumption cycle – much like natural ecosystems such as forests, mountains, or costal areas. The urban ecosystem is characterized by interplay of the built, natural, and socio-economic environment – which separately and collectively generate much of the vulnerabilities that cities face today.

As the later case studies and examples show, the socio-economic opportunities provided by cities enable people from a wide range of income brackets not only to interact and live, but also create vulnerabilities resulting from lack of access to urban goods and services. These dimensions of poverty are also a key contributor to risk that urban residents face, particularly those in the lower income bracket.

Such socio-economic vulnerabilities compound the basic vulnerabilities emerging from physical and built environment of a city, including buildings, infrastructure, and other engineering and development structures. Within this context, the increasing populations of cities present a dilemma – the compactness and density of cities and residential areas could be both an advantage and a disadvantage – it localizes not only the relative vulnerabilities faced by a city's residents, but also increases the actual number of residents exposed to the vulnerability.

We need to understand that at the heart of such risks faced by urban residents is the lifestyles we lead, and everyday consumption choices we make. Through the daily processes of consumption and production that take place within their boundaries, cities, and urban areas made a significant contribution to climate change. They consequently are also affected by climate change impacts directly (flooding, storms) or indirectly (water shortages, air pollution).

But some of these vulnerabilities are highly localized. The tendency of cities is to be located on riverbanks or coastal areas for economic and strategic reasons make them, on the other hand more vulnerable to metro-hydro disasters.

These issues eventually affect the resilience of urban residents to face the impacts of hazards and risks. There is a limit to the capacities of urbanized areas to absorb and tolerate impacts of hazards and risks, and consequently affecting their ability to sustain urban functions and human well-being.

As a result, cities, particularly in developing countries, face cascading vulnerabilities that go beyond the original risk or hazard, whether natural or man-made, drastically increasing the overall impacts on humans and the environment they live in. A "simple" flooding due to inadequate or ill-maintained drainage infrastructure can easily escalate into a major health epidemic due to water contamination and leakage from sewage drains, or an economic downturn can result from blocked roads and destroyed infrastructure and assets.

Such cascading vulnerabilities also result from the disproportionate share of urban areas in industrial output of a nation, that make them vulnerable to industrial accidents, resulting from human negligence or resulting from a natural disaster.

Taken together these points of intersection, it put cities in a unique position to generate both the problem and the solution. The concentration of politico-economic decision-making processes in cities of Asia, particularly capital mega cities, provide greater opportunities to meet the urban vulnerability challenge.

## 4. EMERGING POLICY DIRECTIONS AND STRATEGIES FOR URBAN RISK REDUCTION

Lessons emerging from the field clearly point to a better understanding of natural hazards that are compounded by socio-economic processes in an urban setting. As a recent ISDR report points out, human activities have an impact on the timing, magnitude, and frequency of disasters such as floods and droughts.

A better understanding of the cause–effect relationships between human activities and impacts trigging longer-term global warming and climate change (due to underlying social, economic, political, and environmental factors) have led to policy directions at the micro and local levels that enable urban and city managers to better manage such change.

The urban risk management components presented in this book point the way to development of policies for addressing such change.

One of the key lessons that have directed policies is the fact that disasters and the hazards/risks that urban residents face are natural events, but are also both strongly influenced, and are triggered, by the socio-economic and cultural contexts in which they occur. This is a cyclical relationship – on one hand, production and consumption patterns are modifying and changing the environment we live in, creating degraded environmental hotspots that exacerbate a "simple" disaster event such as a typhoon or an earthquake; on the other, disasters happening in an urban context have had impacts that go beyond the direct impact of that disaster, for example, the disease and health implications resulting from a flooding.

Observations of such integrated and interlinked effects and impacts have called for a more integrated policy approach, particularly of looking at urban areas as complete ecosystems. Such an approach would help in understanding the problems behind the problems, creating solutions with multiple short-term and long-term benefits. Development of environmental infrastructure, therefore, not only helps in maintaining and preserving the urban environment, but also function as a defense against disasters. For example, a river embankment system that controls floodwaters, will also function as a community park and playground area. This thinking is in line with policy approaches governing natural ecosystems such as mangroves and coral reefs. Integrated management of such ecosystems not only helps in maintaining biodiversity, but also acts as natural defenses.

Converse of the above situation is also true – where degraded urban environments (high air pollution, contaminated urban water bodies, blocked and damaged urban sewerage systems, poor waste management, etc.) consequently reduce the ability of urban residents to manage disaster risks. The degraded quality and condition of our urban environment in itself presents a risk that needs to be effectively addressed – not just for the city or urban area itself, but for the entire hinterland and watershed it is located in.

As a result, the policy justifications for improving the urban environment are now being sought not only from the perspective of improving the quality of life in cities, but also from a risk reduction perspective as well.

# 5. URBAN RISK REDUCTION: A FRAMEWORK FOR POLICY AND PRACTICE

As the case studies in Part II will illustrate, there is an urgent need to develop an effective response to the myriad range of problems and challenges in risk reduction faced by cities and urban areas, particularly in developing countries. As the emerging lessons in urban risk reduction have illustrated, this response should take place within a coherent framework for policy and practice, where urban problems that generate these risks are identified and tackled.

The urban risk reduction framework being presented here has a three-fold objective: (a) to develop awareness and educate on issues related to urban risk reduction; (b) to assist in policy and program development; and (c) to facilitate monitoring and evaluation.

For effective development and implementation of the framework, a broad coalition of actors and stakeholders in the urban arena, include government agencies, planners and planning bodies, NGOs, donor agencies, community groups, academics, etc. need to come together. The framework was developed using the case studies, and through discussion meetings undertaken to prepare this book.

*Urban risk reduction poses a challenge for effective distribution and management of global resources.*

The density and population of today's urban areas necessitates the equitable distribution of resources that are needed for its various activities. As mentioned earlier, it is necessary to understand the effects and impacts of an urban area not only within its immediate boundaries, but also on the region and country it is positioned, due to the large amount of resources necessary to sustain it. These in turn generate risks and hazards that have to be.

*For effective urban risk reduction, there is a need to strike a balance between natural and built environments and between ecological and economic objectives.*

Agglomeration and centrality of resources and skills that an urban area offers should not be ignored, but should be balanced with the natural environment and natural resources, such as air, water, land, and minerals. Economic objectives of job creation, income generation and distribution, particularly for developing countries, will have to be tempered with ecological objectives of sustainable living. The priority that developing cities place on economic development and income distribution over that of risk or environmental issues has to be understood from the larger perspective of long-term human development. For example, more than 41 percent of Thailand's GDP is generated in Bangkok and other major cities, but at a huge environmental cost.

*There is a need to develop a structure of goals/visions and a methodology to achieve urban risk reduction in order to identify the action that has to be taken.*

A structure of goals and visions for sustainable urban living to reduce risk that can easily be understood by ordinary citizen, should be developed. This will allow communities and governments to discuss ways in which this can be achieved at a very tangible, community or household level. Goals and visions will also attribute legitimacy and currency to the problems faced in urban areas, and will set the platform on which these problems can be addressed. The scale of urban problems and the risks that they pose should be understood, so that appropriate action can be taken at the appropriate level.

*Steps need to be taken that are relevant in the short-term in order to gain wider acceptability, but keeping long-term goals in mind.*

In relation to the previous point, the urban risk reduction goals and visions have to be divided into immediate, intermediate, and eventual goals, so that the issues are better understood, and tangible/visible results are achieved. This will also ensure stronger long-term participation from all stakeholders. Sharing and cooperating on essential lessons, practices, and technologies is critical to achieving such goals.

*Access, sharing, and dissemination of information has to be a priority to achieve greater understanding of the issues involved.*

The cause-and-effect reasoning of local actions has to be understood from a regional and global perspective. For example, what is the effect of resources consumption and waste generation on the disasters faced by urban residents? Key to achieving this under-standing and exploration is information, and its easy, adequate, and immediate access. Timely and packaged information is key to influencing local decision-making processes – whether at the individual or community/city levels – -which on a cumulative basis, have global repercussions. Appropriate communication and information technologies should also be encouraged, including the widely used Internet.

*Collaborative efforts in "knowledge transfer" at the community-to-community level and city-to-city level has to be encouraged, particularly between developed and developing cities.*

Collaboration with institutions and governments in developed and developing countries for the transfer of urban risk reduction "software" (inspiring ideas and best practices, innovative technologies, practical solutions, including rules, regulations, laws, legisla-tion, and ordinances) has to be encouraged – covering among other issues, policies, programs, skills, local and city governance. Feasibility and transferability of such "software" will have to be studied in depth before collaborative projects are launched.

*There is a need to understand and enact the concept of sustainable development and sustainable living, in all its varied definitions, to achieve urban risk reduction objectives.*

> Wider participation to achieve the goals of sustainable development and living has to be encouraged. This has to involve the community, local governments, and the whole range of non-governmental organizations (including the private sector). Such issues as development of an environmental consciousness, education and training, capacity-building, and environmental governance need to be considered to reduce the consequent risks that it generates. Sustainable living should become a way of life, rather than a fancy concept that is espoused by a "enlightened" few.

*Development of new technologies that are clean, green, and practical has to be encouraged and exchanged between national and city/local governments to combat environmental problems.*

> Consequences of current polluting technologies and lifestyles have to be weighed in terms of their effect on the environment and on the risks that are faced as a result of its use, while transfer of environmental technologies has to be enabled through a variety of governmental and non-governmental forums, including those online. Collaborations with universities and research think tanks have to be enabled so that appropriate technologies are quickly developed to conserve the environment and also reduce risks faced by cities.

While the contents of the framework provides a broad vision, its applicability lies in establishing policies, programs, and projects that operationalize the objectives in the long-term, and set up mechanisms to monitor and evaluate at every stage.

# 6. OPPORTUNITIES FOR REDUCING URBAN RISK

Operationalize the framework presented in the previous section requires an integrated holistic approach to urban disaster risk reduction that is grounded in the pragmatic reality of cities, their environmental conditions and the governance systems with which they are managed.

It is clear from the discussions presented in the previous chapters that urban managers need to be fully engaged and involved in all disaster risk management mechanisms. Disaster risk reduction strategies and programs should integrate urban concerns and be supported by local authorities and agencies.

Risk reduction criteria, particularly those relevant to cities and urban areas, need to be incorporated into urban management frameworks. While these management frameworks address a number of urban issues, including transport, health, education and the environment, risk reduction criteria has to inherently cut across all these issues.

Risk assessments form the basis of risk reduction strategies and action planning, including disaster preparedness. This is a critical starting point for operationalization, and should be a basic and important part of all levels of urban planning and development.

Education and awareness-raising issues are oft-repeated and much abused policy priorities. But the innate abilities of communities to come together at times of disasters, and their close connection to the land and environments they live in, should not be ignored. These are critical ingredients and starting points that need to be used in communication and capacity development programs. Scientific knowledge of the broader picture within which urban risks populate, become corresponding resources that help contextualize the problems.

Effective and targeted education and awareness-raising places further emphasis on research and innovation as well – multidisciplinary and multi-stakeholder interactions at different levels of governance can help develop a better understanding of the issues involved, and spawn a wide variety of solutions adaptable to different situations.

Considering the complexity and interconnectedness of urban risk, cultivating innovative thinking, and fostering innovative ideas, to manage urban risk – for example, the socio-economic, cultural, and environmental dimensions of urban ecosystems management – become a policy objective in itself.

As the case studies have shown, urban technology and engineering solutions for reducing risks also need to take into consideration their own potential environmental impact. Environmentally sound and green design and development practices can go a long way to simultaneously protect the infrastructures from environmental degradation, and also to protect the environment itself.

Ultimately, urban governance and development processes also need to be a critical target of risk reduction strategies. Environmental and disaster risk considerations will have to be taken into consideration in urban and spatial planning. Urban zoning and land use planning, strategic urban management plans need to pay greater attention to the causes and effects of disaster risk and its reduction.

With cities and urban areas emerging as the settlement of choice for a majority of residents, the 21st century is becoming the "urban century." With an increasingly complex and urbanizing world, sustainable urban development and management not only presents considerable challenges, but also potentials, to reduce urban vulnerabilities and risks.

An urban slum can be seen not only as a "problem" that has to be "eradicated" but also as a "solution" that allows its residents to make a balanced trade-off of the risks involved. Understanding the intricacies of the trade-offs – social, economic, environmental, and others – lie at the core of urban risk reduction.

# PART II

## SECTION I
## CASE STUDIES ON DISASTER RISK REDUCTION

# CHAPTER 7

# EARTHQUAKE RISK MANAGEMENT, LOCAL GOVERNANCE, AND COMMUNITY PARTICIPATION IN MANILA

Tomoko Shaw

## ABSTRACT

*Metro Manila, composed of 13 cities and 4 municipalities, is the home of more than 11 million people, and is vulnerable to different types of hazards, including earthquakes and flooding. This chapter focuses on the legal and institutional framework of Metro Manila, and analyzes the effectiveness of local governance in reducing the impacts of earthquake risk in the community level. Although most of the cities are faced with different barriers and challenges with regard to institutional and legal aspects, it is required to mobilize communities and utilize appropriate community leadership to enhance actions at the local level. In case of Manila, barangay or the lowest government body plays a key role in implementing risk reduction measures at community levels, and barangay captain (elected local representative) plays a crucial role in facilitating implementation. A combination of public help, mutual help, and self-help will be able to develop risk reduction strategies at local level.*

Urban Risk Reduction: An Asian Perspective
Community, Environment and Disaster Risk Management, Volume 1, 119–149
Copyright © 2012 by Emerald Group Publishing Limited
ISSN: 2040-7262/doi: 10.1108/S2040-7262(2009)0000001011

# 1. DISASTER SITUATION IN MANILA

## 1.1. Background

Metropolitan Manila, composed of 13 cities and 4 municipalities (Fig. 1), is the political, economic center of the Philippines. The population of the city is approximately 11million at present. It has been developing and is now one of the densely populated areas in Asia. Rapid population growth started in the 1970s, when the population was approximately 4 million. It increased to 6 million in the 1980s, 8 million in the 1990s, and is 11 million at present. The population has increased by 2.5 times in the last 30 years. This rapid population growth is affecting the fringe areas of Metropolitan Manila, and is expected to grow to 25 million by the year 2015 (Santiago, 1996; Oreta, 1996).

## 1.2. Disaster Situation

The Philippines has suffered from various types of natural disasters. Almost 20–80 cases of natural disasters have occurred annually. The types of disasters are flood, typhoon, volcanic eruption, and earthquakes. Among them earthquake is one of the most serious disaster in the Philippines. For the past 40 years, the Philippines have been affected by 10 earthquakes with magnitude greater than 7.0.

Numerous earthquake sources such as the Valley Fault System, Philippine Fault, Lubang Fault, Manila Trench, and Casiguran Fault, are located in and around Metropolitan Manila (Punongbayan et al., 1993, Bautista, 2000; Bautista et al., 2001). Of these faults, the Valley Fault System, which transects west side of the city, is considered to potentially cause the largest earthquake impact to the Metropolitan Manila area.

Recent studies show that the Valley Fault System has generated at least four earthquakes within the last 1,400 years. The approximate return period of these earthquakes is less than 500 years, and no event along West Valley Fault is known after 16th century. There were several recent studies, which point to increasing vulnerability of Metro Manila areas (EQTAP, 2001; MMCS, 2002; Santiago, 2001; Shaw, 2001).

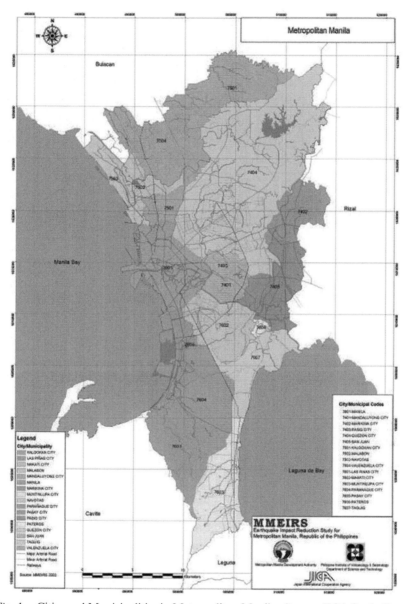

*Fig. 1.* Cities and Municipalities in Metropolitan Manila. *Source:* JICA Study Team.

# 2. LEGAL FRAMEWORK

## *2.1. Presidency Decree 1566*

The basic law and policy framework for disaster management in the Philippines is Presidential Decree 1566 (PD 1566). The incremental accumulation of several laws over a period of 40 years (Executive Order No. 335, Republic Act 1190, and Presidential Decree No. 1) formed the legal historical antecedent of PD 1566. This PD is the operative legal basis for the present disaster risk management system and organizational structure in the Philippines. It also provides guidelines for the organizations and functions of all Disaster Coordinating Councils (DCCs) from the national, regional, provincial, city, municipality, and barangay which is the smallest public administrative unit. This law is complemented by city/municipal ordinances and resolutions legislated by local governments now and then in accordance with the power given to them in the Local Government Code.

PD 1566 was issued to strengthen the Philippine disaster control capability and to establish a community disaster preparedness program nationwide.

Among the salient provisions of the Decree are the following:

- State policy on self-reliance among local officials and their constituents in responding to disasters or emergencies;
- Organization of DCCs from the national down to the municipal level;
- Statement of duties and responsibilities of the National Disaster Coordinating Council (NDCC) (2003), RDCCs, and LDCCs;
- Preparation of the National Calamities and Disaster Preparedness Plan (NCDPP) by Office of Civil Defense (OCD) and implementing plans by NDCC member-agencies;
- Conduct of periodic drills and exercises; and
- Authority for government units to program their funds for disaster preparedness activities in addition to the 2% calamity fund as provided for in PD 474 (amended by RA 8185).

## *2.2. Legal Transition*

In 1941, the late President Manuel L. Quezon, issued Executive Order Nos. 335 and 337. Executive Order No. 335 created the Civilian Emergency Administration (CEA), which was tasked primarily through the National Emergency Commission (NEC) to formulate and execute policies and plans for the protection and welfare of the civilian population under extraordinary and emergency conditions.

In 1954, during World War II, the country's vulnerability to all types of disasters particularly typhoons and floods, and the nuclear arms race of the three superpowers in the 1950s, have prompted the government to promulgate a law – Republic Act 1190, otherwise known as the Civil Defense Act of 1954. Under this law, a National Civil Defense Administration (NCDA) was established which was tasked primarily to provide protection and welfare to the civilian population during war or other national emergencies. To support the NCDA in carrying out its mission, RA 1190 also provided for the establishment of civil defense councils at the national and local levels, namely: the National Civil Defense Council (NCDC) and the provincial, city, and municipal civil defense councils, respectively.

On the other hand, the organization of the local civil defense council was not specifically provided for in the locality but designated the Provincial Governor, City and Municipal Mayor as the Provincial, City and Municipal Civil Defense Director, respectively.

The municipalities and cities which were directly under the supervision of the Provincial Civil Defense Director relative to civil defense services were the main basic operating units for the purpose.

The NCDA, as a planning body under the Office of the President, has been constrained to carry out its functions effectively due to budgetary constraints and the apathy and indifference by the public and the government itself to NCDA's disaster preparedness and prevention programs. But the government's lack of interest to said programs was somewhat reversed when the Ruby Tower building in Manila collapsed in 1968 owing to a powerful earthquake, which led to the creation of a National Committee on Disaster Operation through Administrative Order No. 151 issued on December 2, 1968.

Under this Order, the national committee was created to ensure effective coordination of operations of the different agencies during disasters caused by typhoons, floods, fires, earthquakes, and other calamities. To carry out its functions effectively, the Committee Chairman issued a Standard Operating Procedure (SOP) which prescribed for the organizational set-up for disasters from the national down to the municipal level, their duties and responsibilities and the preparation by concerned agencies of their respective SOPs for the same purpose as the national SOP.

On October 19, 1970, as an aftermath of Typhoon "Sening" which ravaged the Bicol Region, the flooding of Metro Manila for almost three months, a Disaster and Calamities Plan prepared by an Inter-Departmental Planning Group on Disasters and Calamities, was approved by the

President. The Plan has provided, among others, the creation of a National Disaster Control Center.

On June 11, 1978, the National Disaster Control Center, which was created on October 19, 1970, is the forerunner of the NDCC created under PD 1566. It serves as the highest policy-making body for disasters in the country and includes almost all Department Secretaries as members.

### 2.3. Laws and Regulations in Manila

PD 1566 is also the basic law governing disaster coordination in Metropolitan Manila. It provides for the constitution of the Metropolitan Manila Disaster Coordinating Council (MMDCC) and the City/Municipal Disaster Coordinating Councils (C/MDCCs). The functions and duties of the DCCs, while defined in PD 1566 are supported by mayor's executive orders. Policy circulars issued from time to time by the NDCC and the Metropolitan Manila Council also supplement city/municipal ordinances as operating guidelines for the C/MDCCs in Metropolitan Manila. The NDCC has issued various Memorandum Orders on disaster risk management.

### 2.4. Calamity Fund for Disaster Preparedness

In the Philippines, there is a unique and pioneered system of reserve fund that can be utilized for disaster preparedness. Initially, the calamity fund is designed to be utilized for post-disaster activities such as emergency responses, recovery, and reconstruction. The NDCC administers the national calamity fund under the Philippines' General Appropriation Act. The fund shall be used for aid, relief, and rehabilitation services to areas affected by man-made and natural calamities and repair and reconstruction of permanent structures.

However, with the international paradigm shift that more emphasis has been paid on proactive action rather than reactive, some LGU in Metropolitan Manila has started to use this fund for disaster preparedness. For example, street cleaning, clogging the drainage, education campaign has conducted as preparedness activities for flood.

To respond to such situation, Memorandum circular March 2003, stated the following:

Such relief, rehabilitation, reconstruction and other works or services including pre-disaster activities in connection with such man-made disasters may, at the decision of the local government unit, include: preparation of relocation sites/facilities, disaster preparedness training and other pre-disaster activities.

*The calamity fund may also be utilized for undertaking disaster preparedness activities and measures* provided that the Sanggunian concerned shall declare an imminent danger of calamity. In extreme cases and under extraordinary circumstances, such as but not limited to acts of terrorism and outbreak of dangerous and highly communicable diseases such as Severe Acute Respiratory Syndrome (SARS), *the calamity fund may also be utilized for disaster preparedness* without need of a Sanggunian declaration of calamity provided that there is a Presidential proclamation of the existence of an adverse event that would warrant the declaration of the entire country to be under the state of national calamity, which needs to be prevented and suppressed.

Pursuant to the provisions of RA 8185, the amendment is known as "An Act Amending Section 324 (d) of RA 7160", which is popularly known as the Local Government Code of 1991. According to its implementing Rules and Regulations, and Executive Order No. 201 dated 26 April, 2003, it is hereby clarified that 5% local calamity fund of every local government unit (LGU) shall be utilized only for the relief, reconstruction, rehabilitation, and other works and services, in connection with a calamity which occurred during the budget year. Under the aforesaid Act, calamity has been defined as a state of extreme distress or great misfortune caused by adverse event or natural force, causing widespread loss or extensive damage to livestocks, crops, and properties. Accordingly, any adverse event, such as but not limited to acts of terrorism and spread of SARS or other endemics, that could fall within the ambit of the definition of calamity defined by law, can be a legal basis for LGUs concerned to declare their own state of calamity.

The limited budget allocation of the national calamity fund prompted the NDCC to rationalize its use so that urgent and immediate needs in affected areas are duly addressed based on the priority levels set.

PD 1566 defines for the LGUs to program their funds for disaster preparedness activities in addition to the 2% calamity fund as provided for in PD 474. Fig. 2 shows the flow of calamity fund.

## 3. INSTITUTIONAL FRAMEWORK

### 3.1. Institutional Arrangement

The basic Philippine law on disaster management, PD 1566, promulgated in 1978, provides for the organization of multi-sectoral DCCs at every level of

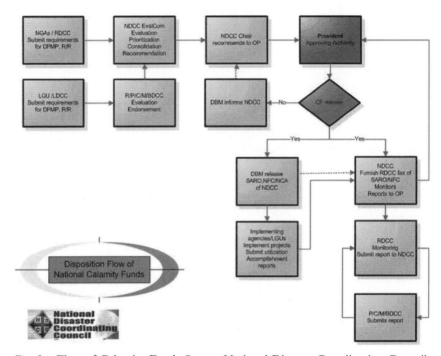

*Fig. 2.* Flow of Calamity Fund. *Source*: National Disaster Coordination Council.

government, from the national level to the barangay (or village) level. Through these DCCs, which are able to link with all relevant government agencies and civic organizations, Philippine communities mobilize resources and capabilities needed to manage disasters.

The DCC approach enables the country to utilize all available means for disaster response, means that are ordinarily used for military and police missions, public service or commercial purposes, but may be rapidly converted into disaster reduction capabilities. It also allows for routine cooperation, sharing of resources, and dissemination of information during periods of extreme stress and emergencies. At the same time, the disaster management coordination approach provides for dedicated technical capabilities for specialized disaster management services as well as confuting attention to disaster preparedness.

At whatever scale of disaster, whether national, regional, provincial, municipal, village, or any levels in between, an appropriate DCC is established, organized, and trained to respond. The NDCC, is the policy-making and coordinating body for disaster management at the national level. It directs all disaster preparedness planning, as well as disaster response operations and rehabilitation, both in the public as well as private sectors. It advises the President on matters related to natural calamities and disasters, including recommendations for the declaration of a state of calamity in disaster-affected areas. It is composed of the heads of 14 national ministries, the Chief of Staff of the Armed Forces of the Philippines, the Secretary-General of the Philippine National Red Cross, and the Administrator of the Office of Civil Defense. The Defense Minister or Secretary of National Defense serves as the Chairman of the NDCC, with the Civil Defense Administrator as Executive Officer (Santiago, 2001).

In each local government of the province, city, or municipality, the local DCC is headed by the elected chief executive, such as the governor or mayor. In the local DCCs, local as well as central government agencies operating at the local level cooperate with civic and nongovernment organizations under the leadership of the highest elected local official. Thus, disaster management is imbedded deeply into the democratic governance of the Philippines. The typical structure of disaster coordination council is shown in Fig. 3 (NDCC, 2008).

## 3.2. Decentralization and Disaster Management

Decentralization and local autonomy in the recent past have been a continuing issue in the Philippines. In the recent disaster risk management, there has been a common understanding that local government and local community are the important focal points. In 1991 the Local Government Code has been enacted, which defines mandates, the functions and powers of provinces, cities, and municipalities including the barangays. The Code authorizes city and municipal mayors to carry out measures as may be necessary during and in the aftermath of man-made and natural disasters and calamities. Under the city and municipality come the smallest public administrative units called barangay in the Philippines. Barangay has its own budget from the local government, and elected officials by the constituents. The barangay captains are likewise authorized and empowered to handle emergencies and disasters.

## 3.3. Barangay and Community in Disaster Risk Management

In the Philippines, the smallest administrative unit is barangay, which is also true in Metropolitan Area. In Metropolitan Manila, there are 1,694 barangays, of which more than half are located in the old city area. Barangays have the

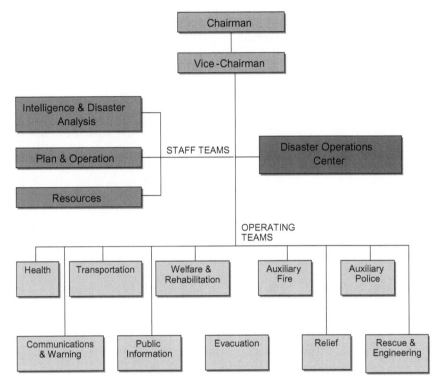

*Fig. 3.* Typical Structure of Disaster Coordination Council. *Source:* National Disaster Coordination Council.

administrative duties of providing community residents with such services as medical treatment, social welfare, public health, environmental improvement, and garbage collection. They are also responsible for the maintenance and management of public facilities, such as culture center, parks, playgrounds, and sports centers. Regardless of the size of barangays, each of them has officers including one barangay captain and seven barangay councilmen (Kagawad) who are elected by the local citizens every three years. They are responsible for implementing various policies through their judicial, legislative, and administrative functions, for maintenance and improvement of lives and for keeping Peace and Order for the barangay constituents.

Other actors are also involved in barangay cleaning, traffic control, and medical assistance.

Community is a certain unit in which people can share their common interests and feel the sense of unity. In a remote area, a village can be a unit of community and it is often a unit of physically formed settlement, consisting of a group of households. However in urban areas, it is very hard to identify the unit of community, in order to demarcate the parish.

Barangay in the Philippines is the unit of community, and it originally means a "sailing boat." Before the Spanish ruled over the Philippines, Malays in the sailing boats arrived and started to live in the islands. Initially barangay consisted of 50–100 family households, which was a preferable size for each member to feel the sense of unity. It served to settle some disputes among the households. The term barangay was changed to Bario during the Spanish governance, but in 1973 Constitution, Bario was renamed barangay again. In this way, barangay has been recognized as the smallest administrative unit.

Nowadays in Metropolitan Manila, size of barangay differs from place to place. The smallest barangay consists of handful to bigger size of several thousand households. National Census data of 2000 indicates that the number of barangay in Manila City is 897, while there are total 1,694 barangays in Metropolitan Manila. The smallest average population for each barangay in Manila City is 1,763, while the largest average population in one barangay is 42,146 in Muntinlupa City. In Manila City, barangay unit is relatively smaller than other cities and municipalities and most barangay captains and councilors know about their neighborhoods and constituents. In such small unit, community is equal to the barangay.

Sitio or Pulok can be found in an old settlement, as smaller unit under some bigger size barangays, while in the newly developed areas, which date back to 20–30 years, like subdivision homeowners association, alley association can be occasionally found. These relatively new units in the new area are not only recognized among their neighbors, but also sometimes in the LGUs, which are in most cases autonomously formed among residents.

In the community-based disaster risk management activities, barangays are regarded as basic units to confront administrative issues, however, in such barangays, smaller units of communities under the barangay need to be identified and considered for disaster management activities.

## 4. DISASTER MANAGEMENT POLICY, PLANS, AND LOCAL GOVERNANCE

### *4.1. National Level Plan*

The National Calamities and Disaster Preparedness Plan delineates the concept of mobilizing existing available resources of all sectors such as public–private before asking higher authorities. It also encourages self-reliance and self-help and collaboration among local officials, general public, and private organizations. The National Plan provides that all tasked agencies and entities are to submit action plans in support of the National Plan, and the inter-agency, multi-sectoral planning, coordination, and operations shall also be conducted.

### 4.2. Metropolitan Manila Disaster Preparedness Plan

This plan is intended to provide an integrated system of direction, control, and utilization of resources, to define the roles and tasks of the MMDCC agencies and NGOs that operate in the National Capital Region (NCR), and to enhance coordination and cooperation among concerned agencies. It establishes that the MMDOC shall be staffed on a 24-h basis and should gather information about a disaster situation and establish contact with the OCD DOC. City and municipality have assigned Disaster Action Officers to report for the duty in the MMDOC.

The plan establishes several control mechanisms: communication links, reporting requirements, and direction and control. The MMDCC utilizes the facilities, staff, and services of the Metro Manila Development Authority (MMDA) as its operating arm, with the support of the OCD, NCR. The MMDCC does not have its own budget but rather operates through the member agencies and the local DCCs.

### 4.3. City/Municipal Level Plan

Each City and Municipality has prepared City Disaster Preparedness Plan and Programs. However, most have not been revised for several years and should be updated. Many of the city and municipal disaster plans and programs are focused more on disasters and emergencies likely to be caused by fire or floods, while only 5 of the 13 cities and 2 of the 4 municipalities specifically address potential disasters triggered by an earthquake. In most of these cases, greater detail with regard to earthquake-induced impacts is needed. Moreover, many of these plans and programs could be strengthened through city or municipal ordinances which formally affix responsibilities with certain entities and individuals.

### 4.4. Barangay Disaster Preparedness Plan

A framework of the disaster management in the Philippines, the PD 1556 clearly defines the role of Barangay Disaster Coordination Council (BDCC).

OCD states that barangay has the inherent responsibility of protecting its members from the effects of disasters affecting community as well as private facilities and that the barangay captain must take necessary precautions to make certain that the community knows how to react in an emergency, and development of barangay preparedness plan is his responsibility.

The Department of National Defense seeks not merely to provide an operational framework to enhance disaster preparedness at barangay level but, by doing so, to strengthen further the imperative of self-reliance at the grassroots level. It also expects the local community to apply their own labors, resources, and capacities toward the welfare of the community.

OCD prepares "Barangay Disaster Manual" and provides appropriate guidelines in the organization and establishment of BDCC which will form the nucleus of disaster activities, especially in emergency response activities. A model BDCC organizational chart and their tasks are defined. The manual defines services such as warning, rescue, evacuation, security, medical, and responsibilities for each service.

This manual can serve as the framework for the community disaster preparedness plan and is designed to provide the barangays general instructions on the organization and implementation of disaster preparedness measures to protect and serve their lives and properties during periods of calamity and natural disasters.

It stresses on using existing capacities that community-wide survey should be made to identify residents with self-protection skills and experiences, and based on these survey, best qualified persons is to be chosen. The basic organization principles are that BDCC should be tailored specially to provide the needs of the community. The BDCC is formed and staffed in accordance with the Barangay Disaster Plan.

# 5. URBAN RISK IN MANILA

## *5.1. Major Urban Risk in Metro Manila*

Metro Manila Earthquake Risk Reduction Study (MMEIRS) was implemented from 2002 to 2004 under the collaborative efforts of the Philippine Institute of Volcanology and Seismology (PHIVOLCS), Japan International Cooperation Agency (JICA), and the MMDA (MMEIRS, 2003a, 2003b, 2004). The objectives of the Study are to: (1) formulate a master plan for earthquake impact reduction for Metropolitan Manila in the Republic of the Philippines and (2) carry out technology transfer to

Philippine counterpart personnel, of MMDA and PHIVOLCS, in the course of the Study (EIRSMM, 2004).

The major contents of the Study are: (1) existing data collection and evaluation, (2) geological survey, (3) social condition survey, (4) building and infrastructure survey, (5) important public facilities survey and dangerous material treatment facilities survey, (6) GIS database development, (7) production of 1:5,000 scale digital topographic maps, (8) analysis of earthquake ground motion and hazards, (9) earthquake damage estimation, (10) preparation of disaster management plan for Metropolitan Manila, and (11) community-based disaster management (CBDM) activities.

The Study developed 18 scenario hazard (ground shaking and liquefaction) maps for the metropolis. The scenarios ranged from possible movement along the various earthquake source zones surrounding or in the metropolis including the Valley Fault System. The worse-case scenario would be M 7.2 movement along the West Valley Fault system. This scenario would result in severe shaking and widespread liquefaction in different areas in the metropolis. Other scenarios included movement along a fault near Manila Bay similar to the 1863 (M 6.5) earthquake and another is an M 7.9 earthquake along the Manila Trench. The study also computed for the projected casualties (death and injuries) including possible disruption to lifeline facilities that may result from the three worst-case scenarios.

The distribution of ground motion, seismic intensity, liquefaction potential, and slope stability was calculated for these 18 scenario earthquakes. Three models, Model 08 (West Valley Fault), Model 13 (Manila Trench), Model 18 (1863 Manila Bay), are selected for detailed image analysis because these scenario earthquakes show typical and severe damages to Metropolitan Manila.

The damage scenario of these three earthquakes is compiled in Table 1. Model 08, which generates 7.2 magnitude earthquake at Manila Fault, is expected to cause heavy damage to 12.7% of residential buildings and 25.6% will be partly damaged. In case of humans, deaths amount to 33,500 and injuries 113,600. Table 1 shows the damage scenario, and Fig. 4 shows some of the results of the study.

*5.2. Local Capacity of Metro Manila MMDA*

At the regional level in the NCR, in 1994 Congress created the MMDA through the passage of Republic Act No. 7924. The Act establishes the State

***Table 1.*** Earthquake Damage Scenario.

| | | | |
|---|---|---|---|
| **Scenario earthquake** | | | |
| Model | Model 08 | Model 13 | Model 18 |
| Magnitude | 7.2 | 7.9 | 6.5 |
| Fault mechanism | Inland fault | Subduction | Unknown |
| **Residential building (1,325,896)** | | | |
| *Damage* | | | |
| Heavily | 168,300 | 1,900 | 14,200 |
| | (12.7%) | (0.1%) | (1.1%) |
| Partly | 339,800 | 6,600 | 52,700 |
| | (25.6%) | (0.5%) | (4.0%) |
| **Population (9,932,560)** | | | |
| *Casualty* | | | |
| Dead | 33,500 | 100 | 3,100 |
| | (0.3%) | (0.0%) | (0.0%) |
| Injured | 113,600 | 300 | 9,500 |
| | (1.1%) | (0.0%) | (0.1%) |
| **Fire** | | | |
| *Outbreak* | 500 | – | – |
| Burnt area and building | | | |
| Wind speed 3m/s | 798ha; 42,100 buildings | – | – |
| Wind speed 8m/s | 1,710ha; 97,800 buildings | | |
| Casualty | | | |
| Wind speed 3m/s | 7,900 (0.1%) | | |
| Wind speed 8m/s | 18,300 (0.2%) | – | – |
| **Bridge 213 (with detail inventory and stability analysis 189)** | | | |
| *Large possibility of falling-off* | | | |
| Bridge | 7 | 0 | 0 |
| Flyover | 0 | 0 | 0 |
| **Flyover 80 (with detail inventory and stability analysis 38)** | | | |
| *Moderate possibility of falling-off* | | | |
| Bridge | 2 | 0 | 2 |
| Flyover | 0 | 0 | 0 |
| **Water supply distribution pipes (total 4,615 km)** | | | |
| Break of pipes or joints | 4,000 points | 0 points | 200 points |
| **Electric power transmission and distribution line (total 4,862 km)** | | | |
| Cut of cables | 30 km | 0 km | 4 km |

***Table 1.*** (*Continued*)

| PLDT telephone Aerial cable (9,445 km) | | | |
|---|---|---|---|
| *Aerial cable (9,445 km)* | | | |
| Underground cable (3,906 km) | | | |
| Cut of cables | 95 km | 0 km | 11 km |
| **Public purpose buildings (hospital 177, school 1,412, fire fighting 124, police 43, MMDCC organizations and 17 LGU city and municipal halls 53)** | | | |
| Heavily damaged | 8–10% | 0–0.2% | 0–1% |
| Partly damaged | 20–25% | 0–0.3% | 2–3% |
| **Mid-rise buildings** | | | |
| *10–30 stories building (981)* | | | |
| Heavily damaged | 11% | 0.3% | 2.3% |
| Partly damaged | 27% | 2.8% | 9.2% |
| **High-rise building** | | | |
| *30–60 stories building (119)* | | | |
| Heavily damaged | 2% | 0% | 0% |
| Partly damaged | 12% | 0.1% | 0.5% |

*Source:* JICA Study Team.

policy of treating Metropolitan Manila as a special development and administrative region responsible for planning, supervising, and coordinating certain basic services, "without prejudice to the autonomy of the affected local government units." As a result, MMDA has jurisdiction over services which have metro-wide impact:

(1) Development planning
(2) Transport (including mass transportation systems) and traffic management
(3) Solid waste disposal and management
(4) Flood control and sewerage management
(5) Urban renewal, zoning and land use planning, and shelter services
(6) Health and sanitation, urban protection, and pollution control
(7) Public safety (including preparedness for preventive or rescue operations during times of disasters, coordination and mobilization of resources, and the implementation of rehabilitation and relief operations in coordination with concerned national agencies)

The MMDA is governed by a board and policy-making body known as the Metro Manila Council, headed by a Chairman appointed by the President

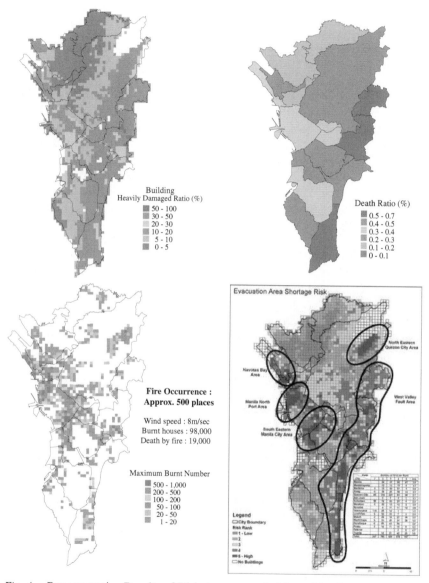

*Fig. 4.* Representative Results of Risk Assessment in Metro Manila. *Source:* JICA Study Team.

and composed of the mayors of the 17 cities and municipalities comprising Metro Manila, the president of the Metro Manila Vice Mayors League, and the president of the Metro Manila Councilors League (Santiago, 2001). In addition, the heads of various national departments attend meetings of the Council as non-voting members. The Council meets regularly and is empowered to approve metro-wide plans, programs, and projects and issue rules, regulations, and resolutions deemed necessary by the MMDA to carry out the purposes of the Act. In view of the Council's composition and power and MMDA's responsibility for disaster preparedness and coordination, the Council has the potential to take a leading role in promoting the strengthening of disaster risk management systems in Metro Manila.

Over the past 50 years, decentralization and local autonomy have been a continuing issue in central–local government relations. In 1991 the Local Government Code was enacted to provide a comprehensive framework for decentralization and exercise of power by local governments. Through the Code, responsibility for basic services and regulatory functions was transferred to the LGUs with the intention of developing self-reliant communities and more effective partners for the attainment of national goals. This principle is consistent with the basic approach to disaster management in the Philippines, which emphasizes local self-reliance through the mobilization of all resources available locally in both governmental entities and civil society.

The law and national plan provide for the establishment of a MMDCC chaired by the MMDA Chairman and with membership determined by the Chairman. MMDCC is responsible, in a disaster, for establishing a Disaster Operations Center (MMDOC) and coordinating from it the disaster operation activities of the local DCCs within Metro Manila.

City and municipal DCCs are to be chaired by the mayor and vice-chaired by the station commander of the INP, with the remaining membership including all city/municipal officials and all national officials working at the city/municipal level. The city and municipal DCCs are also expected to establish a disaster operations center and coordinate from it disaster operations activities, implementing the guidelines set by the NDCC and advising the barangay DCCs regarding disaster management. The barangay DCC has the barangay captain as chairman and leading persons in the community as members. The barangay DCC has similar responsibilities as the higher level DCCs.

The MMDCC, like the city and municipal DCCs in Metro Manila, has no regular schedule of meetings. The most likely reason for this is their reactive character. Disasters that are really metro-wide like major fires or floods seldom occur, although floods are annual occurrences in several districts of Metro Manila. Moreover, DCC members are primarily engaged in the regular, ongoing activities of their agencies, to which disaster-related activities are generally secondary. Also, in general, council members are designated by position rather than on the basis of their individual professional competence or interest in disaster mitigation or risk management.

Also, while the functions and responsibilities of the member agencies of the C/MDCCs are defined on paper, there are few if any examples of detailed manuals or SOPs to guide staff in effectively carrying out specific disaster-related responsibilities. Nevertheless, it has been reported that 3 (Caloocan, Marikina, and Muntinlupa) of the 13 cities in Metro Manila have been evaluated by the DILG-NCR Office as highly performing in disaster preparedness.

Several variables can trigger some DCCs to take initiatives to improve their overall capacities to respond to disasters. DILG-NCR surmised that among these are:

*Leadership of the Mayor*: If the Local Chief Executive takes the lead, the DCC can be made more functional and active, with funding for DCC operations coming from the budget of the Mayor.

*Availability of funds*: Some cities, like Makati or Manila, may more easily provide funds for DCC plans and programs as compared to some other towns with fewer resources.

*Opportunities for cooperation with academic or technical institutions*: The city of Muntinlupa through its initiative has ongoing cooperation with the Tokyo Institute of Technology through which the city has compiled a database on hazards and potential vulnerabilities.

*Awareness of local hazardousness*: The city's awareness as to its position in relation to an earthquake fault like the Valley (Marikina) fault system can trigger more concern on the part of city officials to prepare for disasters.

*Instructions from higher authorities*: At times certain cities or provinces are instructed by the President to prepare contingency plans in anticipation of a crisis or disaster. This is usually done after a crisis or emergency happened in nearby localities.

### 5.3. Local Capacity of Barangay

Barangay functions not only as a grassroot level local community or neighborhood organization but also as the smallest political unit of having public administrative functions, being operated by official budget. Thus, barangay functions as an institutional body. The Local Government Code was enacted in 1991 and it was the milestone of decentralization.

In the Code, the roles of the barangay were clearly defined as the basic political unit, the primary planning and implementing unit of government policies, plans, programs, projects, and activities in the community, and as a forum wherein the collective views of the people may be expressed, crystallized, and considered, and where disputes may be amicably settled. With the added powers and functions, ranging from the enforcement of the laws, maintaining peace and order, ensuring the delivery of basic services, and promoting the general welfare, the barangay can also raise revenue with taxing powers, as well as to impose service charges for barangay-owned facilities and utilities.

Although the decentralization of barangay has been institutionalized for nearly 20 years since the Code, the barangay has not been empowered enough capacities of development roles, since there are no steps or measures shown to put things into practice. The barangay needs to be more proactive, strengthening planning and implementing functions, and not just for problem solving and dispute mediation.

The PD 1566 defines disaster management roles and responsibilities at the barangay level. In addition, barangays have been given additional power for planning and implementation and a new source of revenue by the Local Government Code. CBDM in most countries do not have official status in law and institutions, needless to say about budget, thus these activities tend to become autonomous and sustainability is always a matter of concern. However, in the Philippines, there is an existing official mechanism, where policy and plan can be made at grassroots level.

However, currently, this built-in mechanism has not been observed to be fully utilized. Many barangays have not prepared disaster management plans. It is one of the challenges to revitalize this built-in mechanism, which currently remains in theory, to put it into actual practice.

# 6. ENHANCING SOCIAL RESILIENCE IN THE MEGA CITY

### 6.1. Activity

The pilot communities were aimed to be spearheads to spread similar activities to other communities and barangays in Metropolitan Manila. The community activities started with the social survey, such as key informant survey, and focus group discussions. The community activities are barangay general assembly, community watching, risk and resource mapping, disaster imagination game (DIG), training, and drill. The sequence of the activities is listed in Table 2.

The basic principle of disaster management is self-reliance. Self-reliance means that each individual should protect the safety of oneself and one's own family by oneself, and neighbors should protect their own community by themselves. For community-based earthquake disaster management, certain preparation is needed to mitigate possible damages and prevent secondary hazards such as fires. Neighborhood community organizations are the basic bodies for CBDM activities. Even though Metro Manila citizens are metropolis dwellers, the *bayanihan*[1] spirit, a Filipino traditional communal volunteer spirit that makes seemingly impossible feats possible through the power of unity and cooperation, exists. According to a social survey result, people have the tendency toward fatalism and thinking that someone will help them (Shaw, 2007).

However, the fatalism and dependency on others should be eliminated and self-reliant thinking needs to be primarily stressed. In the pilot community activities, even tough people initially had the sense of fatalism, but after attending several workshops and receiving knowledge and direct perception about earthquake disasters, the fatalism started slowly to vanish.

The fatalism derives from the lack of knowledge; many people simply did not know how to react and what to do to minimize the earthquake impacts. Thus the attitude was fatalistic. However, knowledge is power. Once citizens come to know how to prepare for the earthquake disaster, they will no longer be fatalistic, and they will start taking appropriate actions. The damage estimation results of the number of collapsed houses, casualties, and injuries helped very much in visualizing the situation and gave them the chance to think about how to respond to it to minimize the impact. Resilience and resistance that has been acquired prior to the earthquake event will define the damage conditions at the time of the event and eventually become a precondition that defines the evacuation and recovery processes. Developing resilience and resistance has to be carried out by the individual, family, community, barangay, and LGUs.

DIG is a practical tool for community to understand actual situations and make plans accordingly. There are two major features of the DIG: one is that ambiguous information will be minimized, since any information more or less attributes location. The other is that damage estimation results will

***Table 2.***   Community-Based Disaster Management Activities.

| Activity | Agenda |
|---|---|
| *Social survey* | |
| Key informant survey | ○ Vulnerability and capacity assessment |
| Interview survey | |
| Focus group discussion 1 and 2 | ○ Sharing the residential survey results<br>○ Receiving insights and discussion on key results |
| *Community activities* | |
| General assembly | ○ Explaining damage estimation results<br>○ Showing visual image of possible earthquake damages<br>○ Sharing damage scenario and developing community response scenario |
| Community watching and resource mapping | ○ Identifying resources and risks in the community<br>○ Mapping exercise<br>○ Building regulations<br>○ Introducing building damages and countermeasures<br>○ Emergency community response |
| Disaster Imagination Game (DIG) 1 | ○ Mapping exercise of earthquake hazards<br>○ Sharing vulnerabilities and capacities<br>○ Earthquake emergency risk management planning<br>○ Emergency medical |
| Disaster Imagination Game (DIG) 2 | ○ Earthquake emergency risk management planning<br>○ Presentation on specific topics |
| Training | ○ Training community response in the actual earthquake situation; testing evacuation routes, information management, learning first aid, fire extinguish, organizing community kitchen, etc. |
| Drill | ○ Testing the plan<br>○ Training community response in the actual earthquake situation; testing evacuation routes, information management, learning first aid, fire extinguish, organizing community kitchen, etc. |
| Minutes of Agreement | ○ Identifying roles of PHIVOLCS, MMDA, and LGU for the continuation of the activities<br>○ Discussion and documentation |

be delineated on the map and real situation can be visualized and participants can make realistic and practical plans.

During emergency situations, the following resources are found to be needed: human power, tools for search and rescue, fire extinguishing, emergency medical assistance, life supporting materials like food and water, evacuation facilities, clothes, daily commodities, medical supplies, individual physical strength, decision making, family cooperation and solidarity, local resources, leadership, knowledge about the locality and the weak, aged, and disabled.

Activities of CBDM are categorized in the risk management framework; establish the context, identify, analyze and evaluate risk, treat risk, communicate and consult, and monitoring and review. Table 3 shows major activities of CBDM.

### 6.2. Outcome of the Activities

The basic principle of disaster management is self-reliance. Self-reliance means that each individual should protect the safety of oneself and one's own family by oneself, and neighbors should protect their own community by themselves. For community-based earthquake disaster management, certain preparation is needed to mitigate possible damages and prevent secondary hazards such as fires. Neighborhood community organizations are the basic bodies for community-based disaster. Based on the identified smaller units under barangay, allocation of duties during emergency was prepared.

Resilience and resistance that has been acquired prior to the event would define the damage conditions in time of the event, and eventually become a precondition that defines evacuation and recovery process. This was carried out by individual, family, community, barangay, and LGUs. During emergency situations, following resources are realized: human power, tools for search and rescue, fire extinguish, emergency medical, life supporting materials like food and water, evacuation facilities, clothes, daily commodities, medical supply, individual physical strength, decision making, family cooperation and solidarity, local resources, leadership, knowledge about the locality and the weak, aged, and disabled.

In the planning session, five tasks in emergency time and ordinary time for individual, community, and barangay were identified. The five tasks were search and rescue, emergency medical, information distribution, evacuation, and public awareness. Audiovisual presentation materials that describe the possible earthquake situation will facilitate effective planning opportunities.

**Table 3.** Major Activities of Community Based Disaster Management.

| Risk Management Framework | Description | CBDM Activities | What to do in CBDM Activities | Tools |
|---|---|---|---|---|
| **Action** | | | | |
| Establish the context | Framework for undertaking the process; framework criteria for evaluating risk; understand the environment and local issues, attitude, policies; define the problem to be solved | Strategic group meeting (OCD, PNRC, selected city and barangay officials); workshop (Metro Manila) | Determine participants; organize planning groups; agree on conducting CBDM activities and components; set planning objectives and goals; agree on methodology for evaluating risks; identify problems assess local needs; review LGU master plan; identify development policies | Project Cycle Management (PCM); Strengths, Weakness, opportunities, and Threats (SWOT) analysis |
| **Plan** | | | | |
| Identify risk; analyze risk; evaluate risk | Describe the nature and scope of the hazards, community, and environment; identify factors related to susceptibility and/or resistance to hazards; determine vulnerability, model the risk, estimate likelihood and consequences; evaluate risk against standards or criteria to determine risk treatment | Kick off meeting; social survey; building and infrastructure survey; community watching; community meeting | Identify problems assess local needs; identify role and responsibility; review disaster experience of the local people and draw lessons, analyze and evaluate coping capacities; research, identify and analyze risks and vulnerability on social aspects; local demography, culture, socio-economy, anthropology, leadership, resources, local organizations, past disaster response capacity, etc.; identify, analyze, and evaluate hazards, risks, vulnerabilities by researching | Participatory Rural Appraisal (PRA); questionnaire survey; key informant survey; group interview |

| | | | | |
|---|---|---|---|---|
| | priorities; analyze hazard, risk, resource vulnerability; evaluate hazard, risk, resources | | building structures, infrastructures, roads, open space, physical resources, public utilities, hazardous materials; inspect and recognize local resources, built environment, public utilities, hazardous materials in the community; disseminate damage estimation results; develop knowledge on earthquake disaster preparedness and mitigation; awareness raising that leads to actions | Disaster Imagination Game (DIG) |
| Do<br>Treat risk | Identify, evaluate, and select options; plan and implement measures to reduce risk | Barangay disaster preparedness plan; earthquake scenario; memorandum of agreement; educational materials and poster | Develop management system; determine emergency tasks; determine action plans; prioritize the plan; develop community level earthquake scenario; formalize the plan; document the plan | |
| Check<br>Communicate and consult | Two-way dialogue with stakeholders; ensure their contribution to decision making process | Forum (Metro Manila); seminar (Metro Manila) | Report midterm progress of the CBDM activities; consult opinions and suggestions; share experience of CBDM activities, lessons learned | |
| Check<br>Monitoring and review | Deal with changing conditions; ensure progress | Earthquake drill; map maneuver | Test barangay disaster Preparedness plan | Drill |

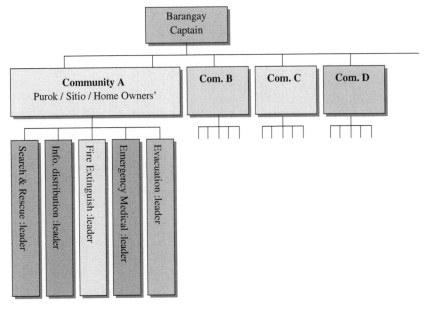

*Fig. 5.* Task Allocation in Barangay.

Knowledge sharing by disaster response agencies also helped participants imagine the precise emergency situation and led to concrete plans. Participants also learned how to prepare for the earthquake and actually have prepared for it (Fig. 5).

Disaster response agencies that can assist in promoting community-based disaster preparedness could get first hand perceptions of community capacity and individual capacity by experiencing the process of planning workshops together with the residents.

The planning process was a training process in which people think about how to react and manage different adverse situations. In emergency situations, people have to react quickly to the changing situations. The planning process gave people opportunity to think how to react, consequently it would be a mind set for emergency risk management.

### 6.3. Implication to Future Activities

Three model barangays were selected to learn lessons to disseminate the similar activities to barangays in Metropolitan Manila. Even though the activities of three model barangays were successful, the safety level of all the barangays in Metropolitan Manila does not mean to be raised. Rather, choosing a community in which typical difficulties and problems may be commonly envisioned in the Metropolitan Manila will provide the suggestive results. Furthermore, establishing the framework of tapping down the activities into other barangays is the ultimate goal. To expand the activities, close collaboration with the local government is essential. At present, formulating barangay disaster preparedness plan and organizing BDCC are clearly defined in the legal form, but the concrete planning steps have not been instructed. This is the main reason why the system remains only in the form but not put into practice.

For such current situations, Minutes of Agreement that ensures further support of communities through LGU were signed with MMDA and PHIVOLCS. MMDA assists to formulate disaster preparedness plan and PHIVOLCS assists technical knowledge about the earthquake disaster.

Further continuous community activities are expected. LGUs are expected to expand the similar activities to other barangays within the city.

In addition to this, MMDA has free training programs within its own budget and writing a request letter addressed to the chairman enables any community or barangay to be trained.

Consequently, the output of the activities and experiences in the three selected communities are ready to trickle down to the other communities.

PHIVOLCS and MMDA signed the Minutes of Agreement for expanding similar activities to other barangays that were willing to be assisted for disaster management activities on the condition that necessary budget was provided by the LGUs.

For the dissemination of CBDM activities, JICA MMEIRS has produced a guidebook titled as "Planning Guide for Community Disaster Preparedness." The main contents explain the concept of participatory planning and the activity guides how to organize community disaster management workshops. Especially procedures for vulnerability and capacity assessment, community watching, risk and resource mapping, DIG, and drills are included.

The guidebook is produced based on the experience of the pilot community activities in three selected areas. The procedures were tested and reviewed in these activities and effectiveness of the planning process has been proved. JICA Study Team has approached Office of Civil Defense, MMDA, and PHIVOLCS for authorization of the guidebook to be utilized as an official guidebook for disseminating community disaster preparedness programs. Along with the Minutes of Agreement, framework for assisting CBDM activities has been established.

The MMIRS project also detailed a Master Plan for Earthquake Impact Reduction that listed 34 frameworks that are broken down to more detailed action plans. Each detailed action plan addressed specific goals and objectives. One of the frameworks regarding CBDM is "to enhance self reliance and mutual help for efficient risk management capacity." It includes (1) developing knowledge about earthquake hazards and vulnerabilities, (2) socializing building safer measures into community practice, (3) enhancing the administrative system supporting community activities such as securing budget, establishing human resource bank, etc., (4) enhancing community governance and linkage with LGUs such as establishing community information and collaborating center, assisting community business, etc., and (5) enhancing potential emergency management capacities such as legitimate local community unit and strengthening social cohesion, promoting business sector involvement.

## 6.4. Conclusion

To pursue mainstreaming efforts in disaster risk management, following are the basic requirements:

- Building capacities of local planners and managers at the metropolitan and city/municipal levels, focus group discussions, trainings and seminars, web-based courses, and e-groups are effective capacity building modes of delivering technical knowledge. Actually, there is also a clamor coming from national planning agencies for capacity building so that in the preparation of national framework plans, Disaster Risk Reduction (DRR) is already incorporated to serve as guide to the national agencies and local governments.
- Establishing pilot cities where demonstration projects can be undertaken and documentation of sound disaster risk management practices documentation is manageable.
- Assistance from higher planning bodies and the international community to metropolitan and small- and medium-sized cities in developing their DRMMP and indicators for monitoring and evaluation.
- Conduct of community consultations with the most vulnerable groups such as those living in informal settlements.
- Continuous advocacy and convincing decision makers and local executives to embrace DRR in urban governance.

In promoting CBDM activities in Metropolitan Manila, following lessons are learned from the pilot activities.

- Requirement of physical assets (such as community centers) to enhance communication and networking in the community
- Introduction of low cost housing program for earthquake safety
- Dissemination of disaster mitigation culture through social and health workers
- Identification and establishment of smaller units and chain of command system within the barangay
- Incorporation of livelihood programs in community activities
- Establishment of synergetic collaboration network to enhance barangay's planning function with the local governments
- Setting up flexible scope of works and time schedule in the community activities
- Inception of priority activity from flood-prone area
- Securing enough time for close interactive dialogue about hazards, building vulnerabilities, and damage estimation results
- Utilizing community global positioning system (GPS) to facilitate map reading and community watching session (need not be owned by the communities)
- Agreement of cost sharing to organize workshops

Above all, making linkage with local government and barangay and building synergetic partnership is necessary. Right now the smallest government body barangay can play an essential role to assess local needs. Therefore, putting local demands and prioritizing them into the development is the suitable task for barangay. More linkages should be made between local government and barangay in terms of public administrative services. This will accelerate effective community governance too.

Community level disaster management is social capital management and it involves development of mutual help and synergetic partnership. Citizens in the Metro Manila are busy urban dwellers who try to make it a better living place. Approaching for upgrading better living environment and amenity will strike residents' hearts more than telling about earthquake disaster management activities. Political will is one of the most important factors in the Philippines and this approach is easier to draw political will.

Even though, CBDM activities become successful to strengthen community bond and to enhance the emergency response capacity, it cannot directly contribute to reduce casualties. Strengthening buildings is fundamental. Convincing the communities that secure living space is of much

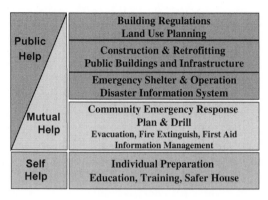

*Fig. 6.*   Conceptual Framework of Community-Based Disaster Risk Management in
Urban Areas.

more priority than retrofit of buildings, to encourage willingness of
strengthening houses, requires long-term efforts and continuous activities.
At the same time, preparing budget for and implementation of the prepared
plans is vital.

Fig. 6 shows the conceptual framework of a sustainable community-based
disaster risk management in the urban context. Three specific types of help
and cooperation are required: public help (government assistance), mutual
help (public–private assistance), and self-help (community, family,
and individual assistance). Building and land use plan, construction and
retrofitting of buildings, public infrastructures, emergency shelters, and
disaster information system are the primary responsibilities of the local and
state government, and with rather low involvement of mutual help.
However, when it comes to the community emergency planning, information exchanges, and drills, a strong collaboration and involvement of the
local community is required. For self-help, it is more to strengthen
individual assets and develop own preparedness. A combination of these
three aspects helps in developing a sustainable system of community-based
disaster preparedness in the urban areas.

# NOTE

1. Bayanihan originally means that neighbors would help a relocating family by
gathering under their house, and carrying it to its new location.

# ACKNOWLEDGMENTS

Part of this chapter comes from the author's experience in the JICA project of earthquake risk reduction in Metro Manila. Collaboration and cooperation from MMDA (Metro Manila Development Agency) and PHIVOLCS (Philippines Institute of Volcanology and Seismology) is highly appreciated.

# REFERENCE

Bautista, B., Bautista, L., Punongbayan, R., & Narag, C. (2001). A deterministic ground motion hazard assessment of Metro Manila, Philippines. *Proceedings of 3rd EQTAP Workshop*, Manila, November.

Bautista, L. (2000). Destructive earthquakes that affected Metro Manila Philippines from 1589 to 1999. *Proceedings of the International Workshop on the Integration of Data for Seismic Disaster Mitigation in Metro Manila*, Quezon City.

EIRSMM. (2004). Earthquake impact reduction study in Metro Manila. A joint study of MMDA, PHIVOLCS and JICA, Tokyo, Japan.

EQTAP. (2001). *Proceedings of Metro Manila Workshop on Earthquake and Tsunami Disaster Mitigation*, July 2001, Manila.

MMCS. (2002). Strategic framework of Metro Manila Case Study, EDM Document, 23pp.

MMEIRS. (2003a). *Earthquake impact reduction study for Metropolitan Manila, Republic of the Philippines*. Interim Report, March 2003.

MMEIRS. (2003b). *Earthquake impact reduction study for Metropolitan Manila, Republic of the Philippines*. Progress Report 2, September 2003.

MMEIRS. (2004). *Earthquake impact reduction study for Metropolitan Manila, Republic of the Philippines*. Final Report (Vol. 1–7), Booklets, March 2004.

National Disaster Coordinating Council (NDCC). Calamities and disaster preparedness plan.

National Disaster Coordinating Council (NDCC). (2003). Contingency planning for emergencies.

National Disaster Coordinating Council (NDCC). (2008). Information on calamity fund, institutional arrangement, organizational set-up and structure. Accessed from http:// ndcc.gov.ph/ndcc/ on January 2008.

Oreta, P. I. (1996). City Study of Manila. In: *Megacity management in the Asia and Pacific region. Policy issues and innovative approaches* (Vol. 2, pp. 153–176). Manila: The Asian Development Bank.

Punongbayan, R. S., Newhall, C. G., Bautista, M. L. P., Garcia, D., & Harlow, R. P. (1993). *Disaster prevention and mitigation in metro manila area*. In: Disaster prevention and mitigation in metropolitan manila area, PHIVOLCS Report, Manila.

Santiago, A.M. (1996). Case study of land management in metro Manila, in Megacity management in the Asia and Pacific region, vol. 1, 437–468.

Santiago, R. (2001). *Metro Manila: An overview*. Third EQTAP Workshop, Manila, November.

Shaw, R. (2001). Metro Manila case study: Development and realization of EqTAP Master Plan. *EQTAP Proceedings*, Kobe (pp. 17–22).

Shaw, R. (2007). Good practice, lessons learned and implications for EAP on undertaking hazard assessments, vulnerability studies and risk analyses and risk financing. ISDR GFDRR Technical Note, 47pp.

# CHAPTER 8

# URBAN DISASTER RISK MANAGEMENT IN KATHMANDU

Jishnu Subedi

## ABSTRACT

*Nepal's urban population is estimated to be around 15 percent. This is a tremendous increment considering that the urban population some 50 years back was just around 3 percent. The rapid increase in urban population in the last five decades has resulted in unplanned and haphazard urban growth. Urbanization causes a shift in employment, from the agricultural sector to the nonagricultural sector. However, in Nepal, despite the increase in the urban population, the economy is still largely dictated by the agricultural sector. Urbanization is creating and adding new risks to the existing risks from natural hazards such as earthquakes, landslides, and flooding. Building a culture of safety is the key to building resilience of communities to disasters and the involvement of the community in managing risks is instrumental in reducing the adverse impacts of these disasters. Public awareness in dealing with disasters and in responding to emergency situations can save a great number of lives.*

## 1. INTRODUCTION

Nepal experiences frequent natural disasters and in the last decade Nepal had also witnessed heavy loss of lives and properties due to armed conflicts.

Urban Risk Reduction: An Asian Perspective
Community, Environment and Disaster Risk Management, Volume 1, 151–166
Copyright © 2012 by Emerald Group Publishing Limited
ISSN: 2040-7262/doi: 10.1108/S2040-7262(2009)0000001012

The major natural disasters that affect Nepal are earthquakes, floods, landslides, fires, windstorms, and avalanches. Nepal is considered a disaster-prone country because of its geography, geology, and location in the tectonic boundary. Nepal lies close to the subduction zone where the Indian plate passes under the Himalayas and hence is susceptible to large-scale earthquakes. In 1934, an earthquake of magnitude 8.4 caused serious damages to the buildings throughout the country and killed more than 9,000 people. Data show that loss of lives as a consequence of natural disasters is more than 20,000 in the span of 20 years. In addition to these natural disasters, other disasters such as road accidents, air accidents, and stampedes also strike regularly and claim many lives and destroy properties. The recent rise in the incidence of armed conflicts has also resulted in more than 10,000 deaths and has heavy impact on infrastructure and development projects. The significance of disaster management in Nepal is increasing, and the country faces challenges in effective disaster management planning and in formulating disaster reduction strategies.

Not only in Nepal, the significance of disaster management is ever increasing in today's world. There are three important reasons: first, risk from the traditional disasters has not decreased much with the advancement of technology. Natural disasters like earthquakes, floods, landslides, and tsunamis still persist and remain a major threat. Although we have been able to cope with them to some extent, we have neither eliminated nor contained them (Carter, 1991). Second, disaster risk has been accumulating historically because of the accumulation of vulnerability in the course of rapid urbanization, particularly in the least developed and developing countries. This is highlighted by the fact that "while only 11 percent of the people exposed to natural hazards live in low human development countries, they account for more than 53 percent of total recorded deaths" (UNDP, 2004a, 2004b). Third, new threats, such as armed violence, terrorism, and other man-made disasters have increased many folds.

## 2. DISASTERS AND POVERTY: THE VICIOUS CIRCLE

The increasing number of disasters has tremendous impact on least developed countries. Hazards, which are potential disaster sources, are distributed, more or less, evenly in developing and developed countries and their occurrence usually do not have any correlation with the economic state

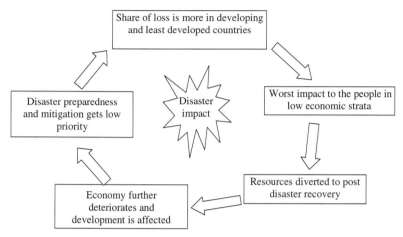

*Fig. 1.* The Vicious Circle of Disaster and Poverty.

of a country. Disasters, which result from the interaction of hazards and the community, are most devastating in developing or underdeveloped countries. The impact of disaster results in loss of life and property, tremendously reducing a country's development potential. The situation is further aggravated by the need to divert resources from essential services and development activities to post-disaster recovery, which taxes a great deal the already limited resources of the developing countries. Furthermore, within the country, people from low-economic groups are the most affected and have the lowest recovery potential. Therefore, disasters further worsen the economic situation of developing countries and within these countries people from lower economic strata are affected most. The developing countries are thus forced into a vicious circle of disaster and poverty as shown in Fig. 1. This vicious circle of disaster and poverty is one of the key issues of urban risk management in developing countries like Nepal.

## 3. URBAN STRUCTURE IN NEPAL

The country is divided into urban and rural areas based on population size and relevant infrastructure facilities (Sharma, 2003).

According to the Municipality Act 1992, urban areas are designated as Metropolis, Sub-Metropolis, and Municipalities. A metropolis is defined as the municipality with a population count of 300,000 or more, with minimum annual revenue of Rs. 70 million

(Nepalese rupees), and with relevant infrastructural facilities. Sub-metropolitan areas are defined as areas with annual revenue of at least Rs. 20 million, with a population of 100,000 or more, and with urban facilities. A municipality is defined as areas with a population of 20,000 or more, with a revenue of at least Rs. 10 million, and with basic urban amenities. Currently, only Kathmandu, the capital city, has received the status of Metropolis city while there are four sub-metropolis and 53 municipalities (Sharma, 2003).

Nepal's urban population is estimated to be around 15 percent and this is a tremendous increment considering that its urban population some 50 years back that was just around 3 percent (Fig. 2a). The rapid increase in urban population in the last five decades has resulted to unplanned and haphazard urban growth.

Despite the increase in urban population by 400 times, Nepal remains one of the least urbanized countries in South Asia. The annual growth rate of the urban population in 2001 was only 3.4 percent, not much compared to the total population growth of 2.44 percent in the same year. The composition of urban and rural populations from 1950 and the growth trend of urban and rural populations are shown in Fig. 2b. Urbanization shows the shift in employment from the agricultural sector to the nonagricultural sector. However, in Nepal, despite the increase in urban population, the economy is still dictated by the agricultural sector.

The increase in urban population can be explained by three factors (Sharma, 2003): (1) definition and redefinition of urban areas by the government; (2) increase in the size of municipalities and merging of neighboring Village Development Committees in the municipalities; and (3) migration of population in search of jobs and opportunities. Therefore, the

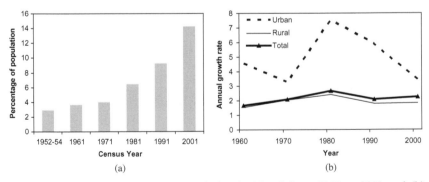

*Fig. 2.* (a) Percentage of Urban Population in Nepal from 1952 to 2001 and (b) Growth Trend in the Rural and Urban Sectors (*Source:* Sharma, 2003).

sudden increase in urban population in 1980–1990 (Fig. 2b) was because of the government decision to raise the status of some rural (village) areas to urban (municipal) areas, thereby increasing the urban population. The trend, therefore, does not directly depict the change in economic activity or development pattern. Furthermore, urban areas do not necessarily have urban facilities and infrastructures as villages were converted to urban areas only by considering their population rather than their qualification to meet urban standards. Moreover, the rise in armed conflicts in remote areas in the later part of the 1990s had been one of the leading factors in the increase in urban population. The influx had been largely in Kathmandu Valley than anywhere else.

With about a population of around 2 million and being the center of business and political activities, Kathmandu Valley holds center stage in the day-to-day affairs of Nepal. Kathmandu Valley comprises one metropolis (Kathmandu), two sub-metropolis (Bhaktapur and Lalitpur), and two municipalities (Kirtipur and Madhyapur). Being located in the vicinity of many active faults, Kathmandu is prone to large-magnitude earthquakes and haphazard urbanization has rendered the city vulnerable.

## 4. EARTHQUAKE DISASTER RISK IN KATHMANDU VALLEY

A loss estimation study of Kathmandu Valley against a major earthquake was carried out as part of the Kathmandu Valley Earthquake Risk Management Project (KVERMP) in 1998. The loss estimation study examined the would be consequences of a 1934-earthquake shaking, which killed more than 9,000 people at that time, if it were to occur in modern-day Kathmandu Valley. The study reported (NSET, 1998):

> Simply applying the percentage of the population killed or injured in the 1934 earthquake to the population of the valley today results in an estimate of 22,000 deaths and 25,000 injuries requiring hospitalization. Applying more recent earthquake casualty figures from cities comparable to Kathmandu Valley results in an estimate of 40,000 deaths and 95,000 injuries. An additional 600,000 to 900,000 residents of Kathmandu Valley are expected to be left homeless by the earthquake due to damaged buildings or fear of being in their homes.

The report further suggested that approximately 95 percent of water pipes and 50 percent of other water system components (pumping stations, treatment plants, etc.) could be damaged seriously. Almost all telephone exchange buildings and 60 percent of telephone lines are likely to be damaged, requiring significant to moderate repair to be operational. Approximately 40 percent of electric lines and all electric substations are likely to be damaged. It could take one month after an earthquake for electricity and telephone utilities to be operational. Water systems will require much more time to repair. It is estimated that most parts of the valley will be without piped water supply for several months and several areas could remain without service for over one year (NSET, 1998).

Japan International Cooperation Agency (JICA) carried out another earthquake scenario analysis as a part of the "Study on Earthquake Disaster Mitigation in Kathmandu Valley" in 2001. The study carried out detailed estimation of damages according to the existing types and numbers of buildings and infrastructures in Kathmandu Valley against three probable earthquakes affecting Kathmandu and made comparison with a simulation of the 1934 earthquake. Among the three probable earthquakes, Mid Nepal Earthquake – set on the existing seismic gap in the middle of Nepal – resulted in the highest number of building damages and death toll. According to the assessment made in the study, the anticipated loss from a Mid Nepal Earthquake would be (JICA, 2002):

1. The number of heavily damaged buildings: 53,000 (21 percent of all buildings).
2. The death toll: 18,000 (1.3 percent of the total population in the valley).
3. The number of seriously injured persons: 53,000 (3.8 percent of the total population in the valley).

The figures are slightly less compared to the projected loss from an earthquake similar to 1934 earthquake in existing condition. The study reported that the numbers of heavily damaged buildings, death toll, and numbers of seriously injured people estimated from the projection of 1934 earthquake in present scenario is 59,000, 20,000, and 59,000, respectively.

# 5. DISASTER RISK AWARENESS IN KATHMANDU

The above two reports suggest that Kathmandu is at very high seismic risk and even conservative estimate places the death toll in thousands. It has been observed from the past seismic history that major earthquakes strike the valley every 75–100 years. Furthermore, there is a long seismic gap zone in the middle of Nepal where energy release through minor quakes has not taken place over a long period. All these suggest that a major earthquake in Kathmandu Valley is inevitable. The only question is whether the community is prepared or not to reduce its impact.

A joint survey was conducted by Nepal Engineering College (NEC) and Center for Disaster Management Informatics Research, Ehime University, Japan in June 2006 to assess the level of natural disaster awareness among residents of Kathmandu Valley. The survey was conducted by under-graduate engineering student volunteers from Nepal in the span of three days. The survey was carried out by handing over a questionnaire directly to the respondents and recording their responses. The three major cities of Bhaktapur, Kathmandu, and Lalitpur were covered in the survey. A total of 1,180 respondents participated. The questionnaire was prepared in English and the volunteers explained the questionnaire, when needed, to the respondents. The sample questionnaire is given in Annex.

When asked whether they agree or disagree (strongly disagree, disagree, agree, or strongly agree) to the statement "Only God knows when the next disaster will happen" (A01 in Fig. 3), 31 percent of the respondents said that they agree (17 percent agree and 14 percent strongly agree) and 69 percent said that they disagree (39 percent strongly disagree and 30 percent agree). When asked whether they agree or disagree to the statement "To come across a natural disaster and remain alive depends on fate or karma" (A09 in Fig. 3), 42 percent said that they agree and 58 percent said that they disagree. Similarly, when asked whether they agree or disagree to "I think that natural disasters cannot be prevented" (A11 in Fig. 3), 50 percent said that they disagree while the other 50 percent said that they agree.

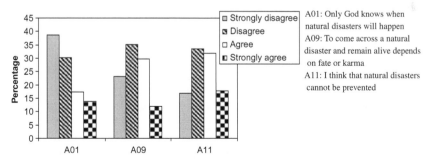

*Fig. 3.* Response to "Describe your Feelings Over the Natural Disaster" Choosing any One of the Options: Strongly Disagree, Disagree, Agree, and Strongly Agree. The Questions are Listed in the Side Box.

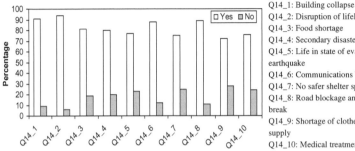

*Fig. 4.* Response on "Do you Feel Insecure about the Following Consequences of an Earthquake?" Different Items are Listed in the Figure, from Q14_1 to Q14_10, with their Brief Description in the Side Box (for Details about the Question Refer Annex).

These results point to the fact that a large proportion of people still think that the occurrence of natural disasters is a God-controlled phenomenon and an even larger number of people think that only fate can decide the consequences.

When asked "Have you ever come across a natural disaster?" 50 percent of the respondents said "no." Interestingly, however, more than 90 percent of the respondents were aware of the possible consequences of a major earthquake in Kathmandu Valley (Fig. 4). The responders felt insecure about the post-earthquake scenario and about damages to building structures, lifelines, food shortage, secondary disasters, shelter place, evacuation, transportation, and emergency facilities (Fig. 4).

In order to assess the level of preparedness among the dwellers of Kathmandu Valley, response was sought on household level preparedness for an earthquake disaster. They were asked to respond on emergency supplies on hand, vulnerable functional components like furniture, evacuation place, communication among family members after an earthquake, provision of fire extinguishers, and structural safety of the building. The results are shown in Fig. 5.

The figure shows that although the level of awareness and knowledge of possible consequences is high, the level of preparedness is at a very low level. Only 31 percent of the respondents have said "yes" in answer to the question about readiness of emergency supplies, whereas 40 percent of residents felt that their houses were designed to withstand earthquake forces. Among the residents of Kathmandu Valley, 60 percent did not have their furniture secured from falling during tremors. Interestingly, 70 percent

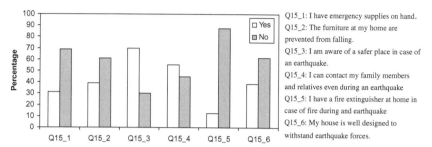

*Fig. 5.* Response to the Questions Related to Household Level Preparedness for Earthquakes. Q15_1 to Q15_6 are Listed in Side Box (for Detail Questions Refer to Annex).

of them know about the safer place in their community. This may be because of the fact that traditional houses in Kathmandu Valley were built with large open space surrounded on all sides by residential buildings. However, such open spaces are dwindling as the land price is increasing very rapidly with the increasing urban population. Using a fire extinguisher is a rare concept in Kathmandu and fire hazard is not considered as severe as inflammable materials are not commonly used in construction except timber. Even in the 1934 earthquake, fire hazard was not so severe. However, currently almost every household uses gas stove these days for cooking which was not the case in 1934 or even 20 years back. Because of the increasing use of gas, fire hazard may also be severe in case of a major earthquake in the future.

It is interesting to note that 40 percent of the people felt that their houses were well designed to withstand earthquake forces (Fig. 5, Q15_6). Houses in Kathmandu can be roughly divided into four categories: traditional houses built with mud-mortar and timber; nonengineered construction with low-quality bricks and minimal use of cement; framed structure without proper engineering consideration; and engineered constructions. There is a tendency to consider framed structures as earthquake safe even though they are designed and constructed with traditional knowledge and without meeting proper engineering requirements. Constructions in the last 20 or so years are usually framed structure, but not necessarily with due consideration to seismic provisions. So, people tend to think that all new constructions are safe from earthquakes. This may be the reason why 40 percent residents feel their structure safe against earthquake. Recent earthquakes in Pakistan and Bhuj, India have shown that framed structures, and even engineer designed structures with improper seismic provisions, are unsafe during an earthquake.

# 6. CULTURE OF SAFETY

Nepal has a long history of destructive earthquakes and the seismic record shows that major earthquakes strike the region in every 75–100 years. The oldest record available of major earthquake dates back to A.D. 1255. Three major earthquakes occurred in Kathmandu Valley in the 19th century in 1810, 1833, and 1866. An earthquake in 1934, believed to be above 8 in the Richter scale, wreaked heavy damage to property and loss of more than 10,000 lives. Despite of this long known history of earthquakes and their devastating effects, the culture of safety and preparedness is lacking among the residents of the valley. The reasons can be explained by three hypotheses:

1. Major earthquakes occur with a gap of 75 plus years and the memory of devastating impacts fades out. People distance themselves from the reality and tend to think of earthquake safety precaution as a waste of money.
2. Influx of migration from areas which are not vulnerable to earthquake might induce a feeling that nothing will happen to them.
3. Low level of awareness among the residents and strong belief in fatalism might lead to the thinking that no matter whatever is done, devastation cannot be prevented.

The reason may be one or combination of more than one of these factors. Whatever the reason, the reality is that the buildings are not constructed considering seismic safety; protection of nonstructural and functional components against tremors gets low priority; and emergency measures for post-earthquake scenario are almost nonexistent.

# 7. DISASTER RISK REDUCTION INITIATIVES

As part of the KVERMP, the Kathmandu Valley Earthquake Management Action Plan, 1998 was prepared by the National Society for Earthquake Technology (NSET) Nepal and Geo-Hazards International, USA. Based on the study, NSET formulated strategy to be implemented in order to reduce the earthquake disaster risk in Kathmandu Valley. The strategies included: building support for the plan and earthquake risk management in general and supporting individual initiatives and revising and keeping the plan up to date.

NSET has been actively involved in School Earthquake Safety Program (SESP), mason training, public awareness creation, and training engineers and architects. The NSET SESP program has been tremendously successful because of the fact that the effect trickles down to the communities. Currently a regional course on Hospital Preparedness for Emergencies (HOPE) is being conducted in Bangladesh, India, Nepal, and the Philippines with assistance of the US Office of Foreign Disaster Assistance (OFDA). NSET has also been instrumental in carrying the message to the community at risk and many ward level communities are now actively carrying out training and drill regularly.

The government of Nepal started preparing a seismic hazard map of Nepal and developed a building code, which was implemented and made mandatory only in 2004. It is now mandatory that new structures in municipal areas are constructed with engineers' consent and following seismic guidelines and building code provisions.

The agenda of disaster risk management has also become a priority of the government. Realizing the challenge ahead and the immediate action required, the government has laid emphasis on disaster management in the Tenth National Plan (2002–2007). The main objective formulated in the Tenth National Plan is "to contribute substantially to make the public life secure by managing the natural and man-made disasters systematically and effectively and by making the development and construction-related programs in the country sustainable, reliable, and highly gainful."

The Tenth National Plan aims to achieve following three targets:

1. Effective disaster risk reduction through international networking and information sharing
2. Hazard map preparation
3. Effective rehabilitation program

In order to achieve these targets envisaged in the plan, the following strategies have been adopted:

• While formulating plans and policies on natural and man-made disaster management, emphasis will be given to the use and development of technologies that lessen harm from natural disasters.
• The relief and rescue activities that are provided to the disaster affected families by the state will be made transparent.
• Emphasis will be given to enhance awareness regarding natural disaster management.

- The seismological measurement center and the natural disaster management center established in the country will be strengthened.

The Tenth National Plan has identified the main cause of failure of past attempts as "the lack of coordination among the authorities involved, adoption of the controlling type of attempt by the management instead of preventive measures, the lack of modern technology that provides pre-disaster information and early warning about possible natural disaster, the lack of topographic survey of possible disaster areas, and the lack of awareness in the management of natural disaster." Although the plan acknowledges the problems in disaster management in the country as the lack of appraisal of natural disaster while selecting development projects, no clear mechanism has been developed to address these gaps. The underachievement of the Tenth National Plan can be explained by the fact that little has been done to improve the situation of seismological measurement and natural disaster management within the planned period. However, it needs to be emphasized that Tenth National Plan has initiated the process of mainstreaming disaster risk reduction in the development planning.

# 8. ISSUES AND FUTURE ACTIONS

The Natural Disaster Relief Act (NDRA, 1982) was the first formal effort to deal with various aspects of disaster management. Although the act primarily addresses the post-disaster relief rather than the holistic concept of disaster management, its positive feature is that it recognizes the importance of local level participation in disaster management. The Ministry of Home Affairs works as the apex body for disaster management and Chief District Officer (CDO) acts as local coordinator at the district level. Although this arrangement is suitable in remote areas, this is nonfunctional in large urban areas like Kathmandu where most of the businesses are carried out by municipal authorities. Strengthening and promoting self-governance of local bodies for risk management is vital for effectiveness of urban risk management strategy. This was also recommended in the study carried out by JICA in 2001–2002 (JICA, 2002).

Although the Tenth National Plan addresses lapses in previous attempts in disaster management and has a clear-cut strategy and objectives, the implementation part is poor. A higher-level mechanism is necessary which can coordinate different ministries, departments, and agencies directly or indirectly involved in different stages of disaster risk management.

There is an urgent need to establish a strong legal base for a comprehensive risk management system. This risk sharing mechanism can reduce the vulnerability of low-income population, which are increasing in number in urban areas.

The National Building Code has been made mandatory, but even the new buildings are not constructed according to the standard. Capacity building at local level is essential for effective implementation of the code. Furthermore, a mechanism of information dissemination at different levels must be established. Raw data should be made available to the scientific community and the research outcome should be disseminated to the communities at risk.

Building a culture of safety is the key in building resilience of communities to disaster and the involvement of the community in managing risk is instrumental in reducing the adverse impact of disasters. Public awareness in dealing with disasters and responding to emergency situation can save a great deal of lives. As major earthquakes happen only in very long intervals, communities might have a tendency to forget the lessons from previous earthquakes. Regular events, e.g., earthquake memorial day at local level and awareness raising campaign, can be effective tools for making people aware of the impending disasters. Schools are effective medium and can serve as focal point for building resilient communities. NGOs and community-based organizations can play roles in initiating the process and ensuring that it will be a sustained process rather than a one-time event. The government and other organizations can support the community initiatives and enhance their long-term capacities.

In conclusion, it should be considered a positive development that the government realizes the importance of mainstreaming disaster risk reduction in development strategies. Translating these realizations into practical achievements is, however, essential in reducing risk of highly vulnerable urban areas like Kathmandu.

# ACKNOWLEDGMENT

Mr. Amod M. Dixit, Executive Director, National Society for Earthquake Technology Nepal has been kind enough to suggest and discuss the contents of this report at different stages. However, any shortcomings, errors, and omissions in this report are the sole responsibility of the author.

# REFERENCES

Carter, N. W. (1991). *Disaster management: A disaster manager's handbook.* Manila: ADB.

His Majesty's Government of Nepal (HMG/N). (1982). Natural Disaster Relief Act (with Second Amendment, 1992) (in Nepali).

Japan International Cooperation Agency (JICA). (2002). The Study on Earthquake Disaster Mitigation in the Kathmandu Valley, Kingdom of Nepal.

National Planning Commission (NPC). (2002). Tenth Five Year Plan. His Majesty's Government of Nepal.

National Society for Earthquake Technology (NSET). (1998). Kathmandu Valley Earthquake Management Action Plan.

Sharma, P. (2003). Urbanization and development. Population Monograph of Nepal, National Planning Commission, HMG Nepal.

UNDP. (2004a). Community disaster management: Introductory booklet (in Nepali).

UNDP. (2004b). Reducing disaster risk: A challenge for development.

# A.1. ANNEX

## *A.1.1. Questionnaire Survey: Natural Disaster Awareness in Kathmandu Valley of Nepal.*

Purpose: To assess the level of disaster awareness among the city dwellers of Kathmandu Valley with regard to the predicted 1934-scale earthquake in Nepal in near future, and make necessary recommendations for the disaster preparedness.

□ PART A

**Please give us your information.**

1) Gender                                  1. Male          2. Female
2) Age (of respondent)                  ____ years-old
3) What is your occupation?
4) What is your education level?

□ PART B

**Please give us your family information.**

5) How many members are there in your family (including yourself)?         _____
6) How many children (under 18 years-old) are there in your family?         _____
7) How many elderly members (over 65 years- old) are there in your family?   _____
8) How many bedridden (always in bed) persons are there in your family?      _____

□ PART C

**Please respond to the following questions in relation with the natural disasters.**

9) Have you ever come across a natural disaster?              1. Yes              2. No

10) If "Yes" in Question 9), please indicate what type of natural disaster it was.

11) Do you think you would participate in disaster drills?              1. Yes              2. No

12) The following 11 statements from **A01** to **A11** describe your feelings over the natural disaster. Please circle the scale from 1 to 4 that refer to the degree of your agreement as follows.

**1. Strongly disagree**
**2. Disagree**
**3. Agree**
**4. Strongly agree**

| STATEMENT | | SCALE | | |
|---|---|---|---|---|
| A01. | Only God knows when natural disasters will happen | 1 | 2 | 3 | 4 |
| A02. | I think the natural disasters are terribly destructive | 1 | 2 | 3 | 4 |
| A03. | I am confident that I can escape during a disaster event | 1 | 2 | 3 | 4 |
| A04. | I feel that large-scale natural disasters will certainly occur in next 10 years | 1 | 2 | 3 | 4 |
| A05. | I feel that the area I live in is safe from the natural disasters | 1 | 2 | 3 | 4 |
| A06. | I have taken enough precautionary measures against natural disasters | 1 | 2 | 3 | 4 |
| A07. | I am aware of the shelter areas in case of a natural disaster | 1 | 2 | 3 | 4 |
| A08. | I don't think I know when a natural disaster will occur | 1 | 2 | 3 | 4 |
| A09. | To come across a natural disaster and remain alive depends on fate or karma | 1 | 2 | 3 | 4 |
| A10. | As the natural disasters are frequent, I secure food and daily commodities | 1 | 2 | 3 | 4 |
| A11. | I think that the natural disasters cannot be prevented | 1 | 2 | 3 | 4 |

13) Do you feel insecure about the following natural disasters (from B01 to B06)? Please circle the scale from 1 to 4 that refer to the level of your insecurity.

**1. Never**

**2. Rarely**

**3. Often**

**4. Always**

| ITEM | | SCALE | | | |
|---|---|---|---|---|---|
| B01. | Flood disaster | 1 | 2 | 3 | 4 |
| B02. | Landslides | 1 | 2 | 3 | 4 |
| B03. | Life-threatening pandemic disease (For example, plague etc.) | 1 | 2 | 3 | 4 |
| B04. | Cyclones | 1 | 2 | 3 | 4 |
| B05. | Earthquakes | 1 | 2 | 3 | 4 |
| B06. | Fire | 1 | 2 | 3 | 4 |

## PART D

14) Please predict the widespread damage during a devastating earthquake. The following items demonstrate damage from the earthquake.

Do you feel insecure about the following consequences of an earthquake?

| | | | |
|---|---|---|---|
| (1) | Building collapse | 1. Yes | 2. No |
| (2) | Disruption of lifeline (such as electricity, roads, water supply, sewerage, etc.) | | |
| | | 1. Yes | 2. No |
| (3) | Food shortage | 1. Yes | 2. No |
| (4) | Secondary disaster (such as fire) | 1. Yes | 2. No |
| (5) | Life in state of evacuation after the earthquake | 1. Yes | 2. No |
| (6) | Communication break | 1. Yes | 2. No |
| (7) | No safer shelter space | 1. Yes | 2. No |
| (8) | Road blockage and transportation break | 1. Yes | 2. No |
| (9) | Shortage of clothes and emergency supply | 1. Yes | 2. No |
| (10) | Medical treatment and medicine | 1. Yes | 2. No |

15) Please respond to the questions related to your preparedness for earthquakes.

| | | | |
|---|---|---|---|
| (1) | I have emergency supplies on hand. | 1. Yes | 2. No |
| (2) | The furniture at my home are prevented from falling. | 1. Yes | 2. No |
| (3) | I am aware of a safer place in case of an earthquake. | 1. Yes | 2. No |
| (4) | I can contact my family members and relatives even during an earthquake | | |
| | | 1. Yes | 2. No |
| (5) | I have a fire extinguisher at home in case of fire during and earthquake | | |
| | | 1. Yes | 2. No |
| (6) | My house is well designed to withstand earthquake forces. | 1. Yes | 2. No |

## ☐PART E

**Please write what you feel about the role the government or disaster management agencies should play.**

# CHAPTER 9

# REDUCING URBAN RISK THROUGH COMMUNITY-BASED APPROACHES IN SHIMLA

Anshu Sharma

## ABSTRACT

*Shimla is a teeming city, with a population of 140,000, in the north Indian Himalayas. It sits in an area of high seismicity that was rocked by a devastating earthquake about a hundred years ago, yet is oblivious of the ticking time bomb below its foundations. Initiating risk reduction in this fast growing urban economic hub is an enormous challenge. SEEDS, a national NGO, started working in the city just before the earthquake centenary in 2005, with an aim to identify ways of reducing earthquake risk through actions that could be carried out by the citizens and the local government, with school children playing a catalytic role.*

## 1. SHIMLA: A CITY OF BEAUTY AND RISK

Shimla once used to be the summer capital of India, when all government offices moved up the hills to escape the summer heat of Delhi. Today tourists flock to Shimla, particularly during the summer months, seeking the

Urban Risk Reduction: An Asian Perspective
Community, Environment and Disaster Risk Management, Volume 1, 167–187
Copyright © 2012 by Emerald Group Publishing Limited
All rights of reproduction in any form reserved
ISSN: 2040-7262/doi: 10.1108/S2040-7262(2009)0000001013

same cool breezes and panoramic views. The views of the snow peaks and green hills, the feel of the quaint European streets and vistas, hot snacks and drinks at the eateries along the Mall Road, all are a tourist delight. Few look beyond, at the embedded risk. Fewer residents notice it, as they go about making additions to their buildings to meet the growing need for space.

Over a hundred years ago, on the 4th of April 1905, an earthquake measuring 7.8 on the Richter Scale hit the Kangra valley in the Indian Himalayan mountain state of Himachal Pradesh. Close to 20,000 people died in the earthquake that rocked villages and cities as far as 700 km away (www.asc-india.org/gq/kangra.htm). This was undoubtedly one of the most devastating earthquakes ever experienced in the region.

Himachal Pradesh lies in Zones IV and V of the Seismic Zoning Map of India. These zones are the most severe seismic damage zones and are also referred to as Very High and High Damage Risk Zones. The issue of greatest concern is that development in the region over the last 100 years has been totally unmindful of this risk. Shimla, the capital city of Himachal Pradesh, is symbolic of this development. Originally designed for a population of 25,000, it today houses 140,000 persons as residents, and another 100,000 or more are present in the city as floating population as it is a regional employment center and an international tourist attraction. Economy has had precedence over safety. Every lane and every view is glaring evidence of the high level of risk the city has created for itself.

Shimla is situated on mountainous Middle Himalayas, which form the last traverse spur of the Central Himalayas, south of the river Satluj. The city is spread across 26 km along a ridge that overlooks terrace-cultivated hillsides. Administratively, the Municipal Corporation looks after the civic management. The municipal area is further divided into 25 wards.

The unique geographic setting of Shimla is bounded by two major thrusts, the Main Central Thrust (MCT) and Main Boundary Fault (MBF). Other thrusts present in the region, such as the Jwalamukhi Thrust and the Drang Thrust, result in several other lineaments piercing the zone into fractured and faulted blocks and active faults enhancing the structural discontinuities. The region has experienced frequent mild tremors and periodic major earthquakes in the past, and will continue to do so in the future.

Shimla can expect maximum peak ground acceleration (PGA) of $4.0 \, \text{m/s}^2$. This suggests that Shimla can expect an earthquake of seismic intensity of VIII on the Modified Mercalli (MM) Intensity Scale. MM VIII indicates that there can be slight damage in specially designed structures; considerable in ordinary substantial buildings; great damage in poorly built structures.

Panel walls can be thrown out of frame structures. Chimneys, factory stacks, columns, walls, and monuments can collapse. Heavy furniture can get overturned. Sand and mud can get ejected in small amounts. Changes can be caused in water levels. Most of the structures in Shimla fall in the "poorly built" classification.

Earthquake-induced ground failure can be expected along the northern slopes of the Ridge, i.e., in Lakkar Bazaar, New Shimla and Vikas Nagar, Ruldu Bhatta, Phingask, Kachhi Ghhati (soft valley), and along the drainage channels. Northern slopes (Snowdown Hospital area) of the Ridge have already experienced subsidence since 1971 and are still considered as a "sinking zone" extending from Scandal Point to Lakkar Bazaar, including the City Bus Stand, Idgah, Longwood, Ruldu Bhatta, and adjoining areas. Soft soil depth is about 10 m at some places in New Shimla, which may also lead to subsidence in the face of an earthquake.

# 2. THE FIRST STEP: ORGANIZING LOCAL RESOURCES

Past experience of many government and NGO-led initiatives clearly indicates the need for local resources and anchoring in order to ensure sustainability of any local initiative. Work carried out by SEEDS itself in the past using Action Planning techniques through field-based project development workshops (Hamdi & Goethert, 1997, p. 145) had resulted in a belief within the project team that the process should start from the ground up. The starting point of the Earthquake Safe Shimla initiative was to find local informers and anchors.

A Planning Team was constituted to help in identifying local problems and finding solutions to reduce the earthquake vulnerability of Shimla. The team comprises project personnel, local experts, prominent citizens, and officials. The Planning Team would also provide credibility to the project locally. The final list of Planning Team members was prepared and the District Collector's office issued an "Office Order" to the effect. The small voluntary initiative now had government legitimacy.

The District Collector's office was identified as the Adopting Entity, the local partner who would own the project. This particular office was chosen because the District Collector is the nodal local officer for disaster management. A Memorandum of Understanding was signed with the Adopting Entity for preparation of an Earthquake Risk Mitigation Plan for Shimla, and for its sustained implementation.

# 3. URBAN EARTHQUAKE RISK ASSESSMENT

Extensive research has been carried out across the globe to develop a suitable method to assess urban earthquake risk. Dr. Rachel Davidson developed Earthquake Disaster Risk Index (EDRI) by using data collected from secondary sources and demonstrated it by evaluating ten cities across the world (www.geohaz.org/radius/understanding2.htm). Risk assessment tools were also identified under the RADIUS (Risk Assessment Tools for Diagnosis of Urban Areas against Seismic Disasters) initiative of the United Nations (www.geohaz.org/radius/). This set of tools translated spatial dimensions or seismic risk data on easy to use spreadsheets. The Understanding Urban Seismic Risk Around the World (UUSRAW) project was carried out as part of the RADIUS initiative (www.geohaz.org/radius/Understanding.htm). It was designed to help cities around the world compare their earthquake risk and to share their experiences and resources in working to reduce the impact of future earthquakes. Geo hazard International (GHI) has also developed a method which is an improved version based on lesson learnt in RADIUS. This method was applied under the Global Earthquake Safety Initiative (GESI) to 21 of the most vulnerable cities across the world (www.hyo-go.uncrd.or.jp/activity/projects/08gesi.htm). Under this method data was collected through questionnaire surveys targeting local professionals.

The SEEDS project reviewed all the mentioned methods and decided to use suitable parts of these along with physical surveys. The method finally applied was primarily based on physical surveys of buildings and infrastructure facilities, backed with information collected through interviews of local professionals. The results were verified through meetings with local community leaders to ensure adherence with ground realities. The complete method was a six-stage process:

## 3.1. Background Research on Earthquake Vulnerability of Shimla

Data was collected from secondary sources and background research was carried out, assessing Shimla's earthquake vulnerability in view of past earthquakes, landslides, soil structure, etc. The research was carried out by the project team with inputs from local experts.

## 3.2. Preparation of Maps for Identification of Risk Zones

Base maps were prepared and subsequently used for GIS-based mapping of risk zones in the city. This primarily covered building typology, land use distribution, elevations, transportation routes, lifeline facilities, etc. Participatory assessment was carried out at ward level with citizen groups. In addition, the project team carried out technical assessment of the buildings. A GIS expert was then engaged to prepare the composite maps.

### 3.3. Questionnaire Survey

The project team carried out questionnaire surveys to assess the capacity of the city with respect to earthquake mitigation, preparedness, and response. Key informants were interviewed for each thematic area, and these informants were drawn from the local academia and concerned agencies. The survey helped estimate potential losses due to likely earthquakes in future. Questionnaires surveys covered the following aspects:

1. Building Data
2. Fire Fighting and Rescue
3. General Emergency Response
4. Hospital Emergency Preparedness
5. Land Use and City Planning[1]
6. Landslides and Avalanches
7. Soil Conditions

### 3.4. Rapid Visual Screening Survey of School Buildings

There was a special focus in the Plan on School Safety. Over 20 school buildings all over the city were surveyed using a specially designed rapid visual screening methodology. Project engineers who had received training on visual screening methods carried out the survey.

### 3.5. Primary Survey of Buildings

Prevalent building types were identified and the project team surveyed the town and collected type wise information on structural features, use, accessibility, age, height, condition, and infrastructure. The survey was carried out in all the 25 wards of the city so that ward level assessments and planning could be done.

### 3.6. Detailed Risk Assessment

Detailed risk assessment was carried out on the basis of the above surveys to arrive at composite risk results.[2] This was done by the project team and a hired GIS expert. These were discussed with local professionals to arrive at consensus on the level of earthquake risk in the city, and its distribution across different neighborhoods.

## 4. CRITICAL FACTORS IDENTIFIED

The risk assessment process threw up results on expected lines. However, what emerged was a detailed scenario of how much risk there was, where it was distributed, and what its causes were.

### 4.1. Rapid Unplanned Growth

Shimla has seen a very rapid population growth in last three decades due to huge housing and tourism demand. This combined with lack of planning and haphazard growth has resulted in the construction of buildings on steep and unstable slopes with improper construction practices. High priority lifeline structures like hospitals, power stations, and telecommunication installations and water supply stations are located in high-vulnerability areas with poor connectivity. Weak enforcement of byelaws and poor emergency management capacity has added the risk.

### 4.2. Skewed Land Use and Building Utilization

The major land use is residential, which is estimated at 75 percent of the total built-up area. Seven percent of the residential buildings accommodate street level commercial activities. Areas such as Mall Road, Lower Bazaar, Krishna Nagar, Summer Hill, and Tatu are highly commercialized where up to 50 percent of total buildings are used for commercial purposes. There is only 4 percent of total building stock that is under institutional and facilities use such as schools, offices, hospitals, post offices, power stations, waterworks, and places of worship, which could double up as emergency community shelters (Gupta & Sharma, 2005). The built-up areas are very congested with multistoried brick masonry

*Fig. 1.*   Haphazard Growth on Unstable Slopes.

houses that have very narrow streets and staircases. There are very few and small open spaces in most of the municipal wards (Fig. 1).

## 4.3. Poor Accessibility within the City

Accessibility within the city is extremely poor. Seventy two percent of total buildings are not accessible by motorable roads. Out of that 38 percent are accessible through pedestrian paths and stairways less than 1 m in width. Certain areas are built on such steep slopes and with such poor accessibility, that in case of a building collapse there will be no escape routes. Many of the motorable roads too are in such locations that in case of earthquake-induced landslides or building collapses on the slopes above the roads, they will get blocked. This can lead to the cutting off of critical rescue and relief routes.

### 4.4. High Vulnerability of Schools

Schools in the city are very highly vulnerable due to multiple factors. Most of the schools are housed in old, dilapidated, and unsuitable buildings that are structurally not strong enough to withstand even a moderate earthquake. They are located in very congested areas and on steep slopes, giving very little open spaces around them for evacuation and refuge purposes. It is also difficult for the already stretched out emergency services to even access these locations. The local awareness on disaster preparedness and response is very low. Many of the actions of the school administration itself are compounding the risk without them even realizing it.

### 4.5. Inadequate Infrastructure and Lifeline Services

There is a serious lack of infrastructure facilities in the city. There is an acute shortage of water, especially in summers, poor sewerage network coverage, and inadequate medical facilities. The primary emergency management service, the fire service, is grossly ill equipped and understaffed. There are 3 fire stations with 6 fire tenders and 100 fire fighters servicing a total population of 140,000 in the city and the surrounding rural areas in addition.

### 4.6. Poor Building Condition

A ban on forest cutting and high price of timber has led to a rapid shift toward alternate construction materials such as bricks, cement, and iron. Reinforced Cement Concrete (RCC) and bricks have become prevalent, but without proper understanding among local construction workers on how to use these materials. Shimla has about 12,700 buildings (Primary survey, February 2005) with an average of 15 occupants per building (Fig. 2). The

*Fig. 2.* Poor Building Condition: Issues of Design and Construction Quality.

building condition is extremely bad in Mall Road, Krishna Nagar, Ruldu Bhatta, Ram Bazaar, Phagi Nabha, Khalini wards. Buildings classified under "very poor" condition in these wards reach up to 70 percent of the total, which is much higher than the city average of 36 percent. One reason behind this is the lack of maintenance due to the fact that tenants are occupying these buildings on very low rents dating years ago, and neither tenant nor owner are willing to invest in maintenance. In older parts of the city poor maintenance, and in newer parts poor workmanship, has resulted in buildings that will be unable to withstand the expected ground shaking.

## 4.7. Inappropriate Building Heights

Building height is very important in calculating risk. Approximately 50 percent of the buildings in Shimla are more than two stories high. Twenty four percent of the buildings are G+3 or more, which are violating the building byelaws. New buildings of three to four stories constructed along steep slopes in the city, 40 percent of which are on loose landfill soil without compaction; pose a grave threat to the occupants and those in the vicinity. The building construction activity itself also has an adverse impact on the soil condition (JAIN, 2003, p. 1), setting a cycle of deteriorating vulnerability.

## 4.8. Old Building Age

Approximately 15 percent of Shimla's buildings were constructed before 1925. The distribution of these buildings varies from 1 percent in new Shimla to 60 percent in the Mall Road area. At the city level, about 20 percent of the houses are more than 60 years old, followed by 13 percent in age group of 50–60 years. Another 25 percent are in the age group of 20–50 years. About 50 percent of the old structures are not properly maintained and are in very poor condition, prone to collapse even due to heavy rains or a minor earthquake. In most of the wooden structures the wood has decayed and joints and other joineries are displaced. The lack of adequate space between buildings increases the vulnerability of structures adjoining these old and unstable buildings.

## 4.9. Poor Enforcement of Laws

About 27 percent of the buildings were constructed before 1971, the year when seismic codes were first introduced by the Public Works Department. Buildings in Shimla flout the codes at design as well as construction stages. Even after the introduction of the codes, most engineers, masons, and other persons associated with building construction are either unaware about the earthquake-resistant constructions practices or are not trained in designing and constructing earthquake-resistant structures. There is a provision for building inspectors to inspect the buildings at different stages of construction, but acute shortage and poor training of staff renders this provision useless. As a result of all this, more than 80 percent of all existing buildings do not meet the seismic code standards.

## 5. MITIGATION PLANNING

Based on the risk assessment, a mitigation planning exercise was launched in partnership with the Planning Team and the Adopting Entity. Local consultation and planning workshops were organized to deliberate upon the study results and to chalk out a plan of action. The approach taken was one of prioritizing critically vulnerable areas, identifying appropriate local-or city-level actions to reduce vulnerability, fixing responsibility with suitable local groups, and concerned government departments, listing tasks, deciding schedules, and finally calculating budgets. Fig. 3 shows the identified risk zones of the city.

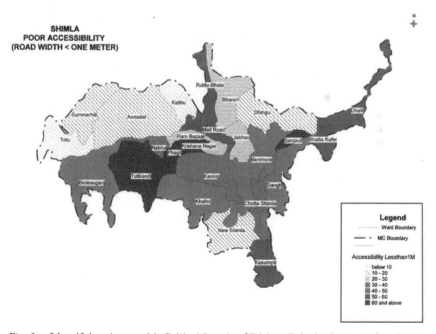

*Fig. 3.* Identifying Areas with Critical Levels of Risk as Priority Intervention Areas.

It was realized that for effective and sustainable implementation of the mitigation plan, it is essential to build the capacity of the communities and urban local government. Locally imbibed mitigation will help in reducing the total loss, which in turn will reduce the resources and time required for response and recovery. The focus of the mitigation planning initiative thus has been on inculcating risk mitigation practices at local level. However, it has also included measures for enhancing local emergency preparedness.

The mitigation plan also tries to bring the city government and the residents together as local disaster managers. The city government should be able to provide critical services in the immediate aftermath of a disaster, and should take responsibility of working to reduce the potential impact of such disasters by governing advance action for mitigation and preparedness. The people, on the other hand, should take responsibility of ensuring that buildings and critical infrastructure at household and neighborhood levels are in line with the city-level mitigation approach, and that local action supports a city-level plan. The two, put together, will form a disaster resilient community.

Local consultations, as part of the planning process, resulted in a well-structured and exhaustive mitigation plan. The next task is to implement this plan. The local government, in partnership with NGOs and international organizations, has initiated some of the activities related more closely to the civil society. Other interventions, requiring shifts in policy at the decision-making level or improved enforcement of regulations by the local government, will need a persistent and long-term push.

Some of the important activities covered by the plan are discussed in the following sections.

### 5.1. Awareness, Education, and Training

- Use of informed media to promote and disseminate accurate information on regular basis, aimed at increasing awareness and reducing panic from rumors
- Provision of tools to home owners for increasing their awareness for fundamental seismic risks and encouraging implementation of mitigation efforts
- Establishing a helpline/building center to provide tips to local citizens
- Demonstrating techniques for cost-effective seismic mitigation
- Designation of 4th April, the anniversary of the Kangra Earthquake, as earthquake safety day

- Conducting orientation sessions and workshops for city officials, community leaders, and other local stakeholders on vulnerability appreciation and loss reduction
- Raising awareness among school children and integrating earthquake education in school curricula
- Providing in-service training to teachers so that they can draw up school disaster management plans

## 5.2. Building Context

- Assessing critical buildings such as hospitals, schools, police stations, fire stations, and designated emergency response offices, and their retrofitting wherever required
- Identifying critically vulnerable buildings and notifying their owners about their vulnerability
- Launching a program to reduce risks in all potentially hazardous poorly built, ill maintained, and hillside residences
- Strengthening or replacement of important city owned and used buildings that are known to have structural weaknesses
- Increasing efforts to reduce fire risk in existing development by improving local management and appropriate fire safety regulation enforcement
- Reducing density in critically high-risk wards through relocation/ redevelopment
- Updating of city building byelaws to incorporate earthquake-resistant guidelines and creation of proper enforcement mechanisms
- Introducing training and certification system for engineers, architects, and building contractors[3]
- Training of masons in safe construction and retrofitting techniques

## 5.3. Public Works Utilities

- Strengthening of critical transportation links to the city
- Creating emergency access route network within the city
- Identification and strengthening of emergency shelters in each locality
- Developing alternate routes for each lifeline building
- Creating aerial access points in the city where helicopters can land in emergency situations

- Establishing emergency drinking water supply network
- Establishing emergency power supply systems for critical facilities
- Establishing and safeguarding multiagency emergency communication system

### 5.4. Emergency Services

- Developing emergency preparedness plans for critical facilities
- Establishing pre-event planning for post-disaster recovery as an integral element of the emergency response plan of the Municipal Corporation and all concerned departments

# 6. SCHOOL SAFETY AS A CATALYST PROJECT

An assessment of the school buildings in Shimla district of Himachal Pradesh indicates a high level of risk in these buildings, similar to the kind of risk that existed in the school buildings of Gujarat prior to the Bhuj earthquake of 2001 that led to the loss of hundreds of school children's lives. This risk arises from three components: structural risk of building collapse, nonstructural risk of injuries from building content, and risk from erroneous human reactions to earthquakes. There are a total of about 750 schools and 97,500 students enrolled in these schools in Shimla district. Since no structural or nonstructural risk mitigation elements have been implemented in any school in the area, it is assumed that all school children are at risk, though the degree of risk may vary from school to school. The project (Fig. 4) addresses this risk and is attempting to reduce it at three levels: through structural retrofitting in select sample schools, through nonstructural mitigation in select sample schools, and through awareness on risk reduction in all schools in the district.

Assessment of an existing structure is much more difficult a task than evaluation of a design on paper. First, the construction of the structure is never exactly as per designer's specifications and a number of defects and uncertainties crop up during the execution. Second, the quality of the material deteriorates with time and the assessment of an existing structure becomes a time dependent problem. A series of assessments, both rapid and detailed, is required to determine the condition of a building. The process of adding extra

**EARTHQUAKE RISK MITIGATION PLAN : SHIMLA**

### Organize Resources

In Shimla, the Project Team identified and signed MoU with the Adopting Entity, Identified members of the Planning Team, appointed the city project leader, conducted first set of meetings

### Assess Risks

Identified predominant building types, conducted rapid visual survey of school buildings, carried out questionnaire surveys of key informants, prepared community profiles, identified high risk zones based on range of hazard and vulnerability factors

### Develop Mitigation Plan

Mitigation Plan prepared through a series of consultations with community representatives, government officials, Planning Team and Adopting Entity. Planning carried out on the basis of the identified risks.

### Implement Plan & Monitor Progress

Public events such as children's drills, community radio programmes, technology demonstrations, retrofitting of school buildings, and training workshops being carried out in 2005 to launch the plan implementation in the year of the Kangra Earthquake centenary.

*Fig. 4.* The Project Process.

features in unsafe structures in order to improve their seismic resistance is termed as "retrofitting." Figs. 5 and 6 shows selected project activities.

The project worked through a four-pronged strategy of:

1. carrying out structural retrofitting in school buildings to prevent their collapse in future earthquakes,
2. implementing nonstructural mitigation measures to avoid injuries from falling hazards in schools,
3. educating school communities and construction workers on safe construction, retrofitting, and nonstructural mitigation practices, and
4. preparing school disaster management plans and training school communities in immediate response, evacuation, and first-aid.

# 7. FROM SCHOOLS TO COMMUNITIES

Over the past decade, school safety has gained ground in the developing world and there have been numerous commendable programs that have demonstrated that schools are a viable entry vehicle for disaster reduction initiatives in any community (UNCRD, Website). The appeal attached to working with children, the universally accepted principle that children must be made safe first, and the concerted efforts of the disaster management community have helped in bringing this agenda to the forefront. Some of the notable achievements in the past years have been:

- In Algeria, following the 2003 Boumerdes earthquake, stories were included in the lessons for the primary school section to teach students about the disaster.
- In Turkey, more than 2,000 volunteer teachers from 50 provinces participated in the Distance Learning Basic Disaster Awareness self-study program from 2003 to 2005.
- In Iran, Earthquake Safety Drills, which started as a pilot project in 1996 to cover 100 schools, have now expanded to cover more than 14 million school students of primary, secondary, and higher schools across the country.

At the same time, such initiatives have paid dividends far beyond the boundary walls of the schools they have worked with. The message given to children travels far, reaching their parents and relatives, and eventually the entire society. Recognizing the importance of community participation, evacuation drills involving the community have been greatly encouraged across countries.

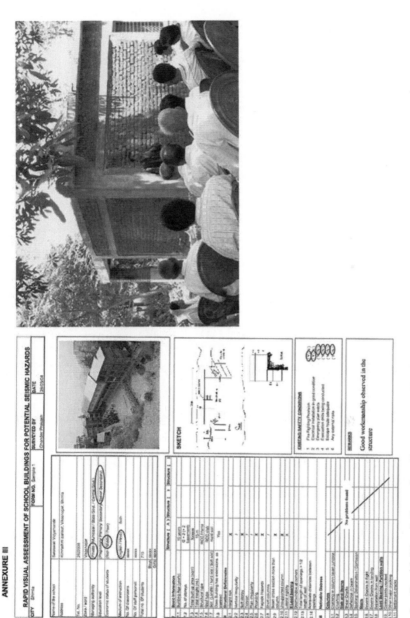

*Fig. 5.* Rapid Visual Screening Formats are Used to Carry Out Structural Assessment of Buildings. Selected Unsafe Buildings Undergo Detailed Assessment and Planning. Retrofitting Work is then Carried Out and Used as a Demonstration and Training Tool for Local Engineers and Masons.

*Fig. 6.*   School Children Conducting a Public Awareness Campaign in Shimla. They Use Street Theatre and Building Models to Inform Local People that "Earthquakes Don't Kill People, Unsafe Buildings Do," and Telling them, "Don't be Scared, be Prepared!"

A school earthquake safety program in Shimla, India, has specifically focused on the involvement of parents in school safety drills. Not only is this good for entire families to know how to respond to a disaster and how to complement each other's actions, it also helps a larger cohesive preparedness action at the community level as it brings various stakeholders together; something that does not happen easily otherwise (Sharma & Gupta, 2008). During the drills, children, teachers, school staff, parents, fire services, civil defense, medical responders, and local government officials all come together and find out through practice how well or poorly prepared they are to face an emergency. They assess, plan, and rehearse together, and learn the value of preparedness at a societal level.

Further initiatives in the region are taking this approach of "school to community safety," wherein an integration of school disaster management plans and community disaster management plans is targeted through measures described above. Community-based disaster management planning has been the focus of many programs over the past decade. They have been organized under Community-Based Disaster Management (CBDM), Community-Based Disaster Preparedness (CBDP), Community-Based Disaster Risk Management (CBDRM), and other banners, but the essence has been constant in terms of community organizations being established, assisted in preparing local disaster management plans, organized into task forces, and trained for specific tasks. The problem with this approach has been that the task forces have remained dependent on external support, and have in most cases ceased to be effective after the external aid agencies have withdrawn. Even linking up with local governance mechanisms has not proved very effective. While local governance institutions lend a stronger sense of legitimacy to the initiatives, they also bring in a high level of politicization.

Convergence of school safety and CBDM programs addresses this problem since schools are present everywhere, and are neutral as well as respected institutions across the board. Their vibrancy is constant over time. The turnover of students ensures a fresh stream of actions and dissemination endlessly, once the systems have been established and the duty bearers have taken it upon themselves to keep them running. Establishing systems of school safety and getting the conviction of the school community has been successfully demonstrated in a number of models across the developing world, some of which are mentioned above in this paper.

# 8. CONCLUSIONS

Shimla's situation is typical of a fast growing town in the Himalayan region. Growing demand for built space, low awareness levels, lack of training opportunities, predominance of informal sector within the construction industry, poor enforcement of laws, and a severe resource crunch within municipal authorities, all add up to give cities so precariously perched, that they will collapse the moment an earthquake of magnitude 6 or more on the Richter Scale hits them. When it is known that such an earthquake visits some place or the other within the Himalayan arc every eight years on an average, the situation is worrisome.

The Earthquake Safe Shimlà initiative is a small beginning to find local means of reducing risk in such cities. It is almost an experimental project that tries to combine technology and local knowledge to arrive at practicable solutions. The project experiences throw up some important lessons.

The main lesson is that bringing together communities and the local government in a partnership mode delivers better results than a recipient–provider relationship. Such partnerships need to go beyond consent to government plans, and need to include an engagement in assessment, planning, implementation, and monitoring activities. Consultation means more than consent.

The second lesson is that technology can deliver very well if adapted to local contexts. Geographical Information Systems can be based on participatory data. In fact, this way they deliver far more, particularly in developing nations where available spatial data is scarce or outdated. Such use of technology also excites local stakeholders and they take a more active part, since the technology gives them a new confidence in the development process.

The third lesson is that schools are the cradles of a society, and are best-suited grounds for inculcating a culture of disaster prevention and preparedness. The approach adopted in Shimla could make schools safer for the children, and also use them as a medium for reaching out to the larger community and the government for overall disaster preparedness.

In a nutshell, urban planning, disaster management, and governance are all people's processes and are best planned and implemented at their level.

## NOTES

1. Land Use and City Planning is one of the core policy issues that have led to the current vulnerable situation of Shimla. The questionnaire survey was targeted at the town and country planners in Shimla and addressed the issues of planned development versus unplanned growth, principles for citing and location of land uses, and conformity and compatibility issues.

2. Risk assessment treated risk as a composite of hazards, vulnerability, and exposure. Earthquakes and landslides were considered as the primary hazards in the city. Building construction contributed to the vulnerability, and land use planning enhanced the exposure of the vulnerable to the hazard. Risk assessment, in this manner, covered aspects of location, type, configuration, construction techniques, materials, age, and usage pattern of buildings. It also covered the environmental setting and inter-building spaces.

3. Current curriculum of architecture, planning, and engineering colleges covers no aspects of disaster management. Some colleges have introduced introductory level

content, mostly as an optional subject, in recent times. There is a national initiative to include disaster management in the formal curriculum of all such institutions, but this move is still underway. Specialized organizations do offer special courses on the subject.

# REFERENCES

www.asc-india.org. Website of the Amateur Seismic Centre, India.

www.geohaz.org. Website of GeoHazards International, USA.

Gupta, M., & Sharma, A. (2005). *Saving Shimla, North India, from the next earthquake*. UK: Open House International.

Hamdi, N., & Goethert, R. (1997). *Action planning for cities: A guide to community practices.* UK: Wiley.

www.hyogo.uncrd.or.jp. Website of the United Nations Centre for Regional Development (UNCRD), Disaster Management Planning Hyogo Office, Japan.

Jain, A. K. (2003). *Limits of acceptable change approach towards conservation of hill capitals*, Technical Paper, Institute of Town Planners, New Delhi, India.

Sharma, A., & Gupta, M. (2008). *Building community resilience through education: School safety as a route to a culture of prevention.* Japan: Regional Development Dialogue, UNCRD.

# CHAPTER 10

# TOWN WATCHING AS A USEFUL TOOL IN URBAN RISK REDUCTION IN SAIJO

Yuki Yoshida, Yukiko Takeuchi and Rajib Shaw

## ABSTRACT

*Many small- and medium-sized Japanese cities are located along the coast and have become vulnerable to both coastal and mountain hazards. The vulnerability is increased by a rapidly growing aging population, low resources, and lack of capacity in the local governments. In this scenario, it is important that the community's potential should be fully utilized through proper awareness raising and capacity building. Town watching is considered as a useful tool to reduce urban risk in small- and medium-sized cities, where local students, teachers, parents, resident associations, and local government members collectively watch both good and bad (vulnerable) parts of their city. This collective watching and participatory mapping enhance the engagement of school children and communities in risk reduction activities. Town watching is considered as a process and it is important to continue the initiative for effective risk reduction at the community level.*

Urban Risk Reduction: An Asian Perspective
Community, Environment and Disaster Risk Management, Volume 1, 189–205
ISSN: 2040-7262/doi: 10.1108/S2040-7262(2009)0000001014

# 1. INTRODUCTION

## 1.1. Small- and Medium-Sized Cities in Japan

In Japan, there are a lot of small- and medium-sized cities. Almost three-fourths of all cities in Japan have less than 100,000 people as population (see Fig. 1). Recently, these minor cities have had many problems, like faltering local economy, weakening local industry, tight local finance, functional decline of urban areas, and so on. These problems are closely related to each other (PRILITT, 2002).

All over the country, the trends of declining birth rate and of aging are continuing. A decrease in the national population in the coming 30 years is quite certain. In 2030, it is estimated that the population will be around 112 million and the aging rate will be around 32.4%. This tendency is more pronounced especially in minor cities because young people are going out of the area (an example is the Shikoku area, see Table 1). Young people are moving to the major cities to get educational advancement and employment. At the same time, old people prefer staying back in the minor cities where they have lived for a long time. Aging affects not only financial issues, but also disaster prevention. Whenever there is a disaster, young people's help is essential. According to of the Ministry of Land, Infrastructure, Transport and Tourism (MLITT, 2005), characteristics of recent heavy rain disasters include the following: many people who need help are affected, the system of

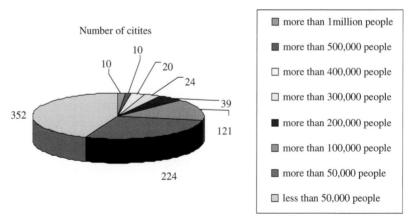

*Fig. 1.* Urban Population in Japan (1998). *Source:* Japan Association of City Mayors.

***Table 1.*** Aging Rate in Shikoku Area (%).

|  | 1975 | 2000 | 2025 |
|---|---|---|---|
| Tokushima | 10.7 | 21.9 | 31.9 |
| Kagawa | 10.5 | 20.9 | 31.4 |
| Ehime | 10.4 | 21.4 | 32.5 |
| Kochi | 12.2 | 23.6 | 33.3 |

*Source:* White Book of Aging Rate (2004).

mutual assistance is poor, risk awareness is low, and so on. So it is important for community people to work together for disaster prevention. But the relationship between urban area and mountainous area becomes poor. Many people living in the urban area have never been to a mountainous area and do not know much about mountainous areas in general. Saijo City in Ehime Prefecture is one of such cities with a mountainous area.

### 1.2. Background of Saijo City

Saijo City is located in the eastern part of Ehime Prefecture. It has an area of 509.04 sq km, with a population of 116,059 (October 2006). On November 1, 2004, Saijo City, Toyo City, Tanbara Town, and Komatsu Town from Shuso County merged to form the new "Saijo City."

The geography of the city is classified broadly into four areas: plain area along the coast; hilly area between Saijo City and Nihama City; hilly terrain ranging in the north side of the median tectonic line along the south side of the plain; and precipitous mountains in the southern side of the median tectonic line. There is Mt. Ishiduchi, the highest mountain in the western part of Japan. Two big rivers, Kamo River and Nakayama River, flow in the center of the city.

Saijo City is famous for its spring water called "Uchinuki." The river water percolates underground and pools, then spouts above ground under pressure. Just by driving a pipe into the ground, water comes out. The amount of flowing water is around 90,000 m$^3$ per day. Due to the little temperature change through all seasons, it is used as daily life water, agricultural water, and industrial water. "Uchinuki" is one of the 100 best waters in Japan.

There is a traditional annual festival called "Saijo Matsuri" in October when almost all people, both young and old, get wildly excited. Each "Jichikai" has its own "Danjiri" (float) and the relationship among people in the communities is strongly felt. A "Jichikai" is a neighborhood association which is organized in each area in the municipality at the people's own initiative. There are 540 Jichikai in Saijo city and they make 28 Jichikai unions.

## 2. SAIJO'S HYDROMETEOROLOGICAL RISK

Climatological analysis of extreme events is carried out to ascertain their long-term trend in a specific location such as a city (IEDM, 2007). Data obtained from the Japan Meteorological Agency indicated that there has been an increase in the heavy rainfall events of more than 50 mm per day in the city of Matsuyama.

A further segregated analysis of these rainfall events suggests an increase in the 50–99 mm rainfall events as against the 100–199 and the >200 mm rainfall events. A similar trend has also been observed in terms of deviation of 50–99 mm rainfall events from the long-term mean for those events, suggesting the influence of climate change. Fig. 2 shows the location of the city and the rainfall pattern. In addition to the heavy rainfall events, Ehime has also been vulnerable to typhoons, as Ehime received devastating typhoons consecutively for three years from 2003 to 2005. Analysis of typhoon events indicates that the frequency of typhoons has been more or less unchanged during 1945–2005 though the trend line shows upward trend due to occurrence of more typhoon events during the later part of the study period.

This brief analysis of the past climate events brings us to the conclusion that there is certainly a change in the mean state of the climate and its behavior in terms of extreme rainfall events and typhoons. The discussions with the meteorologists suggest the following regarding the changing nature of extreme events such as heavy rainfall:

• These extreme rainfall events often occur in localized places.
• They are difficult to predict sufficiently in advance so the disaster management administration may not be alerted with enough time to take appropriate preparedness activities.
• The lack of closely located meteorological observatories makes it even difficult to carry out prediction and impact assessment of such events.
• The interaction of influence of heavy urbanization and the occurrence of heavy rainfall events is much more complex and often it is difficult to attribute the impacts to one single factor.

In 2004, 10 typhoons – beginning with typhoon No. 4 in June, followed by Nos. 6, 10, 11, 15, 16, 18, 21, 22, and 23 – hit Japan. The number is four

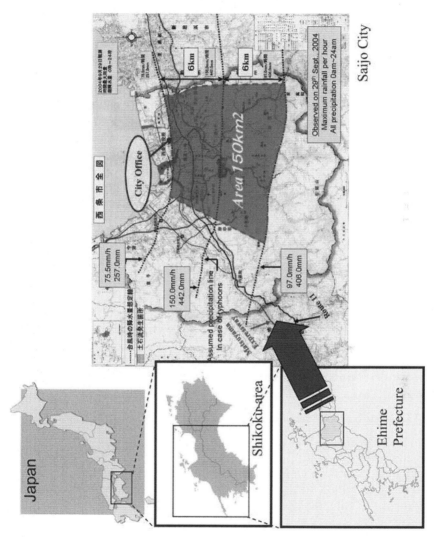

*Fig. 2.* Location of Saijo City and Area Damaged by Typhoon No. 21.

times higher than the usual number of 2–3. It broke a previous record (6, in 1990 and in 1993) since they started to take statistics in 1951. The reason why so many typhoons hit Japan in 2004 is said to be the high-pressure system in the Pacific Ocean that had hung over to the north for a long time. Typhoons moving along the lines of the high-pressure system easily hit Japan. This was also one of the reasons why the typhoons approaching and hitting Japan were able to keep their strength. Rain in a wider area was caused by the higher-than-usual sea temperature in the south part of Japan.

In the summer and autumn of 2004, six typhoons (Nos. 4, 6, 10, 11, 21, and 23), a record high, hit the Shikoku area. (In the Shikoku area, 2 was the most since 1995 and 1.5 was the average.) In the Seto Island Sea area where they do not often have heavy rain, there were many concentrated downpours, landslides, and high tides. A total of 61 persons lost their lives and houses were damaged. Typhoon Nos. 15, 16, 18, 21, 22, and 23 hit Saijo City but Nos. 21 and 23 caused the most damage.

On September 29, 2004, typhoon No. 21 moved across Shikoku area. Because of this, in Saijo City, they had record concentrated heavy rain of 75.5 ~ 150 mm rainfall per hour. There was an avalanche of rocks, earth, and driftwood, which seemed to have occurred due to slope destruction of intermediate and mountainous areas. A lot of driftwood got stuck in the bridge pier and water was held back until it overflowed. As the water level rose suddenly, surrounding houses were flooded. In the flat parts, each area was flooded above or below floor level. In the mountainous areas, numerous landslide disasters occurred, roads were severed, many villages were isolated, and house destruction and human suffering were caused. The dead in Ehime Prefecture due to typhoon No. 21 numbered 14 people. This was the worst record in human suffering caused by typhoons (Fig. 3).

Problems exposed by the typhoon are as follows:

(1) Ill-maintained forest and abandoned thinned wood in the mountains

Numerous small slope failures caused by the concentrated heavy rain of typhoon No. 21 added to the damage. In contrast to "deep-seated landslides," which are not related to the form of forest, "shallow landslides" involve surface soil sliding directly and result from the extent of forest maintenance. In addition, in artificial forests which are not thinned for a long time, sunlight does not reach ground and bottom weeds and young trees have difficulty growing. When it rains there, surface soil is hit directly by raindrops and clogged, and the rain water which cannot soak through the ground runs on the surface. The "water road" caused by the erosion forms valley and finally draws mudslides involving surface soil and fallen trees.

A: Landslide on the mountain
B: The road is blocked by mudslide.
C: Residents hanging laundry on driftwood.
D: The house is destroyed.
E: River water overflowed to the road.
F: Driftwoods get stuck in the bridge.

*Fig. 3.* Damage Caused by the Typhoon. *Source:* Saijo City.

Abandoned thinned wood were also the problem. They were swept into the river by the heavy rain, got stuck in the bridge pier, and water overflowed downstream.

(2)  Concentration of elderly people in mountainous areas

According to the rate of aging in each area of Saijo City, the first to fourth areas are mountainous areas and it means there are many elderly people there. In the typhoons of 2004, mountainous areas were seriously affected. Some areas were isolated because the roads were blocked. In such areas, young people's help was needed by elderly people to evacuate.

(3)  Dangerous shelters

Some designated shelters turned out to be dangerous. For example, in Ofuki area, in the mountainous area, some people evacuated to the community center which was a designated shelter. But one person noticed that the river nearby the center suddenly turned muddy, so they escaped to a different building. One minute after they evacuated, the center was buried in mud (see Fig. 4). Another example, in Funakata area, a mid-mountainous area, the

*Fig. 4.*   Buried Shelter in Ofuki Area.

designated shelter was at the head of a hill and it was difficult to get there. So residents evacuated to a nearby meeting house. Therefore, the designated shelters built by the municipalities should be reexamined and residents should know more about the areas.

(4) Low awareness on disaster prevention

Referring to disaster history of Saijo City, there had been no such large typhoons until 2004. Typhoons first claimed a life in 1976 in the old Saijo City. Fading memory of disasters leads to declining awareness on disaster prevention. Also, judging by one's own experience is dangerous. According to a questionnaire survey in Ofuki area,[2] many people did not evacuate for the reason that they just thought it was not dangerous or they judged based on their long experience and thought it was not dangerous enough to evacuate.

## 3. EDUCATION AS A TOOL TO ENHANCE PARTICIPATION

### 3.1. Participatory Learning

Yamori et al. (2006) states that it is necessary for disaster education in the future to focus on the process of restructuring "communities of practice," not only on the transfer of knowledge and skill between individuals. That is, it should be an important goal of education or learning to establish communities in which both the educator and learner can "participate" together. For example in school, it will be all right just to involve pupils, teachers, or the school system itself to network with experts who can teach about disaster prevention. Teachers or schools themselves do not need to have all about the resources on disaster prevention. One learning tool the schools can adapt is "town watching."

### 3.2. Town Watching

Town watching is a participatory technique used in community or neighborhood planning in the context of a larger administrative unit (such as municipality or city) in order for residents to recognize problems as a group and put forward solutions together. The problem-solving process is guided by at least one expert or professional trained in one or more aspects of planning (Ogawa, 2005). Town watching, which has been developed as a technique practiced by Japanese urban planners in the 1970s, has become popular as a participatory tool in machizukuri (Setagaya Machizukuri Center, 1993). "Machizukuri" has been translated as "community planning" by Evans (2001), and as "town making" participatory community building (Yamada, 2001). "Machi" means town, district, or community and "zukuri" means making or building. The origins of "machizukuri" can be traced as a movement associated with organized citizen actions to fight against pollution in the 1960s in Japan; local authorities needed to adapt to include consultation with its citizens. Lately, machizukuri in some localities evolved into partnerships (Yoshimura, 2002). In recent years, the "machizukuri" movement emerged from Japanese planning practice with a predominant focus on urban design that encourages citizen involvement. Concerns in machizukuri such as access to public road, open space, land use, etc. are well taken into account by town watching. The use of town watching has been extended to dealing with disaster and safety-related physical issues such as safe or unsafe places and evacuation routes. We can call this "disaster town watching."

Also, there is town watching for children. General Insurance Association of Japan has conducted the activity "Exploration Party for Disaster Prevention," "Bosai Tankentai" in Japanese, as one of pillars of disaster education activities and intended to diffuse it (Udagawa, 2004). This program aims to develop children's awareness on disaster prevention through growing interest for their town and also to nurture cherishing relationship among people.

The activity consists of three main steps: "exploration in town," "making disaster prevention map," and "presentation." Children walk around the town in groups and check facilities for disaster prevention and security. After the exploration, they make an original disaster prevention map by writing the location of the facilities and findings, or by attaching photos. At the end, each group makes presentation on the dangerous places and important findings in the town, reviews the activity, and recognizes what they have not noticed before.

# 4. PARTICIPATORY DISASTER EDUCATION AS A RISK REDUCTION MEASURE

## *4.1. Relevance of Town/Mountain Watching in Saijo City*

Because of typhoon Nos. 21 and 23 in 2004, the mountainous area of Saijo City was especially damaged. Land condition and concentrated heavy rain were major factors, but there were other reasons concerning so-called software. In the mountainous area, there lived many elderly people and few young people. So some elderly people had difficulty in evacuating and needed the help of young people. Low awareness of disaster prevention was also a problem. According to the research of OYO Corporation,[1] many people did not evacuate at the time of the typhoon. The same problem was faced in the plain area.

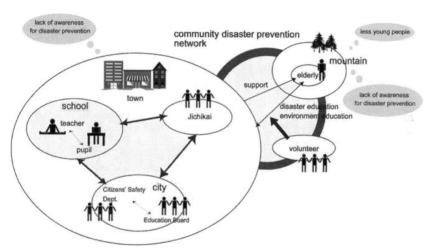

*Fig. 5.* Community Disaster Prevention Network.

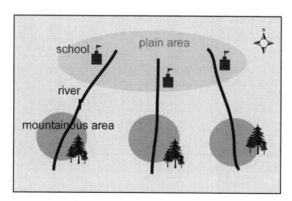

*Fig. 6.* Area of Mountain Watching.

The plain area is rather urban and there are many young people there. So, it is necessary to make "disaster prevention network" (see Fig. 5) between the plain area and the mountainous area, so as to help elderly people in the mountainous area in case of a disaster. As illustrated by the driftwood stuck in the bridge pier causing flood in the plain area, disasters in the mountainous area have bearings on the plain area. Residents of both areas have to know each other's circumstances.

For these reasons, mountain watching was proposed to be implemented in Saijo City. Mountain watching is just like town watching and it is conducted in the mountainous area. The main targets were children, but residents on the mountain, teachers, municipal officials, and forest workers were also involved. The working field was the upper area of a river running along a school (see Fig. 6). Participants watched the site damaged by the typhoon in 2004 and listened to the story of the typhoon victims.

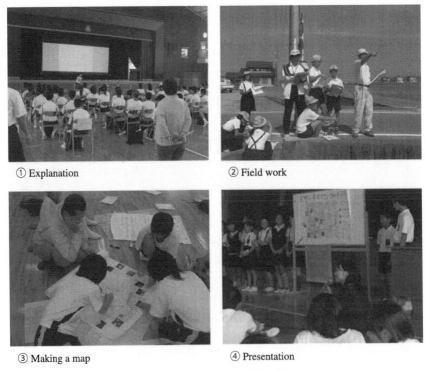

① Explanation                              ② Field work

③ Making a map                            ④ Presentation

*Fig. 7.*   Flow of Town Watching.

At the same time, town watching was proposed to be implemented in the plain area. The main targets were pupils and teachers, parents, the Jichikai, and municipal officers. They walked around the school zone and searched for dangerous places, useful facilities in case of disasters, and favorite places which otherwise did not get noticed in daily life.

Town watching was implemented in five elementary schools and mountain watching in three junior high schools, as the "disaster education program" (Fig. 7).

### 4.2. Outline of Questionnaire Survey

The questionnaire survey was conducted to evaluate the impact of town/mountain watching. The targets were all participants: pupils, teachers, municipal officers, parents, the Jichikai, residents on the mountain, and forest workers. The questionnaire survey was conducted both before going to the field and after the whole process was implemented.[2] It took about 20 min each, and was not read out. For two elementary schools, another questionnaire survey was conducted in November to evaluate pupils' awareness a while after town watching. The total number of respondents in the questionnaire survey is shown in Table 2.

***Table 2.***   Total Number of Respondents.

| Pupils | Teachers | Citizens' Safety Department | Education Board | Jichikai | Parents | Residents on the Mountain | Forest Workers |
|--------|----------|------------------------------|------------------|----------|---------|----------------------------|----------------|
| 435 | 35 | 17 | 9 | 19 | 46 | 0 | 14 |

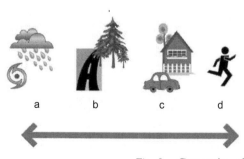

a     b     c     d

a) impact on typhoon itself
b) impact on land and infrastructure
c) impact on houses and properties
d) impact on human

*Fig. 8.*   Categories of Answers.

Pupils were to describe what they know about the typhoon in 2004. As shown in Fig. 8, the answers are categorized in four groups: (a) impact on typhoon itself (e.g., it rained heavily, it caused great damage, etc.), (b) impact on land and infrastructure (e.g., the river overflowed, there were lots of mudslide in mountains, etc.), (c) impact on houses and properties (e.g.,

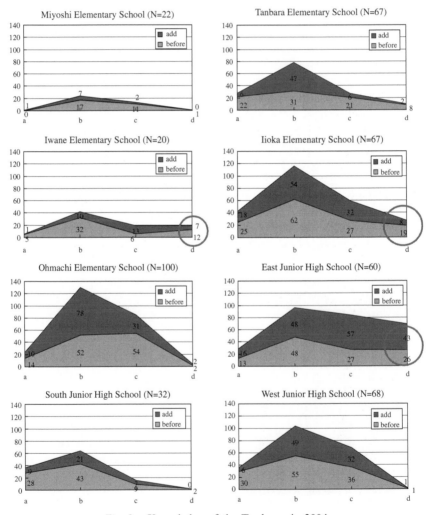

*Fig. 9.* Knowledge of the Typhoon in 2004.

the houses were flooded above the floor level, rice fields were flooded, etc.), (d) impact on human beings (e.g., people evacuated to the school gym, there were a few dead, etc.).

Fig. 9 shows the number of the answers in each school. "Add" area shows the post-answer, excluding the same answer as pre-answer. So, this will correspond to the impact of the town/mountain watching. Each school has different characteristics and these are considered to have resulted from the background of the area where the schools are located.

# 5. CONCLUSION

Small- and medium-sized cities in Japan have some common problems. Young people leave mountainous areas and go to major cities, leaving behind a declining population, making aging a serious problem in mountains. Also, the decline in forestry increases ill-maintained forests. When a disaster happens in such areas, the damage would be serious. Landslides easily occur because of the weak ground condition and some elderly people have difficulty in evacuating without the help of young people. In such cases, help of people from the town is needed. But there is often weak relationship between people in mountainous areas and people in towns. It is important for the community to work together on disaster reduction.

The importance of disaster education becomes well recognized and the number of schools which adopts it increases. But there are some problems in current disaster education, like lack of teachers' training; time pressure in school curriculum; lack of involvement of parents and family; lack of linkage of scientific studies to social issues, in-school education, and events-oriented education; etc.

Town watching or mountain watching is a suitable tool to resolve these problems. It involves many stakeholders, such as pupils in elementary schools and junior high schools, teachers, parents, the Jichikai, residents on the mountains, forest workers, the Citizens' Safety Department, and the Education Board. It provides a good opportunity for them to communicate with each other. In case of a disaster, such relationship is very important. Through town watching, participants get interested in the local area and also get knowledge about disaster prevention.

But town/mountain watching should not end up as only a one-time event. Through a series of continuous actions, it can be improved and will help develop disaster resilience of the area. Clear implementing body and guidelines are necessary for a continuous town/mountain watching.

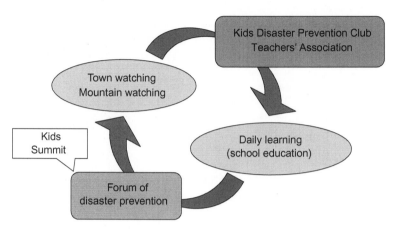

*Fig. 10.*   Continuous Learning Cycle.

In Saijo City, a "teachers' association of disaster education" was set up. This association consists of teachers who have incentive to promote disaster education. They study disaster education and share information. Now they have had several meetings and made a guideline on town/mountain watching, making use of the past experiences.

In addition, a "Kids Disaster Prevention Club" is proposed to be set up here. It is different from boys and girls fire club. It consists of students, teachers, parents, community people, and so on, who get interested in disaster prevention through town/mountain watching. Students can suggest what they want to know more about or they can raise questions that arise in their minds through town/mountain watching during the planning of club activities.

Fig. 10 shows the learning cycle of town/mountain watching. In addition to daily learning, students study about disaster prevention. A forum on disaster prevention, such as the Kids' Summit, is held once or twice a year and students from each school in Saijo City make presentations about what they have learned. In this way, sustainable disaster prevention will start from the school and will involve the entire city.

# NOTES

1. Questionnaire survey conducted by OYO Corporation (2005).
2. Only in Ohmachi Elementary School, the questionnaire surveys were conducted a day before and a day after the town watching.

## ACKNOWLEDGMENT

We would like to express our special thanks to Saijo City: to the Mayor, the Education Department, the Citizens' Safety Department, the schools, the students, and the Jichikai people. Yukiko Takeuchi and Rajib Shaw acknowledge the MEXT/JSPS grants-in-aid (CASIFICA and Water Communities).

## REFERENCES

Evans, N. (2001). Discourses of urban community and community planning: A comparison between Britain and Japan. Sheffield Online Papers in Social Research 3, April 2003. Available at www.shef.ac.uk/socst/Shop/evans.pdf.

IEDM. (2007). *Dealing with uncertainty: Considering climate change risk in disaster management planning*. IEDM preliminary report, Kyoto, Japan (9 pp.).

Ministry of Land, Infrastructure, Transport and Tourism (MLITT). (2005). A subcommittee on the river: The council for maintenance of social capital. A proposal about the promotion of overall heavy rain disaster measures.

Ogawa, Y., Fernandez, A. L., & Yoshimura, T. (2005). Town watching as a tool for citizen participation in developing countries: Application in disaster training. *International Journal of Mass Emergencies and Disasters, 23*(2), 5–36.

Policy Research Institute for Land, Infrastructure, Transport and Tourism (PRILITT). (2002). *For the brand-new and the reproduction of the local city – A proposal to the local city problem solving by seven well-informed people*. Report 2002.

Setagaya Machizukuri Center. (2003). Tool box of participatory design, Tokyo, 2003.

Udagawa, T. (2004). General Insurance Association of Japan, "Activity of Exploration Party for Disaster Prevention". *Fire Disaster, 54*(4), 12–17.

Yamada, M. (2001). A philosophy for community building. *Aichi Voice, 14*, 3–7.

Yamori, K., Ishiwaka, H., Ushiyama, M., Okada, S., Kataoka, S., & Murao, O. (2006). Frontier of disaster education. *Japan Society for Natural Disaster Science (JSNDS), 24*(4), 343–386.

Yoshimura, T. (2002). *Machi-zukuri: New challenge in Japanese urban planning*. Thirtieth International Course in Regional Development Planning, May 16–June 26, 2002. Nagoya: United Nations Centre for Regional Development.

# CHAPTER 11

# URBAN FLOOD RISK MANAGEMENT IN HANOI

Hoang Hung, Masami Kobayashi and Rajib Shaw

## ABSTRACT

*Located at the center of the Red River Delta, Hanoi is the consequence of the unstable balance between soil and water and has witnessed the amicable and adverse relationship between the two elements over a long history. Established as a small town in A.D. 210, Hanoi grew from a harbor on the bank of the Red River to a thriving city and was chosen to be the capital of Vietnam in 1010 as the site had advantageous physical, landscape, and geomancy characteristics. However, the capital had also been confronted with difficulties due to the alluvial process, which raises the level of the watercourse above its normal elevation forcing the inhabitants to take measures such as building a dyke to prevent floods. This chapter analyzes the natural and social conditions as well as several problems that have been affecting urban flood risk management in Hanoi. The chapter ends with practical options and policy measures to address the problems.*

## 1. BACKGROUND

The natural conditions of Hanoi make the city vulnerable to floods. Yet, the recent and future trends of city development do not seem to intend to address

Urban Risk Reduction: An Asian Perspective
Community, Environment and Disaster Risk Management, Volume 1, 207–231
Copyright © 2012 by Emerald Group Publishing Limited
All rights of reproduction in any form reserved
ISSN: 2040-7262/doi: 10.1108/S2040-7262(2009)0000001015

this adverse situation. The various factors leading us to this conclusion are examined below.

### 1.1. Hanoi: Characteristics and Historic Growth

Located at the center of the Red River Delta, Hanoi is the consequence of the unstable balance between soil and water and has witnessed the amicable and adverse relationship between the two elements over a long history (Vuong & San, 1975; Pierre, 2003). Established as a small town in A.D. 210, Hanoi grew from a harbor on the bank of the Red River to a thriving city and was chosen to be the capital of Vietnam in 1010 as the site had advantageous physical, landscape, and geomancy characteristics (Vuong & San, 1975). However, the capital had also been confronted with difficulties due to the alluvial process, which raises the level of the watercourse above its normal elevation, forcing the inhabitants to take measures such as building a dyke to prevent floods. Until the first half of the twentieth century, the dyke was not high and sturdy enough and could only protect Hanoi, which has average elevation of 6 m, from annual water levels varying between 8 m and 12.5 m. Up to 1990, as a result of 40 years of applying technical reinforcements and maintenance, the dyke had been raised from 12.0 m to 15.0 m. Combining with the operation of Hoa Binh reservoir upstream of the Red River, the dyke could protect the city from floods, like the disastrous one in 1971 that brought the water level to 14.13 m.

While often being constrained for implementing flood prevention plans, Hanoi continued to grow in the parts protected by the dyke. The city had expanded during different periods of feudal, colonial, and communist regimes in 1010–1873, 1874–1954, and 1955–1985 (Vuong & San, 1975; Hung & Thong, 1995). From 1986 the capital had experienced significant development as a result of a reform in the country's political economy, which successively changed the planned economy to a market economy and opened the way for a modern consumer society (Luan, Vinh, Brahm, & Michael, 2000). The pace of Hanoi's urbanization exceeded all previous expectations.

Nevertheless, this initial phase of urbanization in Hanoi has exposed the city to many dangers such as spontaneous construction works (Luan et al., 2000). The city's population grew quickly from 1,870,000 in 1985 to 2,685,000 in 1999. This, combined with the growing demand for accommodation, a result of inefficient public housing regime in socialist period, created a boom in house construction by individual households (80%, mostly self-built) with common features of spontaneous diversity and irregularity (Luan et al., 2000;

Hung, 2005). Squatting and illegal construction, which started from the late 1970s, has been spreading across the city and has become a persistent problem (Hung, 2005). Hanoi expanded through uncontrolled suburbanization processes leading to the establishment of settlements in the flood zones outside the dyke called the Riverside Urban Areas.

## 1.2. The Riverside Urban Areas (RUA)

The current RUA is situated in those areas that were inundated in rainy season and cultivated in 1920s. These areas were later on converted into residential areas in the 1970s and spontaneously developed in the 1980s and 1990s. Having altitude in the range of 9.0–11.0 m and located near the central business district, the RUA was considered by poor people and migrants as a place good for livelihood and dwelling due to cheap land prices. Operationalization of Hoa Binh reservoir has further reduced the flood threat to the RUA and it has drawn the attention of rich communities as well. There has been further rise in habitations after the approval of the revised Ordinance on Dyke in 2000 (Table 1) making the RUA the most densely populated area in Hanoi with 24,000 persons per sq km in Chuong Duong ward (Hung, 2005). There has also been persistent expansion of settlements by embanking the riverbank and selling it to new residents (96% in 2003 and 84% in 2004) (Hung, 2005). Subsequently, the human settlements have reduced the river flow, decreased flood discharge capacity, and raised the flood level of the Red River. According to the available data, the flood level of the Red River in Hanoi has been raised by about 0.8 m in 60 years (1939–2000) with the same water discharge. A rapid rise of 0.6 m was observed in the past 30 years (1970–2000) (Nghia & Chau, 2001; Uyen, 2002).

## 1.3. Development Plans of Hanoi

Due to the increasing impact of socioeconomic development, Hanoi has been growing speedily with little attention being paid to the risk of

*Table 1.* Population and Number of Houses in the RUA Since 1925.

|            | 1925 | 1955       | 1975   | 1996   | 2000    | 2001    | 2004    |
|------------|------|------------|--------|--------|---------|---------|---------|
| Population | 0    | Negligible | 33,476 | 75,202 | 107,634 | 140,425 | 160,602 |
| Houses     | 0    | Negligible | n.a.   | 12,533 | 19,569  | 27,700  | 32,012  |

*Source:* Uyen (2002) and Hung (2005).

catastrophic flood. Currently covering an area of 920.97 sq km with a population of 3,055,300, Hanoi is the country's second largest city. The city's population is unevenly distributed: 52.9% live in nine districts of the inner city, which cover only 9.2% of the total municipal area (Hung, 2005). According to the Hanoi Master Plan for the Year 2020, the capital will develop fast with predicted population of 5.1 million by 2020 and 5.9 million by 2030 (HCAO, 1997; Cuong, 2004; JICA, 2005). In the near future, the priority will be given to building Hanoi New Town in the north of the Red River (Fig. 1, right). This will be the first time that the city will be developed over the river, developing the RUA from jumbled areas to being the core of the future city. However, the development plan was not based on an extensive flood risk management plan and might encourage people moving toward the flood-prone areas.

# 2. CATASTROPHIC FLOOD IN THE RUA

A number of catastrophic floods take place each year in different parts of the world leading to very high economic and social losses (Herath & Shaw, 2003). Hanoi is one of such affected cities in Vietnam. Influenced by the Asian monsoon, the average annual rainfall in the Red River Delta and upstream areas is high (around 1,800 mm) and is unevenly distributed (80% during the rainy season). Water discharge in the delta during the rainy season accounts for 75–85% of the annual volume. In some years, during August, it accounts for over 40% of the total volume (MWR, 1994; Imamura & To, 1997; Nghia & Chau, 2001). As a consequence, big floods are a common occurrence during the rainy season.

## 2.1. Catastrophic Flood History

Floods have been the most dangerous and persistent disaster in the delta and in the Hanoi area in the past. From the tenth century to the nineteenth century, there were 188 big floods overflowing the dyke (Vuong & San, 1975; MWR, 1994). Two great floods in the nineteenth century were in 1821 and 1893. The event in 1893, having flood peak of 13 m in Hanoi, caused the heaviest damages (MWR, 1994). From 1902 to 2001 floods regularly occurred and there were two disastrous events in 1945 and 1971 in the delta and Hanoi areas (Fig. 2, Table 2). Though making up only 2% of the total

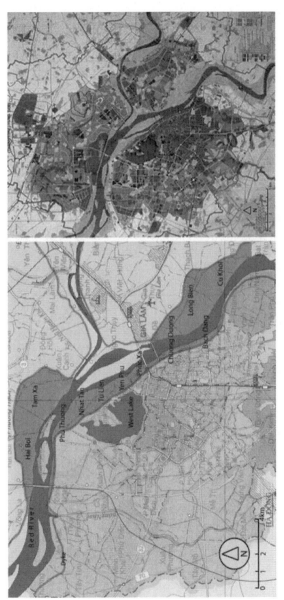

*Fig. 1.* Map of Locality of the RUA's Wards in the Present of Hanoi (Left) *Source:* Hung, H.V.; Base map: Hanoi Administration Map, 2004. Map of the RUA in the Hanoi Master Plan for Year 2020 (Right) *Source:* Cuong (2004).

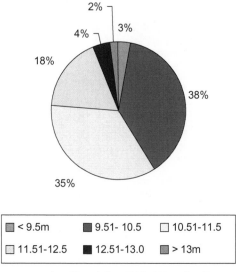

*Fig. 2.* Flood Frequency in Hanoi in 1902–2001 (in Terms of Water Level).
*Sources:* MWR (1994), Nghia and Chau (2001), and Uyen (2002).

*Table 2.* Data of Historical Floods in 1945 and 1971.

| Type of Data | The 1945 Flood | The 1971 Flood |
|---|---|---|
| Flood discharge (Son Tay gauging station) | 34,250 m³/s | 37,800 m³/s |
| Actual flood peak | 13.68 m | 14.13 m |
| Calculated flood peak (in case of no dyke breakage) | 14.43 m | 14.82 m |
| Inundated area | 3,120 sq km | 2,500 sq km |
| Affected people | 3 mil. people | 2.9 mil. families |
| Loss of human life | n.a. | 100,000 people[a] |
| Value of damages (using the exchange rate of 1990) | 51.5 mil. US$ | 79.9 mil. US$ |
| Percentage of national GDP | n.a. | 5.7% GDP |
| Flood return period | 100 years | 125 years |

*Sources:* MWR (1994) and Nghia and Chau (2001).
[a]NOAA (2004).

number of occurrences, these two floods caused the heaviest losses, leaving deep impression on the people, and are evaluated by experts as one of the most catastrophic events of the twentieth century (MWR, 1994; Nghia & Chau, 2001; Uyen, 2002; NOAA, 2004).

## 2.2. Possibility of Future Catastrophic Floods

The possible increase in rainfall magnitude and frequency associated with global climate change suggests higher chances of future catastrophic floods in the Hanoi area that can lead to very high human and economic losses (Thang, Inoue, Toda, & Kawaike, 2004; Tinh & Herath, 2005). With the increase of population and wealth, the city has continuously increased the design targets and constructed a flood control system (e.g., raising height of dyke in Hanoi and constructing reservoirs) that can withstand even higher magnitude floods. Flood frequencies, consequently, has been reduced, attracting more people and investment to the RUA even if it is located outside the dyke. Hanoi is now faced with the dilemma, when it has become extremely difficult to increase design standards any more (Nghia & Chau, 2001; Uyen, 2002), when an event beyond the design level would bring huge loss. The threat of increase in rainfall intensities and magnitudes can amplify the problem. There is a possibility of sudden big floods in case the dams such as Hoa Binh and Thac Ba located upstream of the Red River fail in the event of heavy rainfall and water discharge (Thang et al., 2004; Fahmida, 2005).

# 3. RISK PERCEPTION SURVEY

The overdevelopment of the RUA has mainly been caused by the increase of population and house construction. Regulating policies and implementation processes were unsuccessful in changing people's behavior and the community perception of flood risk. This motivated our study to find out a suitable solution to the future possible flood threat.

## 3.1. Method and Questionnaire

A questionnaire survey was conducted in October and November 2004 to find out how communities in the RUA perceived flood risk. A total of 588 residents of five different wards of the RUA participated in the survey. The sites along the riverbank (between the river and the dyke) that were chosen were Chuong Duong, Phu Thuong, An Duong, Cu Khoi, and Hai Boi (Fig. 1, left). This sequence also reflects the order of density of population, as the first three wards were urban while the remaining two were suburban. The officials of the ward's Construction Section were contacted with the help of Central Committee for Flood and Storm Control (CCFSC) who, in turn, facilitated carrying out the study.

The questionnaires included a mixture of open- and closed-ended questions. Subsection of the questionnaire included questions on advantages and disadvantages of living in the RUA; living conditions; previous experience with, expectation of, and information on flood; individual response to a flood; perception of flood and future flood; and housing information.

## 3.2. Results and Discussion

### 3.2.1. Respondents' Background

Age group of the respondents in the RUA as distinguished with that of Hanoi: the vulnerable (younger than 8 and older than 60) and school group (9–17) were high among the respondents. Respondents had diverse occupation with many of them engaged in agriculture or were unemployed (11% and 8.1%). Among the five wards, An Duong ward had the most number of respondents residing for more than 33 years (32%), who are also well experienced with the past flood incidences. Chuong Duong and Phu Thuong wards have large percentage of respondents residing for less than 5 years (21% and 17%). Respondents possessing medium- and big-sized houses were considerable in comparison with housing indexes of Hanoi, especially 61% respondents in Phu Thuong, An Duong, Hai Boi wards possessed sizeable (120–200 sq m) building plots and three or four storied houses.

### 3.2.2. Satisfaction with Living Condition

Respondents expressed high levels of satisfaction with living in the RUA. They were attracted by the location's advantages such as cheap prices of land and house, cool air, proximity to the central business district, and availability of suitable livelihood options as a number of people in Hai Boi and Cu Khoi wards could cultivate vegetables or flowers sell them to the city's inhabitants. The respondents identified poor infrastructure and frequent flood as disadvantages of living in the RUA and interestingly only 8.2% of the respondents rated the flood as a major disadvantage (Fig. 3). This reflects low level of awareness of hazards and of poor preparedness. Those who have experienced the 1971 flood considered that the risk to their life is low and that the flood mainly causes damage to their possessions.

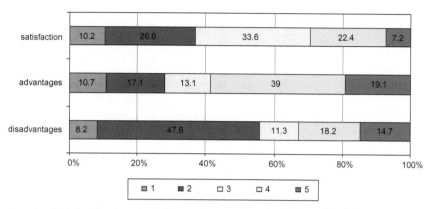

*Fig. 3.* Satisfaction Levels of Respondents with the Living Conditions in RUA. *Satisfaction* – 1: Very good, 2: Good, 3: Fair, 4: Poor, 5: Very poor; *Advantages* – 1: Proximity to the CBD, 2: Cool air, 3: Suitable livelihood, 4: Cheap land price, 5: Do not know; *Disadvantages* – 1: Flood as danger, 2: Flood as inconvenience, 3: Lack of public facilities, 4: Poor infrastructure, 5: Do not know.

### 3.2.3. Flood Risk Perception

Community perception of flood risk was evaluated using two scales: perception of regular flood risks and of catastrophic flood risks.

Flood experience played a major role in shaping the risk perception of the RUA's residents. All the respondents had flood experience and expressed their knowledge of regular flood events. Nearly two-thirds of the respondents took actions to cope with regular flood, e.g., raising the house foundation and lifting possessions to higher places, while a few others prepared small boats for use during flood (Fig. 4). It seemed that living outside the dyke and having experience of regular flood helped residents to take suitable steps to cope with such event.

Majority of the respondents ($n = 567$) expressed chances of possible future flood in the next 20 years. Respondents who had catastrophic flood experience expected higher levels of future flood levels. For instance, the high floodwater level of 1.51–2 m was expected by those people having the 1971 flood experience than people who do not have (34.4% vs. 11.6%). Similarly, more non-experienced respondents (47.1%) expected low future floodwater levels of below 0.5 m than the experienced ones (23.5%) (Table 3). This corroborates with other studies that suggest the importance of flood experience in shaping the perception of flood risk.

However, communities in the RUA had low perception of catastrophic flood risk despite their more frequent experience with the regular flood

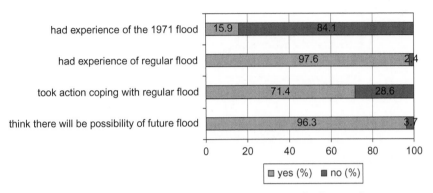

*Fig. 4.* Flood Experience and Perception among the Respondents.

***Table 3.*** Future Flood Levels as Expected by the Respondents.

| Water Levels | No. of Respondents | % | Experience of 1971 Flood | | | |
|---|---|---|---|---|---|---|
| | | | Yes | | No | |
| | | | No. | % | No. | % |
| More than 2.5 m (great) | 0 | 0 | 0 | 0 | 0 | 0 |
| 2.01–2.5 m (high-2) | 13 | 2.3 | 3 | 3.2 | 10 | 2.1 |
| 1.51–2 m (high-1) | 87 | 15.3 | 31 | 34.4 | 56 | 11.6 |
| 0.51–1.5 m (moderate) | 222 | 39.1 | 35 | 38.9 | 187 | 39.2 |
| Less than 0.5 m (small) | 245 | 43.3 | 21 | 23.5 | 224 | 47.1 |

events. Majority of respondents expected the future floodwater levels as below 1.5 m and no one thought that it would surpass the levels of 2.5–3 m, which was observed in 1971. In all 48.9% of the respondents did not believe that flood event of 1971 would occur within next 70 years since they understood that the return period of such flood is more than 100 years. And 37.8% of respondents believed that catastrophic floods could be avoided by using existing reservoirs and other structural solution and 13.3% could not provide a solution to the problem. Regarding possible mitigation measures for the future flood of catastrophic nature, 23.6% ($n = 137$) believed that measures such as raising house foundation, lifting possessions to higher places, and partial small embankments designed for coping with the regular flood would be adequate. Only 65.2% ($n = 383$) could identify the inadequacy of preparedness. However majority of respondents (78.3% ($n = 443$)), believed that their family would be safe in case of a catastrophic flood due to the presence of Hoa Binh reservoir (20.5%) and their houses have been built at higher elevations (57.8%). This suggests that respondents viewed the future possible catastrophic flood in the RUA as less destructive and less terrifying than the one in 1971, just as raising water level higher than regular event.

People are inadequately sensitized on catastrophic flood with a large number of them living there with no experience and without knowing what to expect in a really severe event and suggests poor understanding of natural processes and the impacts on them. This can be compounded by poor judgment regarding the magnitude and frequency or return period of catastrophic flood. Studies elsewhere showed that structural flood protection measures increase the attractiveness of the floodplain for habitation, by increasing the perceived safety or reducing the perceived risk (Michael & Fasil, 2001). However, for people in the RUA, the structural measures were not only reservoirs and other irrigation works provided by the government but also their own private houses (57.8%). The houses as a protection might create a wrong sense of security with people assuming that catastrophic flood (if it occurs) will not affect their lives. Thus, residents of the RUA were more likely to reside and build bigger houses in the areas to cope with flood risk.

# 4. POLICIES ON URBAN DEVELOPMENT AND DISASTER RISK MANAGEMENT

As mentioned above, one of the main reasons of the continued growth of the population and the increase in the number of houses was the low perception about catastrophic flood risk among the communities in the RUA. However, the continued development in the RUA, even after the approval and implementation of Construction Regulations, which deals with illegal construction, and Ordinances on Dyke, which protects the dyke and regulates the growth of the RUA, could not enhance the policy-level preparedness. Hence, the policy goals of Hanoi's urban development, construction regulations, and flood management were analyzed.

Hanoi's developmental plan has a goal of promoting urban development wherever land is available. However, in the case of the RUA, this goal often conflicts with the goal of disaster management, which promotes public safety, as the development of RUA is happening in the most flood-prone area of the city.

## 4.1. Urban Development Policy

Human habitat issues in the RUA used to be a provisional policy under Hanoi City People's Committee (CPC). The establishment of a new Vietnamese government in 1954 created accommodation for the government's staff and city's new inhabitants in Hanoi through establishing collective flat areas in the city including the three locations of Phuc Xa, Chuong Duong, and Bach Dang in the RUA (Fig. 1, left), because they are located near the city's center (Hung & Thong, 1995). In addition, thousands of families in Van Ho, a southern area of Hanoi, were resettled in An Duong (Yen Phu) and Phuc Xa of the RUA for the construction of the government office complex. Resettlement programs for building new housing were undertaken up to 1970 (Hung & Thong, 1995). This must have encouraged the movement of population into the RUA. However, after the heavy toll caused by the catastrophic flood in 1971, no formal housing programs have been encouraged in the RUA.

The human habitations in the RUA did not stop since the area was still considered having many advantages. The stagnation of the country's economy during the 1970s and 1980s had caused the city development plan to focus on available land in the urban core instead of further expansion to suburban areas (Cuong, 2004). The Hanoi Master Plan for the year of 2010, which considers the West Lake area as the center of the city, was approved in 1992. Being in the vicinity of the West Lake, parts of the RUA including Nhat Tan, Tu Lien, and Yen Phu wards became favorable locations. In addition, the reduction of annual flood threat to Hanoi due to the operationalization of Hoa Binh reservoir in 1990 led to use of the available vacant land in the RUA for parks, tourism, and housing. Subsequently, real-estate agencies started investing in housing projects in the RUA leading to the development of Red River City, Phuc Xa, Nghia Dung, and Dam Trau, which were approved by the CPC in 1992 and 1993 (Hung & Thong, 1995).

The Hanoi Master Plan 2020, approved in 1998, further encouraged the development of the RUA. The innovative policies in the 1990s, which directed the country toward an open market economy, have encouraged further growth in Hanoi. As such, the new master plan considers the Red River as the central axis on which the city shall be developed, contemplating the RUA, making up 11% of Hanoi's area, to be the core of the city (HCAO, 1997; NPP, 2003; Cuong, 2004). Henceforth, CPC has been proposing detailed land use plans – a fundamental step of the urban development plan – to rearrange existing residential areas and use vacant land in the RUA for developing new urban areas (NIURP, 1998). Though the proposal has not been approved by the Ministry of Agriculture and Rural Development (MARD) as the foundation for it – a flood management plan for the RUA – was still being prepared (CCFSC, 2004). It attracted huge influx of people seeking accommodation and fortune on speculation, even though most of these activities were illegal (Luan et al., 2000; Leaf, 2000).

## 4.2. Flood Management Policy

Although the goal of the urban development policy for Hanoi has basically been achieved, the same cannot be said of the RUA. The catastrophic flood of 1971 had changed the disaster management policy for the Red River Delta from flood response to flood prevention with the priority on strengthening the dykes. The two Ordinances on Dyke, the Ordinance on Flood and Storm Control, the Strategy and Action Plan for Mitigating Water Disaster, and Decree 62/ND-CP on Regulation of Flood Diversion and Retention for Hanoi have set out the provisions for flood management and enhancing the human security (CCFSC, 2004). Dyke protection took precedence in Hanoi as the city is placed below the level of Red River. Hence, the development of the RUA may affect the safety of the dyke causing an increase of flood levels which may possibly be above the dyke at Hanoi and downstream areas (Nghia & Chau, 2001; Uyen, 2002).

## 4.3. Construction Regulations in Hanoi

Squatting and illegal construction have been a persistent problems in Hanoi since the 1990s, especially in the RUA. Several construction regulations have been issued to regulate squatting and illegal construction, however, these could not rectify the problem. Three reasons could be attributed to this failure as discussed below.

First, the CPC's approach to control squatting and illegal construction has been narrow. The initial approach dealing with the problem was a sole political mobilization called "Civilized Way of Life and New Cultural Family" campaign, which was implemented by ward offices starting from 1978 to encourage the city's inhabitants to voluntarily comply with rules and regulations governing daily living, public awareness, public health, sanitation, traffic, and dissuasion from illegal construction. The campaign was ineffective in reducing squatting and illegal construction (Koh, 2003; Hung, 2005) because it was a one-way propaganda. In this initiative, squatting and illegal constructions were not treated as unlawful activities but like other inhabitants' practices in daily life affecting the tidy urban view.

As the city's political mobilization and education approach did not work efficiently, the CPC changed emphasis to promulgate legal regulations – the Decree 11/XDCB of 1983 governing housing construction and renovation works. Being a symbol of "the modern and civilized Hanoi," collective flat areas were chosen to be the pilot locations for implementation. As a result, the number of illegal construction cases in collective flat areas was reduced in 1983 but increased again starting 1984 (Koh, 2003; Hung, 2005). One reason for these responses to fail in addressing squatting and illegal construction was that the CPC used mobilization approach and legal approach separately as opposed to in combination.

Second, construction regulations had been inconsistent causing misinterpretation among residents. In an attempt to reestablish order on construction matters, in 1987, the CPC issued a set of regulations – Decision 4637/QD-UB. The decision legitimized existing illegal neighborhoods provided the residents pay land taxes and vacate the land when the state requires. Then, it claimed that the city's authorities would strictly control the squatting and illegal construction thereafter without anymore pardon (Koh, 2003; Hung, 2005). However, after failing to deal with squatting and illegal construction, CPC issued Decision 2704/QD-UB and 2771/QD-UB in 1990, which granted further amnesty to offenders. Nevertheless, the new decisions could not reduce the illegal constructions (Koh, 2003; Hung, 2005) since residents interpreted that the state would eventually legitimize all the offenders.

Lastly, complicated construction licensing further contributed to the illegal constructions. As stipulated by the Decision 11/XDCB and 4637/QD-UB, for preparing license application, the residents had to obtain about ten different certificates of their housing need from the ward, district, and government agency offices. Since these multiple authorities have equal power in the process, the decisions were often in gridlock making the application process lasting up to 60 days. This discouraged the residents from applying for the license and most of them had chosen to start the construction without a license (Leaf, 2000; Luan et al., 2000). This process was partially simplified by the Decision 2704/QD-UB and 1431/QD-UB but the needed certificates were still six (Hung, 2005). These drawbacks became stumbling blocks in preventing squatting and illegal construction activities in Hanoi. Moreover, being considered as an isolated location by the city's authorities and some public, the RUA became a haven of squatting and illegal construction.

In 1995 a major public debate was seen in the local media about the possible flood risk to the city as a result of over squatting in RUA. As a result, an enquiry by the officials in Nhat Tan, Tu Lien, and Yen Phu wards revealed 287 illegal constructions encroaching on the dyke section from 1991 to 1994. However, the city's newspapers quoted 1,100 houses as illegal among which 87% houses belonged to the wealthy people who settled there seeking fortune on speculation (Hung, 2005). The huge number of illegal constructions and influential owners made it difficult for the CPC to take strict decisions (Koh, 2003). Since the situation became serious and the fast approaching flooding season was threatening the safety of the capital, the Prime Minister consecutively issued decisions 108-TTg, 158-TTg, 172-TTg, 274-TTg to correct urban and disaster management policies of Hanoi and pointed out the need for protecting the dyke in 1995. As a result, the CPC in cooperation with the Ministry of Water Resources (forerunner of MARD) had demolished the illegal houses so that clear strips of dyke protection land are observed on both sides of the dyke (Koh, 2003).

Nevertheless, the drastic decisions of the central and city governments in 1995 could only restrict squatting and illegal construction within the dyke protection areas but not for the whole RUA since the main consideration was the safety of the dyke. Besides, as mentioned above, the city's approval of four big housing projects in the RUA, in 1992 and 1993, was evidently interpreted by residents that the RUA is a reasonably safe place to live. From 1990 to 1995 there were tens of thousands of squatting and illegal construction cases in vacant land between the boundary of the dyke protection area and the river which were not mentioned by the public media because they were not directly endangering the dyke (Hung, 2005).

### 4.4. Ordinances on Dyke

Ordinance on Dyke is one of the most related policies for regulating the development of RUA and disaster management in Hanoi. There are some factors which made it difficult to implement and coordinate with construction regulation authorities.

The first Ordinance on Dyke, issued in 1989, has set out the provisions for the management and use of dykes. It delineated the dyke protection areas on both sides of the dyke and prohibited construction within these areas. However the ordinance did not exactly provide definition of the dyke protection areas, which totally or partly cover flood-prone areas, instead it left over the task to Council of Minister (central government cabinet). Thus, it could not be fully implemented until the approval of Decree No. 429/HDBT, one year later, promulgating details of the ordinance's implementation in

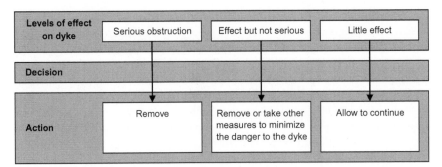

*Fig. 5.* Decision for Continuance or Removal of Illegal Constructions in RUA.

which dyke protection areas were defined as the main body of the dyke and its vicinity of 20 m from the dyke's toe.

Nevertheless, the decree was still not clear for implementation. This subordinate legal documents mandated management task, dealing with the existing houses, to the CPC with vague oriented resolutions (Fig. 5). Again, there were difficulties in execution since the definition of different levels of the effect of housing on dyke was not precisely provided. Thus, the existence of houses in dyke protection areas without any CPC's treatment or resolution likely encouraged more offenders. This, combined with the fact that parts of the RUA were considered by the Hanoi Master Plan issued in 1992 as favorable positions, contributed to the increase of construction activities in the RUA which gradually led to the event in 1995. The ordinance, thus, cannot be described as playing a supporting role for construction regulations to prevent the RUA from encroachments.

In 2000, realizing the fast development in flood-prone areas, a new ordinance on dyke was issued for protecting the dykes and managing flood drainage areas. This ordinance classified flood-prone areas outside dyke into three zones: (1) dyke protection area; (2) from boundary of dyke protection area toward the river course where existence of houses do not directly influence annual floodwater drainage capacity of the river; and (3) next to riverbank where existence of houses directly influence the annual floodwater drainage capacity (Fig. 6). Only existing houses situated in the middle zone were allowed, provided the households obey the dyke protection measures. Yet the task of exactly defining the three zones was again left to the central government, in the coordination of MARD with Ministry of Construction, Ministry of Transportation, and Provincial People's Committee.

Nevertheless, after a delay, Decree 171/ND-CP was promulgated by the central government in 2003, to provide details on the implementation of the

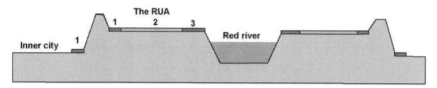

*Fig. 6.* Cross-Section of the RUA Showing Three Zones which were Classified by the Ordinance on Dyke Issued in 2000.

new ordinance. The decree, however, did not have much effect. Thousands of houses had been built illegally in the RUA during the interval between the issuance of the new ordinance and the decree. Available data shows that in 2004, the year in which the real-estate market reached a peak growth rate in Hanoi, the population and the number of houses in the RUA had multiplied 1.5 times from that of 2000. Some of the loopholes in the Decree 171/ND-CP further enhanced the settlements in RUA. The decree envisaged the removal or transformation of existent housing in the third zone, which have an altitude below that of flood Alarm Level 2 (for Hanoi area it equals to 10.5 m), but did not provide exact map of the restricted zone. Thus, offenders have encroached upon the river course and embanked or elevated, by land filling, their land above the Alarm Level 2 prescribed by the decree. In 2003–2004, the CPC and city's newspapers recorded 1,176 squatting and encroaching cases in the riverbank. Many similar other cases have gone unrecorded (Hung, 2005).

In summary the two ordinances on dyke could only gradually restrict the development in the places with direct influence on the dyke, but not in the others. The lack of clear definition of critical areas for dyke protection and flood drainage in the ordinances and their subordinate legal documents had created an obstacle to implement and coordinate the construction regulations. Thus, as shown in Fig. 7, the two ordinances had little effect in preventing the overdevelopment of the RUA.

## 5. SYSTEM OF GOVERNANCE

Public administration in Hanoi and the RUA is complex and governance tasks have not been well coordinated vertically (among authorities at different levels) and horizontally (among authorities at the same level). Moreover, the disaster management in Hanoi had virtually been managed by the central government marginalizing the role of CPC in the flood-prone areas of the RUA.

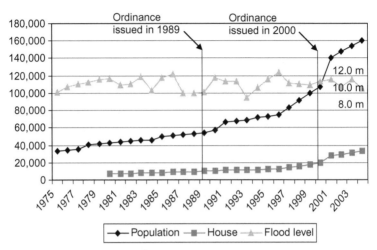

*Fig. 7.* Changes of Population and Housing in the RUA in 1975–2004 and Impacts of the Ordinances on Dyke and Flood Situation. *Sources:* Uyen (2002), CCFSC (2004), and Hung (2005).

The public administration in Hanoi has a three-tier structure (Fig. 8). Governance tasks are directly executed by the People's Committee at each level. Most of the state legislation and directives leave the job of issuing regulations and implementing laws to the city office. Being the contact point between the state and the ordinary people, the ward office has implementation power and may alter the city's policies marginally and make decision on local matters. Situated in the middle, the district office is responsible for decision-making in local matters that exceed the ward's power and for transferring information between ward and city offices (VNNA, 1994).

The three-tier structure has prevented the city's authorities from coordinating vertically to effectively deal with problems such as squatting and illegal construction in the RUA. Hanoi Department of Construction (HDC) and Construction Management Units (CMU) in the district and ward offices implement the city's construction regulations. Depending on the scale and position of a building, a construction license is issued by HDC or the district CMU. The ward CMU monitors the construction process, reports the cases to the district office and implements the final decision of the district CMU. HDC is approached to make the final decision if the case exceeds the jurisdiction of the district. Hence, the ward CMU officials can issue suspension orders but cannot take immediate action such as

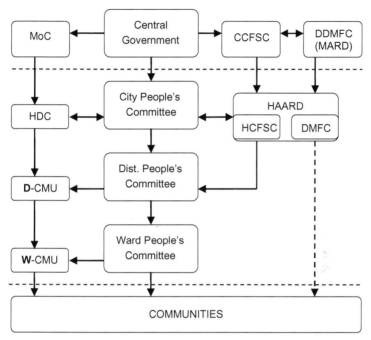

*Fig. 8.* Structure of Governance System in Hanoi. MoC: Ministry of Construction.
*Source:* (VNNA, 1994).

demolition. Due to the lengthy decision-making process, offenders often ignore the ward orders to stop the construction and they are frequently able to complete and inhabit their buildings, thus, the issue become emotional and difficult to solve at this stage (Hung, 2005).

Officials from the district and above could intervene at the ward level. In several cases, offenders are able to use their nexus with the city government officers asking for favors to suspend district or ward orders (Koh, 2003). This was rectified by the Decision 4637/QD-UB which gave more power to the ward office by stressing that the ward office was to be the first authority to deal with squatting and illegal construction. However, ward officials only have a right to destroy illegal construction if the unlawful activity was caught red-handed. As such, offenders usually take up and finish the constructions in the night or during the holidays (Hung, 2005).

This weakness was corrected by the approval of Decree 48-CP in 1997 for fining the violators of regulations related to urban housing and infra-structure management. The decree delegated powers to the Chairperson of the People's Committee at the city, district, and, especially, ward levels to fine offenders and demolish the illegal constructions. This produced relatively good results in keeping squatting and illegal constructions under control in Hanoi in 1998 (Hung, 2005). However, it was not the case in the RUA since ward officials there still have to consult the district when illegal construction interferes with public installations such as the dyke and flood drainages. There were instances that the district officials did not have any motivation to decide and pass on the decision to HDC and CPC (personal communication with the Deputy Chairman of Phuc Tan Ward People's Committee, 2006). Thus, it could be said that, at least in dealing with the problem of squatting and illegal construction, the three-tier structure made the local government more bureaucratic, resulting in official delay.

In addition, there has been lack of cooperation between the CPC and central government agencies. The Department of Dyke Management and Flood Control (DDMFC) and its branch DMFC at the city office are responsible for dyke protection and land use management in the RUA. However, at district and ward levels, DMFC do not have branches to deploy its tasks. Instead, it has to use its limited staff for the inspection of dyke protection areas and depend on the ward officials in dealing with the issue (CCFSC, 2004). When violations were found, the DMFC staff has to report the cases to the ward office and have no authority to intervene directly. The offending cases were handed over to the ward officials for treating based on perception and competency of the cadres and usually left unprocessed (personal communication with the Deputy Head of Hanoi DMFC, 2006). This shows the lack of capacity at the ward level and confusion in the hierarchy of responsibilities.

Moreover, the city office has low motivation in managing development and dealing with illegal construction in the RUA. As the capital city, the safety of Hanoi is the responsibility of the central government represented by the CCFSC. Belonging to CPC and working under the professional supervision of CCFSC, Hanoi Committee for Flood and Storm Control (HCFSC) is in-charge of disaster management in the city. It has tasks of approving and implementing the disaster management plans of the city, which is set up based on the national plan for each year; and organizing activities for preventing and overcoming consequences of hazards in the city following the instructions of CCFSC (2004). To this effect, the HCFSC is only responsible for the response process and not the whole flood risk management. This makes the CPC rely on central government on issues related to risk mitigation in the RUA and consequently lead to the low motivation of the city authorities in managing spontaneous development in the RUA. Concrete instances could be seen in ineffective construction regulations and their implementation processes.

# 6. THE WAY AHEAD

The overdevelopment of the RUA might lead to huge losses if a catastrophic flood should occur. Although there had been considerable concern, as indicated in the approval of several legal documents from 1987 to 2000, the growth of the RUA could not be controlled reflecting the failure of the policies at various levels.

At the heart of the shortcomings lays a discrepancy between the policy goals of urban development and of disaster management, combined with the low perception of catastrophic flood risk among residents reflecting the lack of knowledge base about floods. Moreover, the disagreement of policy goals has been amplified by three weaknesses: ineffective construction regulations caused by inadequate motivation and capacity of authorities in-charge of construction management in the RUA; unspecific factors of Ordinances on Dyke resulting in their narrow scopes focusing on disaster issues only; and ineffective coordination between the local authorities and central government agencies.

The low perception of communities to risks in the RUA implies that the people need to be informed and convinced about the real magnitude of the catastrophic flood before they accept and implement the management strategies and policies. To address this problem, there are two suggested options that can be undertaken at the ward level:

- *Changing the communities' perception of catastrophic flood risk to enhance their preparedness and*
- *Conducting comprehensive hands-on community level education programs* with objectives to provide residents the knowledge of catastrophic flood and its interaction with the overdevelopment of the RUA, interest to take initiative to put that knowledge into practice, and enhanced capacity to respond to future possible catastrophic event.

The overdevelopment of the RUA has ultimately provoked questions of city governance capacity in the dual context of Hanoi's rapid urbanization and the possible increase of flood hazard frequency and severity due to global climate change. The policy deficiencies mean that the city's authorities have not adequately shared decision-making nor sought consensus from the central government and the RUA's residents. The central government's policy tries to prevent the growth of the RUA. However, in reality, due to attractiveness of the RUA for human settlement and mismanagement by the city government, only formal development could be stopped but not the fast spontaneous ones. At present, it is difficult to totally reduce flood risk by keeping flood out of people's way or people out of the flood's way. CPC could not build another dyke to protect the RUA since it might reduce the river's flood drainage capacity, especially in big flood, and consequently endanger Hanoi area by increasing the flood level. On the other hand, given the huge population in the RUA, it is impossible to resettle them all. As such, there should be a "best-mix" of solutions that can relocate residents from the most vulnerable part of the RUA and allow them to use areas with lowest acceptable risk level where could be a trade-off between flood risk and economic benefit. To attain this solution, an urban redevelopment plan for the RUA should be proposed through a new land use planning process. However, the existing policy and governance structure seem to be critical barriers for doing so. Thus, a set of policy measures has been suggested below for dealing with the problem.

- *Build and share a knowledge base on catastrophic flood risk and sustainable ways of coping with the flood*: Knowledge needs to be enhanced about the catastrophic flood and the long-term risk among the communities for enabling fully informed decisions. The central government, city policy-makers, and the RUA's residents need to know about not only the areas subject to the catastrophic flood, but also the existing or proposed use of vulnerable areas. One indispensable information is an acceptable risk level for the RUA, which need to be developed by residents with the participation of experts and local officials. Steps are also needed to ensure that the information is available to and understood by the public. Involving broader stakeholders in the planning process is necessary to share the information in effective ways. Knowledge must be shared with various professional organizations such as the CCFSC, HCFSC, DDMFC, DMFC, HDC, and district and ward offices, whose decisions affect exposure to flood. Targets for improved training materials and courses, especially on the subjects of risk assessment and mitigation techniques, should include professionals from these organizations.
- *Be responsible and develop commitment to manage flood-prone areas in Hanoi*: The central government not only needs to mandate the CPC to undertake a planning process in the flood-prone areas but also can take

actions to foster genuine commitment to manage, through community participation and involvement, flood-prone areas among Hanoi's authorities.

- *Better coordination between urban development and flood management*: Rather than promulgating centralized command-and-control regulations for the development and flood management in the RUA, the city should foster decentralization and call for the establishment of an interagency task force. Land use planning process should form as a coordinating mechanism since various concerns of urban development and flood risk management could be integrated in the process. In that system the city's authorities are required to act in a way consistent with the government agencies such that the sustainability of RUA is enhanced.

# 7. CONCLUSION

The nature of Hanoi makes the city and the RUA vulnerable to floods. The overdevelopment of these high-risk areas has amplified the problem. Hanoi's policies for the RUA contained multidimensional problems. There has been mismatch between the goals of urban development and flood management. This has been amplified by ineffective construction regulations and ordinances on the dyke. Moreover, the structure of governance tasks in the RUA has been complex in which coordination among the city and central government organs has not been effective. The low perception of the RUA's residents of risks has further led to the overdevelopment of the RUA and worsened the flood risk of Hanoi and downstream areas.

Thus, to regulate the overdevelopment of the RUA, there is a need at the community level to: (1) increase community perception of flood, especially catastrophic flood risk and (2) involve local authority and community leaders in conducting comprehensive hands-on community education program. At city level, it is necessary to establish policy measures that are based on sound land use planning encompassing the concerns of urban development and underlying risks. While doing so, the city's authorities must: (1) Build and share a knowledge base on catastrophic flood risk and sustainable ways of coping with floods; (2) Be responsible and develop commitment to manage the flood-prone areas; (3) Develop better coordination between urban development and flood management.

# REFERENCES

CCFSC. (2004). Website of Central Committee for Flood and Storm Control. Available at: http://www.ccfsc.org.vn/ccfsc/vn/. Last accessed in December, 2004.

Cuong, L. M. (2004). Hanoi and its construction planning projects. *Journal of Construction Planning, 10*(4), 16–18 (Vietnamese language).

Fahmida, K. (2005). Flood risk analysis in Hanoi City due to extreme floods under scenario of Hoa Binh Reservoir failure. Paper presented at the International Symposium on Flood in Coastal Cities under Climate Change Condition, Bangkok.

HCAO. (1997). Presentation on the Hanoi Master Plan for 2020. Paper presented in Workshop on Review of the Master Plan and Sectoral Plans, Project VIE/95/050, Hanoi Chief Architect's Office.

Herath, S., & Shaw, R. (2003). Ensuring flood security for sustainable urbanization – Catastrophic flood risk assessment in the Asia-Pacific region. *Proceeding of the UNU-UNCRD Regional Workshop*, Bangkok.

Hung, H. V. (2005). A set of compiling articles of housing and urban issues in Hanoi Moi, Tuoi Tre Thu Do, Dai Doan Ket and Kinh Te Do Thi newspapers from 1983 to 2005, Unpublished Document (Vietnamese language).

Hung, T., & Thong, N. T. (1995). Thang Long Hanoi – Ten centuries of urbanization, construction publisher, Hanoi (Vietnamese language).

Imamura, F., & To, D. V. (1997). Flood and typhoon disasters in Vietnam in the half century since 1950. *Natural Hazards, 15*, 71–87.

JICA. (2005). *Hanoi integrated development and environment programme.* Draft Report. Japan International Cooperation Agency (JICA), Hanoi.

Koh, D. (2003). Illegal construction in Hanoi and Hanoi's wards. *European Journal of East Asian Studies, 3*(2), 337–369.

Leaf, M. (2000). Structure, spontaneity and the changing landscape of Hanoi. In: C. Chifos & R. Yabes (Eds), *Southeast Asian urban environments: Structured and spontaneous* (pp. 73–111). Tempe, AZ: Arizona State University Press.

Luan, T. D., Vinh, N. Q., Brahm, W., & Michael, L. (2000). Urban housing. In: P. Boothroyd & P. X. Nam (Eds), *Socioeconomic renovation in Vietnam – The origin, evolution, and impact of Doi Moi* (pp. 65–113). Singapore: IDRC and ISEAS.

Michael, B., & Fasil, A. G. (2001). Worldwide public perception of flood risk in urban areas and its consequences for hydrological design in Ireland. Paper presented at the National Hydrology Seminar on Flood Risk Management: Impacts and Development, Ireland.

MWR. (1994). *Flood and typhoon control in Vietnam 1890–1990.* Vietnam: The Gioi Publisher.

Nghia, T. T. & Chau, V. H. (2001). Flood control planning for Red River Basin. Paper presented in the First Meeting of FLOCODS Steering Committee, Hanoi.

NIURP. (1998). *Draft of orientation planning for the riverside urban areas.* Hanoi: National Institute for Urban and Rural Planning.

NOAA. (2004). Top global weather, water and climate events of the 20th century, US National Oceanic and Atmospheric Administration. Available at: http://www.noaanews. noaa.gov/stories/images/global.pdf).

NPP. (2003). *Legal regulations on development of the Capital of Hanoi* (Vietnamese language). Hanoi: National Political Publisher.

Pierre, C. (2003). Lessons learned from Hanoi. In: C. Pierre & L. Nathalie (Eds), *Hanoi – Cycle of changes* (pp. 11–17). Hanoi: Technology and Science Publisher.

Thang, N. T., Inoue, K., Toda, K., & Kawaike, K. (2004). Flood inundation analysis based on unstructured meshes for the Hanoi central area. *Annual Journal of Hydraulic Engineering, JSCE, 48*, 601–606.

Tinh, D. Q., & Herath, S. (2005). Urban floods – Challenges. Paper presented at the World Conference on Disaster, Kobe.

Uyen, V. T. (2002). *Planning of drainage system in the Red river of Hanoi, Report* (Vietnamese language). Hanoi: Institute of Scientific Irrigation.

VNNA. (1994). *Law on organization of people's councils and people's committees.* Hanoi: Vietnam National Assembly.

Vuong, T. Q., & San, V. T. (1975). *Immemorial time of Hanoi* (Vietnamese language). Hanoi: Culture and Information Publisher.

# CHAPTER 12

# POST-DISASTER RECONSTRUCTION IN URBAN AREAS IN ACEH

Chiho Ochiai and Rajib Shaw

## ABSTRACT

*On December 26, 2004, a strong earthquake of magnitude 9.0 on the richer scale, hit the Northwest of Sumatra island, Indonesia and caused the Indian Ocean Tsunami. The tsunami struck Aceh and North Sumatra (NAD), caused about 130,000 deaths, 500,000 left homeless, and extensive damage to life, property, and infrastructures. Sumatra is the western tip of island in the Indonesian archipelago. The population of Aceh province is estimated at 4.2 million (2000), or 3% of the Indonesian population and nearly a quarter of the population of Sumatra as a whole. One of the most heavily affected areas is Banda Aceh, which is located at the tip of Sumatra island had a population of 270,000 of which about 25% people lost their lives.*

## 1. BACKGROUND

The number of natural disasters has been increasing every decade since 1970s. Also it is obvious that the impact of natural disasters is on rise by the

Urban Risk Reduction: An Asian Perspective
Community, Environment and Disaster Risk Management, Volume 1, 233–252
Copyright © 2012 by Emerald Group Publishing Limited
All rights of reproduction in any form reserved
ISSN: 2040-7262/doi: 10.1108/S2040-7262(2009)0000001016

increasing number of occurrence, death, affected people, and economic loss based on the data from 1977 to 2001 (CRED, 2006). Every year about 200 thousand people are affected, about 60 thousand people die, and about $400 billion of economic losses are reported. Within five years, about 40% of natural dissenter occurred, 50% of death, 90% of affected, and 50% of economic loss is concentrated in Asian region (JICA, 2005).

This trend continues because of the increase of concentration of population and values in the urban areas. Since 1990, the Chi-chi earthquake, Taiwan in 1999, the earthquake in Maharashtra, India in 1993, the earthquake in Kobe, Japan in 1995, and the Indian Ocean Tsunami, Indonesia in 2004 are some reminders of the devastating natural disasters that occurred and had main impact in urban areas in Asian region. The most of urban areas are heavily dependent on the infrastructures and the services, which give large impact on people's life.

Indonesia was spotlighted by the Indian Ocean Tsunami but the country is also one of the disaster-prone countries that face all types of disasters every year such as earthquake, flood, windstorm, drought, landslide, and tsunami. Table 1 shows the disasters in Indonesia that caused large number of deaths from 1970 to 2006.

These disasters did not necessarily occur in large cities but in small to medium cities. In other words, the urban risks in Indonesia emphasize on

***Table 1.*** Disasters in Indonesia According to Number of Killed (1970–2006).

| Year | Disaster Type | Killed | Location |
|------|---------------|--------|----------|
| 2004 | Tsunami | 130,000 | Aceh, Sumatra |
| 1973 | Wind storm | 1,650 | Flores Sea |
| 2005 | Earthquake | 905 | Nias Island, Sumatra |
| 1976 | Earthquake | 573 | Bali |
| 1981 | Landslide | 500 | Near Java |
| 1981 | Flood | 500 | Mt. Semeru |
| 1997 | Drought | 460 | Irian Jaya Province |
| 1976 | Earthquake | 420 | Irian Jaya |
| 1983 | Earthquake | 360 | Banda Acehat, N. Sumatra |
| 1981 | Earthquake | 306 | Irian Jaya |
| 1982 | Drought | 280 | Irian Jaya/E. Timor |
| 2006 | Flood | 200 | South Sulawesi |
| 2002 | Landslide | 142 | Jakarta |
| 2003 | Flash flood | 140 | Sumatra |

*Source:* ADRC (2008).

small to medium level cities. In Indonesia, small to medium cities also have high concentration of population and values and also many of them are located in coastal areas.

## 2. COASTAL HAZARD AND ITS IMPACT

On December 26, 2004, a strong earthquake of magnitude 9.0 on the richer scale, hit the Northwest of Sumatra island, Indonesia, and caused the Indian Ocean Tsunami. The tsunami struck Aceh and North Sumatra (NAD), caused about 130,000 deaths, 500,000 left homeless, and extensive damage to life, property, and infrastructures (BRR, 2005).

Sumatra is the western tip of island in the Indonesian archipelago. It is also Indonesia's second largest island, covering an area of 473,481 square kilometers. There are approximately 37 million people in Sumatra. The population of Aceh province is estimated at 4.2 million (2000), or 3% of the Indonesian population and nearly a quarter of the population of Sumatra as a whole (Census, 2003). One of the most heavily affected areas is Banda Aceh, which is located at the tip of Sumatra island had a population of 270,000 of which about 1/4 of the people died.

The earthquake and tsunami-affected area is geographically spread along about 500 km long seashore but severely affected areas are limited within about 5 km from the seashore. However, the damage caused by the tsunami is devastating and almost all the houses were washed away totally. In many coastal areas, the land is damaged due to permanent flooding in some residential areas. The Fig. 1 shows the tsunami-affected areas in Aceh Province. The red color shows the inundation area by tsunami. Fig. 2 shows the satellite image of Banda Aceh before and after the disaster. Fig. 3 shows the disaster damage to house and infrastructures in Banda Aceh.

The disaster like Indian Ocean Tsunami is of low consequence but of high disturbance and loss. In Banda Aceh, all the local government office lost their function and all the basic infrastructures and lifeline such as water, electricity, road, and port were destroyed and lost their function. For small to medium city, one disaster could devastate the whole city.

## 3. COMMUNITY-BASED RECONSTRUCTION

Post-disaster recovery is a development opportunity (Shaw et al., 2002). Community-based or participatory approach has been spotlighted and

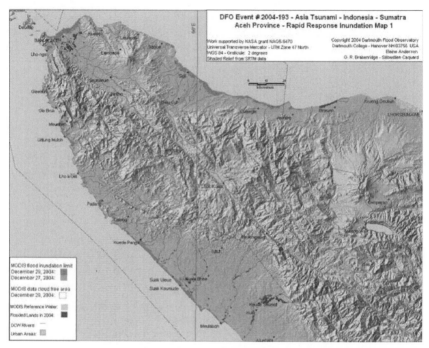

*Fig. 1.* Location Map of Aceh and Inundation by Tsunami (*Source:* http://
www.dartmouth.edu/~floods/images/2004193Aceh.jpg).

adopted in many development projects since 1980s and many positive results
have been reported. The inter-American Development Bank (IDB)'s
"Resource Book on Participation" defines participation as "the PROCESS
through which people with a legitimate interest (stakeholders) influence and
share control over development initiatives, and the decisions and resources
which affect them" (IDB, 1997). The major benefits of participation as
outlined by ADB are: (i) to improve project design and effectiveness, (ii) to
enhance the impact and sustainability of projects, (iii) to improve the
capacity of people and community organization (ADB, 2004).

Disaster recovery is not an exception. Large number of houses and
communities are damaged, destroyed, or affected by large-scale natural
disasters. Housing reconstruction has been a major task and is often raised
at the reconstruction/recovery phase. Quarantelli (1982) pointed out the
importance of house that it has many functions not only as a sheltering
space but also place of the consumption good, subject of speculation as an

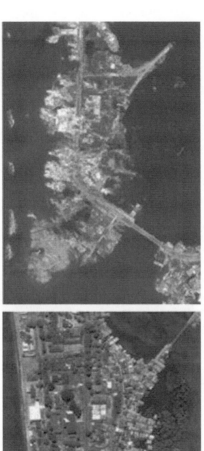

*Fig. 2.* Damage in Aceh Before and After the Disaster.

*Fig. 3.* Damage of Infrastructure and Houses in Aceh (*Source:* iws.ccccd.edu/rgrayson/PhysicalGeology.htm).

investment good, financial security for its owners, a medium through which social relations are produced and reproduced, a cultural structure that constructs the urban environment and a function that plays an important role for the people with the opportunities of living both in and outside of society. Therefore, housing reconstruction is at most people's interest.

However, participatory approach is not adopted in housing reconstruction in post-disaster recovery. Reviewing the housing reconstruction case studies of India, Indonesia, Colombia, and Turkey, (1) time, (2) quality (technical/safety), (3) socio-cultural concern, (4) management, and (5) cost of housing reconstruction, were raised as a major issues for participatory housing reconstruction.

In Aceh, the magnitude of the disaster was extremely large which caused not only many deaths, missing, and locally displaced persons (LDP) but also unrecoverable damage to houses and infrastructures that affected social, economical, and environmental aspects in the region. The Badan Rehabilitasi dan Rekonstruksi (BRR) estimated that 130,000 new houses be needed to be constructed and 85,000 needed to be repaired. Large number of houses and communities are damaged, destroyed, or affected by natural disasters in urban area.

Many organizations such as National governments, international organization, UN, bilateral organizations, and NGOs, intended to support housing reconstruction project taking community-based approach in accordance with reconstruction master plan prepared by the Government of Indonesia (GOI) that encourage to involve the community into the process (BAPPENAS, 2004). People's participation in the housing reconstruction project increases not only the community skills and ties but also the level of awareness to the earthquake-resistant house that will lead to future disaster risk reduction (Tas, Cosgun, & Tas, 2007).

How is the effort of mass-scale housing reconstruction in urban area after the large disaster? Next section introduces the major characteristics related to the housing reconstruction and the World Bank's (WB) effort on community-based housing recovery project after the Indian Ocean Tsunami in Aceh.

# 4. ACEH-SPECIFIC ISSUES RELATED TO HOUSING RECONSTRUCTION

There are several special characteristics of post-disaster scenario in Aceh, which affected the reconstruction after the Sumatra earthquake and Indian

Ocean Tsunami. Some of major characteristics specially related to the housing reconstruction are summarized below.

### 4.1. Former Conflict Area

Aceh has been a conflict area for long historical times. This affects the attitude of people and distrust in national government. In 1976, a rebel movement seeking independence from Indonesia emerged in Aceh. In 1989, GAM reemerged and the central government responded forcefully. Aceh was declared an area of military operation, giving the military wide authority to destroy the movement. Throughout the 1990s, the Acehnese were severely and violently repressed by the Indonesian government and military. Indonesian government established martial law in May 2003 to eradicate GAM and tension between Indonesian Government and GAM had continued until the Indian Ocean Tsunami-affected Aceh.

### 4.2. Identification of Victims and Land Tenure

The identification of victims was difficult since the whole family living in a house was lost or only one or few of the family was able to survive which is very distinctive of this disaster: land allocation, size of house to be reconstructed were affected and caused confusion. Also, many documents including maps and land titles were lost and ownership information became difficult to obtain. This raised not only the land tenure issues but also caused delay in the reconstruction process and caused inefficiency like double counting of beneficiaries.

### 4.3. Coordination

Many national and international organizations flowed aid into the site and intended to support housing reconstruction with different structure, mechanism and methods, which has caused different performances throughout the region. According to BRR report after one year, 100 organizations were involved in housing and it is likely that largest 15 organizations will account for over 80% of houses built. But still, many small organizations were building faster at these early stages and will account for more than half of the permanent houses completed in one year after the Tsunami. Since so many agencies got involved in housing, coordination has been a major challenge for the government and UN organization (BRR, 2006). However, the double counting which many victims registered for financial aid in more than one community caused confusion and one family getting several houses has already raised problem.

## *4.4. Governance*

Since all the governmental functions were affected by the disaster, the initial stage of coordination was conducted by the central government. Five months later, the GOI established BRR to coordinate the reconstruction process. Because of this delay in establishing the organization which is in charge of housing reconstruction, and limited capacity of officers without clear assessment and their own understanding and set of standards, there was confusion in the field and many organizations followed their own standards. It was so because the GOI or BRR delayed providing clear policy guidelines regarding the housing reconstructions to all the organization that conduct the housing reconstruction project in Aceh.

These factors and characteristics were intricately intertwined with each other and caused confusion among government, donor agencies, NGO, and local community. Also disorganized institutions and processes of reconstruction had largely affected the delay in the housing sector in Aceh. All the players had enormous pressure from the public to deliver the assistance. However, the devastation by the disaster was such that, which no one could have organized it in a smooth practice without preplanned scenario. For instance, successful housing reconstruction requires well-planned organizational design and processes, trained staffs and engineers, and land-use and spatial planning. Although several international donors have assisted the GOI and BRR for making the master plan for spatial planning and infrastructure development of the city, it took some time to complete it in the devastating situation.

# 5. POST-DISASTER HOUSING
# RECONSTRUCTION IN ACEH

As mentioned earlier, there are more than 100 organizations involved in housing reconstruction but largest 15 organizations accounted for over 80% of houses committed or built (BRR, 2005). Among others, UN-Habitat

***Table 2.***  Housing Reconstruction Units in Aceh and Nias (Units).

| House/Donor | New House | Repairs |
|---|---|---|
| Housing needs | 130,000 | 85,000 |
| Red Cross and Crescent | 34,000 | |
| Multi Donor Fund (WB project) | 6,000 | 18,000 |
| ADB | 11,000 | 5,000 |
| CRS | 6,000 | |
| IOM | 8–20,000 | |
| GTZ | 4,500 | 975 |
| CARE | 6,500 | |
| Habitat for Humanity | 7,500 | |
| World Vision | 4,066 | |
| Oxfam | 2,100 | |
| Samaritan purse | 2,500 | |
| UN Habitat | 4,745 | |
| UNHCR | 2,622 | |
| Save the Children | 4,000 | |
| Others | 24,200 | |
| Total | > 130,000 | 23,975 |

*Source:* BRR housing sector data collected directly from NGOs and donors (BRR, 2005).

and Multi Donor Fund (MDF) were the two main international agencies that have conducted large-scale community-based housing reconstruction. Specially, MDF collaboration with GOI established the organizational design and utilized local resources to link government, international aid organizations, and the local community. Table 2 shows the donor contributions and the number of new and repair house units.

MDF (WB project) accounted for about 6% of the total new houses to be contracted (the number is later adjusted to new house 8,000 units based on the local needs). The number of house changed in the course of progress. For instance, MDF increased number of new houses from 6,000 to 8,000 on the other hand, number of repaired houses was reduced.

Now closely look at this approach and outline the overall rehabilitation process. Following the unprecedented worldwide support for the victims of the Indian Ocean Tsunami and earthquake, the GOI and the International Community established the MDF to assist in the coordination of funds made available for post-disaster reconstruction (Multi Donor Fund, 2006). The fund pools approximately $650 million of pledges from 15 bilateral and multilateral donors. The projects planned include housing reconstruction, livelihood rebuilding, public service restoring, economy, and sustainable environmental growth support. As a part of housing reconstruction and repair effort, the WB as the main coordinator of MDF has supported the GOI, namely the ministry of public works, to implement the community-based settlement rehabilitation and reconstruction project in NAD and NIAS.

## 5.1. Organizational Structure

In order to coordinate the housing reconstruction process, WB established the implementation structure which was based on the WB poverty alleviation projects which had already been implemented as GOI project since long time and were called Kecamatan development project (KDP) and urban poverty project (UPP). Both projects were WB's assistance program to form the community driven development platform in Indonesia and it was also implemented in Aceh Province (Fig. 4).

The implementation agency of the community-based housing reconstruction project was organized to link government, international donor, and the community as beneficiaries of housing reconstruction. In each ward or village, a village level implementation group selected by the village committee was made responsible for housing reconstruction activities. The housing group was the core group to implement all the project processes with housing facilitator (HF) and also to open a group bank account to manage the fund.

HFs in the field played an important role in supporting socialization process of the community and giving technical verification of housing grant activities and endorsing disbursements requested by the donor. In other words, HF played an intermediate role linking community and donor organizations and government. Their work included to explain the participatory housing reconstruction project, help community to organize groups, support making community plan and drawing the design, prepare the proposal and checking the quality of the construction process. HFs were assigned to villages after receiving technical training including assessment, planning, construction management, information management, etc., by one to several weeks, organized by the BRR which was funded by WB.

In Aceh, HFs were recruited from architectural and engineering backgrounds not only from Aceh province but also from other areas such as central Java and Jakarta. Also, many of them are freshly graduated or years of few experiences in the field.

HFs formed a group which consisted of one senior facilitator and around five facilitators to manage around 200 housing projects that depended on

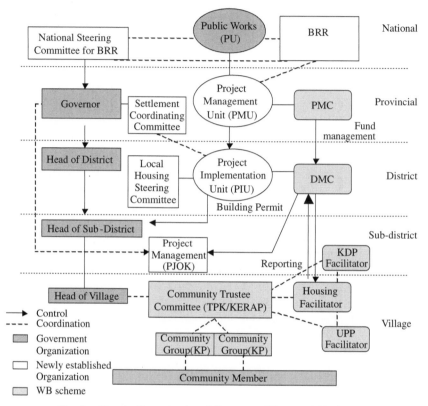

*Fig. 4.* Simple Organizational Structure (*Source:* WB, 2005).

the area and number of houses. HFs were required to prepare weekly reports to give up to date progress of the project which was sent to senior facilitator and was further submitted to consultants who managed at district and provincial levels.

HFs were the one who directly dealt with the community and their role was to ensure that the social concern is met, technical and quality of house is managed and time and schedule is on truck.

When actual construction started, HF was also in charge, together with community group to control the quality of construction. In Aceh case, most of the construction was done by the contractor rather than the community members and actually participated in the construction processes. This could be the special characteristics of urban area. Many of house owners do not have the skill to construct their houses while some of local community still practice construction or at least part of construction work by themselves. Therefore, in urban community, housing reconstruction had to depend on the contractors. In other words, the management and quality control from the technical person became more important.

### 5.2. Processes

The system that supports local communities to conduct community-based housing reconstruction and community need to go through discussion among community members to reach agreement on community leader, the structure of a house and sizes, etc., and this process is essential to community-based reconstruction process. Also it is important for all community members to understand and agree on proper techniques that are used to reconstruct houses and are essential for the reconstruction process.

The project implementation processes are organized into several activities. The process and conditions of housing project implementation vary depending on the land availability, assessment results, etc. However, this is the basic process that community needs to follow and HF-supported communities to conduct the following activities.

(1) Community organization, (2) formulation of committee and working group, (3) community self-survey, (4) community settlement plan, (5) group implementation plan, (6) sign of community support program (CSP) and housing grant application, (7) opening group bank account, and (8) construction activities. These steps are shown with photos in Fig. 5.

It started from forming the working group (KP) of 5–15 households. The community was first asked to form community working groups (KP) and housing reconstruction project committee (KERAP). In UPP project, this committee is called "TPK" but since housing reconstruction project is not permanent project and needed quick decision making, the process of selecting committee member sometimes depended on local existing organization, therefore, the project committee was named KERAP to distinguish from TPK. Also this process is vice versa, in some areas where committee already existed, committee selected the working group (KP).

Then, the community started a self-survey to identify the damage and losses of the houses. In some areas, satellite photos were provided to plot their own land. By identifying the people and family still remaining and plot their own land, community was able to start developing community settlement plan. If land is totally washed away by the tsunami, the process of identifying the land is the most concerning first process. In less-affected

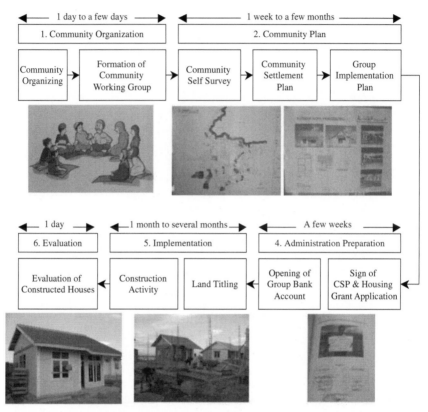

*Fig. 5.* Processes of Participatory Housing Reconstruction in Aceh (*Source:* WB, 2005, modified by author).

areas, in terms of land, plotting the land was completed easier. In community settlement plan, the community discussed location, structure and design of house, public space and roads, etc. The result of community consolidation was posted on the information board for about two weeks to share the information and get an agreement from the community.

After the community settlement plan is completed, the community starts making the implementation plan, how to manage the funds and construction of the houses. During this time, community worked together with facilitators to prepare the proposal for housing. The community group (KP) is asked to open their group account and manage it as a cooperate responsibility. When the proposal is approved, funds are disbursed to their bank account.

After land titling is acquired, the construction process will begin. During and after the completion of housing reconstruction, quality control is conducted by the community together with support from HF to complete house reconstruction.

Even though Aceh is one of the urban areas but because of the conflict situation, it kept strong community ties and strong leadership by the community or village leader. In many urban society community ties are loosen up but Aceh was the special case even the community is becoming the urbanized society. However, tsunami-affected people were placed in different temporary shelters and some people stayed at their family houses. In many cases, people in the community were not able to live close to their original residence. This situation made them difficult to participate in the processes of housing reconstruction.

## 5.3. Timeline of Operation

Based on the interview with WB staff and local consultants, the timeline of operation by WB housing is illustrated. First, the government conducted assessments soon after the disaster, data was gathered from local village leaders and local government office. Similar to UPP/KDP housing and infrastructure project, many NGOs started their housing reconstruction in the second half of 2005 and 2006. UPP/KDP projects had existing budgets available, therefore, they started socialization of community and constructed housing and surrounding infrastructure project.

MDF housing reconstruction project started in year 2006, which was slow compared with UN habitat, Asian Development Bank, and among other NGOs and donors. Proposals for housing reconstruction were prepared in September of 2005, which was approved in March 2006. Soon after the approval, HFs were recruited and training was conducted.

In the end of April 2006, first groups of HFs started the socializing process at the village level. It took about three months to receive the first disbursement. About seven months later, first house was completed by using this process. As a total, it took about two years to complete 1st house by WB after the disaster. The process is still under the progress after three years (January 2008) have passed. This delay has several reasons but major reasons could be the (1) devastation due to the disaster, (2) delay in

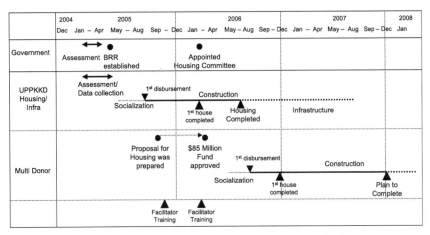

*Fig. 6.* Timeline of WB Housing Reconstruction Project.

establishing the governmental organization which could take lead and decide the policy, (3) delay in establishing the organizational structure and processes with skilled facilitator, and (4) fund management and agreement with government.

Fig. 6 shows the timeline of WB housing reconstruction project.

According to the interview with house owners in 2007, very low percentage of house owners was actually living in the house that was completed. The main reason was that basic infrastructure such as electricity and water was not completed yet and they were not able to move in. This situation clearly explains that housing reconstruction had to be conducted together with basic infrastructure.

### 5.4. Management Information System (MIS)

The WB established management information system called MIS to manage housing reconstruction updates by the database, which is later open to the web-based system. In MIS, the name of beneficiary, progress of housing reconstruction, name of facilitator in charge, etc., can be checked. This helps to manage the implementation of the project more easily and allows taking a direct contact with facilitators and beneficiaries from the office to confirm the situation. Also, in this system, problems and claims from facilitator or house owner is updated for risk management.

## 5.5. Contribution to Five Factors

The contribution to the five key factors from the management side and people's participation side were evaluated and summarized based on the questionnaire survey conducted targeting HFs and beneficiaries of the WB's housing reconstruction project.

The WB's participatory housing reconstruction project established a scheme to encourage the people in the community to participate in the project and it is evaluated that the management side contributed in all five factors. Also, the people in the community participated in the project process and it is evaluated that people contributed in some of factors. Table 3 shows the summary of major issues and related factors and evaluation in Aceh.

***Table 3.*** Major Issues and Related Factors and Evaluation.

| Issue | Item | Management | People |
|---|---|---|---|
| Time/speed | Establishing organizational structure and process | Fair (slow) | – |
| Quality (technical/ safety) | Technical facilitator<br>Process management<br>Participation in the housing reconstruction process increased people's interest and awareness<br>Awareness increased for earthquake resistant houses | Fair (no experience) | Fair/good (limited participation, contractor dependent) |
| Socio-cultural concern | Socialization process<br>Participating planning and construction process<br>Reflecting their needs and suggestions to planning and design<br>Good community relationship to make consensus building | Good | Good (processes participated) |
| Cost | Market price<br>Government policy<br>Labor availability | Fair (high) | – |
| Management | Technical facilitator<br>Management consultants<br>Information management system (MIS)<br>Cooperative responsibility | Fair (system not function well) | Fair/good (village leader or group leader had power) |
| Government leadership | Strong leadership<br>Clear policy and planning | Bad (weak) | |
| Community ties | Community ties and cooperation | | Good (but limited) |

From the evaluation, several external factors that influenced the performance of the housing reconstruction project were pointed out as listed below.

- Damage of disaster and post-disaster situation
- Government's leadership
- Community's socio-cultural and economical background
- Existing community ties and attitude of community
- Existing community skill

## 6. CONCLUSION

Experiencing participatory housing reconstruction in Aceh gave many lessons and also it opened a door for a new era for adaptation of participatory approach in housing reconstruction in the file that was not very much favored in post-disaster recovery. Although many improvements and further careful evaluations are necessary, this study illustrated that WB's participatory housing reconstruction efforts contributed to five key factors of time/speed, quality (technical/safety), socio-cultural concern, management, and cost that were often raised as important issues in the post-disaster housing reconstruction. Also, the survey result shows that people consider building earthquake-resistant house as their main concern. In other words, increasing awareness of earthquake-resistant house and building one could contribute to reduce the urban risks in the disasters in future.

From the case study of Aceh, following points can be summarized:

- Establishing the organizational structure and process helped ensuring people's participation in housing reconstruction process
- HF-supported community in several ways such as technical, social, and management component
- People's participation varies depending on local situation
- Five factors are mutually dependent and each player contributes to ensure each factors.

It can be concluded that the participatory approach is effective in mass-scale housing reconstruction in post-disaster recovery. However, the balance of each players and five factor needs to be considered and adjusted depending on the local situation and the participation of the people need to be encouraged further.

One of the reason WB's housing reconstruction project was able to adopt the participatory approach to the project was that there was an existing community-based project which had been implemented for many years in Indonesia. The know-how and previous experiences helped this whole scheme and mechanism to work in the field. In other words, it is important to recognize that every day practice and preplanning are most effective in post-disaster situation in urban area.

## ACKNOWLEDGMENTS

The authors acknowledge the support from Kyoto University research funding, and logistics support from the World Bank and its partners in Aceh and Jakarta.

## REFERENCES

ADRC. Website http://www.adrc.or.jp/index.php and top 25 natural disasters in Indonesia according to number of killed (1901–2000) (accessed 6 Feb, 2008).

Asian Development Bank. (2004). Effectiveness of participatory approaches: Do the new approaches offer an effective solution to the conventional problem in rural development projects? Special Evaluation Study.

BAPPENAS. (2004). Indonesia: Notes on reconstruction the December 26, 2004, natural disaster. The consultative group on Indonesia 19–20 January 2005. Technical report prepared by BAPPENAS and the international donor committee (http://siteresources. worldbank.org/INTINDONESIA/Resources/Publication/280016-1106130305439/recon-struction_notes.pdf).

BRR. (2005). BRR policy guidelines for the provision of resettlement assistance to victims of the NAD/Nias tsunami and earthquakes.

BRR. (2006). Regulation of executing agency rehabilitation and reconstruction agency and the lives of the people of Nanggroe Aceh Darussalam Province and Nias Island, North Sumatra Province, Number: 19/Per/Bp-Brr/Iii/2006 on house rehabilitation assistance for the victims of earthquake and tsunami in Nanggroe Aceh Darussalam Province and Nias Island, North Sumatra Province.

CRED (Center for Research on Epidemiology of Disasters). (2006). Available at: http://www.cred.be/, accessed on 12th December 2006.

Inter-American Development Bank. (1997). Resource book on participation. Available at: http://www.iadb.org/aboutus/VI/resource_book/table_of_contents.cfm (Date Oct. 2007).

Japan International Cooperation Agency (JICA). (1995). Participation and good governance, section report.

Multi Donor Fund. (2006). Implementing projects, achieving results; 18 months of the multi donor fund for Aceh and Nias. Progress Report III, December 2006.

Quarantelli, E. L. (1982). *Sheltering and housing after major community disasters: Case studies and general conclusions*. Columbus, OH: Disaster Research Center, Ohio State University.

Shaw, R., Kobayashi, M., Kameda, H., Gupta, M., Sharma, A., Nakagawa, Y., & Banda, M. (2002). International cooperation in a post-disaster scenario: A case study from Gujarat, India. *Journal of Natural Disaster Science, 24*(2), 73–82.

Tas, N., Cosgun, N., & Tas, M. (2007). A qualitative evaluation of the after earthquake permanent housings in Turkey in terms of user satisfaction – Kocaeli, Gundugdu Permanent Housing Model. *Building and Environment, 42*, 3418–3431.

The World Bank. (2005). Project appraisal document for a proposed multi-donor trust fund for Aceh and North Sumatra Grant in the amount of US$85 million to the Republic of Indonesia for a community-based settlement rehabilitation and reconstruction project for Nanggroe Aceh Darussalam (NAD) and Nias, Phase 1, Report No: 33585-ID.

# SECTION II
# CASE STUDIES ON ENVIRONMENTAL
# RISK REDUCTION

# CHAPTER 13

# ECO-COMMUNITY AND ENVIRONMENTAL LEARNING IN NISHINOMIYA

Miki Yoshizumi

## ABSTRACT

*Nishinomiya City in Japan is one of the most successful cities in implementing eco-community and has served as a particularly influential model, especially through programs on Education for Sustainable Development (ESD) which the Japanese Ministry of the Environment recognized as the nationwide environmental education program. Nishinomiya City has been implementing a project, "Environmental Learning City," where community-based environmental management has been conducted through environmental education programs. And it established an NPO, "the Learning and Ecological Activities Foundation for Children (LEAF)," to facilitate the programs and build partnerships among citizens, businesses, and the local government. As a result, Nishinomiya's eco-community activities have been sustained, and not only environmental improvement but also social cohesion and mutual learning have been achieved.*

Urban Risk Reduction: An Asian Perspective
Community, Environment and Disaster Risk Management, Volume 1, 255–273
Copyright © 2012 by Emerald Group Publishing Limited
All rights of reproduction in any form reserved
ISSN: 2040-7262/doi: 10.1108/S2040-7262(2009)0000001017

# 1. INTRODUCTION

As cities all over the world have urbanized rapidly after the industrial revolution, most cities have been confronted with various environmental problems, including poor air and water quality, high levels of traffic congestion and ambient noise, poor-quality built environment, derelict land, greenhouse gas emissions, and generation of waste and waste-water. These environmental problems threaten the livelihoods of people. Polluted air, water, and soil have an adverse effect on human health. Recently, it has been recognized that climate change caused by human activities such as overusing fossil fuel and deforestation, has increased environmental risk to natural disasters. According to the Third Assessment Report of IPCC, it is projected that the frequency and strength of extreme weather events would increase in the future due to climate change. As another notable characteristic of Asia and the Pacific regions, up to now, 90% of the world's climate-induced natural disasters have happened in the regions where as much as five hundred thousand people have lost their lives (Ancha, 2005).

These problems are caused by inadequate development plan, which is caused by lack of concern for such environmental problems. As people have been interested only in their own economic benefit, they have become uninterested in community and environmental problems. Governments tend to put their priority on economic issues, and put environmental policies to the back burner, because governments have a tendency to prioritize a policy in which the citizens are interested. For that reason, to tackle the environmental problems and achieve sustainable development, people should learn about environmental issues, be concerned with environmental problems, and act to solve the issues.

In order to raise awareness of environmental problems, education has been recognized as one of the key measures (UN, 1992; UNESCO, 2005; WCED, 1987). The United Nations has been an active advocate in stressing the importance of combining sustainable development and education, and launched the 10-year program "Education for Sustainable Development (ESD)." In addition, it is necessary for people to be interested in their own community in order that they become concerned with environmental problems. If people have not been concerned about their own community, and they do not have a chance to talk about neighboring environment with neighbors, consequently they become unconcerned about environmental issues. On the other hand, a new issue from the social dimension, like dilution of community relationships in urban areas, is becoming a serious problem. Besides, even if people think of environmental issues as serious issues, it is impossible for an individual to solve environmental problems such as polluted river and waste management. Consequently, community actions are very important in solving the environmental problems and impacting government policies. Because of this situation, public participation has been recognized as one of the most important tools to address environmental issues (EC, 1996). This is because local communities know what the problems are in their own areas and governments have limitations to tackle all problems. The community is thus a key actor in tackling environmental problems and achieving sustainable development. The community where people can learn environmental issues through citizen participation and partnership with governments is called an eco-community.

Nishinomiya City in Japan is one of the most successful cities in implementing eco-community and has served as a particularly influential model, especially through programs on ESD which the Japanese Ministry of the Environment recognized as the nationwide environmental education program. Nishinomiya City has been implementing a project, "Environmental Learning City," where community-based environmental management has been conducted through environmental education programs. And it established an NPO, "the Learning and Ecological Activities Foundation for Children (LEAF)," to facilitate the programs and build partnerships among citizens, businesses, and the local government (LEAF, 2004a, 2004b). As a result, Nishinomiya's eco-community activities have been sustained, and not only environmental improvement but also social cohesion and mutual learning have been achieved (Yoshizumi & Miyaguchi, 2005).

The purpose of this chapter is to investigate the key elements that are necessary for the realization of an eco-community by examining the case of a successful program in Nishinomiya City. The paper introduces the eco-community activities of Nishinomiya City within this context. By examining various initiatives of Nishinomiya City, key elements for achieving sustainable development are explored.

## 2. CASE STUDY OF NISHINOMIYA CITY

### *2.1. Background*

The city of Nishinomiya, with a population of approximately 450,000 and an area of 100.18 sq km, lies between Osaka and Kobe in the southeastern part of the Hyogo Prefecture. This is a city where, in 1962, community and local businesses, especially sake brewing industries, protested against the establishment of petroleum complexes and waterfront land reclamation schemes in order to conserve the quality of water in the community. Influenced by an increasing worldwide concern over environmental issues, a community-based environmental learning project called the Earth Watching Club (EWC) was launched in 1992 through the initiative of Mr. Masayoshi Ogawa of the Nishinomiya Municipal Government (LEAF, 2003a). The focus of this environmental program was activities targeting children and the youth.

The Great Hanshin-Awaji Earthquake of 1995, that resulted in over 6,000 casualties, was a turning point for community-based environmental learning projects such as EWC, which began to be perceived not only as effective tools for tackling environmental issues, but also for issues such as crime and natural disaster reduction with capacity building at the local level for disaster preparedness. As a result, the concepts of EWC were further developed and in 1998 led to the birth of a nonprofit organization called LEAF, whose aim is to contribute to the development of a sustainable society by building partnerships among citizens, businesses, and the local government (LEAF, 2004a).

### 2.2. NPO, "LEAF" as Facilitator for Developing Eco-Community

To achieve its stated goal of developing a sustainable society, LEAF initiated environmental learning activities in schools and in local communities, by targeting a wide range of citizens (LEAF, 2004a). In particular, they focus on youth and children as agents of change who will shape the future of their community. LEAF's approach to realizing this goal encompasses (1) establishment of partnerships with various civic groups, the private sector, and government agencies; (2) development of respect for the environment, including nature and culture; and (3) cultivation of a "self-learning ability" through which the individual's capacity to learn independently from the assistance of educational institutions is enhanced and extended to the informal arena of the household, the school, and the community. Specifically, LEAF aims to establish a system that enables people relatively unconcerned about environmental issues to participate in activities of environmental learning through various public events targeting a mass audience. Through their environmental learning activities, LEAF not only seeks to raise people's awareness of environmental issues, but also awareness about community development.

LEAF's operations are supported entirely by external funding, such as donations from members and corporations, as well as national and local government trust funds. Acknowledged as one of the most successful models of practice, LEAF was awarded the 5th Green Purchasing Award in 2002 and the Environmental Grand Prix 2004 for Local Municipalities from the Japanese government.

### 2.3. Activities of Eco-Community

Nishinomiya's various activities can be categorized into five types: (i) community-based education, (ii) nature experience activities, (iii) mutual learning programs, (iv) policy relevant activities, and (v) global partnership. The following section provides an overview of these and cites examples of activities under each category. (See Table 1 and Fig. 1 for an overview of Nishinomiya's activities.)

#### 2.3.1. Community-Based Education

Through their community-based education programs, LEAF invites participants to learn about both global and local environments through active communication at the local level. One of the projects in this category is called the *Eco-Card* (Table 2). This project aims to forge links between school, family, and community through so-called *Eco-Actions*. All elementary school children in Nishinomiya (24,000 enrollment) receive an Eco-Card annually. When children take part in environmentally friendly activities (Eco-Actions), such as purchasing an eco-friendly product or separating recyclable goods in

***Table 1.*** Activities on Environmental Learning in Nishinomiya.

| | |
|---|---|
| 1989 | Citizens' Nature Survey |
| 1990 | Citizens' Nature Survey |
| 1992 | Earth Watching Club Nishinomiya: Model of the Japanese ministry of environment program "Eco-club" |
| 1998 | Established an NPO, "LEAF" |
| 2002 | Established the Environmental Learning City Steering Committee of Nishinomiya City |
| 2003 | Environmental Learning City Declaration |
| 2005 | Published the New Environmental Plan |
| | Enacted city ordinances on the environment |
| | Eco-community project launched |
| | Environmental Plan Steering Partnership Council |
| | Eco-community Workshops were held in 8 areas |
| 2006 | Launched Eco-network meeting |
| | Launched three eco-community meetings |

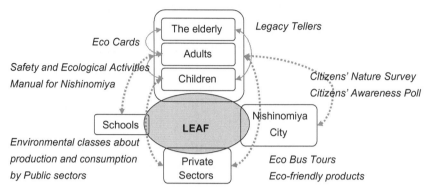

*Fig. 1.* Relationship between LEAF and Other Organizations (Yoshizumi, 2005).

the community, they get a stamp from one of 1,500 *Eco-Stamp Holders*, such as local school institutions, stationery shops, the city hall, and any other institution or adult who is part of the program. After collecting more than 10 eco-stamps on their Eco-Card, children are awarded the title of *Earth Ranger* for their eco-friendly actions. Over 2,000 children are authorized as Earth Rangers each year. In 2004, 2,048 Earth Rangers were delegated in Nishinomiya City alone, and 82,300 were delegated throughout Japan in the same year (Japanese Ministry of the Environment, 2005).

What is interesting about this activity is that these Eco-Stamp Holders decide *by themselves* whether an action by a child should be rewarded as an Eco-Action or not. Thus, while children actively search for what might be considered Eco-Actions, the stamp holders must also continue to learn and develop their ideas on what can be determined as Eco-Actions.

The Eco-Card program is further tailored for each segment of the school population. For example, in order to collect stamps, third and fourth grade students must conduct research and interviews with various people from the public and private sectors concerning environmental issues. The information gathered from these interviews are shared with the community through the *Eco-Messenger* program, which is a student-hosted radio show aired on a local FM station (Fig. 2).

In collaboration with schools, LEAF organizes special classes where students learn about environmental issues from different perspectives. One such class is called *Legacy Tellers* in which the elderly of the community talk about the environment when they were young. By listening to what these Legacy Tellers have experienced, children can compare environmental conditions between the present and the past. Also, children can learn how

***Table 2.*** List of Activities of Nishinomiya Facilitated by LEAF.

| Theme | Activities |
|---|---|
| I: Community-based education | Eco-Card<br>Let us find living things in each season<br>Legacy Tellers<br>Let us travel 50 years in a time machine<br>Walking Tour of Yamaguchi Community with Legacy Tellers<br>"Legacy Tellers" Training Seminar/Legacy Tellers Club<br>Overnight trip for elementary school children with legacy tellers<br>Organizing Eco-Community<br>Safety and Ecological Activities Manual for Nishinomiya<br>Training for local leaders of environmental learning |
| II: Nature experience activity | Walking Tour of Yamaguchi Community with Legacy Tellers<br>Walk along Ancient Shorelines<br>Re-discover Mountains and Rivers in Nishinomiya<br>Safety and Ecological Activities Manual for Nishinomiya<br>Let us find living things in each season<br>Management of Kabutoyama Nature House and Campsite<br>"Miyamizu Junior" Nature Observation Activities<br>"Let us Play Around at Kabutoyama Mountain" Project<br>Arima River Watching<br>Published "Becoming Friends with Nishinomiya's Rivers" |
| III: Mutual learning programs | Eco-Friendly Products<br>Seminars/lectures<br>Nishinomiya, a Story of Sake and Bottle<br>Eco Bus Tours (visiting company sites)<br>"Bus Tour Exploring Lifetime of Bottles," as a part of training for school teachers |
| IV: Policy relevance | Established Environmental Learning City Steering Committee<br>Organize Eco-Community<br>Supported to declare as "Environmental Learning City" in 2003, first case in Japan<br>Collaboration in the municipal Citizens' Nature Survey and the Citizens' Awareness Poll<br>Participation in "the Environmental Learning City Nishinomiya Partnership Program" |
| V: Global partnership | Organized an international conference for Asia Pacific (Eco-Club)<br>Chikyu Kids Environmental Network (www.chikyu-kids.net)<br>EWC Eco-Panel Exhibition<br>"Demonstrating Education for sustainability through community partnerships" joint project between Nishinomiya and Burlington, VT |

*Source:* LEAF (2004a).

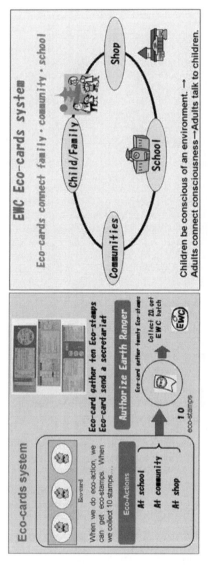

*Fig. 2.* Nishinomiya Eco-Card System (LEAF, 2004a).

the natural environment has changed by taking short excursions, called *town-watch walks*, to various local sites with the Legacy Tellers (LEAF, 2004a).

### 2.3.2. Nature Experience Activities
Nature experience activities allow children to experience the natural environment of their community. For example, the Miyamizu Junior Nature Observation Activities, a program entrusted by the Nishinomiya Board of Education, gives children the opportunity to observe the mountains, rivers, and sea in Nishinomiya through school excursions to these sites. Another project allows children to learn about nature in the mountains through hands-on games and exploratory activities that draw from aspects of the natural environment. Some of these activities incorporate aspects of the Legacy Tellers program through on-site activities that demonstrate how the elders interacted with the natural environment in their youth.

LEAF organizes training seminars for leaders of nature experience activities for community leaders from all over Japan. After the training seminars, leaders are encouraged to develop nature experience activities for their own communities.

### 2.3.3. Involvement of the Workforce
To encourage collaboration between the public and private sectors, Nishinomiya provides opportunities for corporations to become engaged in developing environmental learning programs for elementary and junior high school students. Corporations participate in the project through six different working groups whose themes include clothing, food, housing, energy, eco-friendly stationery, and bottles. Thus corporate employees at various levels are afforded an opportunity to learn about environmental issues through their presentations to children on environmentally friendly products (LEAF, 2003b).

### 2.3.4. Policy Relevant Activities
LEAF also actively involves itself with policy relevant activities that influence municipal development polices. For example, in order to reflect the views of the local community to the policy making level, LEAF conducted a Citizens' Nature Survey and a Citizens' Awareness Poll (City of Nishinomiya, 2003a, 2005). Based on its survey and poll of 5,085 people, including children and youth, LEAF prepared a report that represented the opinions of the local community. The report served as the driving force for the municipal government's revision of environmental policies and led to the

establishment of the new Nishinomiya Environmental Plan and Nishinomiya City Ordinance on city management, both of which were enacted in
March 2005. The Ordinance regulates, with legally binding force, day-to-
day activities that are not in line with environmental guidelines.

The format of the survey and poll succeeded in stimulating and increasing
public awareness on nature issues. They were designed in such a way that
those who were surveyed, numbering 3,993 teenagers and others ranging in
age from 7 to 81, had to investigate and report on local insects and plants in
the Nishinomiya vicinity. In doing so, the survey and poll stimulated
participants' awareness on nature, and thus their mind-set toward
environmental issues. Nishinomiya City has developed a web site with the
results of the surveys and polls conducted in 1991 and 2003, and people can
go online to learn about past and current conditions of the natural
environment in Nishinomiya City (City of Nishinomiya, 2003b). According
to the results of the survey, those who participated reported a deeper
understanding and appreciation of the local natural environment, including
their knowledge of the fish, birds, insects, and plants of Nishinomiya.

In order to promote local participation and involvement in shaping
regional development policies by the municipal government, LEAF also
supported the establishment of the Environmental Learning City Steering
Committee of Nishinomiya, which consists of community leaders and
representatives of the private and public sectors. With the involvement of
this committee, in 2003 Nishinomiya was the first city in Japan to be
declared an "Environmental Learning City" (LEAF, 2004a).

### 2.3.5. Global Partnership

LEAF develops projects beyond the domestic level to foster global partnership
among children around the world. It organizes the Junior Eco-Club Asia-
Pacific Conference each year. In addition, LEAF has created The Chikyu Kids
Environmental Network, a database of children's environmental activities
around the world, spanning over 80 countries. LEAF has also coordinated
joint projects between Nishinomiya and Burlington, VT. These have included
such activities as promoting education for sustainability through community
partnerships (Institute of Sustainable Communities, 2002).

### 2.4. Development of the Framework for Nishinomiya Eco-Community

Nishinomiya City has built a framework for the Nishinomiya Eco-
community. The framework is called the Nishinomiya Environmental

Learning City Partnership which consists of eco-community, eco-network, and the Nishinomiya city government. The members of eco-community are residents in each high school area who are the main actors to promote environmental learning programs and participatory town planning for sustainable development. The eco-network is made up of community groups, school teachers, business sectors, and the city government, and tries to develop a framework for the environmental learning city and programs of education for sustainable development. Moreover, environmental learning steering partnership council was established to coordinate ideas and activities of the eco-community, eco-network, and city government that are built up by leaders of community groups, environmental experts, business sectors, and the city government. Fig. 3 shows the structure of the framework.

Fig. 4 shows the framework of the eco-community. Nishinomiya City thinks that activities of the eco-community are not just a single action, but rather a series of continuous actions particularly combined with learning process.

Town-watching, which is recognized as a tool in participatory town planning, is a key to building an eco-community in Nishinomiya. In town-watching, communities walk around their own areas; learn issues in their own areas which are not only problems but also good points such as historical buildings, beautiful nature, and attractive shops; and develop goal and community action plan toward sustainable development. The objectives

*Fig. 3.* Partnership of Nishinomiya Eco-Community.

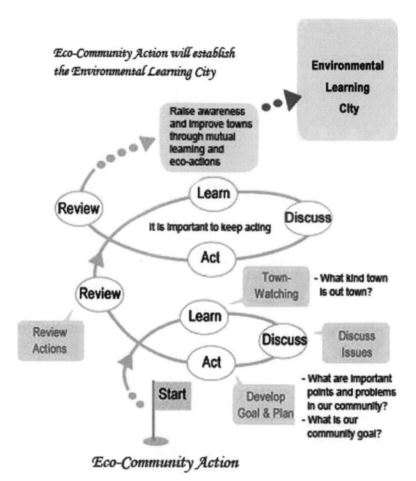

*Fig. 4.*   Evolutionary Process of Nishinomiya Eco-Community (*Source:* Yoshizumi,
based on LEAF, 2004a).

of the town-watching are to:

- Recognize and re-acknowledge communities
- Learn issues in community areas (not only problems but also positive elements)
- Raise awareness about various related issues
- Start actions to solve problems and preserve the positive traits of the community

*Fig. 5.*   Process of Town-Watching.

Fig. 5 shows the process of the town-watching. The important point is that as a learning process, town-watching is not a single action but a series of continuous actions.

Nishinomiya City has already held "Environmental Town-Planning Workshop" in eight sites to promote the eco-community activities. It also established a program to give subsidy to communities that would like to start eco-community. And three communities have already started the eco-community programs by themselves as of 2006.

# 3. ANALYSIS OF THE NISHINOMIYA ACTIVITIES

The four pillars of ESD, as outlined by UNESCO (2003) and described here earlier, provide a useful framework through which to reflect on the accomplishments of Nishinomiya toward achieving ESD. This section discusses Nishinomiya initiatives in the light of these domains of action.

## 3.1. Basic Education

Whereas traditional educational methods in Japan have served primarily to increase basic literacy and numeracy among children, the activities of Nishinomiya have embraced basic education and extended beyond to impart an understanding of the nuanced interaction between the economic, social, and environmental dimensions central to sustainable development. Central to this process is the development of the self-learning capacities of range of participants, as well as the sharing of knowledge, values, and skills toward community decision-making and action involving a variety of stakeholders.

The Eco-Card program, for example, as well as the establishment of the Environmental Learning City Steering Committee are illustrations of how providing a milieu in which sharing knowledge and values between school children and other community members can extend learning beyond the classroom into the informal sector. In addition, Nishinomiya's introduction of the Citizens' Nature Survey and the Citizens' Awareness Poll encouraged residents to learn more about their local environment.

### 3.2. Developing Public Awareness and Understanding of Sustainability

LEAF's engagement of a wide range of citizens has been a critical feature in implementing ESD. Youth and children, commonly viewed as the agents of behavioral change, are typical targets of educational programs. However, LEAF's outreach has extended beyond these participants to sectors of the workforce and the community. Seminars organized in collaboration with private companies have shown that such activities are effective, not only in raising awareness of those students involved, but also in helping employees within such companies to become more environmentally conscious and aware of important elements of sustainable development, such as the intricate interaction between economic activities and social and environmental consequences. This leads to mutual learning opportunities for both students and participating corporate employees.

In 2004, approximately 2,000 Earth Rangers were delegated through the Eco-Card project and about 90 private companies engaged in Nishinomiya's activities. This increase in participation is one indicator that Nishinomiya has been successful in raising public awareness through its various activities. Furthermore, the use of a public radio station as one of the rewards for the Eco-Card activity, has proved to be an effective method for raising public awareness at the local level. To date, more than 1,400 elementary students had joined the radio programs which they have developed themselves. In addition, introducing children to environmental learning activities from various parts of the world, organizing international conferences, and building a global database of youth environmental networks and activities, has expanded the potential for developing awareness and global friendship among children in over 80 countries. Public awareness is therefore an integral component of Nishinomiya activities.

### 3.3. Training

LEAF has actively sought to develop the training component of its initiatives. To this end, LEAF has organized seminars on environmental learning for various groups of citizens and a variety of stakeholders, such as children, youths, adults, the elderly, school teachers, government officers, and private companies, in an effort to enhance the sharing of knowledge, skills, and values for sustainable development at the local level. The seminars and environmental learning programs organized in collaboration with the private sector for elementary students have gained much popularity. At present, approximately 90 private companies have joined the LEAF program. Such activities illustrate the program's engagement in providing continuous training opportunities.

### 3.4. Reorienting Existing Education Programs

At present, Nishinomiya activities do not touch upon the reorientation of existing school curricula, which is considered one of the core elements in realizing ESD (UNESCO, 2005). Although the majority of Nishinomiya activities take place in school, they are not incorporated into the school curriculum itself. Nishinomiya City government involves school teachers, various civil groups, and the private sector; however, mere involvement may not be sufficient to produce a lasting impact on the community. Integrating these community-based environmental learning activities into the school curriculum could provide further reinforcement and development of core concepts and skills.

Analyzing Nishinomiya activities within the UNESCO's framework for ESD provides confirmation of the components of an effective program. However, it also reveals several aspects for further development. The first of these is the need to incorporate ESD programs into formal curricula for reinforcement purposes. Second, while LEAF is involved in several public awareness campaigns, more can be done. For example, the Eco-Messenger program makes excellent use of a local radio station; however, exposure to the public is still limited as the program is not aired regularly. Not only should there be an increase in the frequency of the radio show, but it should also target a wider audience, to include adolescents and adults. Finally, educating the media is of crucial importance. Involving media providers themselves into the ESD program may encourage them to incorporate sustainable development issues into a larger number of awareness programs.

Our analysis of Nishinomiya activities suggests that while there are many underlying components for implementing ESD, the most important element is establishing a mutual learning environment. Mutual learning helps develop public awareness of social, economic, and environmental issues and leads to establishing networks of various stakeholders including students, local residents, local governments, NPOs, and the private sector, allowing them to discuss and address the issues on the same table. Such an environment promotes participation of stakeholders and improves the capacity of participants to learn and address environment and development issues, thus avoiding a common pitfall for many ESD programs – the lack of common terminology and vision, and clear channels of communication.

### 3.5. Reducing Environmental Risks

The activities in Nishinomiya have produced several outcomes to reduce environmental risks through raising environmental awareness. The amount of solid waste per person has decreased since 1997. Green spaces, open spaces, and parks have increased, especially since 1992. It is particularly worth noting that only Nishinomiya, among the cities between Osaka and Kobe, has a natural beach. Besides, air and water pollution level in Nishonimiya has been lower than the national figures.

Nishinomiya has had various natural disasters. In particular, floods had often happened in Nishinomiya, which has 17 class B rivers and 634 regular rivers. After the Great Hanshin-Awaji Earthquake occurred in 1995, Nishinomiya launched the Legacy Tellers activities and developed the "Safety and Ecological Activities Manual for Nishinomiya." By learning geography and history in Nishinomiya in these activities, people in Nishinomiya have learned how people had coped with floods and where the risks are, particularly because some areas which were once sea areas had incurred terrible damages during the Great Hanshin-Awaji Earthquake.

In addition, LEAF developed a webpage, "Bulletin Board of Eco-community Nishinomiya." The activities, progress, and achievements in each area are posted on the web site. People can understand activity condition of their own area, which contributes to an increase in their motivation.

### 3.6. Building Sustainable System Through Partnerships

Nishinomiya environmental learning program was launched in 1992 through the initiative of Mr. Masayoshi Ogawa of the Nishinomiya Municipal Government. He established LEAF to facilitate and promote the environmental activities in Nishinomiya. LEAF has played the role of a facilitator in the activities, involving other citizen groups, schools, private sectors, and national government as well as Nishinomiya City government. LEAF develops activity proposals, attracts people to the activities, facilitates activities, and gives advice on environmental policies of Nishinomiya City government. These days, LEAF has worked not only for Nishinomiya but also for the Japanese Ministry of Environment, Japanese companies such as Kirin Co. and House Co., international organizations such as JICA (Japanese International Corporate Agency) and UNU (United Nations University).

## 4. CONCLUSION

Urban population is growing at a much faster rate than the population as a whole, and by the early years of the 21st century, most of the people in the world will be living in urban areas (UNFPA, 1996). Various urban risks caused by natural disasters and environmental issues have occurred, and the damages to increasing population of urban areas have worsened. In particular, people who live in vulnerable areas, such as people from low-income groups and young people, are easily affected by the urban risks.

In the disaster and environmental management fields, it is recognized that community mutual cooperation can contribute to reducing the risks. However, people in urban areas tend to avoid contacting neighbors and there are few local community activities. As people in urban areas are apt to be interested in their career success and earning money for their own families, it becomes more difficult to promote citizen participation into activities organized by local governments. In these urban areas, damages from urban risks may get worse than that in rural areas.

In view of this, there are lessons learned from the Nishinomiya case study. The analysis of Nishinomiya activities underscores the importance of creating public participation, learning process, and mutual learning environment involving a variety of stakeholders. Unless people interact, learn, and transfer knowledge and values to one another, it will be extremely difficult to build the capacity to realize an eco-community. An efficient way to realize an eco-community is to build such capacity at the local level, rather than through top-down decisions and regulations. LEAF provides such environment for members of the public and private sectors, including children, the youth, the elderly, and other stakeholders such as NPOs.

UNESCO's vision of ESD includes both formal and informal education. In this respect, however, the LEAF program faces the challenge of reorienting school curricula. Nishinomiya activities rely on the participation of people who are already interested in ESD to some extent. At present, they do not reach out to those individuals who are unaware of the issues of sustainable development. There is also a problem of the government's vertical administrative structure, where officers working on city planning and economic development are indifferent to environmental learning. Thus, it is important to institutionalize eco-community at the government administrative level so that more people are given opportunities to participate in eco-community programs. For that, further discussion with the city government and its policy-makers is needed.

While this study of Nishinomiya suggests several effective practical features of a working eco-community model based on the broadly defined and agreed upon theoretical principles of the eco-community, further comparative study of eco-community initiatives in Japan and elsewhere could yield interesting findings regarding common core elements of successful eco-community program design across varying local contexts. Such findings could point to interesting generalized models for modification and local adoption. It is hoped that the current case study contributes in part to this end.

## REFERENCES

Ancha, S. (2005). What's new from IGES? IGES Newsletter, Hayama.

City of Nishinomiya. (2003a). *Civil nature survey in Nishinomiya: Let's find living matters in Nishinomiya*. Nishinomiya, Japan: City of Nishinomiya.

City of Nishinomiya. (2003b). Results of the survey on the local environment. [Online]. Available at: http://ikimono.leaf.or.jp/

City of Nishinomiya. (2005). *New environmental plan for Nishinomiya*. Nishinomiya, Japan: City of Nishinomiya.

European Community. (1996). *European sustainable cities report*. Brussels: European Community Press.

Institute for Sustainable Communities. (2002). *Renkei: Demonstrating education for sustainability through community partnerships*. Vermont: Institute for Sustainable Communities.

Japanese Ministry of the Environment. (2005). *Environmental education and learning in the years to come: Towards sustainable society*. Tokyo, Japan: Japanese Ministry of Environment.

Learning and Ecological Activities Foundation for Children. (2003a). *Eco watching club. Nishinomiya activities report*. Nishinomiya, Japan: LEAF Press.

Learning and Ecological Activities Foundation for Children. (2003b). *Environmental learning assistance of corporate sectors*. Nishinomiya, Japan: LEAF Press.

Learning and Ecological Activities Foundation for Children. (2004a). *Annual action report*. Nishinomiya, Japan: LEAF Press.

Learning and Ecological Activities Foundation for Children. (2004b). *Becoming friends with Nishinomiya's rivers*. Nishinomiya, Japan: International Soro-putimisuto Nishinomiya.

UNESCO. (2003). *United Nations Decade of Education for Sustainable Development (January 2005–December 2014): Framework for a draft international implementation scheme*. Paris: UNESCO.

UNESCO. (2005). Education for sustainable development. [Online]. Available at: http://portal. unesco.org/education/en/ev.php-URL_ID = 27234&URL_DO = DO_TOPIC&URL_ SECTION = 201.html

United Nations. (1992). Agenda 21. [Online]. Available at: http://www.un.org/esa/sustdev/ documents/agenda21/index.htm

United Nations Population Fund. (1996). State of World Population 1996: Changing places: Population, development and the urban future. [Online]. Available at: http:// www.unfpa.org/swp/1996/index.htm

World Commission on Environment and Development. (1987). *Our common future.* New York: Oxford University Press.

Yoshizumi, M., & Miyaguchi, T. (2005). Realizing the education for sustainable development in Japan: A case study of Nishinomiya City. Education for sustainable development: Changes and challenges. *Current Issues in Comparative Education, 7*(2), 22–31.

Yoshizumi, M. (2005). *Challenge on learning activities for sustainable society in Nishinomiya.* Kyoto, Japan: UNESCO and Kyoto University.

# CHAPTER 14

# CONCEPTUALIZING URBAN ECO-VILLAGE IN KAMPONG BAHRU

Rajib Shaw, Siti Omar,
Miki Yoshizumi and Noriati Mat So

## ABSTRACT

*Kampong Bahru is located at the heart of the "golden triangle" of Kuala Lumpur, the capital city of Malaysia. The Settlement was established in 1899 as a result of the expressed desire of the Resident General and the British Resident of Selangor. Initially its objectives were: to educate the children of Malays, to take part in the administration, and to enable them to reap some of the advantages of the prosperity. The new settlement is known as Kampong Bahru (New Village). This chapter describes new innovative ways to revitalize community ties in the urban village context of Kampong Bahru. The concept of eco-communities is analyzed and specific suggested actions are presented.*

Urban Risk Reduction: An Asian Perspective
Community, Environment and Disaster Risk Management, Volume 1, 275–294
Copyright © 2012 by Emerald Group Publishing Limited
ISSN: 2040-7262/doi: 10.1108/S2040-7262(2009)0000001018

# 1. INTRODUCTION: COMMON URBAN ENVIRONMENTAL ISSUES

Cities all over the world are being urbanized rapidly after the industrial revolution, most cities have confronted a variety of environmental problems; to name a few, they are such problems as poor air and water quality, high levels of traffic congestion and ambient noise, poor-quality built environment, derelict land, greenhouse gas emissions, urban sprawl, generation of waste and wastewater.

In particular, cities in the developing world face problems related to the living conditions in which the urban population lives. In the context of urban cities in the developing world, it can be narrowed to the quality of life of living population in the cities. Basically, examples of environmental issues in urban cities include problems such as pollution of local waterways and unfilled land due to uncontrolled release of wastewater, unsanitary conditions of many low-income settlements, low-level of urban solid waste collection, amounts of industrial hazardous waste, or air pollution. These problems are caused by inadequate development plan to avoid the environmental problems as well as urban poverty such as a lack of access to basic services (Davis, 2006).

The environmental and disaster problems in cities are particularly complex as their causes are interrelated. The environmental and disaster problems have an adverse effect on not only health, but also economic activities and social issues. For example, problems related to a poor-quality built environment are often linked to underlying socio-economic problems. In addition, a new issue from social dimension like dilution of community relationships in urban areas is becoming a serious problem. Such dilution of community adversely impacts environmental problems and obstructs implementation of a sustainable city. Although the problems described above are the burning issues related to the urban environment, a few good concepts to solve such issues are observed in the urban setting.

In this chapter, a case study is presented from Kampong Bahru of Kuala Lumpur in Malaysia. Kampong Bahru is an urban village just north of the central part of Kuala Lumpur. The case study demonstrates a unique approach of eco-village conceptualization in Kampong Bahru.

# 2. ECO-VILLAGE: CONCEPT AND EVOLUTION

Ideas to tackle the problems that arose as a result of prioritizing human economic development, and to create villages, where well being of people is achieved, by themselves have emerged. As one of realizations of the ideas, movement of "eco-villages" has started and the eco-villages have been established all over the world. Each village addresses different issues such as the environmental, social, and/or economic issues, pursuing goal of sustainable development and true meaning of "wealth." The eco-villages have been currently drawing attention as archetypal "models" for sustainable societies. In order to explore its significance and to consider its future developments, this paper examines several eco-villages all over the world, as existing examples of possible sustainable societies (Yoshizumi, 2004). The construction of eco-villages all over the world has begun first as an antithesis to the modern forms of industrialization. It seems that there are five different patterns of development, as the earlier attempts became today's eco-villages (see Fig. 1).

The first was E. Howard's Garden City theory, which was an attempt to solve the problems of urbanization. The solution to the environmental and social problems in large cities is said to lie not in centralization but rather in diversification, in urban planning. Such diversification creates cities that are "human scale" and do not negatively affect the natural environment, and such cities are connected through public transportation. In each of the cities the infrastructure and food production facilities are well organized – the patterns of production and consumption are ideally self-sustaining. In this conception, Garden City theory, people escape large-scale cities and live in appropriate-scale cities in balance with nature and lead sustainable lives, can be said to be one of the origins of the eco-village movement.

Next there is a method of society building, based on the Steiner education system in Germany. In this system, society is built through human communication – people work together toward building a society, so that they can learn from one another and help and care for each other. Particularly well known is "Camp Hill," where the disabled and healthy people work together and cocreate the community.

The third approach aims to create a "humaine society," which attempts to overcome the disappointment felt in modern societies based on large-scale industrialization. The attempt to lead a lifestyle in coexistence with nature, stemming from the Hippie movement in the United States in the 1960s, had a large impact on the society at that time. Today there are numerous eco-villages, for example, in the United States, which are based on the ideal of living in rural areas or moving to the developing countries.

Fourth, there is an attempt to revitalize agriculture. As the economic focus shifts toward service-based economy, the tertiary industry, the

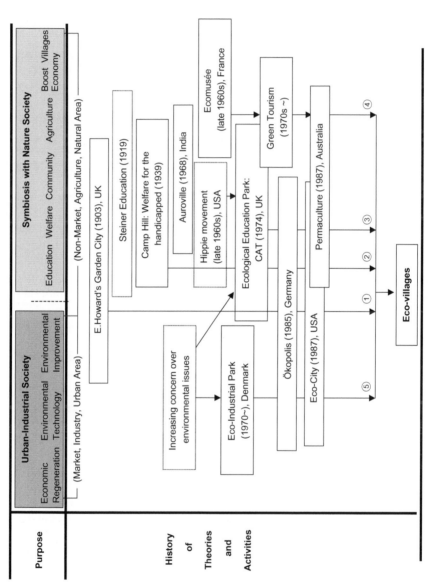

*Fig. 1.* Formations of Eco-Societies (Yoshizumi, 2004).

declination of agricultural villages became a problem. In order to revitalize the villages, various means, such as green-tourism and agro-tourism, were planned; in these types of tourism, the city dwellers might return to the more leisurely life-tempo of the villages, or they refresh themselves by staying in the villages as "tourists" and experiencing agriculture, or they learn the importance of agriculture through experience. Also "Permaculture," which began in Australia, focuses on the importance of the maintenance of human life stemming from nature as experienced in agriculture, and it aims to lead a sustainable way of life by employing non-harmful technologies that utilize the natural workings of nature. This agricultural method has been an important element among eco-villages.

The fifth pattern focuses on establishing space for environmental renewal and education; this was in response to the environmental problems occurring since the late 1960s. There are many favorable examples of developing eco-industrial parks at the former sites of industrial complex in Europe. In Japan also there are Japanese eco-town industries that aims for zero-emission environment in industrial housing developments. In addition, unsuccessful resort area developments in the mountain regions have lead to various revitalization efforts, and in doing so various attempts are under way for developing sustainable eco-villages that integrate environmental education and welfare facilities.

As seen above, there have been several different patterns of eco-villages around the world. In recent years they have come together to form a network, and in 1990, in Denmark, a global-scale network called "Global Eco-village Network" was established. The Global Eco-village Network is a global confederation of people and communities that meet and share their ideas, exchange technologies, develop cultural and educational exchanges, directories and newsletters, and are dedicated to restoring the land and living "sustainable plus" lives by putting more back into the environment than we take out.

In order to solve the problems resulted from prioritizing human economic development to build sustainable cities, various "eco-villages" all over the world came to be established. According to the Global Eco-village Network, "Eco-villages are urban or rural communities of people, who strive to integrate a supportive social environment with a low-impact way of life." Each village addresses different issues such as the environmental problems, social problems, and/or economic problems. But also commonly they share the goal of sustainable development and the pursuit of the true meaning of "wealth." In this light it can be said that today's attempts at eco-villages can be viewed as archetypal "models" for sustainable societies.

## 3. ENVIRONMENTAL LEARNING AND
## SOCIAL CAPITAL

Learning, including formal education, public awareness and training, should be recognized as a process by which human beings and societies can reach their fullest potential. Environmental learning is critical for promoting sustainable development and improving the capacity of the people to address environment and development issues. Communication is the art of expressing and exchanging ideas in speech or writing, or in action. A combination of learning and communication leads to action.

Environmental learning incorporates a human component in exploring environmental problems and their solutions. Environmental solutions are not only scientific, but they also include historical, political, economic, social, cultural, and ethical perspectives. This also implies that the environment includes both built and natural environment. Therefore, environmental learning has following characteristics:

- Rests on a foundation of knowledge about social and ecological systems.
- Knowledge lays the groundwork for analyzing environmental problems, resolving conflicts, and preventing new problems from arising.
- Learning includes the affective domain: the ethics, attitudes, values, and commitments necessary to build a sustainable society.

In addition, environmental learning connects the learning process into actions through community and governance. However, in most cases, due to lack of proper communication, the knowledge remains with a certain group of people, and is not reflected into action. Community refers to all different stakeholders in a certain location: people, government, nongovernment, academic, corporate sector, and many others. Governance includes strategy, policy, regulation, and resource. The interaction between community and governance is very important. The challenging issue of environmental management is turning knowledge into action, and this starts when the environmental issues are incorporated into individual, family, and community actions. Education, culture, and ethics play the most important role in this process.

It is argued that "increasing evidence shows that social cohesion is critical for societies to prosper economically and for development to be sustainable" (The World Bank, 1999). The race to achieve economic-social-political advancement continues to be the main agenda of developing country leaders. Today the role of government as the main provider of services for the citizens is continuously being reviewed. Public Sectors are being reconstructed to accommodate new ideas of administration. Some selected public sector agencies and organizations have been privatized, the local authority included, its exponents believe as the answer to the problem of inefficiencies. The outcome is expected to be a triple win (win–win–win) situation shared by all the stakeholders – the society, the shareholders, and the state. Unfortunately this winning score is sometimes more chaotic than orderly.

Exchanged commitment between people and their social setting is a dynamic two-way process. By the same token, human behavior could not be treated in isolation of the environment. As members of the society, they reside at the "core" of a complicated network of interaction and integration (Omar, 2005a). Any breakdown of these networks may lead to problems such as dissatisfaction and other delinquent behavior such as graffiti, drug abuses, etc. As such man continues to face the challenge of creating the environment, which caters for this need in order to be productive. This is where the study of social capital becomes a necessity (Putnam, 2000), in which Cohen and Prusak (2001) write: "Social capital consists of the stock of active connections among people: the trust, mutual understanding, and shared values and behaviour that bind the members of human networks and communities and make cooperative action possible." (Cohen and Prusak, 2001, p. 4)

# 4. ESTABLISHMENT AND EVOLUTION OF KAMPONG BAHRU

Kampong Bahru is located at the heart of the "golden triangle" of Kuala Lumpur, the capital city of Malaysia (Fig. 2). The Settlement was established in 1899 as a result of the expressed desire of the Resident General and the British Resident of Selangor. Initially its objectives were: to educate the children of Malays, to take part in the administration, and to enable them to reap some of the advantages of the prosperity. In order to carry out these intentions it was decided: to give the Malays English education, and to teach the Malays technical trade apart from agriculture. The British Resident said that he hoped the scheme would result in employment of educated and trained Malays for the clerical services. As a result of the decision, in the year 1990, an area of about 223 acres of land lying between the Klang River and Batu Road was reserved and a Board of

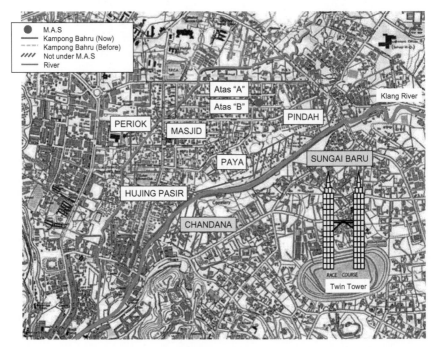

*Fig. 2.* Location Map of Kampong Bahru. The Red Boundary Shows the Outline of the Study Area. (*Source*: Sustainable Eco Development of Kampong Bahru: A Policy Perspective, 2009.)

management appointed to "manage and maintain the settlement." To ensure that the settlement would be properly governed, a set of rules was printed in the Government gazette No. 480 of 19 March 1910, an amendment was made by gazette Notification No. 950 of 22 February 1935.

It was believed that the idea to open the Settlement was mooted by His Highness The Sultan of Selangor in 1897 for similar reasons, which was to provide permanent settlement of the relocated Malays who were requested to leave, so as to make way for tin mining and related activities at the adjoining Klang and Gombak Rivers. Today this area is located around the Kuala Lumpur Mosque at Jalan Tun Perak. This event, however, is unrecorded in history (Personal Communication with MAS, 2007).

Long before the coming of the Chinese miners from Perak invited by Raja Abdullah, the Malays were already involved in businesses and other activities in Kuala Lumpur. As evidence of their presence the roads carry the name "Malay Street" and "Malacca Street," which is now located near the present Masjid India (Indian Mosque) and Bumiputera Commercial Bank (BCB) Headquarters.

The new settlement is known as Kampong Bahru (New Village). Geographically, the village is divided into two areas, high level and low lying. The low-lying land was not favored at that time due to swamp and frequent floods. The high-level land was chosen by early multi sub-ethnic Malay applicants groups who were mostly attached to government services, directly or indirectly. Comparatively, these groups were having more pleasant stay than the low-lying occupiers.

Apart from giving technical skills to the people, the British tried to encourage the people in the low-lying areas to plant padi other than rubber and fruit trees. However, all the efforts failed to materialize due to floods and frequent overflow of the meandering Klang River. Thus, this area was given to the Malay sub-ethnic group of Javanese descents, around 1930s. Their hardworking and endurance of difficulties are proven as now the area is well developed and no more frequent and flash floods occur during rainy season.

Initially, only five sub-kampongs were formed within the Kampong Bahru enclave, namely, Kampong Masjid (Mosque Village), Kampong Hujung Pasir (Sandy end Village), Kampong Pindah (Transfer Village), Kampong Paya (Swamp Village), and Kampong Periok (Pot Village). Later Kampong Masjid was subdivided to establish two more kampongs known as Kampong Atas A (Top Village A) and Kampong Atas (B until today). The names imply that they are indeed original Malay village.

To govern the village, a representative from each kampong was appointed and given the seat in the Board of Management together with other Board Members. Their roles were to voice out grievances and welfare for his respective residents and to exercise the Enactment to the fullest for the betterment of Kampong Bahru. The above practice remained until today minus the British officials.

Mode of selection of the Kampong Representatives requires certain criteria to qualify as has been in practice, until present day, that the person: has to have property in Kampong Bahru, must reside in Kampong Bahru, must be of good character and respectable standing among the residents. Prior to formation of Federal Territories of Kuala Lumpur, Kampong Bahru was under the Selangor State and The Board Chairman was held by the then Chief Minister of Selangor. The post of Chairman without executive power was given to Kuala Lumpur Mayor, when Kuala Lumpur was declared city in 1974.

# 5. CRUCIAL ISSUES OF KAMPONG BAHRU

## 5.1. Physical Infrastructure-Related Issues

The settlement space must be built with a purpose of containing the economic, political, and cultural activities of its dwellers. The government perspective is established in the Kuala Lumpur Structure Plan 2020 (DBKL, 2007), which classifies Kampong Bahru as *Special Areas*. It listed two issues prevalent in Urban Malay Reservation Areas, namely:

(1) Substandard living conditions due to ad-hoc individual development; and
(2) Substandard infrastructure and inadequate community facilities.

A town watching activity conducted jointly by Kyoto University and UiTM (University Technology Mara) and MAS (Malaya Agriculture Settlement) confirmed that the issues mentioned in the Kuala Lumpur Structure Plan are prevalent. Our concern, however, goes beyond the substandard quality of life and regenerating situation of the village. We searched for the answers to the question whether the service providers have breached their responsibilities assigned by the Government, which resulted in the regeneration. Fig. 3 shows the glimpses of the physical condition of Kampong Bahru.

## 5.2. Economic Opportunities

Eighteen respondents are interested in eco-business. This is a positive sign since most of them are already working in the village. Recycling, eco-products, eco-tourism, cleaning, and cleaning services are the businesses that they are interested in.

## 5.3. Social Issues of Kampong Bahru

The city grew around Kampong Bahru converting it into an enclave of sore eyesight. The physical gap between the surrounding environment and the space called Kampong Bahru is quite obvious. As the economy advanced, Kampong Bahru slipped further into a noisy, congested neighborhood of stalls, vehicles, and people. At night the village was awake with people frequenting roadside food stalls built haphazardly by the roadside. Kampong Bahru, once a stopover for rural population who migrate into the city is now in the state of degeneration. The development actors know that the village is

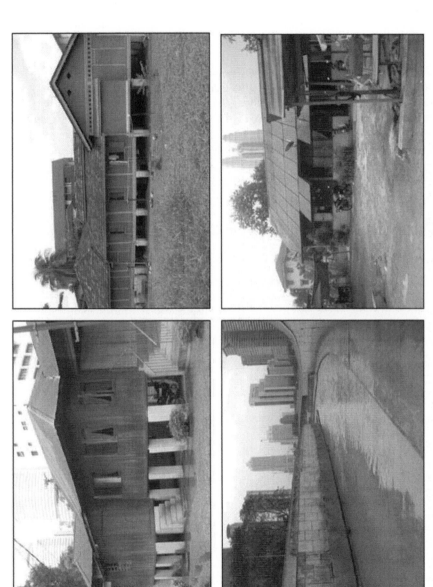

*Fig. 3.* Overview of Kampong Bahru. Top (Left and Right): Traditional Malaya Construction with Elevated Floor to Cope with Flood Risk in the Areas. Bottom (Left): River Passing through Kampong Bahru; (Right): Traditional Shops with a View of Twin Tower of Kuala Lumpur.

an unpolished gem and a huge capital of business opportunities. The Malay Agricultural Settlement Administration Board (MAS) and the community realized these potentials too. The differentiator is the MAS and the community have no structural capital to change their environment.

A simple survey of the residents was conducted by the authors in 2007. Majority of the respondents were dissatisfied with the environmental quality and their environment. The respondents were basically satisfied with the social services available within the vicinity of the village, except on the social services for the underprivileged. Nearly half of the respondents were not satisfied with the effectiveness in the participation of local consultation processes. They are, however, very satisfied with their own place of residence. This is an indication of attachment to their residence despite the environmental problems, which they face. Most of the respondents indicated social relationship as most important. We noted that their activities include participation in the mosques and madrasyah programs. This social networking is also displayed in their affirmative responses to the questions on the social capital.

Kampong Bahru is in dire need of new capital; tangible resources of built environment and belief system-based social capital (see Putnam, 2002 for more literature on social capital). To exist as an urban village, it needs a holistic approach of development that supports a symbiotic relationship between human and his environment. It is therefore, necessary to ask the right questions before we are able to diagnose the real issues of this degenerating urban village, starting with:

- How do we convert the values and artifacts of the urban village into potentials and opportunities?
- How to get an urban village community of Kampong Bahru to enhance their social capital in order to develop their capacity building?
- What would be the framework for capacity building of an urban village community?
- How could the explicit and tacit initiatives that facilitate the cultivation of knowledge and values appropriate to enhancement of social capital and community citizenship be established?

### 5.4. Environmental Issues of Kampong Bahru

The relationship between the Kampong Bahru community and their socio-political environment is complex, with many actors, playing different roles. Except for the Kuala Lumpur Mayor, who sits as the chairperson of the MAS, the village community is the stakeholders of Kampong Bahru. The dissatisfaction of the Kampong Bahru people is externalized in cynicism, apathetic, and distrust of the authority.

The externalized behavior is executed through open burning, graffiti, and vandalism of public properties as manifestation of the stakeholders' dissatisfaction. People carry out open burning of garbage because there is no proper garbage collection system. Public properties are vandalized because there is little or no civic consciousness or community citizenship. These behaviors occur because there is no incentive or opportunity to pull them to behave otherwise.

In the survey, majority of respondents stated that they are dependent on the government to collect their garbage. They admit burning some waste materials, which we have noted during the town watching. Their excuse was that there in no recycling facility in the village. We found one recycling point operated by a private individual. The respondents identified that the most important agency to solve the environmental problems are the local government, the residents themselves, and the community leaders. The most important community action is the education on the promotion of environment, followed by the establishment of a recycling facility and decreasing the amount of garbage.

# 6. ECO-VILLAGE CONCEPTUALIZATION IN KAMPONG BAHRU

For the community of Kampong Bahru, who are Malays (except for traders), the love for the environment is an obligation in their religion: Islam, which for the greedy few, had been put aside through deforestation and desertification of the land. Islam advocates that if human need to create an environment to live or to work in, it must be built with sustainability of nature in mind. The Malay belief system is a complicated web of network consisting of their *adab* [Good behavior, finesse, civil, polite, and civilized, following the procedures and norms], *adat* [A custom or customary laws], and *budi* [specific attribute of a Malay partly internalized within the thought and heart (psychological state) as well as externalized as deeds (social state)]. These values and social artifacts influence the Malays in the ways they express their views, relationships, and overall attitude toward life. They form the foundation of their social capital and community citizenship (Omar, 2005b).

The community of Kampong Bahru is divided into two segments: the elders who hold to old belief system, and the young adults who may not exhibit these attributes, for reasons, which needed investigation. Nevertheless, whichever group one is aligned to, "increasing evidence shows that social cohesion – social capital – is critical for poverty alleviation and sustainable human and economic development" (The World Bank Group, 2005).

To design and construct Kuala Lumpur city to be the economic and tourist hub of the South East Asia, the government turns to solutions provided by the market forces. The city grew around Kampong Bahru converting it into an enclave of sore eyesights. The massive Petronas tallest twin tower in the world with its shops and boutiques of designer clothes and accessories make the village look like a ghetto.

As the k-economy advanced, Kampong Bahru slipped further into a noisy, congested neighborhood of stalls, vehicles, and people. At night the village was awake with people frequenting roadside food stalls built haphazardly by the roadside. Thus the search for a more holistic approach of creating a symbiotic relationship between human and his environment is due. By the same token, the Malay Agricultural Settlement Board was not happy, but their hands are tied by scarcity of fund. Kampong Bahru was once a stopover for rural population who migrate into the city now in the state of disrepair. To address the eco-village in Kampong Bahru, the following questions need to be examined:

(1) What are the main issues of the community?
(2) What are the cultural values and artifacts prevalent among the members of the community?
(3) Could the values and artifacts be converted into potentials and opportunities?
(4) What would be the framework for capacity building of the Kampong Bahru community?
(5) How could a model for enhancement of social capital and community citizenship be developed?
(6) How could the explicit and tacit initiatives that facilitate the cultivation of knowledge and values appropriate to enhancement of social capital and community citizenship be established?

Considering the above situations and questions, it is needed to start some initiatives, which focused on the following issues:

(1) The long-term sustainability of Kampong Bahru against the massive infrastructure of the surrounding area is getting more critical by the day.
(2) No correct socio-cultural framework is available to conceptualize the model of capacity building in which the development of the community must be initiated by the community themselves.

(3) The social capital of the Kampong Bahru community, which could complement the infrastructural and economic model of development are available but obscured.
(4) The various the roles and involvement of the state, agencies, and interest groups in building the social capital and community citizenship of the Kampong Bahru community are unclear.
(5) Limited opportunity for the members of the community to ascend into the economic mainstream and improve the quality of their lives through participation in decision-making.
(6) There is no clear policy for empowerment training for enhancement of social capital for the vulnerable groups such as women and young adults living in Kampong Bahru.

The issue of the community of Kampong Bahru's economic sustainability in urban environment is critical. Yet, without the correct socio-cultural framework it is difficult to conceptualize the model of capacity building in which the development of the community must be initiated by the community themselves. Accordingly, a new approach needs to be developed in order to ensure that the economic survival and synergy of the community be sustained. The Kuala Lumpur City Council (DBKL) has designed a Structural Plan for Kuala Lumpur 2003, which incorporated the Malay Reserve Land of Kampong Bahru. The Plan, nevertheless, is inadequate to deal with the long-term sustainability of Kampong Bahru.

The key issue to eco-village in Kampong Bahru is to focus on enhancing social capital of the community, which could complement the infrastructural and economic model of development. The aim should be to identify and analyse the various roles and involvement of the state, agencies, and interest groups in building the social capital and community citizenship of the Kampong Bahru community. The opportunities of the members of the community to rise into economic mainstream and improvement of the quality of their lives through participation in decision-making need to be examined. It is required to focus on determining the factors that could lead to enhancing the community's abilities to maximize their social capital.

# 7. CONCLUDING REMARKS

Many people speak or write about Kampong Bahru. Some with hidden agenda (as alleged by a member of the MAS governing body) while others have no knowledge on the subject matter at all, but see Kampong Bahru as an unsightly space viewed from the bridge of the twin towers. Supporters of managerialism might offer a "balanced scorecard" approach of solving the problem, while the engineers ponder on the physical problems of waste management and flood mitigation. In case of Kampong Bahru, nothing works unless the community is involved in the decision-making process. One must not forget that the Kampong Bahru community belongs to the K-Economy epoch. They are the descendants, but not similar to the uncomplicated people who had been told by the British Resident of Selangor to move to their present location to make way for the colonialists and their cohorts to prosper.

An urban village is affected by the Government policies and action of the real estate industry team. Indeed, the development actors have difficult yet critical roles to prevent an urban village from degenerating into a ghetto. An integrated approach of built environment, however, could provide the social space not merely through its massive structure, but through its symbiotic relationship with its inhabitants. Yet, developers prefer to build a "selective" style of housing projects, separating the affluent from the poor, resulting in inequality of services and facilities.

A quality social space yields a connected civil society that could enhance people's environmental values, which in turn boost their self-confidence; competency and capacity building. Trust, collaboration, and collective action found in network of relationships with improved management of facilities in built environment are value added to the neighborhood survival and development of citizen's supports system.

The K-Economy epoch provides the impetus for the construction of the K-Community in which people are connected through cyber space. The facilities for sharing of values, trust, and understanding, as the major ingredients of social capital, are not the issues. Today, social capital is critical for poverty alleviation and building a sustainable human and economic development. It is also politically correct to seek for meanings in lives, which encourage the creation of the social, spiritual, and psychological conditions, which recognized that each human is unique.

Studies in the industrialized countries, such as on the redevelopment of Bordesley as an urban village, Birmingham, UK, by Franklin B.J. of Cardiff University and Nishinomiya City of Japan as an eco-city by Miki Yoshizumi of Kyoto University, indicate that more and more intellectuals are talking about sustainable community in different tones and languages, with similar message that people are not islands, but exist in network of complex psychological, political, social, economic, and spatial relationships. If their psychological attachment is to an urban village, that is where their settlement space is. Ghettoizing an urban village injures the spirit that moves the psychological attachment, and indirectly damages the social capital of the villagers.

The Kampong Bahru community speaks of poor waste management and inadequate safety measures, which point to inefficiencies of the agents of the authority in dispensing their parts of the contract. At other point, what you think as sore-eyes, are actually symptoms of deeper sores located at the souls of the villagers, which would inflict our future generations, if not correctly treated and cured. Burdened with environmental and social problems, an urban village could slip into a ghettoized stage. Opportunities for the people of Kampong Bahru are provided to participate in decision-making for their spiritual, psychological, socio-cultural, and economic development. The Malay Agricultural Settlement Management Board (MAS) be empowered to formulate strategies for the development of Kampong Bahru with clear vision on sustainability concern. The hidden social capital of the Malays of Kampong Bahru is placed in its rightful stage to add value to the enrichment of the Malay culture and civilization. Kampong Bahru would assist in the conception of physical artifacts to be utilized as "centers of social learning and control," and can be a model for Urban Eco-Village. The villages face the hazards of flash floods and garbage disposal problems. MAS could not do much if the governance actors are not moving in the right direction to mitigate the problems. It is not that MAS is bent on blaming others, as the villagers are not entirely blameless either. Without proper knowledge, however, villagers would not be aware of the risks of poor garbage disposal system. MAS has taken a step forward by collaborating with a team from Kyoto University, the Mara University of Technology (UiTM), and the MERCY to study our problems. The team from Kyoto University and UiTM arrived to conduct a small workshop on capacity building on the June 17, 2006, followed by "Town Watching" activities on June 18, 2006 (Fig. 4). These programs get the participation of the people as evidence of their willingness to collaborate in projects for long-term sustainable development.

Fig. 5 shows the conceptual framework of the eco-community of Kampong Bahru, which should build on its environmental, economic, and social capital. This should be supported by education, governance, and culture of the local communities. Where the community should be at the core of the implementation of actions, cooperation scheme should be there between government, NGO, people, academic, and corporate world. On the governance side, it should be supported by policy, strategy, regulation, and resources.

Given the significant position of Kampong Bahru in the heart of Kuala Lumpur City, it is timely that a research searching for truth of its real

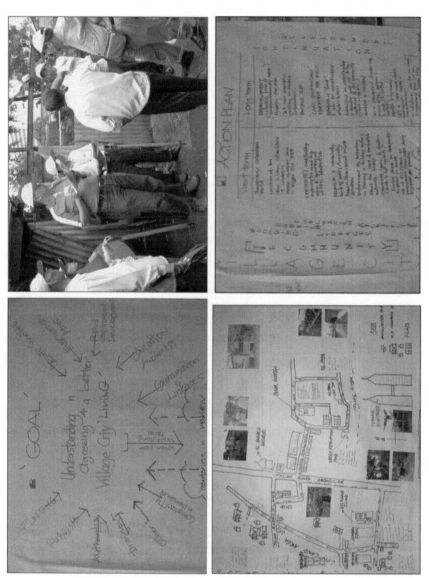

*Fig. 4.*   Town Watching in Kampong Bahru: Process and Product (Maps and Action Plans).

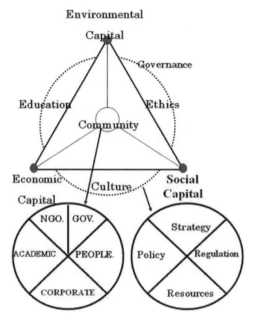

*Fig. 5.*   Sustainability and Eco-Community Framework of Kampong Bahru.

potentials be conducted. It is of profound importance that the issues regarding social capital and capacity building be laid open for discourse. It would be a gross injustice if the community of Kampong Bahru were sidelined, while the businesses in the surrounding area profited from tourism. The government would be able to benefit greatly from such findings, as they could be utilized to improve its performance. It is the obligation of the government to fulfill its social contract, as much as the responsibility of the community of Kampong Bahru to be committed to their social responsibility toward their living environment.

# ACKNOWLEDGMENTS

This research is supported by JSPS-VCC program, and also JSPS/MEXT grant (Water Communities). The authors also acknowledge the support from their individual university resources (both Kyoto University and UiTM).

# REFERENCES

Cohen, D., & Prusak, L. (2001). *In good company. How social capital makes organizations work* (pp. 214, xiii). Boston, MA: Harvard Business School Press.

Davis, M. (2006). *Planets of slums*. London: Verso.

DBKL. (2007). Kuala Lumpur City plan. Available at: http://www.dbkl.gov.my/pskl2020/english/index.htm, accessed on 30th October 2007.

Omar, S. (2005a). Challenges of the K-Era: The psychological contract of knowledge sharing and organisational commitment. *International Journal of Knowledge, Culture and Change Management, 4,* 1061–1073.

Omar, S. (2005b). *Making sense of adat and adages in contemporary Malay Society,* a research commissioned by the Institute of Research, Development and Commercialisation, University of Technology MARA.

Putnam, R. D. (2000). *Bowling alone. The collapse and revival of American community.* New York: Simon and Schuster.

Putnam, R. D. (Ed.) (2002). *Democracies in flux: The evolution of social capital in contemporary society.* New York: Oxford University Press.

Sustainable Eco Development of Kampong Bahru: A policy perspective. (2009). Joint publication of Kyoto University and MAS.

The World Bank. (1999). *Social capital: conceptual frameworks and empirical evidences.* Working Paper No. 5, 49 pages. World Bank, Washington, DC.

The World Bank Group in PovertyNet Library. (2005). Available at: http://www1.worldbank.org/prem/poverty/scapital/home.htm

Yoshizumi, M. (2004). Eco-villages in Europe and the United States. Proceeding of the International Workshop "Capacity Building Workshop on Climate Change Mitigation with Locally Owned Technology and Systems, 14–16 November 2004, the Asia-Pacific Network for Global Change Research (APN) and Kyoto Institute for Eco-sound Social System, Kobe and Kyoto, Japan, pp. 107–118.

# CHAPTER 15

# PARTICIPATORY URBAN ENVIRONMENTAL MANAGEMENT AND SOCIAL CAPITAL IN DANANG

Nozomi Hishida and Rajib Shaw

## ABSTRACT

*The notion of social capital refers to social connections between people, such as networking, trust, norms, etc. Rich and good-condition social capital is supposed to enhance collective action in a society. This is why social capital has attracted more attention in the field of development studies and environmental management studies in recent years. However, the forms and conditions of social capital are different in each society and there is no ideal social capital. Therefore, it is important to know the advantages and disadvantages of the original social capital and how it can be supplemented. In the environmental learning project in Danang, Central Vietnam, social capital was fostered through the activities of the residents' group. New and strong networks of people have been created among broader neighborhoods. The residents' group created multi-dimensional networks (bridges) in the society and helped to foster social capital. Eventually, the residents' group is expected to bring success to the participatory urban environmental project by fostering social capital in the local society.*

Urban Risk Reduction: An Asian Perspective
Community, Environment and Disaster Risk Management, Volume 1, 295–315
ISSN: 2040-7262/doi: 10.1108/S2040-7262(2009)0000001019

# 1. INTRODUCTION

In recent years, more and more discussion and research about social capital have come up. The notion of social capital has attracted attention in the area of development and environmental management, since it is supposed to have a function to promote social cohesion and civil participation. This chapter introduces some major ideas on social capital and discusses its relationship with urban environmental management. The environmental learning project is also introduced, as a case study.

## *1.1. Urban Environmental Management and the Participatory Approach*

Urbanization is one of the vital factors that strongly relates to urban environmental problems in developing countries including Asian countries. Massive population increase seriously affects the life of people living in urban areas and threatens the livability of cities. Large cities in developing countries are often characterized by a lack of infrastructure and investment, making it more difficult for them to improve public services to remedy the situation (Beall, 1997). Ensuring the accessibility of urban environmental services, such as water supply, sanitation, sewage, and waste disposal has been highlighted among many urban governments, because these services are expected to contribute to the remarkable reduction of water and sanitation-related problems, such as diseases and environmental degradation (World Bank, 2003). However, the reality is far from what is expected. Providing necessary infrastructure requires massive costs and a long time. Inadequate provision of environmental infrastructure and services is pressing on urban cities in developing countries, and as a result, it causes number of problems (Nguyen, 2004). With limited resources including financial resources, human resources, institutions and management organizations, and experiences, the cities in developing countries are facing difficulties to solve the urban environmental problems.

The participatory approach has been highlighted as it can be implemented in places with impaired conditions. For environmental management, regardless of the scale of the specific problems, promoting public understanding and participation are the basic requirements since environmental problems originated from human activities. An approach involving lower levels of the society is vital for environmental management. In recent years, the participatory approach in environmental management has been applied all over the world, and importance of overall citizens' participation has been widely discussed. The notion of social capital has received attention lately as one of the factors which affects citizens' participation.

## 1.2. General Concept of Social Capital

Generally, social capital refers to networking, trust, and norms among people, which can be formed in the society. There are various definitions of social capital and its components and functions. Compared to natural capital, economic capital, and human capital, social capital is vastly difficult to be calculated and evaluated. One definition of social capital provided by Social Capital Initiative, World Bank is "*Social capital refers to the internal social and cultural coherence of society, the norms and values that govern interactions among people and the institutions in which they are embedded. Social capital is the glue that holds societies together and without which there can be no economic growth or human well-being.*"

It is said that the concept of social capital was highlighted the first time in a study of Bourdieu. He defined the concept as "*the aggregate of the actual or potential resources which are linked to possession of a durable network of more or less institutionalized relationships of mutual acquaintance or recognition*" (Bourdieu, 1980, 1985). He focuses on the benefit delivered to individuals by virtue of participation in groups and on the construction of sociability for the purpose of creating these resources. The amount of social capital resources people have depends on the scale of the network which each individual join and on the amount of economic, cultural, and social capital owned by the members of the network. The network here refers to families and relatives, personal network and connection, etc.

Coleman, on the other hand, gives rather vague definition. He pointed out that social capital is defined by its function. "It is not a single entities but a variety of different entities, with two elements in common; they all consist of some aspect of social structures, and they facilitate certain actions of actors – whether persons or corporate actors – within the structure" (Coleman, 1988).

For Coleman, social capital can encompass not only family and relatives but also local network as community and norms which is necessary to form and keep the community. In his theory, Coleman mentions two aspects of social capital: one is the structural aspect of social capital, which is indicated in the definition above, and another is cognitive "factors" which exist in the society.

Coleman specially details following factors as social capital:

- Obligation, expectation, and trustworthiness of structure
- Information channel
- Norms and effective sanction

This view of social capital captures not only social structures at large but the ensemble of norms governing peoples' interpersonal behavior (Serageldin & Grootaert, 2000).

After Coleman, Putnam presents the most famous definition of social capital. According to Putnam (1993), "social capital refers to features of social organization, such as networks, norms, and trust, that facilitate coordination and cooperation for mutual benefit." In his famous work in Northern and Southern Italy, Putnam (1993) describes the society which has rich social capital:

> Some regions of Italy, such as Emilia-Romana and Tuscany, have many active community organizations. Citizens in these regions are engaged by public issues, not by patronage. They trust one another to act fairly and obey the law. Leaders in these communities are relatively honest and committed to equality. Social and political networks are organized horizontally, not hierarchically. These "civic communities" value solidarity, civic participation, and integrity. And here democracy works.

Norris (2002) states that most importantly Putnam's theory clearly mentions two phenomena of social capital: one is the structural phenomenon (social networks) and the other is the cultural phenomenon (social norms). Meanwhile, Putnam's definition is often said as the narrow, specific definition on the point that his definition focuses on horizontal network among people, which give positive impact to society and democracy. Serageldin and Grootaert (2000) stated that the definition presented by Coleman covers broader area. They mainly point out that Coleman's concept includes vertical association as well as horizontal, and this wider range of association covers both positive and negative objectives.

Fukuyama (1995, 2001) discusses social capital under an even broader context. He simply defines social capital as "an instantiated informal norm that promotes cooperation between two or more individuals" (Fukuyama, 2001). He shed light on trust and says that social capital can give positive impact on economy in a society, which has strong social trust.

## *1.3. Social Capital and Community Governance*

Social capital is often discussed because of its relevance to governance. Regarding social capital and governance, Putnam's work in Northern and Southern Italy is possibly the most famous. Putnam's explanation for the difference between Northern and Southern Italy on their governance performance is concluded as the difference comes from the type of social capital they have. Putnam mentions that the bridging type of social capital is rich in Northern Italy and it helps governance works well. This study is very significant on the point that it clearly describes the relation between social capital and governance in the case study.

However, his description may need more analysis on interaction between social capital in the civil societies and the governmental sectors. His theory states about the impact which is indirectly given from the civil societies to the governmental sectors but not about the effect which governmental sectors give to the civil societies. There is a lack of viewpoint of vertical interaction between civil societies and governmental sectors.

In their study on social capital and urban governance, Maloney, Smith, and Stoker (2000) discuss about the importance to consider top-down interaction perspective, interpenetration of public authorities, and voluntary community associations. It is said that research on social capital should not focus on only the effect of community-level social capital on government performance, but also the effect of governmental associational relationships on social capital. Here, the need is to supply the top-down perspective to more common bottom-up, horizontal perspective as suggested by Putnam.

Regarding how social capital affects the relationship between government sector and civil societies, Evans (1996) propounds the "state-society synergy." By this concept, he argues that active government and mobilized communities can enhance each other's developmental efforts. What his study claims is that norms and cooperation and networks of civil engagement among citizens, which are core of social capital, can be promoted by public agencies and used for developmental ends.

> Creative actions by government organizations can foster social capital; linking mobilized citizens to public agencies can enhance the efficiency of government. The combination of strong public institutions and organized communities is a powerful tool for development. Better understanding of the nature of synergistic relations between states and society and the conditions under which such relations can most easily be constructed should become a component of future theories of development (Evans, 1996).

Importantly, Evans mentioned that synergy is constructible, regardless of the condition of the preexisted social capital, even in the more adverse circumstances typically found in developing countries.

On the contrary, Bowls and Gintis (2002) take a stance that government and civil society relationship can be explained as complementally relationship. They state that well-working communities require a legal and governmental environment favorable to their functioning, and also says that governmental intervention has sometimes destroyed community governance capacities. So if government and community have well understanding for each other, community governance can be easily enhanced rather than in the case when there is a lack of communication between them. Meantime, government intervention cannot work desirably without an understanding of local context, but tend to damage preexisting community governance.

## 1.4. Social Capital and Urban Environmental Management

In recent years, a number of studies have come up to discuss social capital in context of participatory environmental management. Many studies mentioned that the basic concept of social capital such as trust, norm, and network can be counted as a key factor which contributes to environmental management that often needs peoples' collective action for its success (Kähkönen, 1999; Pargal, Huq, & Gilligan, 1999; Pretty & Ward, 2001).

As an example of the social capital analysis in environmental management, Pargal et al. (1999) describe the case of solid waste management in Dhaka, Bangladesh.

> Using measures of trust and the strength of norms of reciprocity and sharing among neighborhood residents as proxies for social capital is, indeed, an important determinant of whether VSWM systems arise in Dhaka. The effects of norms of reciprocity and sharing on the probability that a VSWM system is created are relatively large and significant, while the role of trust is not identified as a significant factor. Other measures of homogeneity of interests are also important, and interestingly, so is the nature of associational activity. Finally, as would be expected, education levels are strongly and robustly associated with the existence of collective action for trash disposal (Pargal et al., 1999).

In this description, Pargal et al. (1999) stated that norms of reciprocity, sharing on the probability, homogeneity of interest, and education level play a big role in VSWM (voluntary solid waste management), but trust is not a very important factor in this case of Dhaka. Since this example is the original case of Dhaka, it should be clear under different society and different problems that which factors of social capital take what role in environmental management.

From studies and reports about urban environmental problems, it is found that efficiency of governance and participatory management is required to enhance urban environmental condition in developing countries. The government takes a big role to deal with urban environmental problems, since they are main provider of urban environmental services and infrastructures. However, it is clear that there are still great number of people who are not provided adequate services and the government is partly unable to meet the demand. To fill the gap between demand and supply, great needs for community-based, participatory environmental management are raised.

It can be mentioned that efficient governance and participation is necessary for participatory urban environmental government.

However, how are they evaluated – in good condition or not? What figure can be described as a society which has good participation and governance system for urban environmental management? Are there any indicators or ideal model for societies and communities?

The concept of social capital helps to deal with the questions. In this point, some aspects of social capital are highlighted, which help to improve governance and participation and cope with urban environmental management.

# 2. DANANG CASE STUDY

## 2.1. Background

Danang (also called Da Nang) is the biggest city in central Vietnam and is the third biggest city in the whole of Vietnam (Fig. 1). It has a total area of 1,256 km$^2$, a population of 788,500 as of 2006 (General Statistic Office of Vietnam, 2007). Danang has been developing rapidly in recent years. The population of Danang has increased in the last 10 years and is expected to increase further and reach 800,000 in the near future.

## 2.2. Environmental Problems in Danang

Danang has benefited from its development, but at the same time, the city is facing several environmental problems due to urbanization, industrial

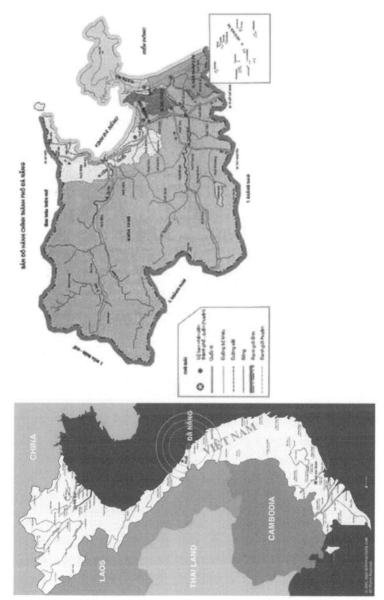

*Fig. 1.* Location of Danang and Map of Danang city (Danang City).

development, and population increase. One of them is air pollution. People in big cities, such as Ho Chi Minh City and Hanoi, use motorbikes for daily commutation. Though Danang is much smaller than these cities, as more and more people here can afford motorbikes, the use of motorbikes is on rise. Hence, air pollution is an important environmental problem in all the three cities. Other environmental problems include waste and water pollution. According to Department of Natural Resources and Environment of Danang City, these two issues are critical environmental problems for the city, and the city government puts an emphasis on these problems. In addition, two main factors are responsible for the increased waste and water pollution of ponds, lakes, rivers, and sea. One is an increase in industrial activity and the other is an increase in the number of households.

In order to solve the pressing environmental problems, a participatory environmental learning project has started in one area of central part of Danang city. The project area, Thuan Phuoc ward, is surrounded by the Han River, Danang Bay, and a fishery harbor. There are lakes and a drainage canal in the ward. Water from the lake flows to the fishery harbor and the sea through the drainage canal. The water is polluted and has a repugnant odor because of the household sewage from the surrounding areas.

The pollution has had serious impact on the health and living conditions of the local communities making them to act upon it with all the resources they have. However, the degree of water contamination has worsened so much that the condition is beyond the capacity of the communities to rectify. The impact of the pollution is such that there is thick sludge at the bottom of the pond, canal, and river; the color of the water turned to white to gray and one can almost find no kind of biological activity in the water due to its high toxic levels.

## 2.3. Environmental Learning Project

Thuan Phuoc ward is facing severe environmental problem due to very high water pollution. There is a need to implement effective interventions to improve the living condition and environmental health in the ward. Hence, this project intends to decontaminate the lake and canal with community participation. As the residents' understanding and cooperation play an important role in enhancing the quality of local environment and ensuring sustainability, enhancing environmental awareness of local communities was taken up as the key objective of this project.

The project, aimed at enhancing the environmental awareness of the residents of the Thuan Phuoc ward, started in August 2006. The project targets the 190 households around the lake and canal, who will be offered training in environmental management, and primary school students in the ward, who will receive environmental education. Hence, environmental training and education are important components of the project. Toward successful awareness rising, citizens' participation is crucial. Therefore, how to involve more residents and to promote interaction between people are the key issues for success of the project, and it should be considered in all processes of the project.

## 2.4. Stakeholders

This project involves several stakeholders in the process: the People's Committee of Thuan Phuoc ward, the Department of Natural Resources and Environment of Danang (DONRE), Vo Thi Sau primary school, the Faculty of Environment of Danang University of Technology (DUT), and the Graduate School of Global Environmental Studies of Kyoto University (KU).

In order to implement the project, they have established two organizations. One is a management group and another is the environmental management system in the local community. The project management group is named as Project Management Board (PMB). The members of PMB include different stakeholders such as the DONRE of Danang city, the DONRE of the district, the People's Committee of Thuan Phuoc ward and Danang University of Technology, and community representatives. Environmental management system is called Environment Protection Committee (EPC) which consists of the leaders of residents' cluster (residents' group) and teachers in the primary school and officer of the ward in the project site. The EPC is the main stakeholder which implements the learning and activities in the project. The members of EPC have monthly meeting for discussion and to share the information and each of the members disseminate the activities in their own resident clusters. As explained later, EPC plays a crucial role in implementation of the project, since EPC is a new network system of the residents and has impact on their relationships.

## 2.5. Strong Leaderships Within Resident Clusters

From observations and preliminary social survey in the planning stage of the project, some features of local community have been extracted. The leadership in the residents' cluster is very strong in this area. The residents' clusters have a big meaning to the resident's daily life, and the neighbor network and social cohesion in one residents' cluster is strong enough to mobilize people to the project activities. These features of the residents' cluster are effective to improve collective action within one resident cluster, and it is a positive factor of the project site. However it may prevent the interaction and cooperation among them. Dissemination of activities and cooperation among people is necessary for participatory urban environmental management, so the lack of cooperation among the residents' clusters is one of the negative factors for the successful implementation of the project. Therefore, ECP activity is expected to provide more opportunities of interaction and cooperation for the residents and bring effective collective action for environmental activities to the community.

### 2.6. Promoting Interaction between Residents Through EPC Activities

There are two major components of the project: environmental education in the primary school and environmental learning and activities for the residents.

As a promoter of the project, EPC has carried out these activities as follows:

- Town watching
- Conducting questionnaire survey
- Clean-up activities around the lake and the canal
- Citizen report card
- Public relations activities
- Monthly meeting
- Water purification by plant filtering (DUT cooperation)

#### 2.6.1. Town Watching
As the first step of the project, town watching was held.

The officers of the ward and representative of the residents walked around the project site and shared their information. They drew the town map and put the information they got on it (Fig. 2(a), and (b)).

By conducting town watching, they found the positive factors and negative factors in their town and defined the problems which they should tackle. Town watching provides new viewpoint to look at their familiar sight and helps them to share the exact situation and problems in their own town.

*Fig. 2.* Glimpses of EPC activities. (a) Town Watching – Observation, (b) Town Watching – Sharing Information, (c) Clean-Up Activities – The Canal, (d) Clean-Up Activities – The Riverside, (e) Environmental Advertisement, (f) Public Relations Panel.

## 2.6.2. Clean-Up Activities

Clean-up activities were one of the major activities which the residents have been doing as a project activity. Cleaning up had been conducted even before the project implementation, however, activities had been carried out in each resident cluster and there were no opportunity to share experiences among different clusters. It can be said that there is lack of community cohesion of the activities. By joining EPC, the residents' leaders discuss the problems and their task, for instance, how they can mobilize the people who tend not to participate in the activities, etc. EPC works as a glue to connect residents' cluster and bring them the feeling of togetherness.

However, in fact, pollution in the lake and the canal is so serious that there are limitations for the residents to keep the conditions under control. It needs budget, tools, and professional technologies to clean the lake and the canal, so affirmative support from the government is needed in order to improve the situation. At this point, EPC also brings to the residents opportunities to report their requirement to government such as the ward and DONRE. Through EPC, problem consciousness and the needs are broadly shared not only among the residents themselves but also between the residents and government. Residents are expected to inform the government about the local problems and needs, which will be vital information for policy making.

## 2.6.3. Public Relation Activities

One of the most emphasized activities of EPC is public relation activity. They create slogan and advertisements for project promotion (Fig. 2(e) and (f)). These advertisements make an appeal to citizens that better environment can be brought by themselves. The promotion has aimed to attract peoples' attention and mobilize more residents to the project. It is expected that the difference of environmental consciousness among the residents is getting smaller by these public relation activities.

The bad odor of the water directly hits the residents who live near the lake and the canal. They suffer more than those who live far from the waterside. As a result, there is a gap between these people about the level of environmental consciousness. However, domestic waste water flows out of not only the houses near the waterside, but also every household in the area. Situation improvement can not be achieved without overall cooperation and efforts of the residents. Therefore the ward office thinks the public relations as crucial activity and strongly supports it.

## 3. UTILIZING SOCIAL CAPITAL FOR URBAN ENVIRONMENTAL MANAGEMENT

### 3.1. Community's Features and the Function of EPC

In the project, social surveys have been conducted twice as of the present. The first survey was conducted in October 2006 and the second survey was carried out in August 2007.

As found in the first survey, the society in the project site has these characteristics:

- Strong leadership of the leaders of resident clusters
- NGOs and volunteer groups are not active or rather rare in the community
- Public sectors are required to take initiative for environmental activities
- Young generation and children are not properly involved in the environmental protection activities
- It is difficult to disseminate the activity to neighbor ward through residents' private relationships

Applying the concept of social capital helps to understand how these characteristics work and affect environmental management in the project site. The culture of top-down implementation is exemplified by less presence of NGOs, volunteer groups, and lack of requirement for public sector's initiatives. Strong leadership of the resident leaders works strongly to mobilize people in their own resident cluster and this is one of the reasons for strong cohesiveness in each resident cluster. This cohesiveness in the cluster can be accelerating the implementation of the project. Therefore the administrative unit has important role in the community structure. Meantime, there are some people for whom it is difficult to be involved in the community activities: young generation and children. They are not efficiently enclosed in the community, so trust and networks that make others participate in the activity do not work for them. These functions of social capital are classified in Table 1.

These characteristics can be classified either as an advantage or a disadvantage according to the circumstances or the stages of the project. Present structure makes residents less positive to join volunteer work, but on the other hand, they are well mobilized under initiative of their leaders and public lead. Therefore, the residents can be mobilized to participate in the community activity in their community (clusters), but they have difficulties to interact with other community due to lack of networking and bridging

***Table 1.*** Condition of Social Capital in the Project Site.

| | Inside the Resident Cluster | Interaction/Dissemination |
|---|---|---|
| Strong leadership of leader of resident cluster | Acceleration: O | Bonding: ☐ Prevent efficient interaction |
| Less presence of NGOs and volunteer groups | Passive: ☐ | No bridging network: ☐ |
| Public sector's initiatives | Leadership and initiative: O | Leader ship of the ward: O |
| | Passive (residents): ☐ | Prevent interaction of wards: ☐ |
| Participation of younger generations and children | Less participation: ☐ | Less participation: ☐ |
| Strong role of administrative units | Acceleration: O | Acceleration: O Prevent efficient interaction: ☐ |

*Note:* O represents positive functions and ☐ represents negative functions.

between communities. In addition, younger generations and children are not well involved in the community activities even in the clusters.

How did this situation come about? One of the reasons is the organization structure of Vietnam. Vietnam's governance system is still strongly centralized and keeps their top-down tradition. In the urban city, the residents are subdivided by the administrative unit system and these groupings become their basic community in their daily life and activity. However, the urban problems including environmental problems occur far beyond these units. Therefore not only the cohesion in one group but also the holistic cohesion of the city is required for participatory management toward environmental improvement.

### 3.2. Comparative Analysis of Social Capital in Project Site

In order to reveal how EPC has worked in the local society, the social survey was conducted in August 2007 when the project had been carried out for almost one year. The survey focused on social capital in the local society of the project site. The main points for consideration are as follows:

- Whether the project has any impact on the residents and social capital between them.
- What kind of role ECP has taken in the project from viewpoint of social capital.

The questionnaire consisted of following nine topics: General questions, Groups, Networking, Trust, Collective action and cooperation, Information, Social tie and cohesion, Public participation and decision making, and Environment.

A total of 397 responses were collected from eight residents' clusters. Four of them have joined the project and EPC since 2006 while the other four have not joined the project. Results of the survey showed that EPC activity has a strong effect on social capital factors. However, there is a difference among social capital factors as far as the magnitude of the effect is concerned. The difference and trends are shown in Table 2. In Table 2, social capital factors are divided into two categories: Bonding and Bridging. The social capital factors belonging to the bonding category explain the condition of social capital in comparatively small neighborhood. On the other hand, the social capital factors in the bridging category indicate the rate in broader network of neighbors. The residents' clusters are divided into two groups: (i) the clusters 13, 14, 15, and 17 – those who have joined the project and are member of EPC (project clusters) and (ii) the clusters 5, 9, 29, and 34 – who have not joined the project nor EPC (non-project clusters).

In Table 2, there is no significant difference between project and non-project clusters in bonding categories. The coefficient of social capital is high overall. It is supposed that the bonding of neighbor and the strong-tie within a resident cluster is a natural condition for the area. Social capital in clusters is originally rich in the area. However, there is an exception: cluster 14 shows low values in Trust, Social-tie, and Participation. Meanwhile, there are different tendencies between project clusters and non-project clusters in the bridging category. The project clusters show higher positive values than the non-project clusters.

# 4. CONCLUSION

## 4.1. The Role of EPC

The project site seems to be lacking in bridging networks beyond the resident clusters compared to a strong administrative network. However, EPC, which was newly established for the environmental awareness rising project, is different from the preexisting administrative structure. What is new about EPC is that it consisted of leaders from different clusters, representatives of the ward and primary school, and even DONRE which generally has no opportunity to join the residents in a meeting (Fig. 3). EPC

***Table 2.*** Impact of EPC in Comparison of the Resident's Clusters.

| Social Capital Factors | | | Non-Project Clusters | | | | Project Site Clusters | | | | X₂ Test |
|---|---|---|---|---|---|---|---|---|---|---|---|
| | | | C.5 | C.9 | C.29 | C.34 | C.13 | C.14 | C.15 | C.17 | |
| Bonding | Network | Neighbor Reliability | ** | ** | * | | * | | ** | ** | 0.00 |
| | Trust | Trust Level: Cluster | ** | ** | ** | ** | * | | ** | ** | 0.00 |
| | | Trust Help: Cluster | | ** | ** | ** | * | | * | ** | 0.00 |
| | | Public Reliability: | | | | | | | | | 0.00 |
| | Collective action | Cooperation | ** | ** | * | ** | ** | ** | ** | ** | 0.00 |
| | | Form of Participation | V | V | V | V | V | R | R | V | 0.00 |
| | Social-tie | Social-tie: Cluster | ** | V | * | ** | ** | R | ** | ** | 0.00 |
| | Participation | Decision Making: Cluster | * | * | | | * | | * | | 0.00 |
| | | Impact on Community: Cluster | * | * | | | | | | *** | 0.00 |
| Bridging | Network | Neighbor Network | * | ** | * | ** | | | | * | 0.00 |
| | Trust | Trust Level: Ward | | * | * | | | | * | * | 0.00 |
| | | Trust Level: District | | | | | | | * | * | 0.00 |
| | | Trust Help: Ward | | | | | | | | | 0.00 |
| | | Trust Help: District | | | | | | | | | 0.00 |
| | | Public Reliability: District | | | | | | | * | | 0.00 |
| | | Public Reliability: City Department | | | | | | * | * | | 0.00 |
| | | Public Reliability: PC of City | | | | | | * | * | | 0.00 |
| | | Public Reliability: PC of Nation | | | | | | * | * | | 0.00 |
| | Information | Information | ** | ** | ** | | ** | ** | | ** | 0.00 |
| | Social tie | Social-tie: Ward | * | | | | * | | | ** | 0.00 |
| | | Social-tie: District | | | | | | | | *** | 0.00 |
| | Participation | Decision Making: Ward | | | | | | | | * | 0.00 |
| | | Decision Making: District | | | | | | | | * | 0.00 |
| | | Impact on Community: Ward | | | | | | | | * | 0.00 |
| | | Impact on Community: District | | | | | | | | * | 0.00 |
| | Action | | * | | | | | | * | * | 0.00 |

*Note:* Indicator: Option ≤3, the most positive option; Option ≥4, two most positive options; * ≥60%; ** ≥80%.

can make a network between the residents (horizontal network), and the residents, ward, and DONRE (vertical network). It even creates new network between the residents and primary school (they have never had a chance to cooperate for environmental activities).

The hypothesis here is that EPC can be an institution that can create and foster the social capital in the society of the project site as a horizontal and vertical bridge among stakeholders. This hypothesis is supported by the results of the second survey:

- There are strong ties among the residents in the residents' cluster.
- Social capital within a resident cluster is generally rich.
- There is weak correlation and trend between social capital and individual attribution.
- There are strong correlations between social capital and EPC activity.
- The positive impact of EPC is especially significant on neighbor network and residents' cluster management.
- Impact of EPC in comparison between project clusters and non-project clusters can be found on social capital in bridging categories.
- The residents who have higher education and higher income tend not to join EPC activity.

From the results, it becomes clear that EPC activity has a positive correlation on social capital. The noted correlation is found in neighbor network and community management in residents' cluster. EPC activity

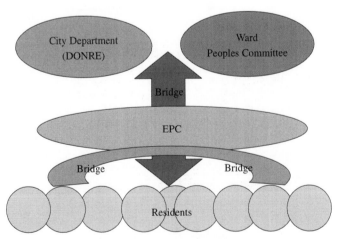

*Fig. 3.* Function of EPC, Creating Bridges in the Society.

affects the creation or strengthens residents' network and also gives the residents more opportunities to join the community management.

Project clusters show the tendency to have more positive values than non-project clusters in bridging categories. It means that EPC activity can foster social capital in broader networks of residents. EPC serves as bridges which create networks among residents and stakeholder in the society. The bridges have two dimensions: horizontal and vertical. Horizontal bridge creates networks among residents, and vertical bridge forms partnership between residents and government. By involving the stakeholders and creating networks among them, EPC is expected to foster social capital and improve comprehensive social cohesion, which is strongly required for participatory environmental management.

## 4.2. Fostering Social Capital and Participatory Urban Environmental Management

In participatory urban environment management, overall participation of the residents in activity is pointed out as one of the crucial factors. If the awareness is not shared among stakeholders and if there is no cooperation toward the solutions, participatory approach cannot be successful. In order for participatory urban environmental management to achieve an effect, it becomes an important subject how residents are involved in activity.

However, in urban areas in which various people gather from every place and where movement of residents is moreover prosperous, it is supposed that social cohesion which brings collective actions to a locality is rather weak. Then, what kind of method is there in order to understand the situation between the residents?

In order to verify the social situation of a location in where a participatory approach is implemented, it is reasonable to observe the relation between the residents, which makes collective action possible and effective. Such relations are explained as social capital, and to verify social capital in a locality is meaningful for a participatory urban environmental management. In case there is rich social capital and strong social cohesion among residents regardless of the difference in each background, effective collective action can be expected even in an urban area. When collective action is performed effectively, it is expected that it has good influence on the residents' participation which is one of the factors of a success of participatory environmental management.

EPC in the Danang case study is one of the good examples where social capital among stakeholders is fostered through the institution (EPC) and environmental management activities. EPC and activities provide them new opportunities for interaction and eventually it is expected to enrich networking and trust among them. Enriched social capital enables more comprehensive participation and brings success to the project. Thus, the viewpoint of social capital is valuable to take into consideration in urban environmental management. Institution, organization, and activities are expected to be planned to have positive impact on social capital, so that the features of social capital in the locality will be well applied to the management plan.

## ACKNOWLEDGMENTS

We would like to express our appreciation to DONRE, People's Committee of Thuan Phuoc ward, Vo Thi Sau primary school, Danang University of Technology, and CECI Danang Office for their cooperation and support to the study. Rajib Shaw acknowledges the support from the JSPS/MEXT grant-in-aid (Water Community) and Gakudo project fund in conducting this study.

## REFERENCES

Beall, J. (1997). Social capital in waste – A solid investment? *Journal of International Development*, *9*(7), 251–261.

Bourdieu, P. (1985). The social space and the genesis. *Theory and Society*, *14*(6), 723–744.

Bowls, S., & Gintis, H. (2002). Social capital and community governance. *The Economic Journal*, *112*, 419–436.

Coleman, J. (1988). Social capital in the creation of human capital. *American Journal of Sociology*, *94*, 95–120.

Evans, P. (1996). Government action, social capital and development: Reviewing the evidence of synergy. *World Development*, *24*, 1119–1132.

Fukuyama, F. (1995). *Trust; the social virtues and the creation of prosperity*. Minnesota, USA: Free Press.

Fukuyama, F. (2001). Social capital, civil society and development. *Third World Quarterly*, *22*, 7–20.

General Statistic Office of Vietnam. (2007). Available at: http://www.gso.gov.vn/default_en.aspx?tabid = 49, accessed in October 2007.

Kähkönen, S. (1999). *Does social capital matter in water and sanitation delivery? A review of literature*. Social Capital Initiative Working Paper No. 9, The World Bank.

Maloney, W., Smith, G., & Stoker, G. (2000). Social capital and urban governance: Adding a more contextualized 'top-down' perspective. *Political Studies, 48*(4), 802–820.

Nguyen, H. T. (2004). *Enhancing water and sanitation services provision in developing cities – The case of Hanoi, Vietnam.* Ph.D. Thesis, University of Hawaii.

Pargal, S., Huq, M., & Gilligan, D. (1999). *Social capital in solid waste management: Evidence from Dhaka, Bangladesh.* Social Capital Initiative Working Paper No. 16, The World Bank.

Pretty, J., & Ward, H. (2001). Social capital and the environment. *World Development, 29*(2), 209–227.

Putnam, R. (1993). *Making democracy work: Civic traditions in Modern Italy.* Princeton, USA: Princeton University Press.

Norris, P. (2002). *Democratic Phoenix: Reinventing political activism.* Cambridge, UK: Cambridge University Press.

Serageldin, I., & Grootaert, C. (2000). Defining social capital: An integral view. In: R. Picciotto & E. Wiesner (Eds), *Evaluation and development: The institutional dimension.* Edison, USA: Transaction Publishers.

World Bank. (2003). *Vietnam environment monitor 2003: Water* (78 pp). Washington DC: The World Bank.

# SECTION III
# CASE STUDIES ON
# ENVIRONMENT-DISASTER LINKAGES

# CHAPTER 16

# ENVIRONMENTAL RISKS IN DHAKA: PRESENT INITIATIVES AND THE FUTURE IMPROVEMENTS

MD. Golam Rabbani

## ABSTRACT

*Dhaka is one of the most populated megacities in the world with a total population of over 12 million and an area of 276 sq km (DCC, 2004). The city is situated at the center of the country and is surrounded by a river system comprising Buriganga, Balu, Turag, and Shitalakhya. The city has a long history dating from the Pre-Mughal, to the Mughal, and, finally, to the Bangladesh period. The growth of Dhaka basically started from the current extreme south and along Buriganga River and then it expanded earlier to the West (Hazaribagh) and the East (Gandaria) and later to the North (Mirpur). However, in the last few decades, the city experienced huge population growth and rapid industrial, commercial, business, residential, and infrastructure development, which have significantly expanded the physical feature of Dhaka. Still many of the development activities are taking place in an informal way within the Dhaka City Corporation (DCC) area, the main part of the megacity.*

Urban Risk Reduction: An Asian Perspective
Community, Environment and Disaster Risk Management, Volume 1, 319–338
Copyright © 2012 by Emerald Group Publishing Limited
ISSN: 2040-7262/doi: 10.1108/S2040-7262(2009)0000001020

# 1. BACKGROUND AND CONTEXT

## *1.1. Background*

The world, with a population of about 6.4 billion is facing multifarious problems and challenges particularly on the environment and on climate change related issues. In Asia, nearly 1.5 billion people of the total 3.6 billion living in urban areas are more or less exposed to natural, man-made, or even technological hazards or disasters (e.g., explosions). The natural hazards like floods, storm surges, tsunamis, earthquakes, volcanic eruptions, cyclones, and tornadoes hit urban cities almost every year. These catastrophic events significantly hinder the economic and social development of the whole world in two phases: first, by damaging the resources, establishments, and infrastructure and second, by obstructing the on-going development, business, and trade. The man-made and technological hazards have become regular events around the world. These hazards (e.g., air, water, and noise pollution, fires in the slums and squatter areas, disease outbreaks, explosions, accidents, etc.) are the added cataclysmic events that aggravate the suffering of the urban people in many countries like Bangladesh.

In Bangladesh, the major environmental issues of the urban areas include air pollution, surface water contamination, declining of the groundwater resources, noise hazards, solid waste management, sewage management, land use violation, drainage congestion, water logging, vegetation management, etc. In addition to these, the urban cities of Bangladesh currently face a number of natural hazards like floods, cyclones, river bank erosion, droughts, northwestern storms, thunderstorms, etc. and are also predicted to be adversely impacted by climate change extreme events. More than 8.5 million people in the coastal urban cities are exposed to some additional risks, e.g., sea level rise, salinity intrusion, etc. The environmental pollution and disaster risk threaten the lives and livelihoods of the urban dwellers in Bangladesh. The indoor air pollution and surface water pollution are a major threat to women and children in the city. Dhaka is significantly threatened.

The concerned government agencies, nongovernment organizations, research and academic institutions, development partners, etc. of different countries are nowadays aware of the urban risks. The Government of Bangladesh (GoB) has recently taken several policy initiatives to reduce the urban risks, especially those that are environment and disaster related. A number of projects and programs of the government are being implemented in many of the urban cities including Dhaka to protect the urban environment. But still many of the issues are not being satisfactorily addressed to protect the city environment. For example, the sewage management, surface water management, indoor air pollution, etc. of Dhaka City. The administrative delay, people's attitudes, lack of transparency and accountability, and limitation of the resources are the key barriers to the risk management and sustainable development of this city.

The NGOs and the civil society representatives of different cities like Dhaka, Chittagong, Khulna, etc. have also come up with specific activities and programs to reduce the urban risks in Bangladesh. Bangladesh Centre for Advanced Studies (BCAS), Waste Concern, International Union for Conservation of Nature-Bangladesh (IUCN-BD), Bangladesh Environmental Lawyers Association (BELA), Forum of Environmental Journalists Bangladesh (FEJB), etc. have awareness, education, solid waste management, etc., environmental programs in different urban areas particularly in Dhaka.

## 1.2. Context

Dhaka, the capital city of the country and one of the largest megacities of the world, accommodates over 12 million people within an area of $1353 \, km^2$. This megacity comprises Dhaka City Corporation (DCC) and five adjacent municipal areas, i.e., Savar, Narayanganj, Gasper, Kadamrasul, and Tongi (UNEP, 2005; BBS, 1991). DCC, the most populated and the central point of the megacity covers $276 \, km^2$ (BBS, 2001). Historically, the human settlement and the infrastructure development started from the southern part of the present DCC in the 16th century, which is currently known as "old Dhaka." During the last centuries, it extended approximately 40 km from south to north and 14 km from the east to the west. Over the 400 years of this long period, the city faced a number of dramatic historical changes in terms of political, demographic, and topographic structure from its beginning until today. There were four regimes who ruled this city from 1608 to 2006. The regimes include Mughal Period (1608–1764), British Period (1764–1947), Pakistan Period (1947–1971), and Bangladesh Period (1971–present).

After 1971, informal development of human settlements, national and international business and trade centers, private and public establishments, industrial and infrastructure, etc., have made Dhaka one of the most unplanned, urbanized, and overpopulated cities in the world. The density of the population of this city is over $8,869/km^2$ (see Fig. 1). To meet the demand of this population, the utility services were established accordingly and also expanded at different periods but not at the same rate as the population and demand increase. This disparity and inequality of the development and management of the utility services, improper management of the natural resources and natural hazards (e.g., floods, excessive rainfall, temperature variation, earthquake) degraded the overall environmental situation of the city. A number of problems and risks that cause environmental degradation to the city have been identified. The major ones are air pollution, surface water contamination, groundwater declination, solid waste management, sewage management, noise hazards, land use violation, water logging, drainage congestion, transport congestion, slums, and squatters. Besides, fires in the commercial establishments and slums, disease outbreaks, building collapse, political strikes and demonstrations, etc. are additional risks for the urban dwellers. A number of driving forces of above contributory factors include poverty, excessive growth of population, rural migration, limitation of resources, mismanagement, technical inefficiency, corruption, lack of transparency and accountability, and bureaucracy. The above features together degrade the natural environment of the city and impose an unhealthy life and livelihood to the city dwellers.

The DCC, Dhaka Metropolitan Police (DMP), Dhaka Water and Sewerage Authority (DWASA), Dhaka Electric Supply Authority (DESA), Titas Gas Limited, Bangladesh Telephone and Telegraph Board (BTTB), Rajdhani Unnyan Kortripakhkha (RAJUK), Dhaka Electricity Supply Company (DESCO), and Department of Environment (DoE) are responsible for specific utility services for the city people (Siddique, Ahmed, Awal, & Ahmed, 2000). The health, education, planning, housing, transportation, and other infrastructure-related organizations do exist in the city area. The NGOs, Development Partners, Corporate Business and Trade Communities, and other related organizations also work on environmental risk reduction in the city.

## 2. MAJOR ENVIRONMENTAL ISSUES

A number of environmental issues have been discussed in several environment-related reports and documents (UNEP, 2005; Nishat, Reazuddin, Amin, & Khan, 2000). This paper identifies 12 issues as the major urban risks facing Dhaka City dwellers. These include air pollution, surface

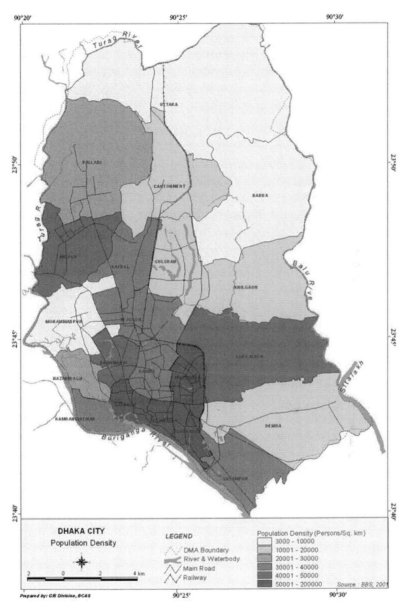

*Fig. 1.* Population Density in Dhaka City.

water contamination, groundwater declination, solid waste management, sewage management, noise hazards, land use violation, water logging/ drainage congestion, transport congestion, slums and squatters, flood, and others as mentioned earlier. This section provides a brief overview of each of the issues mentioned.

## 2.1. Air Pollution

The emission of air pollutants from the motor vehicles, industries, brick kiln, landfill sites, etc., are responsible for degradation of the air quality in Dhaka. Data from the Air Quality Management Project (AQMP) shows that the concentration of particulate matter (PM), nitrogen oxides ($NO_x$), and ozone ($O_3$) are beyond that of the country average standard (AQMP, 2004). The air quality gets worse during the dry season. The main contributors of the air pollutants are motor vehicles of the city.

## 2.2. Surface Water Contamination

Most of the water bodies including rivers (e.g., Buriganga, Balu, Turag, and Shitalakhya), lakes (e.g., Gulshan, Dhanmondi, Ramna), canals, and ponds receive sewage, industrial chemical waste, and solid waste everyday. For example, only 0.12 million $m^3$ of the total 1.3 million $m^3$ of the sewage gets treated and the rest directly or indirectly reaches the surrounding water bodies (UNEP, 2005).

## 2.3. Groundwater Declination

The most dependable natural water resource that supplies drinking water to Dhaka City is under threat due to over exploitation by about 1,100 DTWs belonging to the public and private sectors and low rate of recharge. In 1996, the groundwater level was at a depth of 26.6 m which had gone down to 46.24 m in 2003 (The Daily Star, 2004a, 2004b). Rapid urbanization, particularly the construction of roads, commercial establishments, and human settlements have created huge impervious areas in the city (e.g., the Dhanmondi-Elephant Road-Hatir Pool-Dhaka University area) that does not allow rainwater to get absorbed by the soil. Moreover, open space and small water bodies have been significantly reduced in the city area.

## 2.4. Solid Waste Management

The total waste generation of DCC is around 4,000–5,000 tons/day (personal communication; The Daily Star, 21 June 2004). According to JICA, the existing solid waste generation in the dry season is 3,340 tons/day which may increase to 3,500 tons during summer (JICA, 2004). It should be noted that JICA's study was limited to 131 km$^2$ area of the city whereas DCC's solid waste management service area is more than 276 km$^2$ (JICA, 2004). Nearly 50% of the total generated waste gets dumped in the city landfill sites.

## 2.5. Sewage Management

Dhaka Water Supply and Sewerage Authority (DWASA), under the Ministry of Local Government and Rural Development (LGRD) is responsible for the operation and maintenance of the sewage management within the city area. Only 30% of the city population has access to improved sanitation. As mentioned earlier, more than 1.3 million m$^3$ of sewage gets generated by the city dwellers every day. Most of it directly or indirectly goes to the surrounding water bodies, becoming a major concern of the city people.

## 2.6. Noise Hazards

Studies of World Health Organization (WHO) on noise level at different locations in Dhaka City found them to be beyond the standards in 1999 and 2002 (WHO, 1999, 2002). The noise levels were 70 dB in Dhaka Medical College , 75 dB in Shakhari Patti, 90 dB in English Road, 87.8 dB in Rajuk Avenue, and 85 dB in Tejgaon, though the standard limits for these areas are 50, 55, 60, 70, and 75 dB, respectively. A number of locations were identified as red zones, e.g., the Motijheel and Farmgate areas.

## 2.7. Land Use Violation

The inequality of the land use practices, encroachment by the local musclemen, slums and squatter settlements, and commercial construction are common phenomena in the city area. More than 3,000 slums and squatter areas are located in Dhaka City which accommodates around 3 million people. In 1996, it was reported that around 30% of the people of this city share 80% of the total residential area while the rest of the remaining 70% share only 20% of residential area (Islam, 1996). The situation is assumed to be worse nowadays.

## 2.8. Water Logging/Drainage Congestion

The rainfall causes water logging in most of the areas of Dhaka City nowadays. This may be due to inadequate storm water sewer infrastructure or absence of any sewer system at all. The increase of concrete/metal surface day by day is contributing to the increase in the volume of surface runoff which is worsening the water logging phenomenon.

## 2.9. Transport Congestion

Nearly 0.6 million motor and nonmotor vehicles ply on the city streets daily. They causes heavy transport congestion particularly in the old and central parts of the city.

## 2.10. Slums and Squatter Areas

Slums and squatter areas accommodate the low-income group of people. According to recent estimates done by experts of the Housing and Settlement Directorate and other reports, the existing slums and squatter areas of Dhaka City accommodate no less than 3 million people (Siddique et al., 2004; Akash & Singha, 2003). One of the main concerns in the slums and squatter areas is lack of access to proper water supply and sanitation and solid waste management service. Moreover, the living spaces are too congested and get polluted by biomass fuel burning in adjoining kitchen. The slum people work in the transport, industry, factory, domestic, utility service, business establishments, small shops, supermarkets, petty trading, etc., sectors in the city area.

## 2.11. Flood

The recurring floods disrupt and damage government, nongovernment, and personal property, road-transport system, drainage system, water supply system, and other utility services network in Dhaka City. It has been reported that at least $170 \, km^2$ of the city is below $6 \, m$ mean sea level (unpublished source). The city experienced heavy floods at least 9 times from 1954 to 2004 (Alam & Huq, 2003) causing huge damage and disruption to human lives and livelihoods.

### 2.12. Others

The city dwellers often face fires in the commercial establishments and slums, disease outbreaks, building collapse, demonstrations of the political parties, terrorism, mugging and robbery, etc. as additional risks. These sometimes damage property and kill people.

# 3. MANAGEMENT SYSTEM

As mentioned earlier, the DCC, DMP, DWASA, DESA, Titas Gas Limited, BTTB, RAJUK, DESCO, and DoE have specific roles in providing utility services and relevant risk management. However, the most relevant government agencies for overall environmental management are the DCC, DWASA, RAJUK, and DoE.

The *DCC*, under Ordinance 1983 is responsible for 13 compulsory functions (Siddique et al., 2004). Of these, construction and maintenance of roads, bridges, and culverts; removal, collection, and disposal of refuse, waste, and rubbish; maintenance and watering of public streets; regulation of private sources of water supply; planting of trees on roadsides; regulation of unsanitary buildings; prevention of infectious diseases and epidemics; and control over traffic and public places are main components.

*DWASA* is responsible for supplying safe drinking water and providing sewerage facilities to the city dwellers. Currently, the service area of DWASA is confined to seven zones in the city area. The major functions of DWASA include building, developing, maintaining, repairing, and rehabilitating the necessary infrastructure for water supply and sewage management.

*RAJUK*, under the Ministry of Housing and Public Works, is responsible for preparing the metropolitan plans and providing national counterpart staff. It prepared the Dhaka Metropolitan Development Plan (DMDP) for 1995–2015.

*DoE*, under the Ministry of Environment and Forests, is responsible for policy analysis, planning and evaluation, program coordination, and monitoring and evaluation of the environmental programs. However, the existing management system for the reduction of urban risk can be discussed separately based on the above-mentioned issues.

### 3.1. Air Pollution

In addition to the environment-related laws, policies, guidelines and their amendments in different years, the government has taken a number of policy decisions and programs to address the problem of air pollution in Dhaka City. The Continuous Air Monitoring Stations (CAMS) were established by DoE to record the air quality of the city area under AQMP. The AQMP of DoE is currently conducting a study on policy options to control diesel vehicle PM pollution. The recent major policy decisions to address the air quality of the city are given below (UNEP, 2005):

- Introduction of Compressed Natural Gas (CNG), which has tremendously helped reduce the air pollution of Dhaka City
- Introduction of unleaded gasoline on July 1, 1999
- Notification of lubricant standards on January 1, 2001
- Banning of buses older than 20 years and trucks older than 25 years in Bangladesh from 2002
- Banning of two-stroke engined three-wheeler vehicles from January 1, 2003
- Banning of imported reconditioned cars older than 5 years
- Reduction in the number of nonmotorized vehicles (NMVs) and restriction of movement of such vehicles within certain areas of the city and during specific periods of the day
- Banning of operation of commercial trucks in Dhaka City during day time (8 am–10 pm).

### 3.2. Surface Water Contamination

The Water Resources Planning Organization (WARPO) and DoE are responsible for water resources planning, management, and analysis of water quality. The major water-related policies and acts of Bangladesh include National Water Management Plan 2004, Bangladesh Water Development Board Act 2000, Urban Water Body Protection Law 2001,

Irrigation Water Rate Ordinance 1983, National Water Policy 1999, and Water Resources Planning Act 1992. Recently, the government has decided to relocate the tannery industries, the major source of surrounding river pollution from Hazaribagh to Savar, 30 km away from the city. However, to address surface water contamination, projects, programs, and interventions are lacking. The government may need immediate initiatives to protect surface water resources in and around the city.

### 3.3. Groundwater Declination

The management of groundwater resources is assumed to be very poor as the substantial initiatives for protecting or increasing the rate of groundwater recharge within the city area are to be taken.

### 3.4. Solid Waste Management

The DCC is responsible for the collection, transportation, and final disposal of the solid waste generated within its jurisdiction. Ten zones have been established for the management of solid waste generated in the domestic, commercial, industrial, and medical sectors. The DCC had recently established a Solid Waste Coordination Cell to improve the present management and system of collection. A pilot project was initiated in Rampura (Ward-22) to create awareness among the people regarding proper management of solid waste in Dhaka City through stakeholder participation. The government had banned polythene bags starting January 2002, reducing the solid waste generation of the city. The government, realizing the solid waste-related problems, approved a number of CBOs, NGOs, and private organizations for waste collection, disposal, and recycling.

The government and a few nongovernment organizations, particularly BCAS, Bangladesh Rural Advancement Committee (BRAC), International Centre for Diarrheal Disease and Research of Bangladesh (ICDDRB), Waste Concern, etc. have taken initiatives at different times for creating awareness among the medical professionals on medical waste and its safe handling and disposal. Waste Concern is a leading national NGO working on solid waste management issues in Dhaka. They have established four compost plants with a total capacity of around 15 tons/day in Mirpur, Baily Road, Green Road, and Dhalpur area of the city. Another NGO in Kalabagan started to collect waste from the households for disposal to the municipal depots.

Waste Concern also initiated a waste treatment plant with financial support from DCC and UNDP. National Clean Development Mechanism (CDM) Strategy 2004 had been prepared by the Ministry of Environment and Forest (MoEF) which addresses waste-related issues. According to the strategy, the emissions from landfill sites would be used to generate electricity.

The Solid Waste Management Master Plan for DCC was prepared by JICA in 2005. The Master Plan highlights solid waste management, solid waste associated problems, analysis of costs and benefits, institutional arrangement, and financial aspects, etc. It identified several specific programs to improve the situation. Four of these were taken up for implementation between April 2005 and March 2006. These were Participatory SWM Program, Capacity Building of Collection/Transportation Program, Final Disposal Site Improvement Program, and Solid Waste Administration, and Management Improvement Program.

### 3.5. Sewage Management

DWASA, under the Ministry of LGRD, is responsible for the management of sewerage system and sewage treatment. According to WASA, the existing sewerage system holds 49,803 sewer connections that cover approximately 30% of the city's total population (WASA, 2004). It operates a sewage treatment plant in Pagla, namely Pagla Sewage Treatment Plant (PSTP), which treats only 0.12 million $m^3$ human waste while the total sewage generated by the city is around 1.3 million $m^3$ as mentioned earlier.

The GoB, World Bank (WB), Asian Development Bank (ADB), and Japan International Cooperation Agency (JICA) have taken several initiatives for improving the sanitation services in Dhaka City. The 3rd Dhaka Water Supply Project repaired some damaged sewerage lines and also extended the system (World Bank, 1996). The WB completed a feasibility study on improved sanitation services in South Dhaka in 1996 as part of 4th Dhaka Water Supply Project (Shamsuzzoha, 2002).

### 3.6. Noise Hazards

The government has taken initiatives to control noise level in the city. Some of the major initiatives are as follows:

- Formulation of Noise Control Rules 2004.
- Banning vehicular hydraulic horns.

- Monitoring mechanism at the main traffic points to determine whether the vehicles follow orders or not.
- Removal of 4,000 hydraulic horns by the DMP from vehicles plying the city street (Hasan, 2003).
- Decision on the relocation of the Tejgaon, Gabtoli, Saidabad, Armanitola, and Mohammadpur truck terminals.
- Decision to relocate most of the bus stops, demolish passenger sheds, and build new ones in suitable places.

The WHO conducted two studies in 1999 and 2002 on noise level at different locations in the city.

### 3.7. Land Use Violation

The DMDP has clearly highlighted the sectoral land use practices that need to be followed between 1995 and 2015. However, due to lack of land use policy and the enforcement of existing laws, land use violation is increasing. The land management initiatives are not satisfactorily undertaken by the concerned agencies of the GoB.

### 3.8. Water Logging/Drainage Congestion

The GoB has not yet taken any significant initiatives to reduce the risk of water logging or drainage congestion.

### 3.9. Transport Congestion

The following initiatives were taken by the GoB to address the transport congestion:

- Dhaka Integrated Transport Study (DITS) conducted in 1991–1992 to determine the transport status of Dhaka
- Dhaka Transport Coordination Board (DTCB) established in 2001 to develop innovative transport policies and guidelines for the improvement of the transport status of Dhaka City
- DTCB is currently preparing a Strategic Transport Plan (STP), which will provide a long-term strategic vision for the transport system in Dhaka

- Updating and installation of new traffic signals
- Construction of road dividers and parking facilities
- Construction of bypasses and flyovers (e.g., Mahakhali and Khilgaon). The Gulstan–Jatrabari flyover is under construction
- Decision for amending the Motor Vehicles Ordinance 1983 to provide serious punishment for reckless and drunk driving, illegal parking, using fake driving licenses, and other transport-related crimes
- Construction of a City Center which will provide parking facilities in the Motijheel area.

### 3.10. Slums and Squatters

The relevant government agencies, DCC, and other national and international NGOs are working on different environmental issues particularly water and sanitation services in slums and squatters. The following initiatives were taken by the different organizations at different times to improve the overall situation:

- DCC installed 230 sanitary toilets, 42 tube wells, 9 water reserves, and 8 biogas plants in different slum areas (DCC, 2004)
- Dustho Shastho Kendro (DSK) constructed 75 water points to serve the slum dwellers in Dhaka City (Sharmin & Rainer, 1999)
- Water Aid is also providing water to slum dwellers in Dhaka City
- Plan International installed 17 biogas plants
- Proshika provided community latrines
- Concern-BD also provided community latrines for slum dwellers.

The DCC under the supervision of the Local Government and Engineering Department of the GoB is implementing a project "Slum Development Program" (2001–2006). This program included the following major activities (DCC, 2006):

- Water and sanitation facilities
- Health and nutrition service
- Training program for self employment, legal support, transportation and communication service
- Widening knowledge through educational services
- Women's rights, etc.

## *3.11. Flood*

Experiences indicate that 100% of eastern Dhaka was submerged by the floods in 1998 and 2004 while western Dhaka was nearly 75% affected in the same years. The Dhaka Integrated Flood Protection Project (DIFPP) was implemented by BWDB and funded by ADB and GoB. Under this project, a flood protection embankment cum bypass road was constructed in the western part of Dhaka in 1992–1997. In fact, after the flood tragedy in 1988, the ADB has played an active role assisting the GoB to implement the Flood Action Plan (FAP) and for the better management of existing flood control and drainage infrastructure. The ADB supported GoB with $95.4 million for the Flood Damage Rehabilitation Project. The government has also taken a decision to construct an eastern bypass, which may protect the city from further flood.

The GoB also established the Flood Forecasting and Warning Center (FFWC) to reduce the damages and to create awareness among the people about flood impacts. FFWC keeps records and forecasts the water level of major rivers through the Internet, radio, TV, and other related media services.

On the other hand, the national and international NGOs directly or indirectly, contribute to flood-affected areas by taking part in relief, health care services, and water supply, etc.

# 4. CHALLENGES AND LESSONS LEARNED

Dhaka is a city that is not only plagued with overpopulation and poverty, but it also bears the curses of natural hazards and climate change impacts at the local level. The rural poverty, river bank erosion, etc. cause excessive migration to Dhaka. The utility service providers are unable to meet demand due to lack of resources, which is a big challenge for the GoB. However, the major challenges to manage the urban risks can be stated as follows:

- Limitation of resources (institutional): This includes lack of funds, manpower, and technological knowledge. Due to limitations of resources, there is also limitation in supply of basic utilities such as water, sanitation, health, etc. These challenges hamper the development process.
- Lack of transparency and accountability: This is the most common challenge faced by government and other relevant agencies in Dhaka.

- Technical inefficiency: Technical inefficiency of the different government organizations either delays implementation or leads to improper management of projects or programs.
- Frequent shuffling of government officials: Decision makers and implementers at the government level are often transferred from one agency/organization to another. This creates a gap in knowledge and lack of commitment toward the job.
- Bureaucracy: Bureaucratic system of governance and administration means that there is a long duration between decisions made and their implementation.
- Excessive growth of population: Due to rural–urban migration and natural increase, the population growth rate is above 4.33% in Dhaka while the urban and national growth rates are 3.27% and 1.69%, respectively.
- Poverty: 40–45% people of Dhaka live below the poverty line.

Regarding air quality issues in Dhaka City, the initiatives of the government made a successful history, phasing out the two-stroke three-wheeler vehicles from the January 1, 2003 and introducing CNG vehicles and unleaded gasoline. In fact, the timely policy decisions, enforcement by the government, and advocacy, research, and support of the national and international NGOs made it happen. The Air Quality Standards have also been gazetted by the GoB.

The banning of polythene bags has reduced the surface drainage congestion in the city area. But unfortunately due to lack of strict enforcement these bags are coming back to the market.

The NGOs, particularly Waste Concern and BCAS, and community participation on the solid waste management in Dhaka have been greatly appreciated by concerned people. Waste Concern has established door-to-door collection of domestic waste and recycling plants in the city. These are being replicated in many areas of the city nowadays. BCAS, Waste Concern, and Grameed Shaktis have worked on the process to implement "waste to energy" project using CDM concepts.

The Ministry of Environment and Forests (implementing agency) of the GoB through Waste Concern (sub-implementing agency) initiated community-level solid waste management practices in urban areas of Bangladesh including Dhaka City as a component of the Sustainable Environment Management Program (SEMP), funded by UNDP. Annex 1 shows the summary of the project highlighting its successful history on SWM.

A public–private partnership program called "Beautification of Dhaka City" was launched in 2004. The work is being carried out under supervision of the Prime Minister's office and DCC. The government identified 54 private and 17 government organizations and allotted 105 spots for the beautification of the city. The activities were continued until March 2007 by the organizations at their own cost. This public–private partnership created a win–win situation in the beautification of Dhaka.

Due to lack of enforcement, lack of transparency and accountability, and lukewarm public attitude, etc., the DMDP (second Master Plan) prepared by RAJUK in 1997 is not being properly followed in any development activities in the city area. The first Master Plan for Dhaka was prepared in 1959. This was also not followed in the development activities.

The desired goal of the flood protection embankment cum road was found ineffective during floods that occurred in 1998 and 2004. In fact, some areas in the western Dhaka faced water logging for long time during both events. According to the concerned people and experts, it may be due to lack of proper planning and to the poor design of the embankment.

One of the main goals of the construction of the Mahakhali flyover was to reduce the transport congestion within and around the area. It has substantially reduced the transport congestion in Mahakhali area but significantly increased that along the Cantonment-Farmgate road, about 2 km away from the flyover. The reason may be, again, lack of proper planning.

As mentioned earlier, the government is putting efforts to reduce the risks and to manage the environmental situation of the city in various ways. First, taking policy decisions (e.g., to reduce air pollution, see Sections 2 and 3), implementing rules and regulation to some extent, and consecutive discussions meetings with relevant stakeholders. However, there are many things to be done through involving key stakeholders within the government system and also NGOs/researchers and academics. The government may keep specific budget allocation on urban environmental management especially for Dhaka. The city needs immediate measures on protection and conservation of its surface and groundwater resources.

# REFERENCES

Air Quality Management Project (AQMP). (2004). *Average suspended particulate matter concentration at Continuous Air Monitoring Station (CAMS), Sangsad Bhaban.* Dhaka: Department of Environment (DoE).

Akash, M. M., & Singha, D. (2003). Provision of water points in low income communities in Dhaka, Bangladesh. Paper prepared for the civil society consultation on the 2003 Commonwealth Finance Ministers meeting, Bandar Seri Begawan.

Alam, M., & Huq, S. (2003). *Flood Management and vulnerability of Dhaka city and development issues.* Dana Printers Ltd, Dhaka: Bangladesh Centre for Advanced Studies (BCAS), Dhaka.

BBS. (1991). *Bangladesh Population Census 1991.* Urban Area Report (Vol. 3). Bangladesh Bureau of Statistics.

BBS. (2001). *Bangladesh Population Census 2001.* National Report (Vol. 1). Bangladesh Bureau of Statistics.

BCAS. (2006). Report on local level environmental governance. Prepared for Delegation of European Commission, Dhaka, Bangladesh.

Dhaka City Corporation (DCC). (2004). *Dhaka profile: City growth – Area and population.*

Dhaka City Corporation (DCC). (2006). Slum Improvement Department. Accessed on September 20, 2007 and available at: http://www.dhakacity.org/html/slum_imp_act.html

Hasan, J. (February 21, 2003). Heritage and habitat: Commuting in the capital city: Congestion, frustration and procrastination. *Holiday (The National Weekend Newspaper),* Holiday Publications Limited.

Islam, N. (1996). *Dhaka from city to mega city: Perspective on peoples, places, planning and development issues.* Dhaka: Urban Studies Programme, Department of Geography, University of Dhaka, Bangladesh.

Japan International Cooperation Agency (JICA). 2004. The study on solid waste management in Dhaka city: Overview of preliminary findings, presented on June 17, 2004, Sheraton Hotel, Dhaka.

Nishat, N., Reazuddin, M., Amin, R., & Khan, A. R. (Eds). (2000). *An assessment of environmental impacts of flood 1998 on Dhaka City.* Dhaka: Department of Environment and International Union for Conservation of Nature.

Shamsuzzoha, M. (2002). Dhaka city's waste and waste management scenario. In: A. F. Ahmed, S. A. Tanveer & A. B. M. Badruzzaman (Eds), *Bangladesh environment.* Dhaka: Bangladesh Poribesh Andolon.

Sharmin, L., & Rainer, H. (1999). *An introduction to projects providing the urban poor with water and sanitation* (p. 1212). Mohakhali, Dhaka: BRAC, Research and Evaluation Division.

Siddique, K., Ahmed, J., Awal, A., & Ahmed, M. (2000). *Overcoming the governance crisis of Dhaka City.* Dhaka: The University Press Limited.

Siddique, K., Ghosh, A., Bhowmik, K. S., Siddique, S. A., Mitra, M., Kapuria, S., Ranjan, N., & Ahmed, J. (2004). *Megacity governing in South Asia: A comparative study.* Dhaka: The University Press Limited.

*The Daily Star.* (10 March, 2004a).

*The Daily Star.* (21 June 2004b).

UNEP. (2005). Dhaka City State of Environment Report 2005. United Nations Environment Programme (UNEP).

Water Supply and Sewerage Authority (WASA). (2004). Management Information Report for the month of October 2003. Dhaka.

WHO. (1999). Indoor air pollution status in Bangladesh. Environmental Health Unit.

WHO. (2002). Report on environmental health. World Health Organization, Amman, Jordan.

World Bank. (1996). *Fourth Dhaka Water Supply Project: Feasibility study for improved sanitation services, draft outline terms of reference.* Dhaka, Bangladesh: World Bank.

# ANNEX

---

**Box 1.** Solid Waste Management Practices in Urban Areas including Dhaka

*Project areas:* City, towns, and municipal areas
*Beneficiaries:* Urban poor, informal sector involved in waste recycling, low and middle income communities, private sectors, and farmers.
*Proponents:* Sustainable Environment Management Program (SEMP)
*Implementing Agency:* Ministry of Environment and Forest
*Sub-Implementing Agency:* Waste Concern
*Supported by:* UNDP
*The Objectives:*

i. Development of a community-based solid waste management model with emphasis on recycling and resource recovery;
ii. Development of community–private sector–municipal (GO-NGO) partnerships in solid waste management and recycling for improved environmental sanitation; and
iii. Creation of job opportunities for the neglected poor (especially women) by involving them in waste recycling activities.

*Activities at Local and Grassroots Levels:* Waste Concern started a community-based composting project in 1995 to promote the concept of "4Rs" – reduce, reuse, recycle, and recovery of waste – in urban areas of Bangladesh. It is based on the idea that the organic content of Dhaka's household waste, which accounts for more than 70% of total wastes, can be efficiently converted into valuable compost/soil enricher with the help of simple and low-cost aerobic composting technology.
*Benefits and Outcomes:*

- Changing the mindset of people to look at waste as a resource rather than as a burden.
- Communities enjoying improved, clean environment, and better rental value of their property than before.
- Improved and safe working environment for the informal sector already involved with waste.
- Private fertilizer marketing companies are making profit by marketing eco-friendly product.

*Lessons Learned:*

- Efforts should be made to develop innovative techniques suitable for the local condition, such as enriching the compost to cater to the needs of companies who buy the compost.
- Marketing of the compost was an important feature of this project for its sustainability.
- Resource recovery from waste does not always need expensive centralized mechanical plant. Waste can be managed and recycled in partnership with community groups in decentralized plants, using low-cost and labor-intensive techniques.

*Replicability and Sustainability:* This model is being replicated in Sri Lanka and Vietnam. This model is environmentally and technologically successful, as it has been running since 1995. For communities, this practice has resulted in cleaner neighborhoods, leading to increased property value, and better living environment and the private sector is making profits by marketing an environmentally friendly product, i.e., eco-fertilizer.

*Source:* Waste Concern, 2005 in BCAS (2006).

# CHAPTER 17

# COMMUNITY-BASED URBAN RISK REDUCTION: CASE OF MUMBAI

Akhilesh Surjan, Seema Redkar and Rajib Shaw

## ABSTRACT

*Risk reduction in cities of fast developing nations is both an opportunity and a big challenge. It is an opportunity because cities are considered efficient spatial forms of human habitation where smart interventions can be optimized. However, involvement and ownership of urban society is a big challenge. This paper illustrates these challenges and opportunities with an example of India's largest city – Mumbai. It discusses Mumbai's key drivers of risk, contributing factors to vulnerabilities and places it in the context of the 2005 flood – a disaster of a scale never experienced before. Citizen–government partnerships emanating from community-based small-scale initiatives for improving neighborhood's environment are analyzed. The paper concludes that there are enormous benefits in scaling up the participatory approaches, which result in reducing vulnerabilities and enhancing resilience of cities. Urban risk reduction will remain a daunting task if not built around these existing strengths of cities and their citizens.*

## 1. MUMBAI: AN INTRODUCTION

Mumbai is located on the western seacoast of India. It was originally a cluster of seven islands (of volcanic origin), which were given in dowry by

Urban Risk Reduction: An Asian Perspective
Community, Environment and Disaster Risk Management, Volume 1, 339–354
ISSN: 2040-7262/doi: 10.1108/S2040-7262(2009)0000001021

the Portuguese king to the king of England in the year 1660. Over the years, these islands, which are believed to be inhabited since the Stone Age, have been joined to form present Mumbai covering an area of 438 sq km. The capital of India's Maharashtra state, Greater Mumbai is house to 12 Million (as per Census 2001) people with extremely high average population density of 27,348 people per sq km. Urban Age report (2007) notes that "*Mumbai Metropolitan Region of 18 million residents is the world's fifth most populous metropolitan region. Mumbai is India's entertainment and financial capital, yet also the city with the largest slums. It contributes 40 percent of the national income tax and 60 percent of customs duty. In purchasing power parity (PPP), Mumbai is estimated to have a US$143 billion economy. Per capita income is US$ 12,070, which is almost three times the national average (Maharashtra Trivia, 2007). Traffic congestion, loss of wetlands, and flooding as well as the critical housing issues and slums are key challenges facing Mumbai. Some projections state that Mumbai could overtake Tokyo as the world's largest city by 2050.*"

Mumbai is one of the world's top 10 centers of commerce in terms of global financial flow (Rediff, 2007) and houses important financial institutions, such as the headquarters of many major banks, stock exchange, and the corporate headquarters of many Indian companies and numerous multinational corporations.

As a megacity of magnanimous scale, Mumbai resorts to national, state, and local government for administration of various functions. The state government is directly involved in operating a number of important services in the city, including roads, housing, education, health, environmental services, and policing. The city is administered by the Municipal Corporation of Greater Mumbai (MCGM) headed by an elected Mayor with limited powers. The real executive power is vested in the Municipal Commissioner, who is a civil servant appointed by the state government. The Corporation comprises 227 directly elected Councillors representing the 24 municipal wards. There is a significant overlap between responsibilities at state and city levels. Overall, the city government is less powerful than the state (Urban Age, 2007).

Mumbai experiences tropical savanna climate (MCGM, 2006). The climate of the city, being in the tropical zone, and near the Arabian Sea, may be broadly classified into two main seasons – the humid season and the dry season. The monsoon rains lash the city between June and September, and supply most of the city's annual rainfall of 2,200 mm (85 in.). The maximum annual rainfall ever recorded was 3,452 mm (135.89 in.) in 1954 (GoM, 2007). The highest rainfall recorded in a single day was 944 mm (37.16 in.) on July 26, 2005.

## 2. RISK DOMAIN OF MUMBAI/KEY DRIVERS OF RISK IN MUMBAI

Mumbai is a city in transition; a complex amalgam of first and third-world urban landscapes struggling to transform itself into a modern metropolis (Pacione, 2006). There are a large number of environmental issues and disaster concerns, which collectively make the city vulnerable to both natural and man-made hazards. Much of Mumbai is just above sea level, and the average elevation ranges from 10 m (33 ft.) to 15 m (49 ft.) (Wikipedia, 2007a, 2007b). A recent global screening study by OECD (2007) to rank port cities with high exposure and vulnerability to climate extremes ranked Mumbai top (in terms of exposed population) among the studied 136 cities having more than a million population.

---

### MUMBAI FACT SHEET

- 27,348 person/km$^2$ = average population density of Greater Mumbai
- 17.76 million people live in the Mumbai Metropolitan Region
- 81% of jobs in the service sector
- 55% trips are made by walking
- 344,817 registered cars
- Greater Mumbai area = 438 km$^2$
- 300-km long suburban rail system
- 2% of all trips made in private cars
- 6.5 million people travel on Mumbai's rail system each day
- 11% of Mumbai's surface covered by roads
- 2,893 NGOs
- 43% open green space in Greater Mumbai
- 56% of households lack toilets
- 48% of slums built on private land
- 10 million people in the Mumbai Metropolitan Region live in slums
- 61% of population growth due to natural increase
- 19 persons killed each day in transport-related accidents
- 420% increase in auto rickshaws over the last 15 years

*Source:* Urban Age India Conference (November 2007)

---

Mumbai sits on a seismically active zone owing to the presence of three fault lines in the vicinity. The area is classified as a Zone III region, which means an earthquake of up to magnitude 6.5 on the Richter scale may be experienced. Mumbai lies over more than 10 seismic fault lines. The coastal plain to the east of Mumbai is prone to earthquakes of even "higher intensity, upto 7.5 on the Richter scale" (Mumbai pages, 1998).

Seasonal flooding during the monsoon became a regular feature in many areas of Mumbai. This disrupts many important civic services and infrastructure in addition to paralyzing daily living of significant population. The incessant and torrential rains in the afternoon of July 26, 2005, amounting to 94.4 cm during a span of only 14 h not only caused deluge in Mumbai, but was also a "horrifying memory" for its citizens (Bhagat et al., 2006). Indian Institute of Tropical Meteorology noted that from the year 1876 onwards, incidences of rain in a single day are inconsistently increasing. Climate change experts expressed that such catastrophic flooding events will be more frequent and will also accompany killer winds and towering tides in future. In addition, Indian government also identifies positive tsunami-proneness in Maharashtra state where Mumbai is situated (MHA, 2005).

Proliferation of environmental and social risks further aggravates Mumbai's vulnerability. About 60% of Mumbai's population lives in slums, occupying a mere 8% of land, and their lives are characterized by degraded housing, congestion, inadequate civic services (Parasuraman, 2007). With 300 km, Mumbai's suburban rail system is the most extensive of the subcontinent. Transporting more than 6 million passengers each day, it is also one of the busiest rail systems worldwide, as reported by Urban Age city data (2007). Nine-car trains designed to hold 1,700 passengers travel with up to 5,000 commuters, with an average of 13 people per day killed in rail-related accidents (Rode, 2007).

From time to time, Mumbai also experiences communal violence, riots, serial bomb blasts, mafia/underworld instigated crimes – that not only keep making headlines in international media but shakes the common citizen's sense of security and confidence in law and order.

## 3. WHAT MAKES MUMBAI VULNERABLE?

Urban risk in Mumbai encompasses complex dimensions. Widely acknowledged is the fact that urban hazards and vulnerabilities are greatly interconnected whereas there are many other factors, which contribute significantly as "risk multipliers." Urban hazards in Mumbai vary considerably compared to its counterparts (other mega cities) in developed countries. They are not only represented by one-off events like floods or cyclones but also get exaggerated due to environmental, social, or political stresses or their combination.

To understand Mumbai's vulnerabilities, it may be appropriate to deconstruct the underlying factors making Mumbai more critical than in any other built environment. These factors may be summarized as follows.

### 3.1. Population Growth

Mumbai as a city of opportunity has been attracting people from all over India. Both migration as well as natural population increase, significantly contribute to the enormous population growth of the city. According to the Washington-based Population Institute, the metropolitan region in 2020 will be the world's most populous at 28.5 million, with Tokyo trailing at 27.3 million (d'Monte, 2007). Extremely high concentration of people in Mumbai has far-reaching demographic footprint affecting not only surrounding areas but also far-flung Indian states like Bihar, Uttar Pradesh, and Tamil Nadu, etc. Remittances from Mumbai to these states are exorbitant and hence any risk looming in Mumbai will definitely have telescopic impacts elsewhere.

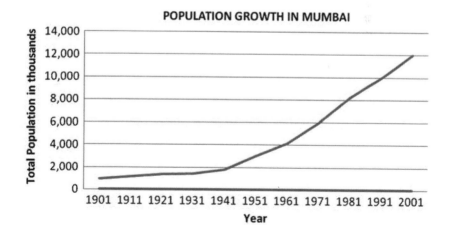

### 3.2. Population Density

Mumbai is one of the "densest cities in the world and hence constitutes a category on its own" (Urban Age, 2007). The population density defined as number of persons living within 1 sq km of area presents striking feature about Mumbai. Although average city density was 27,000 people per sq km for the city, some areas have density astronomically high as 114,001 people per sq km (Parasuraman, 2007). Due to such high population density, population exposure becomes very high even in a small-scale localized disaster.

### 3.3. Urban (mal) Planning

Mumbai is a classic example of unplanned development. Land is scarce and heavily priced resource in Mumbai. Land prices in some pockets are at par with the most expensive real estates in developing country's mega cities. Despite the presence of town planning agency as well as metropolitan development authority, none of the spatial plans could be implemented successfully. The reason for this failure could be numerous starting from short sightedness of planners to political patronage of slum-mafia. As a result, present Mumbai has "unique distinction" of possessing less than one acre of open space for every thousand people, while the norm is four acres or 0.016 sq km (d'Monte, 2007). Committees formed to make an enquiry into Mumbai floods also clearly point at failure of urban planning as one of the major contributor in the disaster.

### 3.4. Reclamation of Low-Lying Areas

Continuous land reclamation in Mumbai for over 300 years (seven islands merged into single landmass) without much scientific approach is continued till today. Even government agencies (at times due to political pressure) are involved in this activity. Illegal dumping of waste including construction waste mainly fuelled by builders and developers for solely opportunist purposes is rampant. Improper dumping by communities in few places is also noticed in recent past. Shrinking drainage as well as inadequate dilapidated drainage system creates havoc even with moderate rainfall. Construction on the flood plains of natural drainage channels, on top of the storm drains and across drainage lines made things worst in almost all low-lying localities in Mumbai. Choking of *Mithi* River with substantial garbage/solids deposits in drains has major impact on drainage capacity of the city. It is a very critical issue, as *Mithi* River provides natural drainage to the city. After the Flood-2005, for three weeks, average load of waste lifted was double the normal daily load. Reclamation of land at the mouth of the sea by development authority to build Bandra–Kurla complex is often cited as a good example of bad urban planning in the city.

### 3.5. Encroachment

Encroachments, especially in the areas of hills and mangroves in Mumbai are leading to decrease in mangroves, wetlands, and forest cover, which are important elements of coastal urban eco-system. Even development authority and local government have been involved in eating up these "soft areas" which are acting as ecological cushion to the city. Intensive violation of Coastal Regulation Zone (CRZ) rules is also often criticized by environmentalists and referred to as one of the root causes of growing flood vulnerability.

### 3.6. Inefficient/Inadequate Civic Services

Negligence in cleaning sewers and drainages is a perennial problem in Mumbai. In many locations, routine cleaning operations are reported to have not been fully undertaken for years together by the local government. The city drainage does not cater to entire city and is also too old and dilapidated to perform. Poor inadequate  solid waste management, crumbling public transport, very high levels of air and noise pollution, interrupted and poor quality and inadequate water supply – are some of the critical issues in congested city of Mumbai aggravating the vulnerability of population on a day-to-day basis.

### 3.7. Poor Civic Sense

General lack of civic sense among communities at large is frustratingly alarming in Mumbai. Despite high proportion of literate population, general sense of hygiene and cleanliness remains poor in most parts of the city. Illegal activities (dumping- mainly by developers and builders, digging – mainly by utilities services providers) by industries, dairies, restaurants, hospitals, and other establishments further add to this problem. Public health constantly has been threatened by such callous attitude of local stakeholders. It is further aggravated by floating population of over three million people which add to pressure on all basic amenities.

### 3.8. Lack of Community-Based Risk Reduction Measures

Mumbai is prone to multiple hazards such as flood, fire, earthquake and house crashes, landslide, road accident, industrial and chemical accident, and cyclone (MDMP, undated; CDP, 2006). Significant proportion of slum population in the city is located on hills, slopes, drains, low-lying areas (with high probability to flood during high tides), coastal locations, under high-tension wires, along highways, along railway lines, within industrial zones, pavements, along water mains, along open drainages, etc. Low income and poor communities often resort to settle on these unsafe locations and become more vulnerable.

Mumbai is the first city in India to have disaster management plan prepared in 1999–2000. *Mumbai Disaster Management Plan* (MDMP) contains city and ward profile, hazard identification, response procedures, etc. right up to the ward level, thus recognizing ward as a lower most identifiable organ in the city. MDMP delves in detail on aspects of disaster preparedness, mitigation, and response yet lays cursory emphasis on community involvement. Since 2003, Indian government and United Nations Development Programme (UNDP) are jointly implementing *Disaster Risk Management* (DRM) program in Mumbai in consultation with state government and MCGM. Although DRM program has been designed to follow Community-Based Disaster Preparedness (CBDP) approach, unfortunately, in its implementation in Mumbai so far, community's pivotal role is a major missing link. MCGM is the nodal agency for disaster management in Mumbai and most of its initiatives have strong bias toward government machineries' capacity building toward response preparedness.

Regrettably, overconfidence of government on availability of disaster management plan document ahead of other Indian cities and reluctance to synergize crosscutting sectors and stakeholders results in recurring disasters year after year. Community-based approach in disaster risk reduction is still a far cry in Mumbai despite its success in other disaster struck regions, partly due to reliance on highly centralized (although inadequate) emergency response services and inhibition of administration to work credibly with urban dwellers.

## 4. MONSOON FLOOD IN MUMBAI: A MAN-MADE DISASTER

From this point onwards, this case study primarily focuses on flood hazards (especially seasonal flooding during the monsoon) in Mumbai. Flooding is not only an annually recurring phenomenon, but it also paralyzes city life, fully or partially and results in loss of working days, drowned property, "house collapse, traffic dislocations, electricity power cuts" and loss of many lives (Pacione, 2006). There are numerous flood points in the busy neighborhoods, which have localized impacts, hence remain unrecognized to be registered as disaster event. In July 2005, this megapolis witnessed most severe flood in the recorded history, which caused death of hundreds of people and paralyzed almost every function for several days. Over 1,000 people lost their lives in the region due to floods and also secondary flood-induced disasters like mudslides, electrocution, wall collapses, car submergence, and water-borne diseases, etc. (Mathur & Sharma, 2005; Bhagat et al., 2006).

There are many arguments behind such deluge like flouting the spatial development plan provisions; reclamation of the low-lying areas; negligence on the part of local government in cleaning sewers and drainages; builders' lobby encroaching the areas of hills and mangroves; irresponsible city dwellers' disregard for their streets, lanes, and sewers; violation of CRZ rules; choking up the Mithi River (which provides natural drainage to the city) by nurturing slum settlements at its banks to become political vote-bank; lack of disaster preparedness; too many people migrating into the city; presence of multiple administrative and development agencies with no clear coordination among them, etc. (Gupta, 2006; Bhagat et al., 2006). Authors also identify natural, human, and administrative causes of this disaster along with garbage problem, over urbanization, development beyond carrying capacity of the city, lack of modern rain gauges etc. to mention a few.

Although there are confronting doubts on uncertain extreme climate events, Mumbai's grave realities through recent experiences put everybody on alert. In the entire gamut of these alarming situations, bizarrely missing link is the citizens of Mumbai and a consideration as how they can play a part in reducing their levels of risk (Mathur & Sharma, 2005).

# 5. NEED FOR PARTICIPATORY URBAN RISK MANAGEMENT

By now it is clear that Mumbai being a coastal city and with its regular monsoon flooding, needs specific attention to deal with hydro-meteorological hazards. A larger study on Mumbai (Surjan & Shaw, 2009) digs into two convincingly realistic options toward suggesting better tomorrow for the city. First, considering an "ideal" situation where institutional bottlenecks, and infrastructure deficiencies are taken care in the city through appropriate political-will; time-bound, resource intensive, high-cost structural and semi-structural strategies; state-of-the-art scientific assessment of risks and corresponding preparedness of civic agencies; and with continuation of present government centric, top-down approach to urban functioning. Second, assuming a more "punctilious and viable" setting where above-mentioned actions will be accentuated while communities are involved to play a part in shaping dreams of their own city – Mumbai.

Further parts of this chapter are heavily drawn from this study. Experiences already proved that well-written plans for disaster and environment management as well as urban development and technocratic solutions for infrastructure improvement and service delivery misrepresent improvement in quality of life. These top-heavy options may well benefit selected sections of the society but ultimately end up increasing vulnerability over a period of time due to their intrinsic transient nature to discard holistic community involvement. Researchers also pointed out that creating an enabling environment for heterogeneous urban communities and empowering them enough to evoke their constructive participation in development decision-making is an incessant process. Instant remedies for civic problems seemingly preferred to fetch immediate political gains at the cost of longer-term community enabling partnership options. In the context of thickly populated city like Mumbai, recognizing and gradually building-up on the existing community-owned institutions hold promise to optimize the efforts and will yield far-reaching results.

# 6. ALM: STRENGTH WITHIN THE COMMUNITIES TO PROTECT DEVELOPMENT GAINS

The Advance Locality Management (ALM) is a unique example of community–government partnership existing in Mumbai since the year 1996 (Baud & Nainan, 2006). This movement was started by motivated citizens who were concerned with neighborhood problems and resultantly growing localized risks. These citizens have encouraged and convinced majority of the locality (neighborhood) to coordinate in improvement of quality of life in surroundings. The collective efforts initially grew fast in the areas facing high environmental degradation including medium and low-income residential settlements. Being a volunteer initiative, people themselves contributed small amount to upkeep the functioning of ALM. Looking at the greater advantages of this growing movement, MCGM's Solid Waste Management Department (SWM) came forward to partner this initiative. "Good urban governance campaign" started as a joint project between the Government of India and MCGM, in collaboration with United Nations Center for Human Settlements (UNCHS) further formalized and boosted this initiative. Finally, since 1997 is a community-based approach for effective management of civic services at the grassroot level (Rathi, 2005). Eventually, in many cases, NGOs/CBOs also joined in and thus, this became 'community–civic society–local government cooperation' for better managing civic services at local level.

In most cases, an ALM is formed by a neighborhood or people living along the common street. A typical ALM usually consists of 100 to 250 houses. This size also enables them to establish direct communication among members. Depending on the size and physical characteristics of the area, the ALM committee members are selected by residents or designees of housing societies in a democratic manner with good representation of women and elderly. In some cases, committee may also include or invite social workers, local corporator, known experts, retired civil servants, and traders from the vicinity to join ALM.

The ALM committee is not a statutory, but an informal voluntary body, and thus, no salary or allowance is paid to the office bearers. Once the committee is formed and functionaries are designated, ALM gets registered with the local municipal ward office. In some cases, where local communities are already found working as voluntary group for some other purpose (such as for celebrating major festivals), an appointed official from MCGM encourage them to form an ALM. MCGM is also responsible for designating a Nodal Officer to attend to citizen complaints, organize meeting of all ALMs in a particular ward or zone, help resolving issues among members, convey important urban improvement measures planed by the local government, etc. The committee can put their suggestions and proposals to improve the civic services, after interacting with the citizens.

City wide filthy environs in general and among residential areas in particular are visibly distinguishable in Mumbai. This fact is further established by the Forbes magazine, which has ranked Mumbai seventh in a list of the world's dirtiest cities (NDTV, 2008). Confirming cleanliness as the utmost priority, in most cases, the first step taken by ALM is to begin to segregate domestic garbage into wet and dry. In addition, major problems addressed through ALMs also relate to garbage clearance, neighborhood level composting, drainage improvement, water supply, beautification of the surroundings, prevention of encroachment, road excavation, pothole filling, road and pavement leveling, surfacing, stray animals, pest control, etc. ALM committee plays a key role in sensitizing the citizens to inculcate the spirit of civic consciousness, and ensure their cooperation to the municipal administration, to implement various projects and programs (CDP, 2006). Their role is most significant to educate the masses. Motivation is a key to success and improved quality of life is the biggest incentive making this initiative sustainable. This is a system, which encourages the citizen to take active role in monitoring the civic administration at every ward level.

ALM, as a system recognized at ward level, provides people with single window access to most civic services. Today, there are about 783 ALM groups (CDP reports 584 ALM committees) covering a population of about 2 million, functioning in the city (Bhagat et al., 2006). This is an ongoing initiative further adopted in the local government Charter in 2006 to scale up as Local Area Citizens Group (LACG) Partnership-2006.

It was evident that ALMs contribute significantly toward segregation of waste at the household level, and as a result, recyclable waste (20% of total waste produced and growing rapidly due to changing lifestyles) is directly picked by identified rag pickers. CDP (2006) recognize that though plastic composes only 0.75% of the total waste generated, it causes maximum nuisance such as clogging of drains. These rag pickers are the local poor and can earn livelihood with dignity through picking recyclable waste including plastic, pet bottles, and cans. Also, at the ALM level, about 55% of the organic/biodegradable waste is composted to convert into organic manure, which is utilized for local gardening. In addition, construction and demolition waste is directed to low-lying landfilling areas for landfill purpose and thus reduce burden to dumping sites. Thus, there is a massive reduction in total waste reaching waste disposal sites and contribute in reducing the burden to already overstressed municipal services. At the same time, the efforts made by collective action of citizens locally have resulted in environmental risk reduction (Bhagat et al., 2006).

There are numerous examples where local flooding impacts are either completely negated or significantly reduced due to better waste management practices prevailing among ALM communities. This has constantly been reported through mass media and also established in academic studies. In fact, local government also has recognized this fact while blaming other severely flood-affected communities for congesting drains with dumping garbage resulting in prolonged localized flooding. Even in cases where well functioning ALM areas got flooded due to downpour, the flood water receded quickly due to clean drains and communities were able to return to normalcy. With very active advocacy and consultation among ALM groups and municipal agency, transparency and accountability is also reflected in the whole process. Harmonizing the local government–ALM relations to smooth functioning of the various activities is crucial in many cases. However, success stories from other areas have set examples to rectify the minor issues in some cases.

# 7. THE LESSONS LEARNT

Building up and sustaining urban community institutions beyond certain time frame is considered very difficult. Success of community-based disaster risk reduction initiatives heavily rely on such established community-owned institutions. Until 2005 flood, the ALM remained a locally recognized entity that helped in garbage management. Ironically, MDMP advocates for community-based risk reduction approaches but overlooked such citizens' committees' possible role. Interestingly, ALMs as organized community group tremendously helped during the 2005 flood (which was among the heaviest flood in last 100 years in Mumbai) by directly involving in rescue, relief, and provision of medical aid, food, and water to affected populations. Had these ALM members oriented beforehand by organizing mock-drills for various disaster scenarios, conducting training and skill development in search and rescue, temporary shelter, mobilizing local resources, and volunteering with other relief agencies, the impact of flood would have been significantly lower. After experiencing disaster, many ALMs voluntarily came forward and searched for capacity building options in disaster management. A few of them also attended training offered by local organizations (like Civil Defence, Red Cross Society, Anirudhdha Academy of Disaster Management, etc.) on their own expense and shared knowledge within their ALM. In one case, an ALM also procured search and rescue equipments and offered training to other ALMs in some parts of the city with own initiative. Appallingly, despite witnessing ALMs important role in reducing severity of disaster and disaster risk itself, there are no sincere efforts (until early 2008) to engage them in preparing CBDP plans and rehearsing regularly.

Further, Mumbai is presently benefiting with cost-intensive infrastructure development projects through various programs like Jawaharlal Nehru National Urban Renewal Mission (JNNURM), Mumbai Urban Transport Project (MUTP), Mumbai Urban Infrastructure Project (MUIP), Mumbai Metro Rail Project (MMRP), etc. Understandably, all these projects aim at improving present-day condition of the city. However, these efforts may go in vain if the projects fail to win the confidence of the community or local people. No one in the city wants to see the newly laid higher capacity drains to be chocked again with polythene, plastic, and other garbage contributing more to devastating floods. In all probability, this is the most suitable time to spearhead massive community sensitization to instill belongingness and civic sense and also to promote new and strengthen existing partnership between government and communities in association with media, corporate sector, civil society organizations, etc.

## 8. THE WAY AHEAD

This ALM practice may not be very innovative in urban context and there may be slightly varying examples of similar nature in different cities of the developing world. This approach can be easily replicated in democratic political settings where local problems and issues are dealt at municipal level in a decentralized manner. The results of this initiative have greatly benefited in improving community-based waste management. The strength of such a great asset created and nurtured over a period of time is and will remain contextual in reducing flood risk at neighborhood and city level. Collective community suffering and action has already generated greater impact during historical flooding (2005) in city in post-disaster cycle. Local government support has also buttressed and catalyzed toward multiplicity of the efforts. It is very convincing and just time to reinforce ALMs by enabling them to effectively contribute in preparedness and mitigation phase as well. Synchronization of inter and intra institutional priorities by establishing close community consultation through ALMs could be the first step toward this goal. Citywide network of ALMs may further be networked with business groups, welfare and charity organizations, government agencies (specially those responsible for physical development, environment management, and risk reduction), informal sectors, corporate groups, media, civil society, etc. for enhanced information sharing and equitable resource allocation. This will also help in testing innovative practices through selected pilot projects from time to time. Through timely and systematic intervention, these citizen groups will not only act as "watchdog" to numerous developmental interventions but may also catalyze people-centered, environmentally responsive, risk-resilient, development of Mumbai. Ultimately, these efforts can be replicated with certain local adjustment in different context as well.

## ACKNOWLEDGMENTS

Akhilesh Surjan acknowledges the Japanese Government (Monbukagakusho: MEXT) scholarship support for carrying out this research. Case Study and Field Campus (CASiFiCA) Project of Disaster Research System (DRS) of Disaster Prevention Research Institute (DPRI) has also provided travel grant to Akhilesh Surjan which helped in conducting field visit during research. The research would not have been possible without the cooperation of communities, CBOs, and local government of Mumbai. The authors would like to convey their sincere thanks to Mr. Dayanand Jadhav and his colleagues of Tri-Ratna Prerana Mandal, Mr. & Mrs. Khatri of Viceroy Park ALM, Mr. Raj Kumar Sharma of M(W) ward ALM, Mrs. Priya Ubale of Clean Sweep for their great support and sharing experiences during the field research. Lastly, Akhilesh Surjan acknowledges Emerald Group's international journal titled "Disaster Prevention and Management" (DPM). Some sections of this paper and Akhilesh Surjan's paper in DPM (Volume 18, Number 4) consists overlapping information.

## REFERENCES

Baud, I. S. A., & Nainan, N. (2006). "Negotiated spaces" for representation in Mumbai: Ward committees, advanced locality management and the politics of middle-class activism. Paper presented to the IDPAD end symposium, Hyderabad, India, November 1–3, 2006. Available at: http://www.idpad.org/html/hyderabad.htm, accessed on 5 May 2007.

Bhagat, R. B., Guha, M., & Chattopadhyay, A. (2006). Mumbai after 26/7 deluge: Issues and concerns in urban planning. *Population and Environment, 27*(4), 337–349.

CDP. (2006). City development plan, Municipal Corporation of Greater Mumbai. Available at: http://www.mcgm.gov.in/forms/tlmenu.aspx?slmno = NjQ%3d-Ty%2bEse9BzqE%3d, accessed on 27 April 2007.

d'Monte, D. (November 2007). A matter of people. Urban Age India Conference, pp. 41–42.

GoM. (2007). *Mumbai disaster management plan*. Mumbai: Relief and Rehabilitation, Division of Revenue and Forests Department, Government of Maharashtra (GoM). Available at http://mdmu.maharashtra.gov.in/pages/Mumbai/mumbaiplanShow.php, accessed on 12 December 2007.

Gupta, K. (2006). Urban flooding: Vulnerability, preparedness and mitigation – 944 mm Mumbai 26/07/2005 event. Keynote presentation at The International Centre of Excellence in Water Resources Management (ICE WaRM), Australia. Available at: http://www.icewarm.com.au/page.php?pId = 188, accessed on 10 December, 2006.

Maharashtra Trivia. (2007). Maharashtra Tourism Development Corporation. Retrieved on 2007-12-07. Available at: http://www.maharashtratourism.gov.in/MTDC/HTML/ MaharashtraTourism/Default.aspx?strpage = ../MaharashtraTourism/Trivia.html

Mathur, S., & Sharma, A. (2005). Mumbai floods: Another wake-up call. Coordinates, Vol. 1, Issue 3, August. Available at: http://www.mycoordinates.org/mumbai-floods-another-aug-05.php, accessed on 14 March 2007.

MDMP. (undated). Mumbai disaster management plan, relief and rehabilitation, division of revenue and forests department, Government of Maharashtra. Available at: http:// mdmu.maharashtra.gov.in/pages/Mumbai/mumbaiplanShow.php, accessed on 12 December 2006.

Ministry of Home Affairs (MHA), Government of India. (2005). Preventive/protection and mitigation from risk of tsunami: A strategy paper. Available at: http://www.ndmindia. nic.in/Tsunami2004/Strategy%20Paper%20on%20Tsunami.pdf, accessed on 10 December 2007.

Mumbai Pages. (1998). The seismic environment of Mumbai. Available at: http://theory.tifr. res.in/bombay/physical/fault.html, accessed on 28 November 2007.

NDTV. (2008). Forbes magazine names Mumbai as city of junk. Available at: http:// www.ndtv.com/convergence/ndtv/story.aspx?id = NEWEN20080043169, accessed on 18 March, 2008.

Organisation for Economic Co-operation and Development (OECD). (2007). Ranking port cities with high exposure and vulnerability to climate extremes: Exposure estimates. Environment Working Paper No. 1, Environment Directorate. Available at: www.oec-d.org/env/workingpapers, accessed on 23 December, 2007.

Pacione, M. (2006). City profile – Mumbai. Cities, 23(3), 229–238.

Parasuraman, S. (2007). Uncovering the myth of urban development in Mumbai. Urban Age India Conference, November 2007, p. 39.

Rathi, S. (2005). Alternative approaches for better municipal solid waste management in Mumbai, India. Waste Management, 26(2006), 1192–1200.

Rediff.com. (2007). Mumbai among world's top 10 financial flow hubs. Available at: http:// www.rediff.com/money/2007/jun/18mumbai.htm, accessed on 18 June, 2007.

Rode, P. (November 2007). Mumbai: The compact mega city. Urban Age India Conference, p. 45.

Surjan, A., & Shaw, R. (2009). Enhancing disaster resilience through local environment management: Case of Mumbai, India. Disaster Prevention and Management: An International Journal, 18(4), 418–433.

Wikipedia. (2007a). Maharashtra. Wikipedia – The free encyclopedia. Available at: http:// en.wikipedia.org/wiki/Maharashtra#Geography, accessed on 25 May 2007.

Wikipedia. (2007b). The free encyclopedia. Mumbai. Available at: http://en.wikipedia.org/wiki/ Mumbai#_note-0, accessed October 2007.

# CHAPTER 18

# RECOVERY FROM TYPHOON DAMAGES IN TOYOOKA

Hari Srinivas, Rajib Shaw and Yuko Nakagawa

## ABSTRACT

*On Wednesday October 20, 2004, Typhoon Tokage (called the "Typhoon no. 23 of 2004" in Japan), one of the deadliest storm in years, swept through most of the southern half of Japan. People were overcome by the massive waves and flash floods triggered by the typhoon's heavy rains and strong winds, which left at least 69 people dead, 20 missing, and some 342 injured, out of which 66 were serious injuries. The number of typhoon-related casualties was the highest in over a quarter of a century, and it further destroyed 50 homes, damaged 1,350 residences, and flooded 26,800 others. Typhoon Tokage was the tenth typhoon to make landfall in Japan in 2004. Storms and floods killed over 100 people in Japan that year, resulting in hundreds of millions of yen in damage, highlighting once again the importance of disaster management in both Japan and in East Asia.*

## 1. THE TOKAGE TYPHOON

On Wednesday October 20, 2004, Typhoon Tokage (called the "Typhoon no. 23 of 2004" in Japan), one of the deadliest storm in years, swept through

Urban Risk Reduction: An Asian Perspective
Community, Environment and Disaster Risk Management, Volume 1, 355–373
Copyright © 2012 by Emerald Group Publishing Limited
All rights of reproduction in any form reserved
ISSN: 2040-7262/doi: 10.1108/S2040-7262(2009)0000001022

most of the southern half of Japan. People were overcome by the massive waves and flash floods triggered by the typhoon's heavy rains and strong winds, which left at least 69 people dead, 20 missing, and some 342 injured, out of which 66 were serious injuries.

The number of typhoon-related casualties was the highest in over a quarter of a century, and it further destroyed 50 homes, damaged 1,350 residences, and flooded 26,800 others. Fig. 1 shows the level of flooding (almost 2.5 m) in some parts of the city. Typhoon Tokage was the tenth typhoon to make landfall in Japan in 2004. Storms and floods killed over 100 people in Japan that year, resulting in hundreds of millions of yen in damage, highlighting once again the importance of disaster management in both Japan and in East Asia.

Coming just months before the World Conference on Disaster Reduction (WCDR) that was to take place in January 2005 in Kobe, Japan – the typhoon, along with the Indian Ocean Earthquake and Tsunami disaster,

*Fig. 1.* A Local Government Official Points to the Level of Flood Waters (Red Line) as a Result of the Typhoon. Such Markers have been Placed throughout the City to Remind Residents of the Dangers of Disasters.

was also a rude reminder of the vulnerability that people faced to climatic events and ensuing disasters.

In the immediate aftermath of the typhoon, the United Nations Environment Program's International Environmental Technology Center (UNEP-IETC) conducted a rapid assessment of the environmental consequences of the typhoon.

A number of key lessons learnt from the study included:

- Need to raise awareness for integration of environment and disaster issues
- Need to document and disseminate examples
- Need to bridge gaps between knowledge and practice
- Need to implement practical examples
- Need to develop guidelines and tools on environment and disaster management
- Need for continuous monitoring

## 2. THREE YEARS ON: HOW DO THINGS STAND?

Considering the unusual severity of the Tokage Typhoon, and of the typhoon season of 2004 as a whole, a number of initiatives were undertaken at the national, prefectural, and local levels, as a result – both to overcome the impacts of the disaster, and to further prevent/mitigate the negative impacts of climatic events such as typhoons.

A follow-up assessment was planned to Toyooka City to document the longer-term measures undertaken by the city administration as a follow-up to the typhoon, and implementing the lessons learnt in the aftermath of the Tokage Typhoon.

After three years, the documentation looked at the following issues:

- The process of Toyooka City's recovery from the typhoon disaster
- Problems faced during the last three years since the Tokage Typhoon disaster
- Long-term disaster prevention measures put in place: landslides, waste/debris management, riverbank management, etc.
- Long-term disaster preparedness measures put in place: community awareness, evacuation procedures, disaster leadership, etc.
- Transferable lessons for other cities that face similar disaster events.

## 3. CONCEPTUAL BACKGROUND FOR TOYOOKA'S DISASTER MANAGEMENT PLANNING

Over the years since the Tokage Typhoon of 2004, Toyooka underwent a number of administrative changes – key among them being the merger of five neighboring cities/towns into one larger urban area, under the banner of "Toyooka City." The towns that were absorbed into and consolidated as Toyooka City were: Izushi, Kinosaki, Hidaka, Banto, and Takeno. This significant change created additional impetus to develop a comprehensive disaster management plan for the "new" and expanded Toyooka.

The responsibility of administering the new Toyooka City was reflected in the views of the Mayor of Toyooka, Mr. Muneharu Nakagai. The Mayor outlined his basic 4-point strategy to develop and sustain the growth of Toyooka. It is interesting to see this strategy as a guiding philosophy that influences and steers local policies, including that of disaster management.

The 4-point strategy covers:

(1) Emphasis on *local endemism* (as city's survival strategy) – Many local cities look same in Japan. There is a need to focus on locally specific history and characteristics as a "survival" strategy. For example, Toyooka uses oriental storks, which roost in the city, as a symbol of the city.
(2) *Living in peace* strategy – Development that is based on long-term prospects, while maintaining the importance of tradition. This is probably opposite to the anonymity of large megacities such as Tokyo (which is also called as "amnesia city" due to the fact that things change or move quickly in Tokyo).
(3) *Innovation from tradition* – Real new innovation draws its inspiration from, and is derived from local tradition. Linked to the first point on local endemism, preserving the local tradition becomes an issue for the city's revitalization.
(4) *Sustainability* – Traditional knowledge and ways of doing things have already the test of time and of sustainability over generations. This is the reason why traditions continue to survive even today. The emphasis and interlinks between sustainability and traditional ways of doing things is an integral and interesting part of the strategy.

For Toyooka, disaster management is therefore looked at from such strategic urban planning scenarios – where both positive and negative aspects of development and nature are taken into account. (For example, the Maruyama river, which runs through the city, has a very small gradient,

*Fig. 2.* Photos Showing Floating Debris from Nearby Mountains and Forests that Blocked Rivers and Damaged Bridges on the Left, and Well-Maintained Rivers and Embankments on the Right.

which enables people to enjoy boating and other water sports, but at the same time increases the potential risk of flooding.) Fig. 2 shows the improvement on physical aspects of the major river after the typhoon.

The three pillars on which Toyooka City's urban planning and development is based on, are:

(1) *Shizen ni idakare te ikiru* ("Living life that is embraced by nature")
(2) Cherish the moment and enjoy everyday life
(3) Take responsibility for future

Such conceptual visions have been a critical part of Toyooka's planning processes for the future, whether for the next 10 years, or for medium-/short-term development plans (three–five years). While the emphasis on traditional values as a counter force to "anonymous modernization" has been a key to Toyooka's image of itself, the problems of the larger environment, such as climate change, cannot be ignored by the city. As the Mayor said in his interview, "I would say it is important to fit it into the local nature. The answers are always in the past. For example, acid free agriculture is our tradition but its technology is completely new" (Fig. 3).

The need to create a unique image and vision for Toyooka was also driven by the merger of the neighboring towns into Toyooka. The Mayor strongly felt that focusing and nurturing local tradition was the right strategy for the city. He citied the case of a junior high school student who told him that "... the merger is a good thing because the circle of helping hands would increase, while at the same time locally specific culture would not disappear. Like in the European Union ...."

*Fig. 3.*   An Old Photo of Toyooka, Dating from the 1960s, Showing the Symbiotic Relationship between Farmers, Farm Animals, and Wild Oriental Storks.

Such thinking has also influenced the disaster management strategies of the city, according to the Mayor. With the new city, when disasters such as typhoons approach, local officers are asked to return to their respective home regions to take emergency decisions such as evacuations, etc. Due to the larger administrative area after the merger, swift monitoring/evaluation has become necessary, and decisions need to be taken as close to the disaster area as possible. The need for disaster education in schools has also taken on added importance – for example, every year, one day is designated as a "Back to Nature" Education Day in nursery, elementary, and junior high schools. Textbooks for teachers and students are also being prepared, aiming to nurture ecological ethics in the children.

## 4. TOYOOKA'S DISASTER MANAGEMENT PLAN

The City of Toyooka established its Disaster Prevention Plan in 2006, and a document was prepared and issued by the Toyooka City Disaster Prevention Council.

After the Typhoon no. 23 of 2004, the idea of "Protect our lives by our joint efforts" was formed and the three basic precepts are as follows:

1. Realize that disaster inevitably happens,
2. Act for damage mitigation, and

3. Treasure local community power.

These were used to create disaster-resistant Toyooka City. These ideas are reflected throughout the Toyooka Disaster Prevention Plan, and detailed and concrete information and guidelines are provided in the area of flood, storm, earthquake, tsunami, snow damage, and large-scale accidents.

It is expected that the Plan works as guidelines to prevent future disasters and mitigate damages when they occur, and inspire citizens and communities to actively and spontaneously involve themselves in disaster management (Box 1).

Toyooka's Disaster Management Plan is operationalized by a process in which detailed and "micro" plans are devised by a number of local entities, governmental, nongovernmental, and community-based.

To understand this process, the following persons/entities were interviewed and a hearing organized to document their responses:

• Disaster Management Department
• Environmental Department
• Urban Planning and Construction Department
• Agriculture and Forest Management Department
• Tourism Department

Besides the above local government entities, the following organizations were also interviewed (Fig. 4):

• Fire fighting community group (*Shobodan* in Japanese)
• Community-based disaster management group (*Jishubosai soshiki* in Japanese)
• Education Department (*Kodomo Kyoiku Ka* in Japanese)
• Nitta Primary School

The following five sections provide an insight into various local entities and organizations that have adopted and operationalized the disaster management plan. It also provides valuable lessons for cities in the region that are planning to adopt similar measures (Box 2).

### 4.1. Disaster Management Department

Much was learnt from the Tokage Typhoon of 2004. The main problems encountered by the city, according to the officials of the department, were

**Box 1.** *Toyooka Disaster Prevention Plan*: "Protect our lives by our joint effort".

The manual consists of six chapters as mentioned below.
Chapter 1: General Rules
Chapter 2: Disaster Prevention Plan
Chapter 3: First-Aid Measures against Flood and Storm
Chapter 4: First-Aid Measures against Earthquake and Tsunami
Chapter 5: First-Aid Measures against Snow Damage and Large-Scale Accidents
Chapter 6: Disaster Recovery Plan

*Chapter 1*
Chapter 1 defines the purpose of the Toyooka Disaster Prevention Plan ("...to protect citizen's life, health, and assets by establishing and promoting comprehensive disaster prevention and mitigation measures"), and provides overall ideas for disaster prevention and mitigation in Toyooka City. The main idea "Protect our lives by our joint effort" is explained, and the three basic precepts (1. Realize that disaster inevitably happens, 2. Act for damage mitigation, and 3. Treasure local community power) are discussed.
   The chapter also discusses damage estimates of hypothetical earthquakes, tsunamis, floods, and tidal waves to reinforce and improve disaster preparedness.
   It predicts vulnerable areas and degree of damages both personal and physical. Detailed information on each community's vulnerability to floods and landslides, as well as information on community shelters and their stock of food, water, etc. are available as an annex of this chapter.

*Chapter 2*
Following the General Rules discussed in Chapter 1, Chapter 2 discusses the Disaster Prevention Plan in six sections.
   These sections are:

(1) Damage mitigation management
(2) Solid disaster preparedness
(3) Improving local disaster prevention and mitigation measures
(4) Adjusting infrastructure for damage mitigation
(5) Passing the experience to the future
(6) Other disaster preparedness measures

In each section, it shows the "division/organization-in-charge" and outlines the actions to be carried out. For example, in Section 2, Department of General Affairs and Fire Department of the City and FM Tajima, a radio station, is responsible for collecting and spreading the news of disasters. The Department of General Affairs appears in almost all sections as the headquarters of disaster management. Other groups, such as Department of Construction, local business, hospitals, doctor's association, fire stations, and local disaster management organizations are also listed as responsible bodies according to each disaster theme.

*Chapters 3, 4, and 5*
These chapters provide countermeasure guidelines in the case of flood and storm (Chapter 3), earthquake and tsunami (Chapter 4), snow damage and large-scale accidents such as nuclear power plant accident (Chapter 5).

Same as Chapter 2, each section of each chapter shows the division/ organization-in-charge, and outlines the actions to be carried out. Each chapter describes information flow within the headquarters/city, cooperation with relevant organizations such as Hyogo prefectural government, Japan Self-Defense Forces and police, as well as rescue and evacuation measures, treatment for food, housing, utilities, medical care, and the wastes generated. It also discusses restoration of school education and psychological treatment for children and adults after the disasters.

*Chapter 6*
Chapter 6 talks about city's responsibilities in helping citizens recover from the disasters. It mainly discusses post-disaster financial assistance, such as condolence money from the city, extension of tax payment deadlines, reducing or exempting payment of tax, fees, and utility bills to lighten financial burdens of disaster victims. Low-cost financing for disaster victims for their housing and businesses are also discussed.

---

(1) the low rate of evacuation by residents despite warnings issued by the city, (2) lack of systematic and concerted information sharing and response, and (3) interorganization coordination within the city.

In view of the above problems, the department has improved its evacuation drills and information sharing process. This includes more

*Fig. 4.* Hearings Organized with City Officials to Discuss their Plans for Disaster
Management in Toyooka City.

intensive interaction with the local communities to organize drills, and
provision of emergency radios to every household in the city.

A detailed disaster management plan (reviewed in Box 1) was prepared by
the department, which was then interpolated into ten localized hazard maps
and plans. The three core components of the plan rests on the city office
being responsible for disaster preparedness, the city's urban service agencies
being responsible for developing/implementing the response mechanism,
and the community at large being responsible for disaster awareness and
education. Fig. 5 shows the low-lying areas in the river, which has close
monitoring in the new disaster management plan .

The importance attached to disaster management was also reflected in the
upgrading of the head of the department to be under the Mayor's office,
effectively making the head equivalent to a Vice Mayor.

But challenges still exist – the key being that the plan focuses more on
preparedness issues in the shorter term, and not on prevention/mitigation
issues of the longer term, particularly of anticipating future disasters or
climate change issues. Disaster management is still implemented in isolation,
and is not integrated into the 10-year development plans of the city as a
whole (Box 3).

**Box 2.** Assessment and Lessons learnt.

The format for developing a disaster management plan at the local level is provided by the central government. Each city/town/village in Japan has to therefore develop a comprehensive plan to prevent, mitigate, and prepare for various disasters that they potentially face.

As shown in the box above, the Plan document is quite comprehensive, covering a range of issues related to risks and hazards that Toyooka faces and countermeasures that are needed to be put in place.

Besides the contents and format of the plan itself, two key features of Toyooka's plan provide interesting lessons – (a) the process of developing the plan in itself provided a number of opportunities for the city administration to review and raise awareness of its residents and integrate it into various other development activities, and (b) a number of organizations and entities, both governmental and nongovernmental, adopted the plan to develop further and more micro plans for the respective communities they served or lived in.

*Fig. 5.* Low-Lying Areas near the Maruyama River that are now being Closely Monitored for Potential Flooding during Heavy Rains and Typhoons.

---

**Box 3.** Assessment and Lessons learnt (Disaster Management Plan).

A key aspect of the follow-up measures after the Tokage Typhoon, was the enhancement of the role that the Disaster Management Department played, and its proximity to senior management officials of the city, including the Mayor's office itself. The head of the department in fact reports directly to the Mayor – a change from previous practice, where the department was part of the construction department.

The key feature of the plan is outlining of the specific and enhanced roles that city service agencies have to play in the case of a disaster. This division of labor is critical and provides interesting lessons for other cities in the region. It also includes citizens and community organizations.

In the Plan, the city office is itself responsible for disaster preparedness as a whole, while the city's different urban service and infrastructure agencies are responsible for developing and implementing the disaster response mechanism. The community at large also has a role to play in being responsible for disaster awareness and education.

---

### 4.2. Environmental Department

With the huge volume of wastes generated during the Tokage Typhoon, one of the key areas focused on by the department is that of waste generated during future disasters. Specifically, the effective separation of wastes, its temporary storage, and proper disposal and recycling.

The department quickly learnt that clearing off the waste debris is a critical priority for rebuilding program to commence (Fig. 6). The awareness of local residents on waste separation and proper disposal is a critical starting point for speedy recovery after a disaster.

The department strongly felt that there was a need to put in place a Disaster Waste Treatment Plan, which it developed and implemented in May 2006. Some of the key features included:

- Separate different types of wastes at three levels: (1) in front of the house itself by the resident or by volunteers, (2) in the designated temporary waste-dumping site by the waste department, and (3) in the final incinerator by the waste management company.

*Fig. 6.* Before-and-after Photos of a Temporary Debris Storage Area. The Area is now Designated for Temporary Waste Storage after Disasters.

- The prior designation of vacant areas a temporary holding of waste debris for further processing to be recycled or processed.
- Agreement between neighboring cities and cities in the region to help each other to dispose waste in the aftermath of a disaster.
- Determine and designate the categories of waste that residents/volunteers will have to separate into, for recycling/processing.

There were many additional steps that the department was planning to take in the future, or was not doing currently. These included:

- Simulation exercises to determine the kinds and volumes of waste generated after different kinds of disasters.
- Development of waste management plans on future disaster scenarios, and not based on past experiences alone.
- Strengthen the intrinsic link between waste plans and disaster management plans.
- Increase awareness among residents on issues related to disaster debris and the role that they have to play in effective and speedy waste clearance for recovery (Box 4).

### 4.3. Urban Planning and Construction Department

The Urban Planning and Construction Department of Toyooka City is primarily responsible for the overall physical development and growth of the city. The department felt that its key role in disaster management programs lay in reconstruction plans after a disaster, and in future

***Box 4.*** Assessment and Lessons Learnt (Waste Management).

Many of the lessons learnt from the clean-up in the aftermath of the Tokage Typhoon have been adopted and incorporated into the disaster management plan.

Effective and timely clearance of waste and debris was a key focus of the department as a critical pre-condition for the residents to recover from a disaster. An important measure taken by the department is the development and implementation of a disaster debris clearance plan.

As outlined in the text above, besides the preparation of a basic disaster waste management plan, some of the features that can be adopted by other cities in the region include: (a) a system of separation of wastes into its component streams, (b) designation of temporary waste handling sites, (c) agreement between neighboring cities' waste management departments to help each other in the case of a disaster.

The future plans outlined by the department also provide insight into measures that can be taken by a city's waste management agency to also handle disaster debris.

development plans that influence the ability of a community to mitigate and prevent disasters.

The key operating mechanism of the department is the 10-year Master Plan for the city, outlining the land use and zoning patterns, transportation routes, etc. Within the process of developing the plan, several potential vulnerability issues can and has been incorporated in the designs and plans, including safe neighborhoods, disaster facilities, localized plans for prevention, hill development, etc.

The department still faced a number of challenges, including the fact that only 60 percent of the current area of Toyooka was actually planned, and the other 40 percent remained "unplanned." It was also of the opinion that links to local economy and to construction investment that inherently took disaster issues into account, needed to be strengthened (Box 5).

### 4.4. Agriculture and Forest Management Department

The Agriculture and Forest Management Department is responsible for the planning and management of forests and agriculture lands in and around

---

**Box 5.** Assessment and Lessons Learnt (Urban Planning).

Vulnerability of communities to risks and disaster events is primarily caused as a result of the *proximity* of human settlements to such hazards and risks. Infrastructure and urban development processes can either increase this risk, or help mitigate it.

An in-depth internal assessment carried out by the department has resulted in a better understanding of the intrinsic linkages between infrastructure and urban development, and disaster hazards/ risks for their programs and projects. An important outcome of this assessment is the resultant stronger integration of disaster risk mitigation measures into the department's medium- and long-term planning processes.

The opinions and views expressed by the department also highlight the importance of involving the private sector in ensuring that disaster risk reduction is made an integral part of the construction and development process of a city.

The "unplanned" areas of a city – particularly those used by lower income households, continue to pose a challenge to most local governments, and illustrate the importance of involvement of local community groups and NGOs assisting them in disaster planning and preparedness exercises.

---

the Toyooka City. An assessment of the damages caused by the 2004 Tokage Typhoon showed that a key cause was the improper pruning and maintenance of the forests that surrounded Toyooka, eventually leading to their flooding the rivers and breaching the dykes.

A better understanding of such inter-linkages has led the department to focus its attention also on disaster management issues, without loosing the focus on its "regular" issues such as improving the natural environment, fostering environmentally friendly agriculture, etc. Fig. 7 shows the balance of land use management.

The Department, for example, has designed a special eco-label, based on the city's symbol – the oriental stork – as a logo. Agriculture produce that is "friendly" to the storks and do not damage the environment is designated as a "Stork Friendly" item – an eco-product.

It has also taken action to petition the national Ministry of Agriculture, Forestry and Fisheries (MAFF) to designate Toyooka as a "Bio Mass

*Fig. 7.* Balancing Agricultural Land Use and Forests/Mountains is Critical for
Long-Term Recovery. Photo Shows Agricultural Fields Recovered after Extensive
Silting.

Town."[1] The city's biomass town strategy calls for the revitalization of
forestry and improving access to forests (Fig. 8).

The department has promoted Shimin Kumiai or forestry cooperatives
among the residents in order to network and improve access of the
community to forest's resources and to create jobs during the off-season.

The ownership registration of properties in forests and nearby areas was
also considered important by the department in order to facilitate
community involvement in maintaining forests in the longer term. A
corporate "green tax" was also implemented to revitalize the mountains and
forests on a continual basis.

Challenges that the Department faced were essentially related to a lack of
awareness and appreciation of the links between proper maintenance of the
local environment, and the potential externalities in disaster prevention and
mitigation. It was obvious that much more needed to be done to increase the
knowledge and awareness both within the department as well as with
various stakeholders in the public, private, and community sectors of the
city (Box 6).

*Fig. 8.* Forests Surrounding Toyooka City that is Targeted for Better Maintenance to Reduce Debris being Washed into the River along with the run-off.

### 4.5. Tourism Department

For a city that extensively depended on domestic tourists for its economic growth, tourism plays a very important role not only in the economic sense, but also in preserving traditional assets and ways of living.

For example, Izushi is well known in the region for *soba* (buckwheat) noodles and pottery; Kinosaki is famous for hot springs and crab dishes; Toyooka itself is well known as a roosting place for the almost extinct oriental storks.

But disaster events such as the Tokage Typhoon severely affected the city. During the typhoon, there was a 30 percent drop in tourist arrivals in Toyooka, and the city has not yet recovered, even now, to the pre-typhoon levels. Mass media unfortunately played a critical role in creating an image that discouraged travelers from coming to Toyooka.

This is why the department has increasingly focused on local events, traditions, products, and features as attractions for visitors, but simultaneously also promoting an image of "safety" and "ecologically friendly and secure city" by offering farmers' day events, home stays, eco-tourism, etc.

***Box 6.*** Assessment and Lessons Learnt (Forest Management).

The key cause of flooding during the Tokage Typhoon was the run-off from nearby forested mountains surrounding Toyooka City, which blocked rivers and inlets to streams, and consequently resulting in a breach of the river embankments.

This understanding and post-disaster assessments have provided the department with valuable lessons, as outlined above, for it to better mitigate and be prepared for disasters in the future.

Improving access to nearby forests, and streamlining ownership of pockets of forested lands are cornerstones of the policies that other cities can learn from. For Toyooka, such an approach has brought the local community closer to the forests, and hence to closer monitoring of potential degradation and maintenance problems.

It also includes a more systematic integration of the city's image and vision into features derived from the forests, mountains, and agricultural areas that surround the city.

A key challenge that the department continues to face, and so will other cities adopting such an approach, will be the lack of awareness of the local communities and hence their active participation and involvement in the department's activities to reduce/mitigate the disaster risks and hazards that Toyooka faces.

***Box 7.*** Assessment and Lessons Learnt (Tourism Department).

A key lesson learnt by Toyooka's Tourism Department is the role that tourism inflows play in enhancing the city's image and the pride that local residents have in the city. This will consequently increase the pressure to take measures that will ensure safety of the city's assets and residents/visitors during a disaster.

The plans of the department in integrating environment, safety and local culture, and in projecting this impression to the outside world are an important lesson that can be learnt.

The fact that tourism program/plans in themselves have a role to play in disaster management – in bringing about greater participation of the local community in enhancing the city's image, and in ensuring safety and security, is an important lesson to be understood.

For example, a small town such as Toyooka will soon play host to a group of 400 students from China.

The successes of all these initiatives depend heavily on proper disaster management and safety of not only the local residents, but also of tourists – during and in between disasters. The need to balance the environmental impacts of tourism on a fragile local environment was also a concern of the department (Box 7).

# NOTE

1. More information on Japan's Biomass town initiative can be found on the MAFF website at: http://www.maff.go.jp/